This study presents the first broad coverage of Indian experiences in the American Revolution rather than Indian participation as allies or enemies of contending parties. Colin Calloway focuses on eight Indian communities as he explores how the Revolution often translated into war among Indians and their own struggles for independence. Drawing on British, American, Canadian and Spanish records, Calloway shows how Native Americans pursued different strategies and endured a variety of experiences, but were bequeathed a common legacy as a result of the Revolution.

# The American Revolution in Indian country

CAMBRIDGE STUDIES IN
NORTH AMERICAN INDIAN HISTORY

*Editors*

Frederick Hoxie, The Newberry Library
Neal Salisbury, Smith College

*Also in the series*

# The American Revolution in Indian country

## Crisis and diversity in Native American communities

COLIN G. CALLOWAY
*University of Wyoming*

CAMBRIDGE
UNIVERSITY PRESS

Published by the Press Syndicate of the University of Cambridge
The Pitt Building, Trumpington Street, Cambridge CB2 1RP
40 West 20th Street, New York, NY 10011–4211, USA
10 Stamford Road, Oakleigh, Melbourne 3166, Australia

First published 1995

Printed in the United States of America

*Library of Congress Cataloging-in-Publication Data*
Calloway, Colin G. (Colin Gordon), 1953–
The American Revolution in Indian country: crisis and diversity
in Native American communities / Colin G. Calloway.
p.    cm. — (Cambridge studies in North American Indian
history)
ISBN 0–521–47149–4
1. Indians of North America—History—Revolution, 1775–1783.
2. Indians of North America—Government relations—To 1789.
3. Indians of North America—History—18th century—Sources.
I. Series.
E83.775.C35   1995
973.3′ 150397—dc20                    94–28669
                                           CIP

A catalog record for this book is available from the British Library.

ISBN 0–521–47149–4 hardback

For Marcia, Graeme, and Megan

"That event was for us the greatest blow that could have been dealt us, unless it had been our total destruction."
　　　–Chiefs of the Iroquois, Shawnee, Cherokee, Chickasaw, Choctaw and Loup Nations to Francisco Cruzat, governor of Saint Louis, August 23, 1784.

# Contents

# Figures and maps

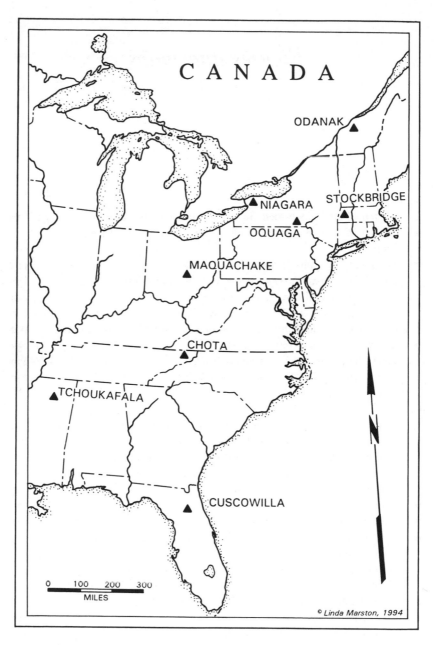

Map 1. Approximate location of the eight Indian communities.

# Preface

As a British citizen living in the United States and studying the American Revolution, I frequently encounter widely divergent views on that event. Taking account of polar British and American perspectives can be a relatively simple matter. Defeat becomes victory; villains become heroes, and a tragic loss of empire translates into the triumphant birth of a new nation. However, taking account of the perspectives of people who do not fall so easily into Whig and Loyalist camps can be much more difficult. Where does one stand when the conventional positions on the Revolution offer no solid ground?

The American Revolution occupies a central place in American history, historiography, and mythology. Nevertheless, more than two hundred years after the event, the full story of many of the people who lived through it remains to be told. Recent historians have addressed this omission and investigated popular movements, the participation of African Americans, the experiences of women, the tales of local communities, and so on, to get a better sense of what was going on backstage in revolutionary America while the two Georges and their generals acted out their historic roles on center stage. The political upheaval and social ferment of the times involved much more than throwing off the imperial authority of Great Britain, and was not confined to the cities of the eastern seaboard. Historians have looked to the peripheries of revolutionary America to examine those people who invaded Indian lands in defiance of first imperial and then federal authority, who challenged or ignored the control of eastern elites, and who protested the distribution of rewards in postrevolutionary society or questioned the dominant society's vision of a new republic.[1]

However, with few exceptions, revolutionary revisionism and recognition of

---

[1] For example: David Szatmary, *Shay's Rebellion: The Making of an Agrarian Insurrection* (Amherst: University of Massachusetts Press, 1986); Thomas P. Slaughter, *The Whiskey Rebellion: Frontier Epilogue to the American Revolution* (New York: Oxford University Press, 1986); Alan Taylor, *Liberty Men and Great Proprietors: The Revolutionary Settlement on the Maine Frontier* (Chapel Hill: University of North Carolina Press, 1990); Michael A. Bellesiles, *Revolutionary Outlaws: Ethan Allen and the Struggle for Independence on the Early American Frontier* (Charlottesville: University Press of Virginia, 1993).

the far-reaching nature of the American Revolution has not yet embraced American Indians. In general, historians of the Revolution have not been particularly interested in Indians, and scholars of Indian history have not paid much attention to the Revolution. Historians who have considered Indians in the Revolution have focused on the competition for tribal allegiances, the Indians' role in the fighting, their contribution to the outcome of the struggle for independence, and the symbolic significance of their involvement. They have considered Indians as military and political units, but rarely have they asked about the experiences of Indian people caught up in the conflict, examined the effects of the war on the Indians' home front, or considered Indian groups as human communities.[2] Alternatively, when scholars focus on Indian experiences, the eight years of the Revolutionary War often receive short shrift. The recent *Blackwell Encyclopedia of the American Revolution* contains two essays on Indians: one covers the twenty years before the Revolution; the other focuses on the period after the Revolution.[3] Although some events – the Indian removals of the 1830s, the Dawes Allotment Act of 1887 – figure prominently as landmarks in American Indian history, the Revolution tends to get lumped together with everything else that was going on in late-colonial or early national America. After all, this was a "white man's war" and only secondarily involved or affected Indians.

The national mythology accords Indians a minimal and negative role in the story of the Revolution: they chose the wrong side and they lost. Their contribution to the outcome of the Revolution was therefore negligible, and their

---

[2] Barbara Graymont's twenty-year-old study of the Iroquois in the Revolution and James O'Donnell's slim narrative of the southern Indians' participation remain the standard texts. Other essays and papers have struggled to find a framework that will make sense of the complexity and confusion of American Indians and the American Revolution. Barbara Graymont, *The Iroquois in the American Revolution* (Syracuse, N.Y.: Syracuse University Press, 1972); James H. O'Donnell, III, *The Southern Indians in the American Revolution* (Knoxville: University of Tennessee Press, 1973); S. F. Wise, "The American Revolution and Indian History," in John S. Moir, ed., *Character and Circumstance: Essays in Honour of Donald Grant Creighton* (Toronto: Macmillan, 1970), 182–200; Francis Jennings, "The Indians' Revolution," in Alfred F. Young, ed., *Explorations in the History of American Radicalism* (De Kalb: Northern Illinois University Press, 1976); idem, ed., *The American Indian and the American Revolution* (Chicago: Occasional Papers of the Newberry Library Center for the History of the American Indian, 1983); Kenneth M. Morrison, "Native Americans and the American Revolution: Historic Stories and Shifting Frontier Conflict," in Frederick E. Hoxie, ed., *Indians in American History* (Arlington Heights, Ill.: Davidson, 1988), 95–115; Bernard Sheehan, "The Problem of the Indian in the American Revolution," in Philip Weeks, ed., *The American Indian Experience* (Arlington Heights, Ill.: Forum, 1988), 66–80; Andrew McFarland Davis, "The Indians and the Border Warfare of the Revolution," in Justin Winsor, ed., *Narrative and Critical History of America*, 8 vols. (Boston: Houghton Mifflin, 1884–9), vol. 6: 605–84.
[3] Peter Marshall, "The West and the Indians, 1756–1776," and James H. Merrell, "Indians and the New Republic," in Jack P. Greene and J. R. Pole, eds., *The Blackwell Encyclopedia of the American Revolution* (Oxford: Blackwell Publisher, 1991), 153–60, 392–98. Likewise, Francis Jennings, "The Indians' Revolution" is rooted firmly in midcentury.

treatment after the Revolution justified. Because many Indians sided with the British, they have, from the Declaration of Independence onward, been portrayed as allies of tyranny and enemies of liberty. Yet Indian people in revolutionary America, whether they sided with rebels, redcoats, neither, or both, were doing pretty much the same thing as the American colonists: fighting for their freedom in tumultuous times. The Revolution was an anticolonial war of liberation for Indian peoples too, but the threat to their freedom often came from colonial neighbors rather than distant capitals, and their colonial experience did not end with American independence.

We cannot tell the full story of revolutionary America without including American Indians, and we cannot begin to grasp the reality of the Revolution for Indian people without shifting our focus to Indian country and to Indian communities. Any broadly brushed treatment of Indian involvement and experiences is likely to obscure and distort local diversity; only by looking at different groups and communities can one get a sense of the range of experiences of Indian peoples in these times. Indian villages, as much as New England towns, were communities living in and responding to revolutionary conditions, although getting at their story is, of course, much more difficult.

Scholars who have tried to view the Revolution from an Indian standpoint have found it understandably difficult to divorce the years 1775–83 from the changes affecting Indian America throughout the eighteenth century. For Indian people in eastern North America, the entire century was an age of revolution, a pivotal era in which "the balance tipped irrevocably away from the Indian."[4] In some ways the Revolution only intensified familiar pressures on Indian lives and lands. The Indians' "War of Independence" was well under way before 1775, was waged on many fronts – economic, cultural, political, and military – and continued long after 1783.

War was nothing new in Indian country in the eighteenth century, but the Revolution generated new sources of conflict and new levels of violence that destroyed much of the world Indians, and non-Indians, had created there. As elsewhere in North America, old structures, traditional patterns of behavior, and long-standing alliances broke down in a climate of tumult and change. Religious ferment and dissension split Indian congregations and communities as well as white ones. Dissident groups challenged established authority in Indian country as well as in colonial society. Refugees from war and hunger choked forts and villages. By the end of the Revolution, Shawnees from Ohio were living in Missouri, New England Indians were living among the Oneidas in New York, and there were two Iroquois leagues: one in New York State, the other on the Grand River in Ontario. Stockbridge Indians from Massachusetts,

---

[4] James H. Merrell, *The Indians' New World: Catawbas and Their Neighbors from European Contact through the Era of Removal* (Chapel Hill: University of North Carolina Press, 1989), 280.

who had been loyal allies of the crown in earlier wars against the French, now turned away from the king and made common cause with the rebels, defying the authority of their Mohawk "fathers" in doing so. In the meantime, their home community underwent final transformation into a white man's town. Abenaki Indians who had been driven north and suffered bitter losses at the hands of New Hampshire rangers in the Seven Years' War now returned south and served alongside the rangers in defense of the Connecticut Valley, while their relatives who remained at Odanak evaded British recruitment efforts. Delaware and Shawnee chiefs who counseled moderation found themselves swept aside by the current of events in the Ohio Valley. Young Cherokee warriors challenged the authority of older chiefs and joined hands with militants from the north. Alliances that cut across old tribal lines became the norm.[5] Seminole communities in northern Florida asserted autonomy from the parent Creek confederacy and engaged in their own version of "nation building." Chickasaw headmen who had been steadfast in loyalty to Britain throughout the century found that, by 1783, they needed to develop new foreign policies to preserve their independence in a region now coveted by both Spaniards and Americans.

Anthropologists remind us that social beings exist "not in a world of events but in a world of meaning,"[6] and scholars of Indian history struggle increasingly to develop sensitivity to the emic realities of native societies, and to guard against their own etic preconceptions. A former president of the American Society for Ethnohistory has questioned "whether the American Revolution was a real event for American Indians," or whether it represented only "the paternal substitution of George the First for George the Third."[7] It is true that the American Revolution in Indian country can be understood only in the context of a longer-term and larger turmoil, and that the American winning of independence did nothing to alleviate this turmoil. But to see the Revolution only as substituting a president for a monarch is to place too much weight on its outcome and on what Anglo-Americans saw as its most importance consequence. It ignores the searing impact that the Revolution had *in Indian country*, and the significance of the events that occurred there for the people whose lives they disrupted. The substitution of President Washington for King George may not have been an important event for Indian people, but burning villages in the course of the conflict that produced the substitution undoubtedly was, and the new situation resulting from the substitution had far-reaching repercussions in Indian country. When Indian chiefs told the Spanish governor of Saint Louis

[5] Gregory Evans Dowd, *A Spirited Resistance: The North American Indian Struggle for Unity, 1745–1815* (Baltimore: Johns Hopkins University Press, 1992).

[6] Henry S. Sharp, "Memory, Meaning, and Imaginary Time: The Construction of Knowledge in White and Chipewyan Cultures," *Ethnohistory* 38 (1991), 162.

[7] Raymond D. Fogelson, "The Ethnohistory of Events and Nonevents," *Ethnohistory* 36 (1989), 142.

in 1784 that the American Revolution constituted "the greatest blow that could have been dealt us," they were talking about a real event and they called it that, but for them the important point about the Revolution was the flood of American settlers it unleashed onto their lands.[8] Indian people were deeply affected both by the consequences of the Revolution and by its course, irrespective of its outcome. The meaning of the Revolution, for them, was very different; the event itself was all too real.

In the end, white Americans excluded Indians from the republican society the Revolution created. Despite their absence from much of the historical literature, Indian people were everywhere in colonial America.[9] In 1775, Indian nations, despite intrusive and disruptive pressures unleashed by European contact, still controlled most of America west of the Appalachians. In 1783, when Britain transferred that territory to the new United States, most of it was still in Indian hands, but a new era had begun. The American revolutionaries who fought for freedom from the British Empire in the East also fought to create an empire of their own in the West. Contention over Indian land was an old story by 1775, but the Revolution elevated acquisition of Indian lands into a national policy. The new nation, born of a bloody revolution and committed to expansion, could not tolerate America as Indian country. Increasingly, Americans viewed the future as one without Indians. The Revolution both created a new society and provided justification for excluding Indians from it.

The American Revolution generated new policies, new ideologies of republicanism, and new social experiments, all of which affected Indian people directly and indirectly. To do justice to these issues would expand this book beyond manageable limits and carry the story well into the nineteenth century. Many of the chapters in this book look before 1775 and beyond 1783, but the Revolutionary War years remain its core and its focus. My purpose is not to present a complete narrative of events during these years, but rather to examine a number of Indian communities as case studies of how Native Americans fared during the conflict, and to offer suggestions as to what the American Revolution meant for these people.

"Indian country" has a range of legal, economic, cultural, and political meanings. It is used here simply to mean where Indian people lived. This broad definition permits inclusion of the Stockbridge Indians, who by the time of the Revolution lived in a town surrounded by white settlements, as well as the Chickasaws, who at the end of the Revolution still dictated which and whether outsiders should enter their country. The term "Indian country" is not intended to indicate the existence of separate Indian and white worlds.

---

[8] *Spain in the Mississippi Valley* vol. 3, pt. 2: 117.
[9] James H. Merrell, "Some Thoughts on Colonial Historians and American Indians," *William and Mary Quarterly*, 3d series, 46 (1989), 94–119. See also James Axtell, "Colonial America without the Indians: Counterfactual Reflections," *Journal of American History* 73 (1986–7), 981–96.

My use of "community" is similarly loose, referring usually, but not always, to a group of people living in face-to-face association and occupying a common location, either permanently or seasonally. What Europeans called tribes were often aggregates of communities; many Indian communities were also multiethnic units rather than members of a single tribe. A community sometimes comprised several villages in a particular area rather than a single town in a single location. Names of communities should often be regarded as "addresses" rather than tribal designations. Native Americans were accustomed to accommodating a variety of groups and individuals within flexible bonds and fluid social structures. Approaching the Revolution in Indian country on a community-by-community basis rather than a tribe-by-tribe one seems to better reflect the social and political realities of Indian society. As Richard White has pointed out, Indian country was largely a world of villages.[10]

Although sympathetic to the view that one should call people what they call themselves, I have retained the names of individuals and groups in the form I thought would be most readily identifiable for most readers. Where a person's Indian name appears regularly in the records I have retained it; so, for example, Little Carpenter appears as Attakullakulla in this book. Otherwise I have used the English name, for example White Eyes instead of Koquethagecton.

The author does not pretend to try and tell the "Indian side of the story." Nor, in concentrating attention on Native Americans, does he forget that this was a civil war for others too. As the experience of thousands of Loyalists, or a glance at the war in the southern backcountry reminds us, Indian communities were not the only ones to suffer and fracture during these calamitous times.[11] This is a non-Indian view of Indian history, and a non-American view of American history, written by an expatriate Briton who holds no brief for British colonialism but who believes that distance and objectivity can be as valuable as "inside information" in writing good history. The communities discussed in this volume represent small patches of a huge tapestry. That tapestry must be fully pieced together before we can begin to appreciate the experiences of all the participants in the American Revolution or understand the full meaning of the story of this nation's birth.

[10] Richard White, *The Middle Ground: Indians, Empires, and Republics in the Great Lakes Region, 1650–1815* (Cambridge University Press, 1991).
[11] For example, Ronald Hoffman, Thad W. Tate, and Peter J. Albert, eds., *An Uncivil War: The Southern Backcountry during the American Revolution* (Charlottesville: University Press of Virginia, 1985); John S. Pancake, *This Destructive War: The British Campaign in the Carolinas, 1780–1782* (University: University of Alabama Press, 1985), esp. 83–90.

# Acknowledgments

Most of the research for this book was done in the East; most of the writing was done in the West; much of the thinking about it was done on long trips across country. I am grateful to my family – on both sides of the Atlantic – for accepting my way of life, which has taken me out of *their* lives so often and for so long, and to my colleagues at the University of Wyoming for putting up with my frequent absences.

I have accumulated many other debts over the years of work that have gone into this project. The University of Wyoming supported and recognized my research with a faculty grant-in-aid in 1989, basic research grants in 1987, 1988, and 1992, Alumni Association awards in 1987 and 1988, a Cardoso faculty award in 1992, and a research merit award in 1991. Other support came in the form of a visiting fellowship at the Beinecke Library, a research fellowship at the David Library of the American Revolution in Washington Crossing, Pennsylvania, a National Endowment for the Humanities summer stipend, a Phillips Fund grant from the American Philosophical Society, and an Archie K. Davis fellowship from the North Caroliniana Society.

This study has benefited greatly from the expertise, collegiality, and helpfulness of people at a wide range of institutions. I am grateful to the University of Wyoming's William Robertson Coe Library, and particularly the interlibrary loan staff, who invariably pursued my requests with diligence and effectiveness; the British Museum and Public Record Office; the Library of Congress; the Newberry Library; the William L. Clements Library at the University of Michigan, where Rob Cox helped make a short visit productive beyond my expectations; Yale's Stirling and Beinecke libraries; the Massachusetts Historical Society, Massachusetts Archives, and Boston Public Library; the New Hampshire Historical Society; the Vermont Historical Society; the David Library of the American Revolution, where David Fowler and Ezra Stone made my visits pleasant as well as productive; the New York Public Library, Rare Books and Manuscript Division; the New York State Archives; the Connecticut State Library, Archives Department, and the Connecticut Historical Society; the National Archives of Canada; Dartmouth's Baker Library; the Stockbridge town library, where Pauline Pierce provided quick and efficient help, and Stockbridge town hall; Hamilton College, where Frank Lorenz was a perfect guide; Harvard's Widener and Houghton libraries; the Southern Historical Collection and H. G. Jones, Curator of the North Caroliniana Collection, at the Wilson Library, University of North Carolina at Chapel Hill; the North Carolina Department of Cultural Resources, Division of Archives and History; Duke University's William Perkins Library; the Tennessee State Library and Archives; the Mississippi Department of Archives and History, and Bruce Chapell at the P. K. Yonge Library at the University of Florida in Gainesville.

Many other people have provided help, inspiration, and guidance, reading portions of the manuscript, offering information, sharing ideas, or simply responding to enquiries. Frederick E. Hoxie encouraged me to stay with the Revolution at a time when the northern plains were beckoning strongly, and he and Neal Salisbury both made valuable suggestions that greatly improved this book. Cambridge editor Frank Smith displayed an early interest in the project and did some useful editing of the final manuscript. Cary Groner did a thoughtful job of copyediting the manuscript and Camilla Palmer steered the book through production. Robert Grumet read large portions of the manuscript and was generous with his time and comments. Others who deserve mention include Barry O'Connell, colleague and good friend from our first meeting; Michael Green, Reginald Horsman, Robert Scott Davis, Jr., John Sugden, John Moody, Fredrika Teute, Patrick Frazier, Daniel Mandell, Earl Olmstead, Phil Hoffman, William L. Anderson, James A. Lewis, Joan Greene Orr of the Museum of the Cherokee Indian, Mary Druke Becker, Alan Taylor, William Autry, Patricia Galloway, Dolores Elliott, Marjory Barnum Hinman, Barbara Sivertsen, Barbara Covey, Peter C. Mancall, James H. O'Donnell, III, Ronald Schultz, Terry Barnhart, and Dennis Farmer, who walked me over the grounds of Fort Niagara on a chilly spring morning and showed me the location of the Indian refugee camps.

Ideas and versions of chapters were tried out before audiences at meetings of the American Society for Ethnohistory, the Organization of American Historians, the Conference for Iroquois Research, the Dublin Seminar for New England Folklife, and the New England Historical Association, as well as at the David Library of the American Revolution, Brown University, the Capitol Historical Society, the University of Wyoming, Dartmouth College, Keene State College, and the Yorktown Victory Center.

At the University of Wyoming I have been blessed with three successive departmental chairs – the late Lawrence Cardoso, Herbert Dieterich, and William H. Moore – who ensured that university administration did not get in the way of research, writing, and teaching. Sharon Brown was always patient with my computing ineptitude and helped solve many problems. Linda Marston prepared the maps, and my colleague and good friend Phil Roberts compiled the index. The university encouraged my research, accommodated my rather un-orthodox academic life-style, and, in times of tightening budgets, managed to boost my morale with awards for teaching and research.

My thanks go to all of the people who have helped, directly or indirectly, to make this book possible. They share credit for whatever is good in it, and bear no responsibility for whatever is not. During most of the years when this book was taking shape in Wyoming, Marcia kept together our home in Vermont, while trying to maintain a career of her own. Our children, Graeme and Megan, arrived while the book was being researched and written, and have made me understand, as never before, what events such as those described here meant for people who were parents.

# Abbreviations

AGI, PC

Archivo General de Indias, Seville, Papeles Procedentes de Cuba. Transcripts of parts of this collection are available in several archives in the United States. The P. K. Yonge Library at the University of Florida at Gainesville holds a microfilm edition of the collection. The author consulted the microfilm calendar of the collection at Duke University's Perkins Library (M5989); specific documents were obtained at the North Carolina Division of Archives and History, Raleigh, and the Library of Congress.

*American Archives*

Peter Force, comp. *American Archives* 4th series, 6 vols. Washington D.C., 1837–46, and 5th series, 3 vols., Washington D.C., 1848–53.

*ASPIA*

Walter Lowrie and Matthew St. Clair Clarke, eds., *American State Papers, Documents, Legislative and Executive, of the Congress of the United States (1789–1815), Class II, Indian Affairs.* Washington D.C.: Gales & Seaton, 1832.

C.O. 5

Public Record Office, Kew, England. Colonial Office Records, Series 5: America and the West Indies. Over the years, the author has consulted the original manuscripts at the British Public Record Office (C.O. 5), transcripts of the Library of Congress (LC, C.O. 5), and the printed documents relating to the American Revolution (*DAR*).

| | |
|---|---|
| Carleton Papers | Public Records Office, Kew, England, Gifts and Deposits. Carleton Papers or Headquarters Papers of the British Army in America: P.R.O. 30/55 (also available on microfilm). |
| Clements Library | William L. Clements Library, University of Michigan, Ann Arbor. |
| Clinton Mss. | Henry Clinton Papers, William L. Clements Library, University of Michigan, Ann Arbor. |
| *DAR* | K. G. Davies, ed., *Documents of the American Revolution, 1770–1783* (Colonial Office series), 21 vols. Shannon: Irish University Press, 1972–82. |
| Draper Mss. | Lyman Copeland Draper Manuscripts, State Historical Society of Wisconsin. On microfilm. |
| *Frontier Advance* | Louise P. Kellogg, ed., *Frontier Advance on the Upper Ohio, 1778–1779*. Madison: Wisconsin State Historical Society, 1916. |
| *Frontier Defense* | Reuben G. Thwaites and Louise P. Kellogg, eds., *Frontier Defense on the Upper Ohio, 1777–1778*. Madison: Wisconsin State Historical Society, 1912. |
| *Frontier Retreat* | Louise P. Kellogg, ed., *Frontier Retreat on the Upper Ohio, 1779–1782*. Madison: Wisconsin State Historical Society, 1917. |
| Gage Papers | Thomas Gage Papers, William L. Clements Library, University of Michigan, Ann Arbor. |
| Haldimand Papers | Correspondence and Papers of Governor General Sir Frederick Haldimand, 1758–91, British Museum, London, Additional Manuscripts 21661–21892. |
| Hand Papers | Library of Congress, Peter Force Transcripts, Series 7e, reels 13–14, items 55–7, Edward Hand Papers, 1775–1846. |
| H.M.C. | Historical Manuscripts Commission, London. |
| *Johnson Papers* | James Sullivan et al., eds., *The Papers of Sir William Johnson*, 15 vols. Albany: SUNY Press, 1921–65. |

| | |
|---|---|
| L.C., C.O.5. | Colonial Office Records, Series 5, transcripts in Library of Congress. |
| Mass. Archives | Massachusetts Archives. In the Massachusetts State Archives at Columbia Point, Boston. |
| Morgan Letterbooks | Carnegie Library of Pittsburgh, Colonel George Morgan Letterbooks, 3 vols., 1775–9. |
| *MPA, FD* | *Mississippi Provincial Archives, French Dominion.* Vols. 1–3, edited by Dunbar Rowland and A. G. Sanders (Jackson: Mississippi Department of Archives and History, 1927–32); vols. 4–5, edited by Dunbar Rowland, A. G. Sanders, and Patricia Kay Galloway (Baton Rouge: Louisiana State University Press, 1984). |
| *MPHC* | *Collections of the Michigan Pioneer and Historical Society,* 40 vols., 1874–1929. |
| NAC, C-1223 | National Archives of Canada, Records Relating to Indian Affairs (R.G. 10), second series, microfilm reel C-1223: Minutes of Indian Affairs, 1755–90. |
| *NYCD* | E. B. O'Callaghan and Berthold Fernow, eds., *Documents Relative to the Colonial History of the State of New York,* 15 vols. Albany: Weed, Parsons, 1853–87. |
| NYPL | New York Public Library. |
| North Carolina Colonial Records | William L. Saunders and Walter Clark, eds., *The Colonial and State Records of North Carolina,* 30 vols. Raleigh: Secretary of State, 1886–1914, vols. 1–9. |
| North Carolina State Records | Saunders and Clark, eds., *Colonial and State Records of North Carolina,* vols. 10–30. |
| *PCC* | Papers of the Continental Congress, 1774–89, National Archives Microfilm, No. M247. |
| *Penn. Archives* | *Pennsylvania Archives,* first series, 12 vols., Philadelphia, 1852–6. |
| Report on American Mss. | "Report on American Manuscripts in the Royal Institution of Great Britain," 4 vols. *Historical Manuscripts Commission,* |

59. London: His Majesty's Stationary Office, 1904–9.

*Revolution and Confederation*    Colin G. Calloway, ed., *Revolution and Confederation*. Vol. 18 of Alden T. Vaughan, gen. ed., *Early American Indian Documents: Laws and Treaties*. Frederick, Md.: University Publications of America, 1994.

*Revolution on the Upper Ohio*    Reuben G. Thwaites and Louise P. Kellogg, eds., *The Revolution on the Upper Ohio, 1775–1777*. Madison: Wisconsin State Historical Society, 1908.

Schuyler Papers    NYPL, Philip Schuyler Papers, Indian Papers, 1710–96, boxes 13–15, reel 7.

*Spain in the Mississippi Valley*    Lawrence Kinnaird, trans. and ed., *Spain in the Mississippi Valley, 1765–1794: Translations of Materials from the Spanish Archives in the Bancroft Library, University of California, Berkeley*. American Historical Association, Annual Report for the Year 1945 (Washington D.C., 1946–9.), vols. 2–4: Part 1: The Revolutionary Period, 1765–1781; Part 2: The Post-War Decade, 1782–1791; Part 3: Problems of Frontier Defense, 1792–1794.

*Virginia State Papers*    William P. Palmer et al., eds., *Calendar of Virginia State Papers and Other Manuscripts Preserved in the Capitol at Richmond*, 11 vols., Richmond: James E. Goode, 1875–83.

*WHC*    Wisconsin State Historical Society Collections.

*Writings of Washington*    John C. Fitzpatrick, ed., *The Writings of George Washington from the Original Manuscript Sources, 1745–1799*, 39 vols. Washington, D.C.: Government Printing Office, 1931–44.

Note: In order to keep notes to a manageable length, names of correspondents and dates of correspondence have been omitted in cases where page or folio numbers serve adequately to locate the documents.

# Prologue

## *New worlds for all: Indian America by 1775*

In the summer of 1775, as news of the opening conflicts in the American Revolution spread west, a young Englishman recently arrived from Derbyshire in search of good land traveled to the "Indian country" of the Ohio Valley. Nicholas Cresswell went with a party that consisted of two Englishmen, two Irishmen, a Welshman, two Dutchmen, two Virginians, two Marylanders, a Swede, an African, and a mulatto. On August 27, Cresswell visited a mission town of Moravian Delawares at Wal-hack-tap-poke or Schönbrunn, a settlement of sixty log houses covered with clapboards, arranged along neatly laid-out streets, and a meeting house with a bell and glass windows. The parson preached through an interpreter, the Indian congregation sang hymns in Delaware, and the service was conducted with "the greatest regularity, order, and decorum, I ever saw in any place of Worship in my life." Four days later, Cresswell was at the Delaware town of Coshocton, where he participated in an Indian dance. The beating of drums, the gourd rattles, the rattling of deer hooves on the knees and ankles of the male dancers, and the jingling of the women's bells struck Cresswell's ears as "the most unharmonious concert that human idea can possibly conceive," and the sight of an "Indian Conjuror" in a mask and bear skin was "frightful enough to scare the Devil."[1]

Indian America by 1775 was a landscape of cultural polyphony, or more accurately perhaps, cultural cacophony, a country of mixed and mixing peoples. Cresswell's brief sojourn among the Delawares exposed him to some of Indian country's diversity and to its mixture of change and continuity. He saw Indians who wore European clothes but retained traditional loincloths and nose rings. He noted that they had learned to curse from Europeans, observed that white traders cheated them blind whenever they could, lamented the destructive effects of alcohol, and learned that smallpox had "made terrible havoc." He traveled with Indian girls who served as guides during the day and bedfellows

[1] *The Journal of Nicholas Cresswell, 1774–1777* (New York: Dial, 1924), 87, 106, 109. Henry Warner Bowden, *American Indians and Christian Missions* (University of Chicago Press, 1981), 160, identifies the mission.

at night. He witnessed Indian orators in council, and became something of an ethnographic observer. He had "been taught to look upon these beings with contempt," but instead developed "a great regard for the Indians" and felt "a most sensible regret in parting from them." Three months in a changing Indian world changed a visiting Englishman.[2]

The next year, a New Jersey captain in Iroquois country was struck, as Cresswell had been among the Delawares, by the contrast between the quiet and orderly church services of the Oneidas, and the noise, drumming, and chanting of Seneca, Cayuga, and Onondaga ceremonies. Many Oneidas by this time were Presbyterians, although traditional beliefs and rituals survived intact. Some people were literate in both English and Iroquoian. Some Oneida children attended school, many Oneidas were skilled carpenters and farmers, and trade with Europeans was a major economic activity.[3]

Other Indian communities throughout the eastern woodlands displayed similar blends of old and new. Single-family log cabins had replaced, or coexisted with, traditional wigwams and communal longhouses. At the mission village of Lorette on the Saint Lawrence, for example, the Huron Indians "built all their houses after the French fashion." In New England, Indian families who still lived in wigwams likely had their share of European-manufactured household goods, and even European-style furniture.[4] The palisaded villages of the seventeenth century had often given way to more open and dispersed settlements in which kin groups settled near their fields and livestock rather than around the village council house. Indian towns sometimes comprised clusters of small hamlets; sometimes they were large multiethnic trading centers.[5]

Indian America had always experienced changes, of course, but their tempo and impact increased dramatically after the arrival of European and African

[2] *Journal of Nicholas Cresswell*, 49–50, 105–6, 108, 113, 118–19, 120–2.

[3] Mark E. Lender and James Kirby Martin, eds., *Citizen Soldier: The Revolutionary War Journal of Joseph Bloomfield* (Newark: New Jersey Historical Society, 1992), 90–1; David Levinson, "An Explanation of the Oneida–Colonist Alliance in the American Revolution," *Ethnohistory* 23 (1976), 280.

[4] Robert S. Grumet, *National Historic Landmark Theme Study. Historic Contact: Early Relations Between Indian People and Colonists in Northeastern North America, 1524–1783* (National Park Service, 1992); Daniel K. Richter, *The Ordeal of the Longhouse: The Peoples of the Iroquois League in the Era of European Colonization* (Chapel Hill: University of North Carolina Press, 1992), 261; William S. and Cheryl L. Simmons, eds., *Old Light on Separate Ways: The Narragansett Diary of Joseph Fish, 1765–1776* (Hanover, N.H.: University Press of New England, 1982). xxx; Adolph B. Benson, ed., *Peter Kalm's Travels in North America*, 2 vols. (New York: Wilson-Erickson, 1937), vol. 2: 462; William Sturtevant, "Two 1761 Wigwams at Niantic, Connecticut," *American Antiquity* 40 (1975), 437–44; Kathleen J. Bragdon, "The Material Culture of the Christian Indians of New England, 1650–1775," in Mary C. Beaudry, ed., *Documentary Archaeology and the New World* (Cambridge University Press, 1988), 128–9.

[5] Benson, ed., *Peter Kalm's Travels*, vol. 2: 619; Marvin T. Smith, *Archaeology of Aboriginal Culture Change in the Interior Southeast* (Gainesville: University Presses of Florida, 1987), 94; Michael N. McConnell, *A Country Between: The Upper Ohio Valley and Its Peoples, 1724–1774* (Lincoln: University of Nebraska Press, 1992), 24–7.

people, producing what James Merrell has aptly described as a "new world" for Native Americans. "It is strange what revolution has happened among them in less than two hundred years," remarked Hector De Crèvecoeur. At first contact, America was what John Winthrop called a land "full of Indians." By the end of the colonial period, the Indians of the eastern woodlands numbered perhaps 150,000 people in a world teeming with immigrants. Most who survived did so by adjusting in some measure to Europeans and their ways.[6]

Adjusting to Indian country and Indian people also created a new world for the newcomers. Like the rest of colonial America, Indian country was an arena in which a "kaleidoscope of human encounters" generated a web of cultural exchanges as Indians, Africans, and Europeans made what T. H. Breen has called "creative adaptations" to new places and new peoples.[7] Those Indians, Africans, and Europeans were not representatives of monolithic groups, but individuals of different ethnicity, geography, gender, and status. "Indians" were Abenakis, Delawares, Senecas, and Cherokees; "Africans" were Ibos, Ashantis, and Yorubas; "Europeans" were Swedes, Germans, Scots, Irish, and English – and Englishmen from London were very different than Englishmen from Cornwall or Yorkshire.

Mohawks shared their villages with individuals from other tribes, and their valley home with people of Dutch, German, Scottish, Irish, and English descent. Delawares lived alongside Swedes and Finns before Germans, Scotch-Irish and Welsh settled their lands. Franco-Indian communities and individuals persisted long after the collapse of New France. Catholic Indians often spoke French and bore French names, wearing crucifixes as well. Cosmopolitan French communities that embraced both Indians and blacks dotted the landscape from the Saint Lawrence to the mouth of the Mississippi. Non-Indians lived and trespassed in Indian country, with or without the Indians' consent. Scotch-Irish borderers competed with Cherokee and Shawnee hunters in the latter's traditional hunting territories; Cherokee and Shawnee villages were home to Scots and Irish Indian agents; adopted white captives took their place in the kinship network of Indian societies. Runaway slaves added an African strand to the fabric of southeastern Indian communities. People who intruded on Indian country often

---

[6] James H. Merrell, *The Indians' New World: Catawbas and Their Neighbors from European Contact through the Era of Removal* (Chapel Hill: University of North Carolina Press, 1989); idem, "'The Customes of Our Countrey': Indians and Colonists in Early America," in Bernard Bailyn and Philip D. Morgan, eds., *Strangers within the Realm: Cultural Margins of the First British Empire* (Chapel Hill: University of North Carolina Press, 1991), 117–56, esp. 122–4; J. Hector St. John De Crèvecoeur, *Letters from an American Farmer* (New York: Dutton, 1957), 102–3.

[7] T. H. Breen, "Creative Adaptations: Peoples and Cultures," in Jack P. Greene and J. R. Pole, eds. *Colonial British America: Essays in the New History of the Early Modern Era* (Baltimore: Johns Hopkins University Press, 1984), 195–232. For discussion of creative adaptations between Native Americans and African Americans see J. Leitch Wright, Jr., *The Only Land They Knew* (New York: Free Press, 1981), ch. 11.

pursued their own independence from eastern authorities and rendered ineffective much of colonial and early national Indian policy.

Indian people likewise participated in shaping colonial and revolutionary
American society. They served in colonial armies as soldiers and scouts, traveled
to colonial capitals as ambassadors, attended colonial colleges as students, walked
the streets of colonial towns as visitors, came to settlements as peddlers, and
worked as slaves, servants, interpreters, guides, laborers, carpenters, whalers,
and sailors. The proximity and interconnectedness of Indian and colonial communities throughout large areas of North America gave the backcountry warfare of the Revolution a face-to-face nature that heightened its bitterness.

The "changes in the land" described by William Cronon in colonial New
England were replicated with variations on other frontiers in the wake of European contact. Ecosystems, like cultures, experience perpetual change, and Indian
people had been clearing and cultivating fields for hundreds of years before
Europeans arrived. But the colonists, and in the South their African slaves,
introduced new plants, new techniques of forestry, new agricultural practices,
and domesticated livestock, which generated far-reaching changes in the physical
world Indian people inhabited. Indians in Maryland had complained to the
General Assembly in the seventeenth century that the colonists' cows ate their
corn. "Your hogs & Cattle injure Us," they said. "We Can fly no farther let
us know where to live & how to be secured for the future from the Hogs &
Cattle." Later generations of Indian people incorporated cows and pigs into
their economies. Old World grazing animals not only contributed to deforestation; they also brought new grasses like Kentucky bluegrass. English colonists
in the south found Indians cultivating peach trees, introduced by Spaniards
and diffused northward along native trade routes, as if they were indigenous to
the region. Charles Woodmason noted that the Carolina backcountry had begun
to "wear a new face" by the 1760s as colonists carved farms and fields out of the
forest.[8]

For thousands of Indian people, the new world that Europeans created was
also a graveyard. European and African people brought with them lethal diseases
common in the Old World but unknown in America. Smallpox, plague, measles,

[8] William Cronon, *Changes in the Land: Indians, Colonists, and the Ecology of New England* (New York: Hill & Wang, 1983); Timothy Silver, *A New Face on the Countryside: Indians, Colonists, and Slaves In South Atlantic Forests, 1500–1800* (Cambridge University Press, 1990); *Archives of Maryland* 2 (1884), 15; David J. Weber, *The Spanish Frontier in North America* (New Haven, Conn.: Yale University Press, 1993), 309, 311–12. See also M. Thomas Hatley, "The Three Lives of Keowee: Loss and Recovery in Eighteenth-Century Cherokee Villages," in Peter Wood et al., eds., *Powhatan's Mantle: Indians in the Colonial Southeast* (Lincoln: University of Nebraska Press, 1989), 241. Carolyn Merchant explains how the "colonial ecological revolution" in New England was succeeded by the "capitalist ecological revolution" and the onset of urbanization and indus-trialization in the early national period in *Ecological Revolutions: Nature, Gender, and Science in New England* (Chapel Hill: University of North Carolina Press, 1989).

influenza, pneumonia, tuberculosis, diphtheria, yellow fever, and a host of new diseases took hold in Indian America and produced one of human history's greatest biological catastrophes. Whole communities perished. Others lost 50 percent, 75 percent, or 90 percent of their population. Recurrent epidemics of the same or different diseases prevented population recovery. European travelers in Indian country saw abandoned villages and met stunned survivors. The new world of death even produced changes in burial practices.[9] Not all Native American populations dropped at the same rate in the wake of European invasion; in the lower Mississippi Valley, among the Creeks, and in some areas of the Great Lakes, Indian populations were actually on the rise in the eighteenth century, in part because they absorbed refugees from other areas.[10] Nevertheless, European invaders confronted Indian people whose capacity to resist often had been seriously eroded before they laid eyes on the enemy.[11] British Indian superintendent Sir William Johnson had the Mohawks inoculated against smallpox, but "contagious Distempers" continued to thin Iroquois numbers.[12] Most Europeans simply accepted the slaughter; but on at least one occasion the British actively promoted it. When two Delawares came into Fort Pitt for talks during Pontiac's War in 1763, "we gave them two Blankets and an Handkerchief out of the Smallpox Hospital," wrote William Trent in his journal. "I hope it will have the desired effect." It did.[13]

The new world that emerged in the wake of European contact was also one of unprecedented violence. Social disruption created random individual violence; warfare reached new levels of intensity. Indians fought each other for access to European guns, then turned the guns on their enemies with deadly effect.[14] Increasingly dependent upon European allies for the goods and guns vital to

*violence*

---

[9] Wright, *The Only Land They Knew*, 228–9.

[10] See, for example, Peter H. Wood, "The Changing Population of the Colonial South," in Wood et al., eds., *Powhatan's Mantle*, 56–60, 66–72; Richard White, *The Middle Ground: Indians, Empires and Republics in the Great Lakes Region, 1650–1815* (Cambridge University Press, 1991), 145.

[11] There is now an extensive literature on Native American demography and epidemiology. Standard works include: Russell Thornton, *American Indian Holocaust and Survival: A Population History since 1492* (Norman: University of Oklahoma Press, 1987); Henry F. Dobyns, *Their Number Become Thinned* (Knoxville: University of Tennessee Press, 1983). Some of the most recent scholarship is reflected in John W. Verano and Douglas H. Ubelaker, eds., *Disease and Demography in the Americas* (Washington, D.C.: Smithsonian Institution Press, 1992).

[12] Milton W. Hamilton, ed., "Guy Johnson's Opinions on the American Indian," *Pennsylvania Magazine of History and Biography* 77 (1953), 326; cf. Carl F. Klinck and James J. Talman, eds., *The Journal of John Norton* (Toronto: Champlain Society, 1970), 274.

[13] "Journal of William Trent," in John W. Harpster, ed., *Pen Pictures of Early Western Pennsylvania* (University of Pittsburgh Press, 1938), 103–4. See also Bernard Knollenberg, "General Amherst and Germ Warfare," *Mississippi Valley Historical Review* 41 (1954–5), 489–94, 762–3.

[14] See, for example, J. Frederick Fausz, "Fighting 'Fire' with Firearms: The Anglo-Powhatan Arms Race in Early Virginia," *American Indian Culture and Research Journal* 3 (1979), 33–50; and Patrick M. Malone, *The Skulking Way of War: Technology and Tactics Among the Indians of New England* (Lanham, Md.: Madison, 1991).

survival in a dangerous new world, they found it difficult if not impossible to avoid becoming involved in the wars for empire waged in North America. George Morgan, American Indian agent at Fort Pitt, knew that Indian neutrality in the Revolution was unlikely: "They have long been taught by contending Nations to be bought & sold."[5] Intertribal warfare escalated and, again, Europeans sometimes worked to curtail it, sometimes actively encouraged it as part of a "divide and conquer" strategy.[6]

Endemic warfare disrupted normal patterns of life. Communities that diverted their manpower into war felt the repercussions in lost sons and husbands, in reduced economic productivity and increased dependence on allies, in disrupted ceremonial calendars and neglected rituals, and in diplomatic chaos and political upheaval. War became normal, and the warrior culture that was ingrained in many societies as they battled their Indian and European enemies created a stereotype of Indians as warlike, which in European eyes justified treating them as "savages." In some societies, the influence of women declined as Europeans dealt exclusively with males as the hunters and warriors; in others, women's traditional roles escaped relatively undisturbed and provided a much-needed measure of stability.[17]

In a world of escalating violence, war chiefs rose in status as civil chiefs lost influence. Richard White has painstakingly reconstructed the attempts of French and Algonkian people living in the Great Lakes region in the late seventeenth century to create a "middle ground" of common understanding and accommodation in a world of upheaval. Chiefs struggled to maintain peace, knowing that the alternative to coexistence and mutual dependency was a bloodbath. First the French, then the British, learned that success in this middle-ground world required mediation, moderation, and generosity, not force and coercion. But the Franco-Indian alliance unraveled as the Ohio Valley, once a haven between

---

[5] Carnegie Library, Pittsburgh, George Morgan Letterbook, vol. 2: 2.

[6] E.g., Thomas Gage to John Stuart, Jan. 27, 1764, Clements Library, Gage Papers.

[17] Theda Perdue, "Cherokee Women and the Trail of Tears," *Journal of Women's History* 1 (1989), 14–15. Paula Gunn Allen, *The Sacred Hoop: Recovering the Feminine in American Indian Traditions* 2d ed. (Boston: Beacon, 1992), 30–42, discusses "the overthrow of the gynocracy" with reference to the Iroquois and Cherokees. Kathryn E. Holland Braund, *Deerskins and Duffels: Creek Indian Trade with Anglo-America, 1685–1815* (Lincoln: University of Nebraska Press, 1993), 131–2; idem, "Guardians of Tradition and Handmaidens to Change: Women's Roles in Creek Economic and Social Life During the Eighteenth Century," *American Indian Quarterly* 14 (1990), 239–58; Robert S. Grumet, "Sunksquaws, Shamans, and Tradeswomen: Middle Atlantic Coastal Algonkian Women During the 17th and 18th Centuries," in Mona Etienne and Eleanor Burke Leacock, eds., *Women and Colonization: Anthropological Perspectives* (New York: Praeger Scientific, 1980), 43–62. See also Thomas Hatley, "Cherokee Women Farmers Hold Their Ground," in Robert D. Mitchell, ed., *Appalachian Frontiers: Settlement, Society, and Development in the Preindustrial Era* (Lexington: University Press of Kentucky, 1991), 37–51; and Carol Devens, *Countering Colonization: Native American Women and Great Lakes Missions, 1630–1900* (Berkeley and Los Angeles: University of California Press, 1992), 16–18.

empires, became an imperial battleground, and chiefs found it increasingly difficult to control their warriors.[18]

Warriors now made commitments that undermined the consensus politics that traditionally guarded against rash decisions.[19] Seneca warriors who traveled to see Sir William Johnson in the spring of 1762 explained that their sachems had not made the trip because the roads were very bad, but informed the superintendent, "We, are in fact the People of Consequence for Managing Affairs, our Sachims being generally a parcell of Old People who say Much, but who Mean or Act very little, So that we have both the power & Ability to settle Matters."[20] New leaders emerged as villages and bands coalesced in the reshuffling of population that European contact generated. Opportunists sometimes generated political fragmentation of their own: "We have been unhappy in loosing our old Chiefs who Conducted our affairs," said Pitchibaon, a Potawatomi chief in 1773; "we who are appointed in their place are no more listened to, every one sets up for Chief and make Towns and Villages apart."[21]

Chiefs who lacked traditional sanction often assumed influential roles as intermediaries and brokers with European colonists; older village chiefs found that these same roles offered new sources of authority.[22] As traditional bases of power weakened, European agents and traders cultivated client chiefs, giving them medals and gifts to buy and bolster their support. Chiefs always had acted as redistribution agents, maintaining influence not by accumulating wealth but by giving it away, thereby earning respect and creating reciprocal obligations. The gifts client chiefs gave now came from European backers and represented their sole source of influence; without allies to supply them they often fell from power. By the eve of the Revolution, British Indian superintendent John Stuart was virtually appointing chiefs among the Choctaws, where traditional patterns and functions of leadership had collapsed amid a European scramble for allies within the nation.[23] He handed out medals to Choctaw and Chickasaw chiefs at

---

[18] White, *Middle Ground*.

[19] For a study of the rise of a "common warrior" to a position of leadership, and his dismantling of traditional power structures in a world complicated by war and diplomacy, see Richard White, "Red Shoes: Warrior and Diplomat," in David G. Sweet and Gary B. Nash, eds., *Struggle and Survival in Colonial America* (Berkeley and Los Angeles: University of California Press, 1981), 49–68.

[20] *Johnson Papers*, vol. 3: 698; cf. William N. Fenton, "Locality as a Basic Factor in the Development of Iroquois Social Structure," in Fenton, ed., "Symposium on Local Diversity in Iroquois Culture," *Bureau of American Ethnology* Bulletin 149 (Washington D.C.: Smithsonian Institution, 1951), 25.

[21] *Johnson Papers*, vol. 8: 888.

[22] McConnell, *Country Between*, 13; White, *Middle Ground*.

[23] Richard White, *The Roots of Dependency: Subsistence, Environment, and Social Change among the Choctaws, Pawnees, and Navajos* (Lincoln: University of Nebraska Press, 1983), 40, 42, 73–82; cf. in the Great Lakes region, idem, *Middle Ground*, 177–80.

the Mobile congress in 1765; at the same congress in 1772 he convened the Choctaws to fill vacancies in the ranks of Britain's client chiefs created by war and old age:

> The competition and anxiety of the candidates for medals and commissions was as great as can be imagined and equalled the struggles of the most aspiring and ambitious for honours and preferment in great states. I took every step to be informed of characters and filled the vacancies with the most worthy and likely to answer the purposes of maintaining order and the attachment of this nation to the British interest.

Such interference further undermined traditional leadership structures: two years later Stuart was complaining that chiefs lacked the influence to control their young men.[24] The inroads of alcohol also deafened young men to the wisdom of their elders, and sachems lamented their inability to control their warriors in this new world of chaos and opportunity.[25] Challenges to traditional authority and declining political deference were not unique to colonial white society in the years before the Revolution.

The pressures unleashed by European invasion threw the jigsaw map of Indian America into the air, and Indian people tried to rearrange the falling pieces into some kind of coherent world. Ancient communities collapsed; new, multiethnic communities grew up out of the ruins of shattered societies. New villages grew up around French missions on the banks of the Saint Lawrence as Abenakis and other people from New England pulled back from the northward-pushing English frontier.[26] Iroquois towns seemed to absorb all comers.[27] Shawnees, Delawares, and Senecas who turned their backs on colonial society and resettled the upper Ohio Valley early in the eighteenth century acquired new identities as little-known "Ohio Indians."[28] In the Great Lakes region, the Ohio and Susquehanna valleys, and the South Carolina Piedmont, remnant groups, their old identities often all but lost to history, amalgamated. Europeans identified the new polyglot societies as "tribes." By the time William Bartram traveled through the South on the eve of the Revolution, the loose Creek Confederacy consisted of "many tribes, or remnants of conquered nations,

---

[24] Dunbar Rowland, ed., *Mississippi Provincial Archives, 1763–1766: English Dominion*, vol. 1 (Nashville: Brandon Printing Co., 1911): 229, 254; *DAR*, vol. 5: 37; vol. 7: 102; vol. 8: 110; "Papers Relating to Congress with Choctaw and Chickasaw Indians," *Publications of the Mississippi Historical Society* 5 (1925), 158.

[25] *Johnson Papers*, vol. 12: 1035; White, *Roots of Dependency*, 74–5; idem, *Middle Ground*, 321–2.

[26] Colin G. Calloway, *The Western Abenakis of Vermont: War, Migration, and the Survival of an Indian People, 1600–1800* (Norman: University of Oklahoma Press, 1990).

[27] Francis Jennings, *The Ambiguous Iroquois Empire: The Covenant Chain Confederation of Indian Tribes with English Colonies from Its Beginning to the Lancaster Treaty of 1744* (New York: Norton, 1984), 95.

[28] McConnell, *Country Between*, ch. 1.

united."[29] Indian country was a world of villages, bands, and clans, but European pressures and the need to deal with distant capitals demanded increasingly unified responses at a time when traditional structures often were in flux.[30]

The localism of Indian politics did not confine Indian people to local activity. On the contrary, Indian communities throughout the eastern woodlands became more closely interconnected. By the middle of the eighteenth century, eastern Indian horizons had widened considerably from the world of small villages and narrow loyalties that had occupied their attention a century before.[31] Competition between European powers for Indian allegiance, and between Indian nations for European trade, dominated Indian politics and foreign policies throughout most of the eighteenth century. Indian nations aligned and realigned themselves with European allies, played rival nations against each other to ensure their neutrality and survival while retaining a flow of trade goods, and divided into factions. "To preserve the Ballance between us & the French is the great ruling Principle of the Modern Indian Politics," wrote Peter Wraxall.[32] Indian warriors and diplomats, following an extensive network of trails and water courses, traveled, talked, and fought on a semicontinental scale. Iroquois diplomacy ranged from the Great Lakes to Quebec; Cherokee towns hosted ambassadors from other nations. Henry Hamilton, the British governor of Detroit early in the Revolution, sketched an Indian whose name he forgot but whom he remembered as "one of those characters, always to be found among the Indians – He travels from Village to Village, being provided with news"[33] (Fig. 1). A multitribal conference that assembled on the Scioto plains in southern Ohio in 1770 to discuss united defense of Indian lands brought together "the Chiefs of the most powerfull Nations on the continent."[34] The cross-tribal nature of

[29] William Bartram, "Observations on the Creek and Cherokee Indians, 1789," *Transactions of the American Ethnological Society* 3, pt. 1 (1853), 12.

[30] White, *Middle Ground*, ch. 1; Merrell, *Indians' New World*, ch. 3; McConnell, *Country Between*, 225–9; Laurence M. Hauptman, "Refugee Havens: The Iroquois Villages of the Eighteenth Century,' in Christopher Vecsey and Robert W. Venables, eds., *American Indian Environments: Ecological Issues in Native American History* (Syracuse, N.Y.: Syracuse University Press, 1980), 128–39. Michael N. McConnell, "Kuskusky Towns and Early Western Pennsylvania History, 1748–1778," *Pennsylvania Magazine of History and Biography* 116 (1992), 33–56, examines one example of prerevolutionary change in Indian communities. The phenomenon is further discussed in White, *Middle Ground*, and Gregory Evans Dowd, *A Spirited Resistance: The North American Indian Struggle for Unity, 1745–1815* (Baltimore: Johns Hopkins University Press, 1992).

[31] John Sugden, *Blue Jacket and the Shawnee Defence of the Ohio*, unpublished manuscript.

[32] C. H. McIlwain, ed., *Peter Wraxall's Abridgment of the New York Indian Records* (Cambridge, Mass.: Harvard University Press, 1915), 219. For examination of the complex relationship between play-off politics and factionalism among the eighteenth-century Choctaws, see White, *Roots of Dependency*, ch. 3; and Patricia K. Galloway, "Choctaw Factionalism and Civil War," *Journal of Mississippi History* 44 (1982), 289–327.

[33] Henry Hamilton, "Drawings of North American Scenes and North American Indians, 1769–1778," Harvard University, Houghton Library, pf. MS Eng. 509.2.

[34] *NYCD*, vol. 8: 281.

Figure 1. Sketch of an unidentified Indian, "one of those characters, always to be found among the Indians – He travels from Village to Village, being provided with News." From "Drawings of North American Scenes and North American Indians," by Henry Hamilton. Houghton Library pf MS Eng 509.2. By permission of the Houghton Library, Harvard University.

Indian communities and Indian actions would become even more apparent during the Revolution.

Most Indian communities were economically dependent upon Europeans to some degree by 1775.[35] The rate and extent of dependency varied, but Cherokees in the mountains of the interior were no more willing or able to do without European trade goods than were coastal groups surrounded by European settlers. A Cherokee headman named Skiagunsta told the governor of South Carolina in 1753 that his people could not survive without the English: "The Cloaths we wear, we cannot make ourselves, they are made to us. We use their Ammunition with which we kill Dear [sic]. We cannot make our Guns, they are made to us. Every necessary Thing in Life we must have from the white People."[36] Skiagunsta probably exaggerated for his audience – Indian peoples in New England, the Ohio Valley, and the Southeast had learned to overcome total dependence on Europeans by repairing and maintaining their own firearms and metal tools[37] – but the language of abject poverty and dependence was common in Indian speeches up through the Revolution. Captain Ouma of the Choctaws said his people were as "helpless as the Beasts in the woods," without British goods; Handsome Fellow of the Oakfuskie Creeks acknowledged in 1777 that "we have been used so long to wrap up our Children as soon as they are born in Goods procured of the white People that we cannot do without it."[38] Dependency rendered Indian people vulnerable to abuse: Choctaws at the Mobile congress in the winter of 1771–2 complained graphically that traders shortchanged them so often that the flaps of cloth provided as loin cloths "dont cover our secret parts, and we are in danger of being deprived of our manhood by every hungry dog that approaches."[39]

As Indian peoples became tied into the trade networks of western Europe, they also became participants in a consumer revolution that brought the products of industrializing Europe to frontier America. A "pan-Indian trade culture"

[35] Braund, *Deerskins and Duffels*, provides an in-depth examination of the extent to which trade with Europeans became the economic lifeblood of Creek society.

[36] John Phillip Reid, *A Better Kind of Hatchet: Law, Trade, and Diplomacy in the Cherokee Nation during the Early Years of European Contact* (University Park: Pennsylvania State University Press, 1976), esp. 196; William L. McDowell, Jr., ed., *Colonial Records of South Carolina: Documents relating to Indian Affairs, Vol. 1 (1750–1754)* (Columbia: South Carolina Archives Department, 1958), 453.

[37] Malone, *Skulking Way of War*, 67–74; McConnell, *Country Between*, 218; Braund, *Deerskins and Duffels*, 66.

[38] "Papers Relating to Congress with Choctaw and Chickasaw Indians," 150; Talk from the Handsome Fellow of the Oakfuskeys, June 18, 1777, North Carolina State Archives, Raleigh: Treasurer's and Comptroller's Records, *Indian Affairs and Lands* (box 1), Cherokee Nation, 1739–1791.

[39] "Proceedings of a Congress held by John Stuart with the Chickasaw and Choctaw Nation, Dec. 31, 1771, enclosed in Stuart to Gage, May 23, 1772, Clements Library, Gage Papers, vol. 137, item 14: 5; "Papers Relating to Congress with Choctaw and Chickasaw Indians," 148.

emerged in many areas of the country.⁴⁰ When William Tapp or Taptico, last werowance of the Wicocomoco Indians of Chesapeake Bay, died, he left behind English clothing, a house furnished with tables, chairs, and chests, four feather beds, and "a parcell of Olde Books,"⁴¹ By the time of the Revolution, according to one observer, the Fort Hunter Mohawks lived "much better than most of the Mohawk River farmers." Oneida Indians cooked in metal kettles and frying pans, ate with spoons from pewter plates at meals illuminated by candlesticks, sipped out of teacups filled from teapots, served beverages from punch bowls, combed their hair with ivory combs while looking in glass mirrors, wore white flannel breeches, used silk handkerchiefs, and lived in "a very large framed house [with a] chimney at each end [and] painted windows."⁴² Overhill Cherokees used combs, mirrors, scissors, pewter spoons, and a variety of metal tools and jewelry. White Eyes of the Delawares and Oconostota of the Cherokees both wore eyeglasses.⁴³ European trade goods were so pervasive in eastern Indian communities before the Revolution that archaeological deposits often reveal little distinction between Indian and non-Indian sites.⁴⁴ Native Americans, like their backcountry colonial neighbors, had been drawn into a larger Atlantic economy that shaped their tastes, their lives, and ultimately their landscape.⁴⁵ For many Indian peoples, the most pressing question posed by the outbreak of the Revolution was not who should govern in America but who would supply the trade goods on which they had come to depend. For many of their colonial neighbors, the material wealth to be found in Indian communities by 1775 provided an economic incentive for going on campaigns into Indian country.

The fur and deerskin trades not only introduced new commodities to Indian America; they also introduced alien systems of value and meaning. New economic

⁴⁰ George Irving Quimby, *Indian Culture and European Trade Goods: Archaeology of the Historic Period in the Western Great Lakes Region* (Madison: University of Wisconsin Press, 1966).

⁴¹ Stephen R. Potter, *Commoners, Tribute, and Chiefs: The Development of Algonquian Culture in the Potomac Valley* (Charlottesville: University Press of Virginia, 1993), 224–5.

⁴² William Campbell, ed., *Annals of Tryon County* (New York: Dodd, 1924), 130. On the material culture of the Oneidas see Massachusetts Historical Society, Boston: Timothy Pickering Papers, reel 62: 157–74.

⁴³ Gerald F. Schroedl, ed., *Overhill Cherokee Archaeology at Chota-Tanasee* (Knoxville: University of Tennessee, Department of Anthropology, Report of Investigations No. 38, 1986); Paul Gleeson, ed., *Archaeological Investigations in the Tellico Reservoir, Interim Report 1969* (Knoxville: University of Tennessee, Department of Anthropology, Report of Investigations No. 8, 1970); and idem, ed., *Archaeological Investigations in the Tellico Reservoir, Interim Report 1970* (Knoxville: University of Tennessee, Department of Anthropology, Report of Investigations No. 9, 1971). An inventory of White Eyes's personal effects is in *Frontier Advance*, 168.

⁴⁴ Grumet, *National Historic Landmark Theme Study*, 183.

⁴⁵ James Axtell, "The First Consumer Revolution," in his *Beyond 1492: Encounters in Colonial America* (New York: Oxford University Press, 1992), ch. 5; McConnell. *Country Between*, 211–15; Timothy H. Breen, "An Empire of Goods: The Anglicization of Colonial America, 1690–1776," *Journal of British Studies* 25 (1980), 467–99; Elizabeth A. Perkins, "The Consumer Frontier: Household Consumption in Early Kentucky," *Journal of American History* 78 (1991), 486–510.

incentives undermined old spiritual relationships between hunters and their
prey.[46] Indian hunters and European traders combined to deplete deer and beaver
populations; native and European economies intersected.[47] In areas and eras of
shrinking animal populations, consumption outstripped production, and Indians
who had become commercial hunters often became debtor-hunters.[48] Traders
and their alcohol brought death and disruption to Indian communities, as *alcohol*
village chiefs and colonial officials realized. From Maine to the Mississippi and
throughout the century, Indian spokesmen complained about abuses by traders
and the alcohol they peddled in Indian society. Christian Penobscots said "it
hurts our souls." "You may find graves upon graves along the Lake," an
Iroquois leader lamented to Albany officials in 1730, "all which misfortunes are
occasioned by Selling Rum to our Brethren." In 1738 the Shawnees staved in
all the kegs of rum in their villages and sent word to all French, British, and
Indian traders that they would destroy any rum they brought. A chief from the
Hudson River apologized to the Mohawks in 1756 for his inexperience in
council proceedings, explaining "the Rum we get from the English hath drowned
the Memory of all antient Customs & the Method of treating on public affairs."
A Choctaw chief said rum "pours upon our nation Like a great Sea from
Mobille and from all the Plantations and Settlements round about"; another
admitted that "When the Clattering of the Packhorse Bells are heard at a
Distance our Town is Immediately deserted young and old run out to meet
them Joyfully crying Rum Rum; they get Drunk, Distraction Mischief Confusion and Disorder are the Consequences and this the Ruin of our Nation."
Another Choctaw said "he had lost above a thousand people by excessive
drinking in little more than 18 months." A British agent in the Choctaw towns
in 1777 saw "nothing but Rum Drinking and Women Crying over the Dead
Bodies of their relations who have died by Rum." By the time of the Revolution,
according to Richard White, the Choctaws "quite simply, hunted for liquor,"
and chiefs were powerless to halt the social chaos that resulted. In Cherokee
society, too, drunkenness increased the aggressiveness of warriors and served as
a way of challenging traditional leaders who could not keep peace in the villages.[49]

[46] Calvin Martin, *Keepers of the Game: Indian–Animal Relations and the Fur Trade* (Berkeley and
Los Angeles: University of California Press, 1978); and Shepard Krech, III, ed., *Indians, Animals,
and the Fur Trade* (Athens: University of Georgia Press, 1981).

[47] Peter C. Mancall, *Valley of Opportunity: Economic Culture along the Upper Susquehanna, 1700–
1800* (Ithaca, N.Y.: Cornell University Press, 1991), 59, 70; Daniel H. Usner, Jr., *Indians,
Settlers, and Slaves in a Frontier Exchange Economy: The Lower Mississippi Valley before 1783*
(Chapel Hill: University of North Carolina Press, 1992), ch. 5.

[48] Braund, *Deerskins and Duffels*, 136–8.

[49] Mass. Archives vol. 29: 535; Charles Hanna, *The Wilderness Trail*, 2 vols. (New York: Putnam,
1911), vol. 1: 309; vol. 2: 307; Penobscots, see Colin G. Calloway, ed., *Dawnland Encounters:
Indians and Europeans in Northern New England* (Hanover, N.H.: University Press of New
England, 1991), 202; for the Iroquois, see Richter, *Ordeal of the Longhouse*, 263–8, quote at 266;
for the Shawnees, see Donald H. Kent, ed., *Pennsylvania Indian Treaties, 1737–1756*, in Alden

Colonial officials lamented alcohol's effects but recognized its usefulness in destabilizing Indian communities.[50]

The forces of change challenged people's spiritual lives. Missionaries from different countries and denominations entered Indian country to compete for a harvest of Indian souls. They promoted social revolution and produced factions in Indian communities.[51] The divisions became further complicated after the Great Awakening in the colonies in the 1730s and 1740s severed ties with a single established church. In the 1760s, a Seneca warrior named Onoquadeahla told Presbyterian missionary Samuel Kirkland in no uncertain terms that his presence "would be distructive to the nation, & finally over throw all the traditions & usages of their Forefathers & that there would not be a warior remaining in their nation in the course of a few years." Another Seneca named Isaac, "painted black and red on each side of his face," took a shot at Kirkland.[52] Indian peoples confronted Christian invaders with movements of spiritual revitalization and cultural resistance such as those led by Neolin, the Delaware Prophet, and the Munsee Wingenund in the 1760s.[53] Others embraced Christian messages in Indian ways. Many of the Indians who fought in the Revolution were Christians.

Everywhere, though, there was continuity in the midst of change.[54] Indians who donned European clothes often retained traditional hairstyles, slit ears, and facial tattoos. New trade goods were fashioned into traditional motifs or endowed with traditional meanings. Traditional lithic and ceramic technologies declined, but basket making and wood carving survived and even were stimulated by European demand. Some Indians continued to prefer birch-bark containers to metal pots for maple sugaring. Moccasins and canoes were unmatched by European substitutes for travel along forest paths and lakes. People still found guidance in dreams and believed in the efficacy of spirits, ceremonies and

---

T. Vaughan, gen. ed., *Early American Indian Documents: Laws and Treaties* (Frederick, Md.: University Publications of America, 1984), vol. 2: 5–6; for the Hudson River, see *Johnson Papers*, vol. 7: 348; vol. 9: 464; for the Choctaws, see "Papers Relating to Congress with Choctaw and Chickasaw Indians," 148–51; *DAR*, vol. 8: 127; vol. 13: 81; vol. 14: 113; C.O. 5/78: 126, 128, 130; White, *Roots of Dependency*, 74–5, 85; for the Cherokees, see Tom Hatley, *The Dividing Paths: Cherokees and South Carolinians through the Era of the Revolution* (New York: Oxford University Press, 1993), 48–51. Peter C. Mancall, "'The Bewitching Tyranny of Custom': The Social Costs of Indian Drinking in Colonial America," *American Indian Culture and Research Journal* 17 (1993), 15–42.

[50] Peter C. Mancall, "'Abominable Filthyness': The Liquor Trade and the Course of Empire in British America," paper presented at the annual meeting of the American Historical Association, 1992.

[51] Devens, *Countering Colonization*, suggests that missions also disrupted formerly reciprocal gender relations among Great Lakes communities.

[52] Walter Pilkington, ed., *The Journals of Samuel Kirkland* (Clinton, N.Y.: Hamilton College, 1980), 38.

[53] McConnell, *Country Between*, 220–3; Dowd, *Spirited Resistance*, ch. 2.

[54] E.g., Richter, *Ordeal of the Longhouse*, 276–80.

omens, though missionaries urged them to look to the Bible for direction. Ancient rituals continued to renew the world and maintain harmony; participation in those rituals helped define community identity in a world where so much else was in flux.[55] Old ways made strong crutches as people ventured down new paths.

The forces of contact, cultural exchange, transformation, and dependency operated along two-way streets. As Indian people traded for European cloth, guns, and alcohol, Europeans adopted Indian-style clothing, canoes, and foods. As Indian people adopted domesticated livestock, European colonists adopted Native American corn culture and hunting practices. British commander-in-chief, General Thomas Gage, realized on the eve of the Revolution that the intrusions of backcountry colonists onto Indian lands was due, in large measure, to the fact that they lived Indian-style, by hunting.[56] Indian and colonial economies affected each other and became interdependent. European traders needed Indian hunters and customers; European and colonial armies needed Indian scouts and allies, and, in time, adopted Indian methods of waging war;[57] European missionaries needed Indian neophytes; colonial whaling industries employed local native laborers;[58] settlers relied on Indian neighbors for their knowledge of the use of wild plants, and native herbal cures sometimes proved effective where European medicine failed;[59] colonial schools even needed Indian students to help secure funding.[60] In some areas of New England, Indians not only worked in the colonial economy but also lived with white families;[61] in some areas of the South they worked alongside Africans as plantation slave laborers.[62]

---

[55] Cf. Jay Miller, "Delaware Integrity: The History and Culture of the Gamwing (Big House Rite)," unpublished manuscript.

[56] John Mack Faragher, *Daniel Boone: The Life and Legend of an American Pioneer* (New York: Holt, 1992), 21; C.O. 5/90: 87.

[57] Richard R. Johnson, "The Search for a Usable Indian: An Aspect of the Defense of Colonial New England," *Journal of American History* 64 (1977), 623–51; James Axtell, *The European and the Indian: Essays in the Ethnohistory of Colonial America* (New York: Oxford University Press, 1981), 299–302.

[58] Daniel J. Vickers, "The First Whalemen of Nantucket," *William and Mary Quarterly* 3d series, 40 (1983), 660–83, esp. 577; idem, "Nantucket Whalemen in the Deep-Sea Fishery: The Changing Anatomy of an Early American Labor Force," *Journal of American History* 72 (1985), 277–96.

[59] Antoni Pace, trans. and ed., *Luigi Castiglioni's Viaggio: Travels in the United States of North America 1785–87* (Syracuse, N.Y.: Syracuse University Press, 1983), 352, 358–9, 424; H. L. Bourdin and S. T. Williams, eds., "Crèvecoeur on the Susquehanna, 1774–1776," *Yale Review* 14 (1925), 581–2; Virgil J. Vogel, *American Indian Medicine* (New York: Ballantine, 1970), 33–87; Hugh Talmage Lefler, ed., *A New Voyage to Carolina by John Lawson* (Chapel Hill: University of North Carolina Press, 1967), 17–18, 26, 134, 226, 230.

[60] Margaret Connell Szasz, *Indian Education in the American Colonies, 1607–1783* (Albuquerque: University of New Mexico Press, 1988); James Axtell, "Dr. Wheelock's Little Red School," in *European and the Indian,* 87–109.

[61] John A. Sainsbury, "Indian Labor in Early Rhode Island," *New England Quarterly* 48 (1975), 379.

[62] James H. Merrell, "Some Thoughts on Colonial Historians and American Indians," *William and Mary Quarterly* 3d series, 46 (1989), 102–7, 110; Wright, *The Only Land They Knew,* ch. 6.

As old Turnerian notions of the frontier as a line of advancing settlement diminish, we can better understand the persistence and presence of Indian people in colonial cities, and better appreciate the tapestry of colonial life. Not only did Indian diplomats regularly visit colonial capitals from Quebec to New Orleans, but Indians living in the neighborhood of emerging towns actively participated in the urban economy. They sold food, plants, baskets, and firewood in market squares, and earned wages as day laborers, servants, and dockworkers. As traditional economies were disrupted and the fur and deerskin trades declined, many Indian people resorted to "a cycle of itinerant economic activities." Some actually moved closer to colonial towns, relying on the urban economy in hard times of readjustment. They learned new skills as bricklayers, coopers, wheelwrights, blacksmiths, and seamstresses, and they adopted traditional skills to meet new demands, as wood carvers, potters, and basket makers.[63]

Throughout Indian country, Europeans lived in and around Indian communities. Traders who went into Indian country to do business often found that they were most successful if they married into the kinship networks of Indian societies. Like other colonists who lived with Indians, many found themselves living as Indians. Rev. David Jones found 20 whites living at the Shawnee town of Chillicothe in the winter of 1772–3; as many as 300 English and Scots were living among the Creeks by the beginning of the Revolution.[64] Scotsman Alexander Cameron married a Cherokee woman and lived with the Overhill Cherokees so long that he "had almost become one of themselves" by the time of the Revolution."[65]

Many other captives, traders, Indian agents, and even occasional missionaries underwent similar "conversion" to Indian ways. Like many of his Jesuit colleagues, Sebastian Rasles, missionary to the Abenakis at Norridgewock in Maine in the early eighteenth century, spent most of his adult life in Indian country. He spoke the Abenakis' language and shared their homes and hopes, food and fears, even as he sought to convert them. "As for what concerns me personally, Rasles told his brother, "I assure you that I see, that I hear, that I speak, only as a savage."[66]

"White Indians" often aroused fear and contempt in colonial society, but found a place in Indian country and exercised considerable influence as culture

---

[63] Daniel H. Usner, Jr., "American Indians in Colonial New Orleans," in Wood et al., eds., *Powhatan's Mantle*, 104–27; Wright, *The Only Land They Knew*, 154, 166.

[64] White, *Middle Ground*, 329; Martha Condray Searcy, *The Georgia–Florida Contest in the American Revolution, 1776–1778* (University: University of Alabama Press, 1985), 20, 200, n. 98.

[65] *DAR*, vol. 12: 194; *Colonial Records of North Carolina*, vol. 10: 767; C.O. 5/82: 114; Clements Library, Gage Papers, vol. 137, item 8.

[66] Calloway, ed., *Dawnland Encounters*, 75–80; Reuben G. Thwaites, ed., *The Jesuit Relations and Allied Documents*, 73 vols. (Cleveland, Ohio: Burrows, 1896–1901), vol. 67: 85–97, 143–5.

brokers.[67] James Dean, who served as an American interpreter during the Revolution, spent his boyhood among the Oneidas and learned to speak their language without a trace of an accent.[68] Simon Girty, captured as a boy by Senecas in 1755, made his home in Indian country and built a career as culture broker and interpreter that gave him far-reaching influence in Indian country during and after the Revolution.[69]

Intermarriage between Indians and Europeans, and between Indians and Africans, produced "new peoples" of mixed ancestry. Most were incorporated into Indian communities, but many suffered psychological stress as racial conflicts increased.[70] Some lived with racism in colonial communities; some developed separate communities and formed an ethnic identity of their own.[71] Interaction between different peoples produced new languages in these new worlds. Refugee communities sometimes produced a babel of different dialects. Trade jargons emerged. Indians adopted Spanish, English, Gaelic, Dutch, French, and African words; Europeans incorporated Algonkian, Iroquoian, and Muskhogean terms into their vocabulary.[72] In the 1750s, at Stockbridge, Massachusetts, where an Indian blew a conch shell every Sabbath to call the faithful to worship, the missionary's son heard so much more Mahican than English spoken that he frequently found himself thinking in the Indians' language.[73] Traveling in New York in 1776, Joseph Bloomfield, then a captain in the Third New Jersey Regiment and later governor of New Jersey, heard spoken on a daily basis English, High Dutch, Low Dutch, French, Mohawk, Oneida, Seneca, Cayuga, Onondaga, and Tuscarora.[74]

Even where whites did not live with Indians, the influence of Indian country and the evidence of cultural exchange was strong. In the Delaware Valley, Finns and Swedes lived closely with Indian neighbors, acquiring from them corn (and the knowledge of how to plant, cultivate and prepare it), gourds,

[67] On mutual conversions in Indian country see Axtell, *European and The Indian*; idem, *The Invasion Within: The Contest of Cultures in Colonial North America* (New York: Oxford University Press, 1985); also Calloway, ed., *Dawnland Encounters*, ch. 6; and idem, "Neither White Nor Red: White Renegades on the American Indian Frontier," *Western Historical Quarterly* 17 (1986), 43–66.

[68] *Revolution and Confederation*, 560, n. 48.

[69] Colin G. Calloway, "Simon Girty: Interpreter and Intermediary," in James A. Clifton, ed., *Being and Becoming Indian: Biographical Studies of North American Frontiers* (Chicago: Dorsey, 1989), 38–58.

[70] Hatley, *Dividing Paths*, 60–1.

[71] Jacqueline Peterson and Jennifer S. H. Brown, eds., *The New Peoples: Being and Becoming Metis in North America* (Winnipeg: University of Manitoba Press, 1985); Terry G. Jordan and Matti Kaups, *The American Backwoods Frontier: An Ethnic and Ecological Interpretation* (Baltimore: Johns Hopkins University Press, 1987), 88.

[72] Jordan and Kaups, *American Backwoods Frontier*, 89–90.

[73] Patrick Frazier, *The Mohicans of Stockbridge* (Lincoln: University of Nebraska Press, 1992), 95.

[74] Lender and Martin, eds., *Citizen Soldier*, 91.

pumpkins, squash, turkeys, furs and skins, sassafras tea, bayberry candles, and maple syrup. "They adopted wholesale the Delawares' knowledge of edible and medicinal wild plants," and spoke a Delaware-derived pidgin. Intermarriage was common and Indian children were reported living in Swedish homes on the Schuykill before the end of the seventeenth century. Long before Scotch-Irish and Welsh people came to dominate the midland backwoods population, Finns and Swedes set the pattern of trade, tolerance, and mutual acculturation "that was essential to the piecing together of a successful woodland pioneer culture." Later arrivals noted that the Swedes and their Indian neighbors were "like one people."[75] Things were not too different elsewhere. Ranger Robert Rogers recalled that growing up in a frontier town in New Hampshire in the early part of the century, he "could hardly avoid" gaining some knowledge of Indian ways and languages.[76]

*– hunting*

Colonists from Europe, where hunting was a gentleman's sport, learned from Indians how to hunt for a living. Colonial hunters who operated in Indian country pulled on Indian leggings, breechclouts, and moccasins, dressed their long hair with bear grease, and sometimes donned war paint. Anglican preacher Charles Woodmason denounced settlers on the Carolina backcountry as being "hardly one degree removed" from their Indian neighbors. General Thomas Gage reckoned backcountry settlers on the Ohio River "differ little from the Indians in their manner of life." Missionary David McClure said that backcountry Virginians were "generally white Savages, and subsist by hunting, and live like the Indians." Whereas Indians in Canada took to wearing jackets and waistcoats like their French neighbors, Frenchmen traveling in Indian country "generally dressed like the natives," exchanging their trousers for leggings and loincloths. Young men in backcountry Virginia were proud of their "Indian-like dress," and even wore leggings and breechclouts to church, which apparently sparked the interest of young women in the congregation. When George Rogers Clark and his Virginians arrived at Kaskaskia in 1778, they were dressed Indian style, "in hunting shirt and breech cloth." Their appearance surprised the Spanish governor of Saint Louis but was not unusual for men accustomed to life in Indian country.[77] In the Mohawk Valley in the 1760s, Peter Warren Johnson

---

[75] Jordan and Kaups, *American Backwoods Frontier*, 87–92.
[76] *Journals of Major Robert Rogers* (London, 1765), vi–vii.
[77] Faragher, *Daniel Boone*, 20–1; Axtell, *European and the Indian*, 297–9; Richard J. Hooker, ed., *The Carolina Backcountry on the Eve of the Revolution: The Journal and Other Writings of Charles Woodmason, Anglican Itinerary* (Chapel Hill: University of North Carolina Press, 1953), 61; C.O. 5/90: 87 (Gage); McClure quoted in White, *Middle Ground*, 341; Benson, ed., *Kalm's Travels in North America*, vol. 2: 462, 560; David Hackett Fischer, *Albion's Seed: Four British Folkways in America* (New York: Oxford University Press, 1989), 681; Lawrence Kinnaird, ed., "Clark-Leyba Papers," *American Historical Review* 41 (1935–6), 95, 97. Euro-American hunters nevertheless differed from Indians in their disregard of Native American ritual with respect to the prey.

met Europeans who tattooed their faces and chests like their Indian neighbors, "which is done by pricking the Skin with Pins, till the Blood comes, & then applying Gunpowder to it, which will remain for ever." French fur traders in Canada likewise tattooed their bodies.[78] Cultural boundaries between Indians and Europeans, and between Indians and Africans (as between Indians and other Indians), were often fuzzy and porous.

The mixing of peoples and cultures did not erase differences or eradicate conflict. Surveying the inventory of things colonists borrowed from Indians, James Axtell reminds us that "Their goal was not to become Indian, nor did their selective and piecemeal adaptations of native techniques and technology make them so."[79] The same can be said of Indians who borrowed from European culture: they did not intend to, nor did they, become Europeans. In fact, conflict between Indian and European cultures was increasing steadily by the eve of the Revolution, as growing pressure on Indian lands eroded previous patterns of coexistence.

As the eighteenth century wore on, Indian people and Indian cultures were being engulfed by an ocean of European and African people. The powerful Six Nations, renowned warriors and past masters of the art of playing European rivals against each other, had long been "sinking into irrelevance in a region more and more dominated by Euro-Americans."[80] As Indian numbers dwindled, immigration and natural increase sent America's non-Indian population skyward. The population of British North America doubled every twenty-five years and increased 400 percent between 1700 and 1750. The population of North Carolina shot from 45,000 in 1750 to 275,000 in 1775. Five thousand Scots migrated to North Carolina alone in the decade before the Revolution. By 1775 as many as fifty thousand whites lived west of the Appalachians.[81]

The newcomers included Pennsylvania Germans and American-born Virginians, but increasingly in the eighteenth century the Europeans-turning-Americans on the frontier came from the Celtic fringes of the British Isles, propelled by failed rebellion, a decaying clan system, agrarian transformation and sheep enclosures, high rents, poverty, and famine. After their kinsmen and their dreams of a Jacobite restoration died in the sleet at Culloden, many Highland Scots came to America as soldiers, the only profession that permitted them to wear a tartan and gave steady employment in bleak times. Others joined victims of wrenching economic changes from the Lowlands, the north

---

[78] *Johnson Papers*, vol. 13: 194; Benson, ed., *Kalm's Travels in North America*, vol. 2: 577–8.
[79] Axtell, *European and the Indian*, 302.
[80] Richter, *Ordeal of the Longhouse*, ch. 11, quote at 271.
[81] James Axtell surveys the shift from a population that was predominantly brown to one that was increasingly white and black in "The Columbian Mosaic," in his *Beyond 1492*, 217–40. Mancall, *Valley of Opportunity*, 73; Bernard Bailyn, *Faces of Revolution: Personalities and Themes in the Struggle for American Independence* (New York: Knopf, 1990), 172–3; White, *Middle Ground*, 340.

England borders, Ireland, and Wales, migrating to America in such numbers
that authorities in Britain worried the exodus would empty Scotland of its
people. Accustomed to lives of hardship and cultures of violence, Scotch-Irish
and North Country immigrants brought their clan rivalries, blood feuds, and
Old Testament sense of justice to the American frontier, where, said Quaker
James Logan, they made "hard neighbors to the Indians." Colonial authorities
steered Scotch-Irish immigrants toward the frontier, knowing they would provide effective defense against Indian attacks. Alternatively, they made excellent
shock troops for the invasion of Indian lands.[82]

Land, of course, was the main source of contention between Indian people
and their new neighbors. In the seventeenth century, although some colonial
governments passed laws to protect Indian lands, others used deeds to legitimize the acquisition of Indian lands by trickery, coercion, and corruption –
what Francis Jennings refers to as "the deed game." Many Indians learned the
terms and implications of selling land to Europeans, struck the best deals they
could in the circumstances, and endeavored to slow the rate of land loss, but
they could not halt the pressure.[83] The problem increased in intensity throughout the eighteenth century. Long before the Revolution, Indians found themselves sucked into the practice of selling off lands to satisfy debts accumulated
in trade with their colonial neighbors. Creek Indians called their Georgian
neighbors "Ecunnaunuxulgee" – "people greedily grasping after the lands of
the red people."[84]

---

[82] On the Celtic and borderland migrations to colonial America see, for example: Fischer, *Albion's Seed*, 605–782; Bernard Bailyn, *Voyagers to the West: A Passage in the Peopling of America on the Eve of the Revolution* (New York: Knopf, 1986); Angus Calder, *Revolutionary Empire: The Rise of the English-Speaking Peoples from the Fifteenth Century to the 1780s* (New York: Dutton, 1981), esp. 677–8; Kerby A. Miller, *Emigrants and Exiles: Ireland and the Irish Exodus to North America* (New York: Oxford University Press, 1985), ch. 4; Ned C. Landsman, "Border Cultures, the Backcountry, and 'North British' Emigration to America," *William and Mary Quarterly* 3d series, 48 (1991), 253–9; Forrest McDonald and Ellen Shapiro McDonald, "The Ethnic Origins of the American People, 1790," *William and Mary Quarterly* 3d series, 37 (1980), 179–99; Duane Meyer, *The Highland Scots of North Carolina, 1732–1776* (Chapel Hill: University of North Carolina Press, 1961); Eric Richards, "Scotland and the Uses of the Atlantic Empire," and Maldwyn A. Jones, "The Scotch-Irish in America," both in Bailyn and Morgan, eds., *Strangers within the Realm*, 91–5, 284–313. Jones quotes Logan at 297. See also Governor Josiah Martin's views on Scottish immigration in 1775, *DAR*, vol. 9: 71–4. For colonial use of the Scotch-Irish as frontier defense, see Kenneth W. Keller, "What is Distinctive about the Scotch-Irish?" in Mitchell, ed., *Appalachian Frontiers*, 69–86, esp. 76–7.

[83] Francis Jennings, *The Invasion of America: Indians, Colonialism, and the Cant of Conquest* (New York: Norton, 1976), 128–45; Emerson W. Baker, "'A Scratch with a Bear's Paw': Anglo-Indian Land Deeds in Early Maine," *Ethnohistory* 36 (1989), 235–56; Robert S. Grumet, "An Analysis of Upper Delawaran Land Sales in Northern New Jersey, 1630–1758," in William Cowan, ed., *Papers of the Ninth Algonquian Conference* (Ottawa: Carleton University Press, 1978), 25–35; and Grumet "'We Are Not So Great Fools': Changes in Upper Delawaran Socio-Political Life, 1630–1758," Ph.D. diss., Rutgers University, 1979.

[84] Michael D. Green, *The Politics of Indian Removal: Creek Government and Society in Crisis* (Lincoln: University of Nebraska Press, 1982), 26.

The British victory in the Seven Years' War opened Indian country to a flood of settlement that the Royal Proclamation of 1763 and other official measures barely even checked. In the wake of their victory, British ministers in Whitehall tried to implement a program that would provide security for their colonies by maintaining garrisons in the West, establishing an Indian reserve, and regulating an equitable trade with the Indians. Their efforts to finance the program by such measures as the Stamp Act contributed to the challenge to British imperial authority that culminated in the Revolution.[85]

The irony of British policy in the years between the Seven Years' War and the Revolution was that "although it aspired to control Indians, it foundered on the British government's inability to control its subjects." The victorious British at first rode roughshod over the traditions of the middle ground, but Pontiac's War in 1763 taught them a bitter lesson, and they worked to reconstruct the social and diplomatic arrangements they had thought they could do without. Even as they did so, however, the old middle ground was rapidly giving way to a world of violence as Anglo-American settlers swarmed into Indian country.[86]

A younger generation of colonists in the midst of an economic recession found that there were too many sons and not enough land in their home communities. The abundance of frontier land, combined with the scarcity of land at home, undermined fathers' traditional authority over their sons, and over daughters for whom they could no longer ensure a place in the world.[87] British policymakers were no more able to control frustrated and ambitious young settlers than were those setters' own fathers.[88] In 1772, the acting governor of Georgia, James Habersham, took measures to remove from Indian lands "a parcel of stragling northward People" who threatened to frustrate the orderly transfer of those lands to the crown.[89] However, few colonists were willing to acquiesce in royal attempts to keep them from western lands. Scotch-Irish settlers who had emigrated to escape English domination paid little heed to an English proclamation in their new world. Veterans of the "French and Indian wars" were not about to be deprived of the fruits of their hard-won victory. British policies that tried to regulate the frontier often only aggravated the tensions, alienating backcountry settlers and ensuring that many of them would throw in their lot with the rebels once the Revolution began. Although settlers

[85] Jack M. Sosin, *Whitehall and the Wilderness: The Middle West in British Colonial Policy, 1760–1775* (Lincoln: University of Nebraska Press, 1961).

[86] White, *Middle Ground* 344; e.g., *DAR*, vol. 8: 113–14.

[87] Robert A. Gross, *The Minutemen and Their World* (New York: Hill & Wang, 1976), 82, 89, 100, 106–7.

[88] The situation was not entirely new: in 1749 the Onondaga spokesman Canasatego pointed out in meetings with commissioners from Pennsylvania that "white People are no more obedient to you than our young Indians are to us." Kent, ed., *Pennsylvania Indian Treaties*, 205.

[89] "The Letters of James Habersham, 1756–1775," *Collections of the Georgia Historical Society* 6 (1904), 199.

could ignore the proclamation, land speculators could not, and it helped push into rebellion Virginia gentry with western lands to sell.[90]

New boundaries negotiated in the North at the Treaty of Fort Stanwix in 1768, and in the South at Augusta and Hard Labor in 1768 and 1770, did little or nothing to stem the tide. The Treaty of Fort Stanwix in particular infuriated Shawnees and others who felt the Six Nations had sold their lands out from under them.[91] In the fall of 1770, Indian trader, agent, and land speculator George Croghan reported, "Last year, I am sure, there were between four and five thousand [new settlers] and all this spring and summer the roads have been lined with wagons moving to the Ohio."[92] Settlers and land speculators opened up new frontiers everywhere. Daniel Boone founded Boonesborough in April 1775, "opened a land office, disposed of over half a million acres in a few weeks, founded three more settlements, and convened a legislature before the year was out."[93] By the eve of the Revolution, Kentucky constituted a wedge of colonial settlement thrust into the heart of Indian America. The new settlements not only threatened Indian hunting territories but divided northern and southern tribes, disrupting old networks of trade and communication.[94] Most of the settlers coming to Kentucky came from North Carolina, which was itself being settled from Pennsylvania, West Virginia, and Scotland.

Such constant movement, settlement, and resettlement alarmed Indian people struggling to hold onto their lands.[95] Anglo-American history for generations has portrayed pioneers as settlers, Indians as nomads. But Indian people in the eastern woodlands, who lived in settled communities reliant upon a mixed subsistence economy that almost always included agriculture, must surely have regarded Scotch-Irish and Anglo-American invaders as the true nomads of colonial America. Others did: after the Revolution, Spanish officials regarded American backwoodsmen on Florida's northern frontier as "nomadic like Arabs and . . . distinguished-from savages only in their color, language, and the superiority of their depraved cunning and untrustworthiness."[96]

[90] Woody Holton, "The Revolt of the Ruling Class: The Influence of Indians, Merchants, and Laborers on the Virginia Gentry's Break with England," Ph.D. diss., Duke University 1990, ch. 2.

[91] *NYCD*, vol. 8: 111–37; Peter Marshall, "Sir William Johnson and the Treaty of Fort Stanwix, 1768," *Journal of American Studies* 1 (1967), 149–79; *Johnson Papers*, vol. 7: 184; Louis De Vorsey, Jr., *The Indian Boundary in the Southern Colonies, 1763–1777* (Chapel Hill: University of North Carolina Press, 1966).

[92] Quoted in Thomas P. Slaughter, The *Whiskey Rebellion: Frontier Epilogue to the American Revolution* (New York: Oxford University Press, 1986), 65–6.

[93] Bailyn, *Faces of Revolution*, 172.

[94] George C. Chalou, "George Rogers Clark and Indian America 1778–1780," in *The French, the Indians, and George Rogers Clark in the Illinois Country* (Indianapolis: Indiana Historical Society, 1977), 36.

[95] E.g.: C.O. 5/90: 78.

[96] Quoted in Weber, *Spanish Frontier in North America*, 272.

By the eve of the Revolution, Indian people from Quebec and Maine to Georgia and the Floridas were complaining in vain to colonial authorities about trespasses on their land, and about schemes to get it.[97] Indians from the seven New England "praying towns" were "reduced to such small pittances of land, that they could no longer remain there," and moved to New York to take up land granted to them by the Oneidas in 1774.[98] Delawares, Munsees, and Mahicans warned the governors of Pennsylvania, Maryland, and Virginia in December 1771 that the flood of settlers across the mountains was likely to produce disaster: "Unless you can fall upon some method of governing your people who live between the Great Mountains and the Ohio River and who are now very numerous, it will be out of the Indians power to govern their young men, for we assure you that the black clouds begin to gather fast in this country."[99]

"I know of nothing so likely to interrupt and disturb our tranquility with the Indians," reported John Stuart, "as the incessant attempts to defraud them of their land by clandestine purchase." The British authorities recognized the justice of the Indians' complaints and identified the roots of the problem, but could do little about it.[100] Frontier people came to believe that the British government and its agents favored Indians and the Indian trade over settlers; John Stuart's efforts to extend imperial control into the Indian country generated rumors that he was planning to use Indians against the colonists. By 1775 the southern backcountry was ready to explode.[101] When the Revolution broke out, American patriots called it a war for liberty. Most Indian people knew, and the British reminded those who didn't, that it was also a continuation of the struggle about Indian land and who was to get it. Violence was always close to the surface in Indian–white relations. Indians and whites alike had long struggled to avert it, but by the eve of the Revolution, murder and revenge, not mediation and accommodation, typified relations. As Richard White sees it, the common world "yielded to a frontier over which people crossed only to shed blood."[102] Young warriors defied the authority of older chiefs by killing frontiersmen, who

[97] Mass. Archives, vol. 29: 531–2; *Johnson Papers*, vol. 7: 949–51; vol. 8: 840; vol. 12: 173, 1027; "Report of Congress with the Creek Indians [Feb. 1771]," *Publications of the Mississippi Historical Society* 5 (1925), 120–1, 129; also see this volume, 225–6.

[98] Hamilton College Library, Brothertown Records, 1774–1804; *American Archives*, 4th series, vol. 2: 1047.

[99] *DAR*, vol. 3: 254–5.

[100] *DAR*, vol. 5: 202–4; vol. 9: 90; Clarence Edwin Carter, ed., *The Correspondence of General Gage*, 2 vols. (New Haven, Conn.: Yale University Press, 1931–3), vol. 1: 334–6.

[101] Edward J. Cashin, "Sowing the Wind: Governor Wright and the Georgia Backcountry on the Eve of the Revolution," in Harvey H. Jackson and Phinizy Spaulding, eds., *Forty Years of Diversity: Essays on Colonial Georgia* (Athens: University of Georgia Press, 1984), 233–50; J. Russell Snapp, *John Stuart and the Issue of Empire on the Southern Frontier* (Louisiana State University Press, forthcoming).

[102] White, *Middle Ground*, 456; McConnell, *Country Between*, 258–9.

themselves ignored distant governments, killing Indians and occupying their lands.

In 1774, American frontiersmen lured a party of Mingo Indians into their camp, got them drunk, and then killed and scalped them, mutilating the pregnant sister of a Mingo chief known as Logan.[103] The act was the most brutal in a spate of killings along the Ohio that spring. Despite Delaware efforts to avert it, and amid considerable diplomatic scrambling in Indian country, open war exploded between Virginia and the Mingoes and Shawnees. Lord Dunmore's War was both the latest in a series of escalating frontier conflicts and a precursor of the one to come.

Anglo-Americans were not the only people experiencing times to try men's souls by 1775. In Indian country, too, people wrestled with challenges to traditional sources of authority, felt the repercussions of religious ferment, struggled to deal with demographic changes, felt squeezed by economic strangleholds, resented growing threats to their liberty, and worried about the kind of world their children would inherit. Indian people had had plenty of experience of colonialism, and they had already fought their share of anticolonial wars. Choosing the winning side in the new war that broke out in 1775 was crucial but, as in past wars, victory was hardly a realistic goal. The best Indian people could hope for was damage control, but they could not know the extent of the damage the Revolution would cause to the worlds they and their colonial neighbors had created.

Most of North America was still Indian country in 1775. Indian people still dominated most of the continent and walked the streets of colonial towns. Much of colonial life involved Indians; much of colonial war, diplomacy, and commerce revolved around them. Writing to fellow revolutionary John Adams in 1812, Thomas Jefferson recalled that in Williamsburg before the Revolution, Indians "were in the habit of coming often, and in great numbers to the seat of our government, where I was much with them."[104] The Revolution that erupted in 1775 was bound to affect and involve Indians; but it also ushered in a new era and a new society from which they were to be increasingly excluded. The interethnic societies and cultural mixings that characterized much of Indian America by 1775 had been a long time in the making. The Revolution did not terminate them overnight, but did produce a new government and society increasingly committed to the notion that Indian country east of the Mississippi should cease to exist.

At the beginning of May 1775, before news of Lexington and Concord reached him, Major Arent Schuyler De Peyster, commanding officer at the

---

[103] James H. O'Donnell, III, "Logan's Oration: A Case Study in Ethnographic Authentication," *Quarterly Journal of Speech* 65 (1979), 150–6.

[104] Lester Cappon, ed., *The Adams–Jefferson Letters*, 2 vols. (Chapel Hill: University of North Carolina Press, 1959), vol. 2: 307.

remote British outpost at Michilimackinac, sat down to pen a report to General Thomas Gage. It had been an unusually mild winter on the Great Lakes, he wrote. "To use the Indian Phrase, the World seems to have had a great shove to the Southward."[105] There would be no more mild winters for De Peyster or his Indian neighbors for many years. In fact, their world never would be quite the same again.

[105] De Peyster to Gage, May 5, 1775, Clements Library, Gage Papers, vol. 128.

# 1

## Corn wars and civil wars: the American Revolution comes to Indian country

### The Revolution becomes an Indian war

In Indian country the American Revolution often translated into an American civil war. While British regulars and Continental troops fought campaigns in the East, in the backcountry – which usually meant the Indians' backyards – whites killed Indians, Indians killed whites, Indians killed Indians, and whites killed whites in guerilla warfare that was localized, vicious, and tolerated no neutrals.[1] Dissension and disruption in Indian councils increased as militant voices drowned out words of moderation.

In Indian country and Indian communities the outbreak of the Revolution usually generated division and confusion, not united tribal action. Some people saw in the Revolution and the promise of British support a chance to drive Americans from their lands; others hoped to keep out of it; still others volunteered to fight alongside American neighbors. Abenakis in western Maine debated night after night as to what to do now that Englishmen were killing one another. One Abenaki woman said she thought the world was coming to an end.[2] Catawba Indians in South Carolina "were alarmed, and could not tell what to make of it."[3] George Morgan found Indians in the Ohio Valley "much

---

[1] On the nature of the Revolutionary War and partisan conflict in the southern backcountry see, for example: Ronald Hoffman, Thad W. Tate, and Peter J. Albert, eds., *An Uncivil War: The Southern Backcountry during the American Revolution* (Charlottesville: University Press of Virginia, 1985), xii; Sylvia R. Frey, *Water From the Rock: Black Resistance in a Revolutionary Age* (Princeton, N.J.: Princeton University Press, 1991), passim, e.g. 101–3, 132–3; and Rachel N. Klein, *Unification of a Slave State: The Rise of the Planter Class in the South Carolina Backcountry, 1760–1808* (Chapel Hill: University of North Carolina Press, 1990), ch. 3. See also Richard White, *The Middle Ground: Indians, Empires, and Republics in the Great Lakes Region, 1650–1815* (Cambridge University Press, 1991), 378 and ch. 9.
[2] Letter from Henry Young Brown, May 16, 1775, American Antiquarian Society, Worcester, Mass., U. S. Revolution Collection; *American Archives*, 4th series, vol. 2: 621; *Collections of the Maine Historical Society* 14 (1910), 279.
[3] William Moultrie, *Memoirs of the American Revolution, as Far as it Related to the States of North and South Carolina and Georgia*, 2 vols. (New York: n. p., 1802), vol. 1: 81.

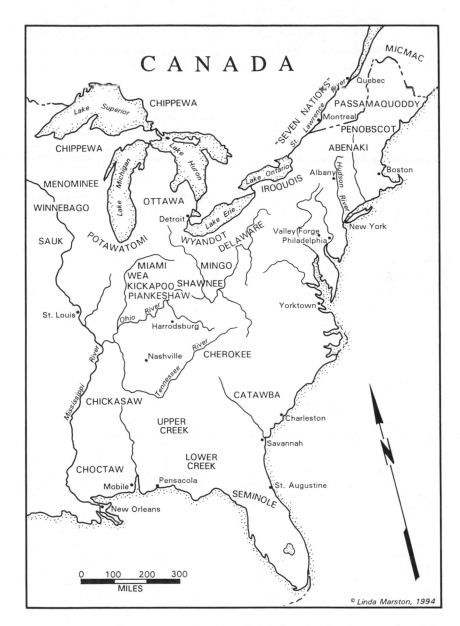

Map 2. Indian country during the American Revolution, showing the approximate locations of major tribes

confused and unsettled in their Resolutions" in the spring of 1776.[4] The Spanish governor of Saint Louis, Fernando de Leyba, told the governor of Louisiana, Bernardo de Galvez, in the summer of 1778 that the war was "causing a great number of Indian tribes to go from one side to the other without knowing which side to take."[5]

Not all Indian people were living in Indian country when the Revolution broke out, and Indians responded to the event as individuals, not just as tribal units. Joseph Burd Jaquoi, a Mohegan Indian from Connecticut, had served in the Seven Years' War and was in England on a lieutenant's half pay when the Revolution began. He was offered a captain's commission in the British army but, he said in a later petition to the government of Connecticut, "refused to serve in that unnatural contest." He gave up his lieutenancy, forfeited his half pay, and returned to America. Taking up residence in North Carolina, he joined the American army to fight against his former comrades in arms when the British invaded the Carolinas.[6] Other Indians also enlisted in the American cause as individuals. "Lewis Indian" and "James Indian" volunteered for service in New Hampshire companies in the first months of the war. "Peter Indian," a Dartmouth graduate, enlisted in a New Hampshire company to fight Burgoyne in 1777. Others, with distinct Indian names or with names no different from their colonial comrades, joined up in other colonies; still others may have enlisted with their Indian identity unrecorded.[7]

When "this island began to shake and tremble along the Eastern shore," the American Revolution looked very much like an English civil war to Indian eyes. Most Indian people seem to have regarded it as a family quarrel in which they had no business meddling.[8] Mohegan preacher Samson Occom wished the whites "would let the poor Indians alone, what have they to do with your Quarrels."[9] British and American agents encouraged a non-involvement on the

[4] Morgan to commissioner of Indian Affairs, May 16, 1776, Letterbook of George Morgan, 1776, Pennsylvania Historical and Museum Commission. Morgan's 1776 letterbook is reproduced in Francis Jennings et. al., eds., *Iroquois Indians: A Documentary History of the Diplomacy of the Six Nations and Their League*, 50 reels (Woodbridge, Conn., 1985), reel 32.

[5] *Spain in the Mississippi Valley*, vol. 2, pt. 1: 298.

[6] Connecticut State Library, Hartford, Connecticut Archives: Indian Series, 2, vol. 1: 66.

[7] Russell Lawrence Barsh, "Native American Loyalists and Patriots: Reflections on the American Revolution in Native American History," *Indian Historian* 10 (Summer 1977), 9–19; *New Hampshire State Papers, Revolutionary Rolls*, vol. 1: 265; vol. 2: 619; Eric P. Kelly, "The Dartmouth Indians," *Dartmouth Alumni Magazine* 22 (Dec. 1929), 123. Listings of individual Indians who served in the patriot cause are provided in a series of pamphlets entitled *Minority Military Service*, published by the National Society of the Daughters of the American Revolution: *Connecticut* (1988), *Rhode Island* (1988), *Massachusetts* (1989), *Maine* (1990), *New Hampshire and Vermont* (1991).

[8] Speech of American commissioners at Albany in August 1775, quoted in William L. Stone, *The Life of Joseph Brant*, 2 vols. (New York: Blake, 1838), vol. 1: xvi–xvii; *Revolution and Confederation*, p. 14; Edmund C. Burnett, *Letters of Members of the Continental Congress, 1774–1789*, 8 vols. (Washington, D.C., 1921–36), vol. 1: 113–14; Mass. Archives, vol. 144: 311–12.

[9] Harold Blodgett, *Samson Occom* (Hanover, N.H.: Dartmouth College Publications, 1935), 164–5.

part of the Indians in the early months of the war, when they were soliciting
neutrality rather than support from the tribes. Before long, however, British
and American, then Spanish and French, agents began to lobby Indian peoples
for their active support, justifying their actions with the argument that if they
did not employ Indians as allies, the enemy would.[10] The Continental Congress
resolved in December 1775 to call on Indians "in case of real necessity." The
British likewise pleaded necessity in enlisting Indian support for the defense of
Canada, and in forest warfare, where their enemies employed Indians.[11] Where
Indian support was not forthcoming, British and Americans naturally preferred
to factionalize tribes than to see them swing into the enemy camp.

Faced with an ongoing struggle to preserve their cultural and territorial
boundaries, some Indian peoples needed little encouragement to take up arms
against the Americans. Others were more cautious. Little Abraham of the
Mohawks told American commissioners at Albany in August 1775 that his
people intended to remain neutral: "We mind nothing but Peace," he said, and
reiterated the sentiment the following year.[12] When British Indian agent John
Butler attempted to enlist Seneca support at Niagara early in June 1776,
Cawconcaucawheteda, or Flying Crow, head war chief of the Allegheny Senecas,
treated his arguments with disdain, declaring that the Indians were at peace
with the Americans and intended to remain so as long as they could.

> It is true they have encroach'd on our Lands, but of this we shall speak to
> them. If you are so strong Brother, and they but as a weak Boy, why ask
> our assistance. It is true I am tall and strong but I will reserve my strength
> to strike those who injure [us] . . . You say they are all mad, foolish, wicked,
> and deceitful – I say you are so and they are wise for you want us to
> destroy ourselves in your War and they advise us to live in Peace.[13]

The Seneca chief Kayashuta agreed, saying, "We must be Fools indeed to
imagine that they regard us or our Interest who want to bring us into an

[10] Clements Library, Clinton Papers, vol. 10: 15; Dorothy V. Jones, *License for Empire: Colonialism by Treaty in Early America* (University of Chicago Press, 1982), 127–8; Andrew McFarland Davis, "The Employment of Indian Auxiliaries in the American War," *English Historical Review* 2 (1887), 709–28; *American Archives*, 4th series, vol. 5: 989; vol. 6: 975. Congress established three Indian departments at the beginning of the war, later reduced to two; Worthington C. Ford and Gaillard Hunt, eds., *Journals of the Continental Congress, 1774–1789*, 34 vols. (Washington, D.C., 1904–37), vol. 2: 123, 175. On the work of one of them see James F. and Jean H. Vivian, "Congressional Indian Policy During the War for Independence: The Northern Department," *Maryland Historical Magazine* 63 (1968), 241–74.

[11] Ford and Hunt, eds., *Journals of the Continental Congress* 3 (1775): 401; Robert S. Allen, *His Majesty's Indian Allies: British Policy in the Defence of Canada, 1774–1815* (Toronto: Dundurn, 1992), ch. 2; Sydney Jackman, ed., *With Burgoyne from Quebec* (Toronto: Macmillan, 1963), 127–9.

[12] *Revolution and Confederation*, 17–18, 29, 34, 52; *American Archives*, 4th ser. vol. 3: 485–8.

[13] Quoted in Barbara Graymont, *The Iroquois in the American Revolution* (Syracuse, N.Y.: Syracuse University Press, 1972), 99.

unnecessary War." Recognizing that taking sides in the conflict would set off a destructive cycle of revenge and retaliation, Kayashuta worked tirelessly to keep his people out of the fight. At Fort Pitt in July 1776 he tried to argue Indian neutrality from a position of strength and to implement the kind of diplomacy that had served the Iroquois well in past wars, "We will not suffer either the English or Americans to march an army through our country," he declared. That autumn, he warned the Americans to restrict their fighting to the coast and "not come into our Country to fight, lest you may stumble and fall on us so as to wrest the Chain of Friendship out of our hands."[14]

But Indians could not keep the war out of Indian country. As Britons, Americans, and other Indians demanded to know "who are friends and who are not," many Indians already had come to the sad realization that "it is impossible for them to continue much longer in a state of neutrality." The competition continued throughout the war and throughout the eastern woodlands.[15]

Winning Indian allegiance was one thing; retaining it amidst shifting fortunes of war and competing diplomacies required constant attention to gift giving, protocol, and local chiefs.[16] In the spring of 1777, British agent William Caldwell warned the Senecas not to "regard anything the Bigknife [Americans] might say to them for tho he had a very smooth Oily Tongue his heart was not good." Two years later, American commander Daniel Brodhead warned the Shawnees that the British would tell them fine stories but had come three thousand miles only "to rob & Steal & fill their Pockets."[17] As long as Detroit remained in British hands, securing the support or at least the neutrality of the French and Indian inhabitants of the Illinois country was vital to the American war effort. Pulled between British and American agents, many tribes in the Wabash and Illinois country "got divided among themselves part for us others

---

[14] Kayashuta's July speech is in Morgan Letterbook 1776 (July 24): 38; reprinted in J. Almon, *Remembrancer* 1776, pt. 3: 53–4; his autumn speech is in "Council at Pittsburgh, Oct. 15–Nov. 16, 1776," Yeates Collection, Historical Society of Pennsylvania. Both are reprinted in *Revolution and Confederation* 121–2, 134–6.

[15] *American Archives* 4th series, vol. 6: 764; *PCC*, reel 172, item 153, vol. 2: 203; Carl Berger, "The Campaign to Win the Indians' Allegiance," in his *Broadsides and Bayonets: The Propaganda War of the American Revolution* (Philadelphia: University of Pennsylvania Press, 1961), 52–83.

[16] E.g.: Louise Phelps Kellogg, "Indian Diplomacy during the Revolution in the West," *Transactions of the Illinois State Historical Society* 36 (1929), 47–57; Paul L. Stevens, "'To Keep the Indians of the Wabache in His Majesty's Interest': The Indian Diplomacy of Edward Abbott, British Lieutenant Governor of Vincennes, 1776–1778," *Indiana Magazine of History* 83 (1987), 141–70; idem, "'To Invade the Frontiers of Kentucky?' The Indian Diplomacy of Philippe de Rocheblave, Britain's Acting Commandant at Kaskaskia, 1776–1778," *Filson Club History Quarterly* 64 (1990), 205–46. See also White, *Middle Ground*, for the complexities of Indian diplomacy; and Haldimand Papers 21765: 383–4 for an inventory of Indian councils held at Detroit, Niagara, and other posts between 1778 and 1783.

[17] *Revolution on the Upper Ohio*, 67–70; Robert L. Scribner et al., eds., *Revolutionary Virginia, the Road to Independence: A Documentary Record*, 7 vols. (Charlottesville: University Press of Virginia, 1973–83), vol. 4: 129–30; Draper Mss. 1H54.

for the English," recalled George Rogers Clark. Having won many of the
Indians over by his hard-line diplomacy, Clark realized that they "required
great attention to keep the Flame from cooling too soon."[18]

Discourse and discord were part of the normal process by which Indian
societies reached consensus. However, the issues raised by the Revolution were
such that consensus could not always be reached. The divisions of colonial
society that John Adams summarized as one-third patriot, one-third loyalist,
and one-third neutral were replicated with numerous variations in countless
Indian communities in North America. As elsewhere on the frontier, the pressures imposed by the Revolution revealed existing fissures as well as creating
new ones.[19] Mohawk and Onondaga speakers asked Congress to ignore the
actions of individuals who went against the consensus of the Iroguois League.
In 1779 the Delawares asked Congress to distinguish between their nation as a
whole, which was still friendly, and the actions of a few individuals who, like
the Tories in the states, sided with the British and had been obliged to leave the
nation.[20]

As provocations increased, neutrality became increasingly precarious, even
impossible, forcing Indians to choose sides. Neutrality was not a viable option
for people who were not economically independent.[21] A Cherokee headman
indicated the degree of dependency to which his people had succumbed by
the beginning of the war when, suddenly cut off from trade and ammunition,
"I had recourse to the bow & arrow for my subsistence and defence – these
weapons my boy understands the use of better than myself."[22] Most of the
Indians who eventually sided with Britain did so after American acts of treachery, inability to provide trade, and continued pressure on their lands convinced
them they had no choice in the struggle for survival but to support the crown.
In colonial times the crown had established a record of protecting Indian
country; its colonial subjects, those now in rebellion, had posed the major threat
to Indian lands. Moreover, Britain possessed the economic resources Indian
peoples needed. Commitment was never unanimous and, council-fire rhetoric
aside, Indians fought for their own reasons, to protect their lands and people

---

[18] James Alton James, ed., *George Rogers Clark Papers, 1771–1781* (Springfield: Illinois State
Historical Society, 1912), 248.

[19] Cf. Hoffman, Tate, and Albert, eds., *Uncivil War*, xii.

[20] *Revolution and Confederation*, 35; Draper Mss. 1F50; 1H91–3; *Frontier Advance*, 352; *PCC*, reel
183, item 166: 446.

[21] *PCC*, reel 173: 372–83, reprinted in Maryly B. Penrose, comp., *Indian Affairs Papers: American
Revolution* (Franklin Park, N.J.: Liberty Bell, 1981), 158–61; Robert W. Venables, "The Indians'
Revolutionary War in the Hudson Valley, 1775–1783," in Laurence M. Hauptman and Jack
Campisi, eds., *Neighbors and Intruders: An Ethnohistorical Exploration of the Indians of Hudson's
River* (Ottawa: National Museum of Man, 1978), 231–3; Daniel H. Usner, Jr., *Indians, Settlers,
and Slaves in a Frontier Exchange Economy: The Lower Mississippi Valley Before 1783* (Chapel
Hill: University of North Carolina Press, 1992), 142.

[22] Carleton Papers, P.R.O. 30/55/60, No. 6742: 5.

from invasion, or to secure vital supplies, rather than to carry out the wishes of their British "father." A Seneca chief who had just returned from visiting the British at Niagara declared, "When our white Brethren call us to meet them at their Towns, we all flock like Bees – not that we want to take strong hold of their Friendship but to share the Goods they bring with them." After France entered the war, French emissaries circulated among the tribes of the Great Lakes region in an effort to secure Indian allegiance to the United States. But long-standing French influence could not outweigh American failure to match promise with performance when it came to supplying their Indian allies. North-western Indians assured Godfroy de Linctot in 1780 of their fidelity to the king of France, but asked pointedly:

> If our father is allied to the Americans, why do these allow us to be in want
> of everything; must we die together with our wives and children while
> rejecting the offers which the English make to us. . . . On the one hand we
> are forgotten, abandoned; on the other hand we are solicited and at times
> threatened by the English; in such a situation what can we do, what ought
> we to do?[23]

Any overview of Indian dispositions and allegiances is difficult and hazardous. Militants throughout Indian country saw the Revolution as an opportunity for a British-supplied-and-supported Indian alliance to recoup many of the losses of past generations. Deputies ranged far and wide promoting intertribal unity against American expansion.[24] However, most people fluctuated in their senti-ments, and participation in the fighting was often relatively brief. Enthusiasm for the British cause waxed and waned with the fortunes of war. Indian leaders displayed considerable statecraft in steering their people through the treacher-ous diplomatic waters churned up by the Revolution.[25] Emerging on the win-ning side was a vital consideration for Indian people, who knew they would have to live with the winners.

Some of the groups most consistently hostile to the Americans were actually bands composed of what Americans termed "renegade" warriors from various tribes. One of the first communities to wage war against the Americans was Pluggy's Town on the Oletangy River, where Chippewas, Wyandots, and Ottawas joined the Mingoes (Ohio Iroquois), and where Americans found it was often "difficult to tell what Nation are the Offenders." Like the Mingo chief Logan,

*[handwritten margin note: renegade warriors (mostly) consistently hostile]*

[23] Morgan Letterbook 1776 (July 26); Clarence W. Alvord, ed., "Kaskaskia Records, 1778–1790," *Collections of the Illinois Historical Society* 5 (1909), 164–5.

[24] Gregory Evans Dowd, *A Spirited Resistance: The North American Indian Struggle for Unity, 1745–1815* (Baltimore: Johns Hopkins University Press, 1992), ch. 3; *DAR*, vol. 12: 202; William A. Evans, ed., *Detroit to Sackville, 1778–1779: The Journal of Normand MacLeod* (Detroit, Mich.: Burton Historical Society, 1978), 117; White Eyes to George Morgan, July 13, 1776, Morgan Letterbook 1776.

[25] White, *Middle Ground*, 367, 398.

Pluggy had good reason for his hostility, having returned from peace talks after Dunmore's War to find "his blood relations lieing dead" at the hands of Virginians. Pluggy's Mingoes caused consternation among Americans and among neighboring tribes who blamed them for corrupting their young men and threatening to embroil them all in war. The Americans wanted to destroy. Pluggy's Town but held off for fear they would spark a general Indian war.[26]

The League of the Iroquois or Six Nations – the confederacy of Mohawks, Oneidas, Tuscaroras, Onondagas, Cayugas, and Senecas that stretched across upper New York State – had managed to maintain a pivotal position in North American affairs by preserving formal neutrality and essential unity of action in previous conflicts, but was unable to do so in this one. According to British agent Daniel Claus, the sudden death of superintendent Sir William Johnson on the very eve of the Revolution left the Iroquois "scattered like a flock of helpless sheep."[27] Presbyterian missionary Samuel Kirkland heard many Indians say that "they never knew a debate so warm & contention so fierce to have happened between these two Brothers, Oneidas & Cayugas, since the commencement of their union."[28]

In 1775 the Oneidas and other Iroquois took a neutral stance, but two years later they were killing each other. Mary Jemison, an adopted white captive living with the Senecas, recalled how her people returned from meeting the Americans at German Flats, where they had pledged their neutrality late in the summer of 1775, "well pleased that they could live on neutral ground, surrounded by the din of war, without being engaged in it."[29] But in 1777, after pestilence struck Onondaga, the central council fire was ritually extinguished for the first time in the league's history, and civil war erupted. Jemison said the British invited Iroquois warriors "to come and see them whip the rebels" at the siege of Fort Stanwix, but instead of "smoking and looking on, they were obliged to fight for their lives" in the bloody battle at Oriskany. The memory of the hand-to-hand fighting haunted Seneca chief Blacksnake into his old age:

[26] Draper Mss. 2D122; "In Congress, Dec. 3, 1777," NYPL, Schuyler Papers, reel 7, box 14; Edward G. Williams, ed., "The Journal of Richard Butler, 1775," *Western Pennsylvania Historical Magazine* 47 (1968), 39–40; Edward De Schweintz, *The Life and Times of David Zeisberger* (Philadelphia: Lippincott, 1870; New York Times and Arno Press reprint 1971), 445; *Revolution on the Upper Ohio*, 236–7; *Pennsylvania Archives*, 1st series, vol. 5: 260; Morgan Letterbook, vol. 1: 23, 47–50, 56–9, 61, 71–3, 76; vol. 2: 45; Library of Congress, Edward Hand Papers, reel 13, item 55, vol. 262: 47.

[27] Claus to Haldimand [?], Dec. 2, 1774, NAC, Claus Papers, reel C-1478; quoted in John C. Guzzardo, "The Superintendent and the Ministers: The Battle for Oneida Allegiances," *New York History* 57 (1976), 282.

[28] Samuel Kirkland to Philip Schuyler, March 11, 1776, Hamilton College, Kirkland Papers 64b; Guzzardo, "Superintendent and the Ministers," 255–83.

[29] Mass. Archives, vol. 144: 311–12; June Namias, ed., *A Narrative of the Life of Mary Jemison. By James Seaver* (Norman: University of Oklahoma Press, 1992), 98. The proceedings of the German Flats conference are in *PCC*, reel 144: 1–43, *American Archives*, 4th series, vol. 3: 474–90, and *NYCD*, vol. 8: 605–8.

"There I have Seen the most Dead Bodies all it over [sic] that I never Did see, and never will again [.] I thought at the time the Blood Shed a Stream Running Down on the Descending ground During the afternoon." The Senecas suffered heavy losses, and Jemison remembered the "sorrow and distress" in her community after the battle. Pro-British warriors burned Oneida crops and houses in revenge; Oneidas retaliated by burning Mohawk homes. The Oneidas themselves split into factions; most supported the Americans, but some joined the British. The Tuscaroras also supported the Americans, whereas the Cayugas lent their weight to the crown. The Onondagas struggled to maintain neutrality until American troops burned their towns in 1779. For the Iroquois, the Revolution was a war in which, in some cases literally, brother killed brother.[30]

Massachusetts and Connecticut exempted Indians from their wartime drafts, along with blacks, mulattoes, schoolteachers, and students at Harvard and Yale.[31] Nevertheless, Indian towns surrounded by colonial neighbors in southern and central New England rallied to the American cause and served steadfastly, despite suffering heavy losses. William Apess, a Pequot Indian writing in the next century, said that the small Indian town of Mashpee on Cape Cod furnished twenty-six men for the Patriot service, all but one of whom "fell martyrs to liberty in the struggle for Independence." Pequots and Mohegans from Connecticut suffered similar high casualties: roughly half the Pequots who left to fight in the Revolution did not come home. Indian women widowed by the war were forced to look outside their communities for husbands, intermarrying with European and African American neighbors.[32]

Indian responses in northern New England and eastern Canada were more ambiguous. Abenakis seemed ambivalent. Some served with George Washington,

[30] Namias, ed. *Mary Jemison*, 100; Graymont, *Iroquois in the American Revolution*; idem, "The Oneidas and the American Revolution," in Jack Campisi and Laurence M. Hauptman, eds., *The Oneida Indian Experience: Two Perspectives* (Syracuse, N.Y.: Syracuse University Press, 1988), 39; Joseph Priest, *A True Narrative of the Capture of David Ogden, among the Indians, in the Time of the Revolution* (Lanesborough [Mass.?]: n.p., 1840), 10 (Oneidas split); Anthony F. C. Wallace, *The Death and Rebirth of the Seneca* (New York: Knopf, 1970), ch. 5; William T. Hagan, *Longhouse Diplomacy and Frontier Warfare: The Iroquois Confederation in the American Revolution* (Albany: New York State Bicentennial Commission, 1976); George F. Stanley, "The Six Nations and the American Revolution" *Ontario History* 56 (1964), 217–32; *NYCD*, vol. 8: 720, 723–6; Haldimand Papers 21767: 104; 21773: 101; Draper Mss., vol. 14: 248–51; *PCC*, reel 183: 387–93; *DAR*, vol. 14: 251; Thomas S. Abler, ed., *Chainbreaker: The Revolutionary War Memoirs of Governor Blacksnake, As Told to Benjamin Williams* (Lincoln: University of Nebraska Press, 1989), 69, 87, 91, 144; quote at 128–9; Clements Library, Clinton Papers, vol. 26: 32; NYPL, Schuyler Papers, reel 7, box 14.

[31] *Acts and Resolves of the Province of Massachusetts Bay*, 21 vols. (Boston: Wright & Potter, 1869–1922), vol. 21 (1779–80): 33–5, 397–9; *Public Records of the State of Connecticut* (Hartford: Lockwood and Brainard 1894) vol. 1: 91.

[32] Barry O' Connell, ed., *On Our Own Ground: The Complete Writings of William Apess, A Pequot* (Amherst: University of Massachusetts Press, 1992), 239–40; Colin G. Calloway, "New England Algonkians in the American Revolution," *Annual Proceedings* of the Dublin Seminar for New England Folklife, 1991 (Boston University, 1993), 51–62, esp. 55; Jack Campisi, *The Mashpee Indians: Tribe on Trial* (Syracuse, N.Y.: Syracuse University Press, 1991), 88–91.

others joined the British.[33] The Indian communities on the Saint Lawrence known as the Seven Nations of Canada displayed similar reluctance. Most of them had fought against the "Bostonians" during the Seven Years' War, but their exposed position meant they had much to lose and little to gain in this conflict. British and American agents campaigned to win their allegiance. Warriors from the Seven Nations served with Burgoyne; some also sided with the Americans. But the Seven Nations as a whole resurrected the old system of playing off rival powers, and avoided declaring openly for either side, considering this their best strategy for surviving the war intact. As the Revolutionary War escalated in Indian country, this meant steering a middle course between warring Six Nations relatives as well as between redcoats and Bostonians.[34]

The village of Caughnawaga or Kahnawake near Montreal, which was also the site of the Seven Nations' council fire, became a major conduit for the passage of intelligence, and a key community in the contest for Indian allegiance in the north.[35] According to one report from Montreal in March 1775, the Caughnawagas refused British requests "to fight Boston," in part because of kinship ties to New England resulting from captive taking in the French and Indian wars: "They are a very Sinsible Polliticke People and say that if they are obliged for their own safety to take up arms on either side that they shall take part on the Side of their Brethren the English in N. England; all the Chiefs of the Caughnawaga Tribe being of English extraction captivated in their infancy." That some Caughnawaga youths were attending Dartmouth College served as an additional disincentive to attacking the New England frontier. But the Caughnawagas were equally reluctant to fight for the Americans. Ethan Allen said they acted on sound political principles and, like the French, were "watching the scale of power."[36] The entry of France into the war produced the additional pull of old ties, and Caughnawagas visited General Rochambeau's

---

[33] See this volume, ch. 2; Colin G. Calloway, The *Western Abenakis of Vermont, 1600–1800: War, Migration and the Survival of an Indian People* (Norman: University of Oklahoma Press, 1990), ch. 11; idem, "Sentinels of Revolution: Bedel's New Hampshire Rangers and the Abenaki Indians on the Upper Connecticut," *Historical New Hampshire* 45 (1990), 271–95.

[34] Lawrence Ostola, "The Seven Nations of Canada and the American Revolution, 1774–1783," M.A. thesis, University of Montreal, 1989. The Seven Nations included the Mohawks of Caughnawaga, the Mohawks and Algonkins of Oka or Lake of Two Mountains, the Hurons of Lorette, the Abenakis at Odanak, and the Cayugas and Onondagas at Oswegatchie. When the Oswegatchie mission closed, the inhabitants moved to Saint Regis (Akwesasne), which then became part of the Seven Nations.

[35] Paul Lawrence Stevens, "His Majesty's 'Savage' Allies: British Policy and the Northern Indians During the Revolutionary War. The Carleton Years, 1774–1778," Ph.D. diss., State University of New York at Buffalo, 1984; *PCC*, reel 172, item 153, vol. 1: 31, 71–2, 98, 176–7, 200; vol. 2: 107–8; *DAR*, vol. 11: 166; Otis G. Hammond, ed., *Letters and Papers of Major-General John Sullivan*, 3 vols. (Concord: New Hampshire Historical Society, 1930–9), vol. 1: 233.

[36] *Collections of the Maine Historical Society* 2d series, 14 (1910), 240; Hammond, ed., *Letters and Papers of Major-General John Sullivan*, vol. 1: 287; Michael A. Bellesiles, *Revolutionary Outlaws: Ethan Allen and the Struggle for Independence on the Early American Frontier* (Charlottesville: University Press of Virginia, 1993), 125.

forces when they landed at Newport, Rhode Island, in 1780.[37] But Caughnawagas also had ties to both sides in the Iroquois civil war.

In Maine and Nova Scotia, Passamaquoddies, Micmacs, and Maliseets were reluctant to become involved in a war that had little to offer them. Massachusetts passed a resolution in July 1776 that five hundred Micmac and Maliseet (Saint Johns) Indians be employed in the continental service. Maliseet chiefs Ambrose St. Aubin and Pierre Tomah sometimes spoke as if they were engaged in a common cause to protect their lands and liberties, but eastern Indians often deftly avoided the belligerents' recruiting efforts. Delegates who attended the Treaty of Watertown in 1776 exceeded their authority in committing the tribes to the American cause. The tribes split as British power and British goods exerted increasing influence. About a hundred principal men of the Micmac, Maliseet, and Passamaquoddy tribes took an oath of allegiance to King George between September 1778 and January 1779.[38] With chief Orono "hearty in our cause," a company of Penobscots served with the United States and figured prominently in the action at Penobscot in 1779.[39] A dozen Pigwackets from western Maine petitioned Massachusetts for permission to enlist.[40]

In the strategically crucial Ohio country, Indians and whites began (or rather continued) killing each other as soon as the Revolution broke out.[41] The Indians were the prize in a diplomatic tug-of-war between Henry Hamilton, the British commander at Detroit, and George Morgan, the American Indian agent at Fort Pitt.[42] The Delawares, neutral at the outbreak of the war, soon came under

[37] Durand Echevirria, "The Iroquois Visit Rochambeau at Newport in 1780: Excerpts from the Unpublished Journal of The Comte De Charles," *Rhode Island History* 11 (1952), 73–81.

[38] *Revolution and Confederation*, 40–2, 44, 57–8; *Acts and Resolves of the Province of Massachusetts Bay* 19 (1775–6), 525–6; *American Archives*, 5th series, vol. 1: 838–50; vol. 3: 800–7; Sir Guy Carleton Papers, 1777–1783, 107 reels (University Microfilms International), reel 5, No. 1690; reel 6, No. 2158. *DAR*, vol. 13: 266; Frederic Kidder, ed., *Military Operations in Eastern Maine and Nova Scotia during the Revolution, chiefly compiled from the journals and letters of Colonel John Allen* (Albany: Munsell, 1867), esp. 55; *Dictionary of Canadian Biography*, vol. 4: 693, 735–6; James Phinney Baxter, ed., *Documentary History of the State of Maine: Collections of the Maine Historical Society*, 2d series (Portland: Maine Historical Society), vols. 14 and 15; "The Catholic Indians in the American Revolution," *American Catholic Historical Researches* 4 (1908), 193–230; Library of Congress, Peter Force Transcripts, series 7E, reel 20, item 81: 3; James S. Leamon, *Revolution Downeast: The War for American Independence in Maine* (Amherst: University of Massachusetts Press, 1993), 91–9.

[39] *American Archives*, 4th series, vol. 2: 1005; Mass. Archives, vol. 144: 382; Massachusetts Historical Society, Solomon Lovell Papers. A payroll of the Indians who served at Penobscot, reprinted from Mass. Archives, vol. 37: 145, is given in "Maine Indians in the Revolution," *Sprague's Journal of Maine History* 6 (1918–19), 105–12.

[40] Calloway, *Western Abenakis of Vermont*, 208.

[41] Clements Library, Clinton Papers, vol. 12: 51.

[42] On Hamilton see Bernard W. Sheehan, "The Famous Hair Buyer General: Henry Hamilton, George Rogers Clark and the American Indian," *Indiana Magazine of History* 79 (1983), 1–28; Nelson Vance Russell, "The Indian Policy of Henry Hamilton: A Reevaluation," *Canadian Historical Review* 11 (1930), 20–37; and John D. Barnhart, ed., *Henry Hamilton and George Rogers Clark in the American Revolution, with the Unpublished Journal of Lieut. Gov. Henry*

pressure from American and British agents and from other tribes, particularly *Delawares* pro-British Wyandots under Half King to the north. The war and the question of an American alliance became linked to old divisions over embracing Euro-American culture. Following the deaths of chiefs Custaloga and Netawatwees in the fall of 1776, the Delaware council began to fragment. British policy had *old allegiance* formerly sought to control the Ohio tribes by working through the Iroquois Confederacy, who claimed ancient hegemony and maintained a lingering influence in the region. Now White Eyes and some other Delawares saw an American alliance as an opportunity to assert independence from the Six Nations and challenge their claims to lands west of the Ohio. A group of young Delaware warriors under Wandahela defected to the British, but even General Hand's infamous "squaw campaign," in which American militia attacked camps of Delaware women and children, did not destroy the tribe's commitment to peace. The Delaware capital at Coshocton became a refuge for Indian people who wanted to distance themselves from those who had sided with the British. The United States signed a treaty with the Delawares in 1778 in an effort to secure their neutrality and a right of passage across their lands, but many Delawares complained they had been deceived into taking up the hatchet for the United States in a treaty that George Morgan described as "villainously conducted." White Eyes and John Killbuck of the Turtle clan displayed continued pro-American sympathies, but Captain Pipe of the Wolf clan moved with many of his followers to the Sandusky River in northwestern Ohio, closer to the Wyandots and the British. The Americans murdered White Eyes, their strongest supporter in the Delaware national council, and failed to provide the trade they promised and that the Delawares needed. Pipe gained influence among his hungry and disillusioned people, and the British were able to lure Delaware warriors into their orbit.[43]

*Hamilton* (Crawfordsville, Ind.: Banta, 1951.) Gregory Schaaf, *Wampum Belts and Peace Trees: George Morgan, Native Americans, and Revolutionary Diplomacy* (Golden, Colo.: Fulcrum, 1990) looks at Morgan's Indian relations in 1776. Morgan's papers, which give much fuller information, are in the Carnegie Library, Pittsburgh; the Pennsylvania Historical and Museum Commission; the Library of Congress, Draper Mss.; and the Kellogg and Thwaites collections of documents relating to the Revolution in the Ohio Valley. On Fort Pitt, see Edward G. Williams, "Fort Pitt and the Revolution on the Western Frontier," *Western Pennsylvania Historical Magazine* 59 (1976) 1–37, 129–52, 251–87, 379–444.

[43] On Iroquois claims to hegemony and the Ohio tribes see Francis Jennings, *The Ambiguous Iroquois Empire: The Covenant Chain Confederation of Indian Tribes with English Colonies from its Beginnings to the Lancaster Treaty of 1774* (New York: Norton 1984) and Michael N. McConnell, "Peoples 'In Between': The Iroquois and the Ohio Indians, 1720–1768," in Daniel K. Richter and James H. Merrell, eds. *Beyond the Covenant Chain: The Iroquois and Their Neighbors in Indian North America, 1600–1800* (Syracuse, N.Y.: Syracuse University Press, 1987), 93–112. On the Delawares in the Revolution and the schisms within the nation see C.A. Weslager, *The Delaware Indians* (New Brunswick, N.J.: Rutgers University Press, 1972), ch. 13; Dowd, *A Spirited Resistance*, 65–89; and the Brodhead Papers, Draper Mss., H Series, esp. 1H22–3, 47–8; *Frontier Defense*, 27–9, 95–7, 100–1, 215–20; *Frontier Advance*, esp. 20–1, 112–13, 117–18,

*Am. failure*
*to supply*
*goods during*
*wartime*

Nothing hurt the pro-American and neutral Delawares more than the United States's failure to supply them with goods and trade in time of war. "Great Stress is laid on your inability to supply our wants," Captain Pipe told Morgan in 1777, "& we are ridiculed by your Enemies for being attached to you who cannot even furnish us with a pair of Stockings or a Blanket – this obliges us to be dependent in a great measure on them." Delaware chiefs who visited Daniel Brodhead at Pittsburgh two years later were nearing the end of their tether: "The poor wretches are quite destitute of clothing, and unless they can be supplied by us, they will be compelled to submit to such terms as our enemies may impose on them."[44] The Americans were unable to match bombast with either goods or action. In 1778, in council at Fort Laurens at the head of a bedraggled army and at the tail end of an abortive campaign against Detroit, General Lachlan McIntosh warned the Shawnees, Delawares, Wyandots, Ottawas, and Chippewas that they had fourteen days to come and make peace or else suffer the consequences, "upon which declaration they Set up a General Laugh."[45]

A detachment of Delawares served the United States through the final years of the war, and Brodhead warned Delaware chiefs not to be deceived by the British or alarmed by the Wyandots: " As to the speech of the half King it is a Great discharge of wind, he dare not hurt a hair of your head."[46] But war and hunger rendered continued neutrality impossible in the Ohio Valley. Anticipating a general war in 1780, Brodhead decided to strike first. "The Delawares have acted a double part long enough," he declared. American troops guided by Killbuck (who had turned increasingly toward the United States as his people turned to the British), attacked the cluster of villages around Coshocton and burned the Delaware capital. The inhabitants fled "half-naked" to the militant Wyandots and Delawares around Sandusky, who received them with open arms and British supplies. Killbuck's followers took refuge at Fort Pitt, where they not only suffered hunger and hardship but also were exposed to danger at the hands of American frontiersmen.[47]

157, 187–8, 202–5, 224–6; George Morgan Letterbook, Carnegie Library, esp. vol. 1: 18–22, 46, 49–51; vol. 3: 148–51, 162–5; LC, Hand Papers, reel 13, item 55: 90–1. John Heckewelder, *A Narrative of the Mission of the United Brethren among the Delaware and Mohegan Indians* (Philadelphia: McCarty & Davis, 1820) provides a firsthand pro-American account of developments in Delaware country.

[44] George Morgan Letterbook, vol. 1: 80; vol. 2: 88; vol. 3: 27; *Penn. Archives*, lst series, vol. 12: 190. See also *PCC*, reel 183, item 166. 411–17, 445; *Frontier Advance*, 317–18.

[45] *Frontier Advance*, 180.

[46] "Pay Roll of the Delaware Indians in Service of the United States, June 15 1780–Oct. 31, 1781"; Revolutionary War Rolls, 1775–1783, National Archives Microfilm M246, roll 129; Draper Mss. 2H57; *Frontier Retreat*, 237.

[47] Draper Mss. 3H19; 5D80, 86, 99, 142; *Penn. Archives*, lst series, vol. 8: 640; vol. 9: 161–2; *Frontier Retreat*, 337–43, 353, 376–81, 399; *Penn. Archives*, lst series. vol. 9: 161–2; Neville B. Craig, ed., *The Olden Time*, 2 vols. (Cincinnati: Clarke, 1876), vol. 2: 378–9, 389; *MPHC*, vol. 10 (1886): 476, 478; Dowd, *Spirited Resistance*, 82–3; Consul W. Butterfield, ed., *The Washington–Irvine Correspondence* (Madison, Wis.: Atwood, 1882), 179.

*[handwritten margin notes: Anglicized Delawares clinging to neutrality]*

Those Delawares who had converted to Christianity and lived in separate villages under the guidance of Moravian missionaries also clung to a neutrality that cost them dearly. The Wyandot Half King warned the Moravian Delawares in 1780 that "they were sitting between two powerful, angry gods, who, with their mouths wide open, were most ferociously looking at each other!" and that they were in peril of being attacked and devoured by one or both of them. Two years later, American militia marched to the Moravian Delaware town of Gnadenhütten, rounded up the inhabitants, and bludgeoned to death ninety-six men, women, and children.[48] In 1782, American borderers, perhaps the same party who massacred the Moravians, attacked the Delawares living on Smokey or Killbuck Island near Pittsburgh. In the ensuing confusion, the wampum belts and other records that constituted the tribal archives were lost in the river. They were never replaced, and Delaware unity suffered another blow.[49]

Having assiduously endeavored to avoid entanglement in the war, Delawares had good reason to be bitter. In a speech recorded by Moravian missionary John Heckewelder at Detroit in November 1781, Captain Pipe, now fighting alongside the British, turned angrily on commander Arent Schuyler De Peyster, roundly denouncing Britons and Americans alike for dragging the Indians into their quarrel.

> Father! Many lives have already been lost on *your* account! Nations have suffered and been weakened! Children have lost Parents, brothers, and relatives! Wifes have lost Husbands! It is not known how many more may perish before Your war will be at end![50]

*[handwritten margin note: Shawnee]*

The neighboring Shawnees had been involved in long resistance against encroachment on their lands and had just fought a costly war against Lord Dunmore and Virginia. Early in the Revolution, Shawnee emissaries traveled to Cherokee country in an effort to form a confederacy against American expansion. However, the Shawnees themselves were divided over the question of further resistance. The Shawnee chief Cornstalk tried to preserve his people's fragile neutrality, but confessed he was unable to restrain his "foolish Young Men." American frontiersmen displayed their peculiar penchant for murdering key friends at key moments. After Cornstalk was killed under a flag of truce in 1777, most Shawnees made King George's fight their own.[51]

---

[48] Heckewelder, *Narrative of the Mission of the United Brethren*, 236–7; *PCC*, reel 73, item 59, vol. 3: 49–51; Draper Mss. 5D42; 11S146–9; *Penn. Archives*, lst series, vol. 9: 523–5; Schweintz, *Life and Times of David Zeisberger*, 537–8; Butterfield, ed., *Washington–Irvine Correspondence*, 99–109.

[49] Jay Miller, "Delaware Integrity: The History and Culture of the *Gamwing*," unpublished manuscript, p. 161.

[50] James H. O'Donnell, III, ed., "Captain Pipe's Speech: A Commentary on the Delaware Experience, 1775–1781," *Northwest Ohio Quarterly* 64 (1992), 126–33.

[51] Colin G. Calloway, "'We Have Always Been the Frontier': The American Revolution in Shawnee Country," *American Indian Quarterly* 16 (1992), 39–52; and this volume ch. 6.

Closer to King George's outposts, Half King of the Wyandots played an apparently ambiguous role. When the Americans were planning expeditions against Detroit, he warned them to steer clear of the Wyandot towns or he would be unable to restrain his young men. He sent messages to the Delawares urging neutrality and warned them against listening to the British.[52] At other times, he threatened the Delawares if they did *not* join the British, declared for the British in 1777, and stood as Britain's foremost ally in the Sandusky region as Wyandot war parties passed through Delaware towns en route to the American frontier.[53] Moravian missionary David Zeisberger blamed the British, but another report was probably closer to the truth in identifying a consistent motivation. The Wyandots apparently were playing for time until they could move their women and children to safety and "untill such times as their Corn gets hard, and they have brought it out of Your Way, after which their Tomhawk will be as Sharp against You as ever."[54]

Farther west, Indian people living on the Wabash, Illinois, and Mississippi rivers had not yet felt the full threat of American expansion, and many were cool to British overtures. Nevertheless, the reverberations of the Revolution were felt at the western reaches of the woodlands and beyond. On the Mississippi, British and Spanish agents competed for Indian allegiance, sending flags, medals, and presents into Indian villages and courting the support of tribes as far distant from eastern battlefields as the Otoes, Iowas, and Missouris.[55] In the spring of 1776, De Peyster, then commanding at Michilimackinac, sent his agents to drum up Indian volunteers from the Ottawas, Chippewas, and Menominees at Green Bay, then dispatched them to resist the American invasion of Canada. The Indians traveled to Montreal only to find that the invaders had already been repulsed. Indians from the western Great Lakes participated in Burgoyne's campaign in 1777, and De Peyster despatched another 550 warriors to Montreal in 1778.[56] The Miami Indians were pulled by the opposing appeals of Americans and British at opposite ends of the Wabash, and the Miami council at Kekionga struggled to maintain a united front against American expansion in the area. Wabash Indians and some Great Lakes tribes swung to the crown when Henry Hamilton arrived in the region, but fell away after

---

[52] Draper Mss. 1H16–17, 47–8; *Frontier Advance*, 187, 265–6; George Morgan Letterbook, vol. 3: 86–7.

[53] *Frontier Defense*, 27–8; *Frontier Advance*, 117, 233, 265–7; LC, Hand Papers, reel 13, item 55, vol. 262: 51; Heckewelder, *Narrative of the Mission of the United Brethren*, 154, 159–60, 166.

[54] George Morgan Letterbook, vol. 2: 88–90; *Frontier Advance*, 328–83; *Penn. Archives*, 2d series, vol. 3: 305–6.

[55] *WHC*, vol. 18: 412–14, 424; Louis Houck, ed. *The Spanish Regime in Missouri*, 2 vols. (Chicago: Donnelley, 1909), vol. 1: 175–6.

[56] David A. Armour and Keith R. Widder, *At the Crossroads: Michilimackinac During the American Revolution*, rev. ed. (Mackinac Island, Michigan: Mackinac Island State Park Commission, 1986), 54–56; *MPHC*, vol. 10: 261–3; *WHC*, vol. 11: 111, 133; vol. 18: 355–8.

George Rogers Clark brought the Revolutionary War to their doors and captured Hamilton in 1779, and a Franco-Indian force destroyed Kekionga in 1780. In the wake of Hamilton's "miscarriage" and the Franco-American alliance, many of Britain's allies in the region seemed "quite disheartened" and ready to desert. Although they continued to profess loyalty to the king, "they frame Excuses for not going to War." In the western Great Lakes region, the later years of the Revolution became a duel for Indian allegiance, waged between Clark and British agent Charles Langlade.[57]

The Potawatomi response to the Revolution reflected existing divisions. The Detroit Potawatomis supported Britain throughout the war. However, the Illinois and Wisconsin bands resisted British overtures, swung to the Americans when Clark occupied Illinois in 1779, and maintained ties to the French and Spanish in Louisiana. The Potawatomis of the Saint Joseph River fell under competing British, American, and Spanish influences during the course of the war, but ultimately joined the Detroit band in supporting Britain and resisting American expansion.[58] Like Indian peoples throughout eastern North America, they did not throw themselves blindly into the fray but weighed the words and actions of both parties. When the Potawatomi chief Siggenauk or Black Bird met Clark at Kaskaskia in November 1778, he was eager to hear the American side of the story so that he might judge for himself. "To satisfy this inquisative [sic] Indian," wrote Clark, "I was obliged to begin almost at the first settlement of America and to go through almost the whol [sic] History of it to the present time particularly the cause of the Revolution." It took him half a day. Siggenauk asked pertinent questions and had to be "satisfied as to every point."[59] The Wabash Kickapoos gave Henry Hamilton their support in 1778 but, with Illinois Kickapoos supporting Clark, they defected at Vincennes. However, as the flood of American settlers increased, the Kickapoos, like the Potawatomis, turned

[57] Bert Anson, *The Miami Indians* (Norman: University of Oklahoma Press, 1970), 84, 91; White, *Middle Ground*, 399; *MPHC*, vol. 9: 383, 395–6; vol. 19: 411, 423, 497, 537; *Frontier Retreat*, 122–3; Barnhart, ed., *Henry Hamilton and George Rogers Clark*, 124; George C. Chalou, "George Rogers Clark and Indian America, 1778–1780," in *The French, The Indians, and George Rogers Clark in the Illinois Country* (Indianapolis: Indiana Historical Society, 1977), 34–46; Haldimand Papers, 21717: 37–8, 52–3; Louise Phelps Kellogg, "Wisconsin Indians during the American Revolution," *Transactions of the Wisconsin Academy of Sciences, Arts and Letters* 24 (1929), 47–57. *Collections of the Illinois Historical Society* 1 (1903) contains documents relating to "Clark's Conquest of the Illinois," and "Letters from the Canadian Archives" relating to the contest in the area.

[58] R. David Edmunds, *The Potawatomis: Keepers of the Fire* (Norman: University of Oklahoma Press, 1978), 99–115; *MPHC*, vol. 9 (1886): 392–6, 454; vol. 10: 349–51, 380–1, 453–5; Houck, ed., *Spanish Regime in Missouri*, vol. 1: 175. Potawatomi relations with De Peyster at Detroit are in NAC, C-1223, vol. 13.

[59] James, ed., *George Rogers Clark Papers, 1777–1781*, 253–4. Clark mistakenly described Black Bird or Siggenauk as a Chippewa, but cf. White, *Middle Ground*, 397, and James A. Clifton, *The Prairie People: Continuity and Change in Potawatomi Indian Culture, 1665–1965* (Lawrence: Regents Press of Kansas, 1977), 164–6.

back to the British and became increasingly active in the northwest Indian confederation.[60]

Sauk and Fox Indians on the upper Mississippi were counted British allies, but also tried to maintain relations with the Americans and with Spaniards at Saint Louis.[61] Farther west, the Santee Sioux were accustomed to sending chiefs each summer to Michilimackinac to strengthen alliances. The Mdwekanton Santee chief Wabasha, described by the British as "a prince of an Indian," apparently visited Governor Carleton in Quebec in 1776 and was given a general's commission in 1778.[62] The Anglo-American war was not always the conflict foremost in the minds of western Indians: Winnebagoes who turned out for the British in 1779 were anxious lest the Chippewas and Sauks attack their villages in their absence.[63]

A force of about a thousand British and Indians attacked Saint Louis in May 1780. The Indians were mainly western tribes, including about two hundred Sioux under Wabasha, Chippewas led by Matchekewis,[64] and a group of Sauk and Fox warriors recruited en route from their villages. The failure of the attack dealt a serious blow to British prestige among tribes that were already vacillating. The Sauk and Fox recruits proved reluctant allies at best, but a Spanish–American expedition burned their crops and village at Saukenuk on Rock River in retaliation. Many Sauk and Fox people switched allegiance from Britain to Spain in the fall. Meanwhile, the new Spanish lieutenant governor, Francisco Cruzat, initiated a vigorous Indian policy based on the belief that securing Indian friendship constituted the best defense for Saint Louis. When two Indian chiefs from the Milwaukee region, known to the Spaniards as El Heturno and Naquiguen, visited Saint Louis and urged an expedition be sent against the British post at Saint Joseph, Cruzat consented. A force of Spanish volunteers and Indian allies took Fort Saint Joseph by surprise in February 1781, held it for a day, and returned to Saint Louis after raising the Spanish colors. Spanish prestige among the tribes climbed as Britain's declined. Tribal leaders surrendered their British flags and medals, and Cruzat replaced them with Spanish

---

[60] Arrell M. Gibson, *The Kickapoos* (Norman: University of Oklahoma Press, 1963), 35–40.

[61] Haldimand Papers, 21756: 22; *Spain in the Mississippi Valley*, vol. 2, pt. 1: 398; *WHC*, vol. 11: 126, 163; vol. 18: 365, 412–15.

[62] Paul L. Stevens, "Wabasha Visits Governor Carleton, 1776: New Light on a Legendary Episode of Dakota–British Diplomacy on the Great Lakes Frontier," *Michigan Historical Review* 16 (1990), 21–48; Gary Clayton Anderson, *Kinsmen of Another Kind; Dakota–White Relations in the Upper Mississippi Valley, 1650–1862* (Lincoln: University of Nebraska Press, 1984), 65; Haldimand Papers 21757: 284–92, 332; 21771: 108–9; *WHC*, vol. 11: 147–8; vol. 18: 413–14.

[63] Haldimand Papers, 21756: 12–13; *WHC*, vol. 11: 132.

[64] Matchekewis or Madjeckewiss (c. 1735–c. 1805) had participated in the capture of Fort Michilimackinac during Pontiac's War. Making his peace with the British, during the Revolution he had assisted in Burgoyne's expedition as well as raids into the Illinois country. David A. Armour, "Madjeckewiss," in Richard L. Blanco, ed., *The American Revolution, 1775–1783: An Encyclopedia*, 2 vols. (New York: Garland, 1993), vol. 2: 1008.

ones.[65] As the Revolution brought continuing shifts in power on the Mississippi, a young Kaskaskia chief, Jean Baptiste de Coigne, enlisted "under the flag of his fourth allegiance." Having dealt with first France and then Britain before the conflict, he now shifted allegiance to Spain and then to Virginia. In de Coigne's view, Virginians, French, and Spaniards were "all as one."[66]

In many areas of the southern backcountry, the war was "from start to finish, an Indian war."[67] British Indian superintendant John Stuart at first refrained from employing Indians, even as patriots spread rumors that he intended to do so and propelled backcountry settlers into the rebel camp.[68] The Catawbas in South Carolina, surrounded by settlers who "intend to seize their women and children the moment they hear they attempt violence," did the sensible thing and supported the Americans.[69] The Cherokees already had grim experience of the consequences of becoming involved in the wars of non-Indian neighbors. With trouble brewing, they were "very uneasie About their Women and Children, saying that if any rupture should happen between them and the white people the Women &c would run to the wood[s] and Starve."[70] Nevertheless, with settlers encroaching on their lands, younger Cherokee warriors led by Dragging Canoe launched attacks on the American frontier, with disastrous results. After expeditions from Virginia as well as North and South Carolina destroyed Cherokee towns and crops, the older chiefs regained the initiative and sued for peace. Refugee Cherokees fled to the Creeks, the Chickasaws, and to Pensacola. The nation split along generational lines as many younger warriors followed the lead of Dragging Canoe. Some five hundred families seceded to

[65] Abraham P. Nasatir, "The Anglo-Spanish Frontier in Illinois Country During the Revolution, 1779–1783," *Journal of the Illinois State Historical Society* 21 (1928), 343–50; Don Rickey, "The British–American Attack on St. Louis, May 26, 1870," *Missouri Historical Review* 55 (1960), 35–45; Lawrence Kinnaird, "The Western Fringe of Revolution," *Western Historical Quarterly* 7 (1976), 268–9; idem, "The Spanish Expedition against Fort St. Joseph in 1781: A New Interpretation," *Mississippi Valley Historical Review* 19 (1932), 173–91; *Spain in the Mississippi Valley*, vol. 1: 431–4; *WHC*, vol. 18: 412–15; Houck, *Spanish Regime in Missouri*, vol. 1: 167, 175–7.

[66] Stanley Faye, "Illinois Indians on the Lower Mississippi, 1771–1782," *Journal of the Illinois State Historical Society* 35 (1942), 57–72.

[67] Edwin J. Cashin, " 'But Brothers, It is Our Land We Are Talking About': Winners and Losers in the Georgia Backcountry," in Hoffman, Tate, and Albert, eds., *Uncivil War*, 245.

[68] Clements Library, Clinton Papers, vol. 16: 35; "Letters from Governor Sir James Wright, 1774–1782," *Collections of the Georgia Historical Society* 3 (1873), 189; Philip M. Hamer, "John Stuart's Indian Policy During the Early Months of the Revolution," *Mississippi Valley Historical Review* 17 (1930), 351–66. For the motivations of backcountry settlers, see Edward J. Cashin, "Sowing the Wind: Governor Wright and the Georgia Backcountry on the Eve of the Revolution," in Harvey H. Jackson and Phinizy Spalding, eds., *Forty Years of Diversity: Essays on Colonial Georgia* (Athens: University of Georgia Press, 1984), 233–50.

[69] James H. Merrell, *The Indians' New World: Catawbas and Their Neighbors from European Contact through the Era of Removal* (Chapel Hill: University of North Carolina Press, 1989), 215–21; Gibbes, ed., *Documentary History of the American Revolution*, vol. 1: 197; *DAR*, vol. 11: 118; *Remembrancer*, 1776, pt. 3: 180.

[70] LC, C.O. 5/77: 184.

form new communities on the Chickamauga River.[71] The Chickamauga towns
became the core of Cherokee resistance, attracting warriors from other towns
and supporting the war effort of the Shawnees and their northern allies.[72] Other
Cherokees suffered as a result of Chickamauga resistance, some helped the
Americans, and the Revolution became a Cherokee civil war.

Elsewhere in the south, the Chickasaws were accounted ancient friends of the
British, but, distant from the main theaters of conflict, they took little part in
the early fighting.[73] The Choctaws, with a population of perhaps thirty thousand in 1775, and a key strategic position on the lower Mississippi, attracted the
attention of British and Spanish rivals. The Anglo-Spanish contest allowed the
Choctaws to play European powers against each other as they had in the past as
a way of maintaining independence and securing trade goods, but once again
the nation split into factions. The majority supported King George, but the Six
Towns district, closest to New Orleans, favored Spain. According to James
Colbert, there was "hardly a Blackguard in the Six-towns but has Medals, Gorget,
& Red Coats given them." British agents always feared losing them, and Choctaws
from opposing districts came into conflict during the Revolution.[74] Moreover,
before British agents could set about securing Choctaw warriors as allies against
the Americans, they had first to arrange an end to a Choctaw war against the
Creeks that they themselves had fomented several years earlier when British
Indian policy had aimed at keeping Indian tribes divided against themselves
rather than united against the Americans.[75] By 1780, Choctaws were fighting
alongside British soldiers. Several hundred Choctaws fought in the defense of
Pensacola against Spanish attack early in 1781, where Spaniards found the
woods "sown with Indians." However, the Choctaw chief Franchumastabie was
infuriated that British exertions did not match those of his warriors.[76]

---

[71] See this volume, ch. 7.
[72] James Paul Pate, "The Chickamaugas: A Forgotten Segment of Indian Resistance on the Southern Frontier," Ph.D. diss., Mississippi State University, 1969.
[73] See this volume, ch. 8.
[74] C.O. 5/79: 137; Richard White, *The Roots of Dependency: Subsistence, Environment, and Social
Change among the Choctaws, Pawnees, and Navajos* (Lincoln: University of Nebraska Press, 1983),
81, 87–8, 107; Duane Champagne, *Social Order and Political Change: Constitutional Governments
among the Cherokee, the Choctaw, the Chickasaw, and the Creek* (Stanford, Calif.: Stanford University Press, 1992), 77. On Spanish–Choctaw relations, see Manuel Serrano Y Sanz, *España Y
Los Indios Cherokis Y Chactas en la Segundo Mitad de Siglio XVIII* (Seville, Tip. de la Guia
Oficial, 1916), esp. 19–20.
[75] Clements Library, Clinton Papers, vol. 15: 40; *DAR*, vol. 9: 90–1; vol. 11: 167; vol. 12: 79, 143,
191, 220, 224, 239–40, 247; vol. 19: 62.
[76] Bernard de Galvez, "Diary of the Operations against Pensacola, 1781," *Louisiana Historical
Quarterly* 1 (1917), 59; James H. O'Donnell, III, *The Southern Indians in the American Revolution*
(Knoxville: University of Tennessee Press, 1973), 104–5, 113; C.O. 5/82: 118–19, 130–1, 205,
210; *DAR*, vol. 20: 59–60, 149–50. Kathryn Holland examines the motives of the Indians in
coming to the defense of Pensacola in "The Anglo-Spanish Contest for the Gulf as Viewed from
the Townsquare," in William S. Coker and Robert R. Rea, eds., *Anglo-Spanish Confrontation on
the Gulf Coast During the American Revolution* (Pensacola, Fla.: Gulf Coast History and Humanities Conference, 1982), 90–105.

According to British Indian superintendent John Stuart, the key location of the Indians of Georgia and Alabama meant that they had "always been courted by different interests."[77] Creeks expressed their desire for neutrality early and often, but the Revolution brought renewed diplomatic pressures. At Picolata in December 1775, Governor Patrick Tonyn told the Creeks that Britain loved Indians like a mother loved "the Child hugging the Nipple," whereas Americans pretended to love them but "would kill & destroy them afterwards." At Augusta in May 1776, American trader-agent George Galphin assembled two hundred Creeks and urged them to stay out of the war. Though Cussita and some other Lower Creek towns accepted Galphin's talks, British agent David Taitt said the delegates were plied with rum and threw the nation into "great confusion" when they returned home. The Augusta meeting was testimony to the divisions among the Creeks rather than to any real possibility of neutrality. Stuart and Taitt waged diplomatic warfare against Galphin, who distributed gifts from his trading post at Silver Bluff. Galphin's diplomatic efforts were undermined by Georgian aggressions against the Creeks, and most Upper Creek towns were pro-British. In the spring of 1776 Creek warriors were reported to be "Enraged to a degree of Madness to be at the Mad Children as they term the rebels." But the Creeks were at war with the Choctaws, and the Cherokee experience, reinforced by American emissaries, gave them warning of the dire consequences that their entry into the Anglo-American conflict might precipitate.[78] The Spanish also continued to exert influence in Creek towns, and opposing coalitions almost came to blows over what strategy to pursue.

Creek warriors eventually turned out for British campaigns against both the Americans and the Spaniards, and the neutralist party began to disintegrate. Creeks who had migrated to Florida earlier in the century and were in the process of becoming Seminoles generally supported the British; nevertheless, the Creeks were cautious participants at best in this white man's war. In David Taitt's assessment, most Creeks opposed the Americans "yet do not seem hearty in joining against them but would much rather wish to enjoy the advantages of a neutrality by being paid from both parties." John Stuart complained they were "a mercenary People, Conveniency & Safety are the great Ties that

[77] C.O. 5/79: 67.
[78] Tonyn to the Creek Nation, Dec. 6, 1775, North Carolina State Archives, Secretary of State – General Records [Provincial] Council of Safety, 1775–1776, box 306. Galphin's meeting with the Creeks at Augusta is in North Carolina State Archives, Secretary of State Records, *Continental Congress*, 1774–1779 (S.S. 317), and in *Revolution and Confederation*, 210–11. Taitt's account of the meeting is in *DAR*, vol. 12: 159–60, and in *Revolution and Confederation*, 212–13; Lillian M. Hawes, ed., "The Papers of Lachlan McIntosh, 1774–1779," *Collections of the Georgia Historical Society* 12 (1957), 59–60; Clements Library, Clinton Papers, vol. 10: 3; vol. 11: 5, 14; vol. 16: 14; O'Donnell, *Southern Indians in the American Revolution*, 39–40. See also Talks by Old Tallassee King's Son and the Handsome Fellow, June 18, 1777, North Carolina State Archives, Treasurer and Comptroller's Records, Indian Affairs (box 1), Cherokee Nation, 1739–1791; and Robert Scott Davis, Jr., "George Galphin and the Creek Congress of 1777," *Proceedings and Papers of the Georgia Association of Historians* (1982), 13–29.

Bind them." As historian Michael Green points out, the Creeks were simply following the consistent goals of their foreign policy: preserving Creek territory intact and maintaining ample trade for manufactured goods.[79]

In June 1778, the Continental Congress found that the nations at war against them in the West included "the Senecas, Cayugas, Mingoes and Wiandots in general, a majority of the Onondagas and a few of the Ottawas, Chippewas, Shawnese & Delawares, acting contrary to the voice of their nations." A month later, delegates from the Shawnees, Ottawas, Mingoes, Wyandots, Potawatomis, Delawares, Mohawks, and Miamis accepted a war belt from Henry Hamilton at Detroit. While Delawares, Oneidas, Tuscaroras, and other Indians friendly to the United States gathered "to guard against the impending Storm," and called on the Americans for protection, Thomas Jefferson and others advocated using friendly Indians to wage war against hostile ones.[80]

## Carrying the war to Indian country

The American Revolution was not only a civil war for many Indian peoples; it also amounted to a total war in Indian country. Indian and non-Indian nations were at war, on the brink of war, or arranging alliances in expectation of war. American history has paid little attention to the impact of this war on the Indians' home front. Operating out of Detroit and Niagara, the British utilized Indian allies and terror tactics to demoralize American frontier settlements, but Indian country suffered more than its share of killing, ravaging, and destruction. George Morgan recognized that whatever policies the United States might try to pursue toward the Indians, "many persons among ourselves wish to promote a War."[81] Indian leaders appealed to American leaders to "restrain your foolish young Men," just as whites appealed to Indian chiefs to restrain

[79] C.O. 5/79: 113; *DAR*, vol. 12: 159–60; Michael D. Green, "The Creek Confederacy in the American Revolution: Cautious Participants," in Coker and Rea, eds., *Anglo-Spanish Confrontation on the Gulf Coast During the American Revolution*, 54–75. See also: David H. Corkran, *The Creek Frontier, 1540–1783* (Norman: University of Oklahoma Press, 1967), 275, 282–5, 296, 316–25; Dowd, *Spirited Resistance*, 56; Kathryn Holland Braund, *Deerskins and Duffels: Creek Indian Trade with Anglo America* (Lincoln: University of Nebraska Press, 1993), 167; Champagne, *Social Order and Political Change*, 80; Carleton Papers, reel 3A, No. 925; Haldimand Papers, 21761: 134. cf. Jonathan Bryan's assessment in 1781 that, except for a few of the Cussita towns, the Creeks were well disposed to the Americans; Bryan to Greene, Aug. 27, 1781, Nathanael Greene Papers, Duke University, Perkins Library.

[80] Horatio Gates Papers (New York: Microfilming Corporation of America, 1978), reel 7: 764–6; Ford and Hunt, eds. *Journals of the Continental Congress*, vol. 11: 587–8; *MPHC*, vol. 9 (1886): 442–58; Julian P. Boyd, ed., *Papers of Thomas Jefferson* (Princeton, N.J.: Princeton University Press, 1950), vol. 3: 276; Clarence W. Alvord, ed., "Kaskaskia Records, 1778–1790," *Collections of the Illinois State Historical Society* 5 (1909), 147. A summary of limited tribal commitments is provided in White, *Middle Ground*, 399.

[81] Morgan Letterbook, vol. 1: 76.

their warriors, with equally ineffective results.[82] American commissioners warned Creek headmen in 1777 "We look to you to stop the killing, or our own beloved men & warriors will not hinder a just retaliation."[83] The chiefs could do little and retaliation begat retaliation. According to Richard White, "Murder gradually and inexorably became the dominant Indian policy" as backcountry settlers took the law into their own hands, killing mediation chiefs and noncombatants, and undermining the work of George Morgan and the policies of Congress.[84]

When war came, American strategy – like that of the French and the British before them, and of the Spanish in dealing with recalcitrant tribes west of the Mississippi at this time – aimed to carry the war into Indian country, destroy Indian villages, and burn Indian crops late in the season when there was insufficient time for raising another crop before winter.[85] Despite the adoption of commercial hunting and the addition of fruit, potatoes, cattle, pigs, and domestic fowl to their diet and their economy, the sacred "three sisters" of the Iroquois – corn, beans, and squash – remained the staff of life for many woodland Indians. Trader James Adair said corn was an Indian people's "chief produce and main dependance." Corn was also at the core of many tribes' spiritual wellbeing: Cherokees recalled the mythical female origins of their agriculture in the story of Selu, a woman whose name means "corn"; and annual Green Corn ceremonies ensured ritual purification of the community. Like the buffalo in Plains Indian culture and economy, corn for eastern woodland Indians was the basis of life and prosperity but was also an Achilles' heel, providing enemy armies with a target that could be hit time and again with devastating effect. In the Revolution, American armies waged war against Indian cornfields. Daniel Brodhead maintained that marching a thousand men into Indian country was a more effective means of protecting the frontier than employing three times that number as garrisons. General Armstrong agreed that carrying the war to the Indians' homes and families had an adverse effect on their morale: the Indians might flee their towns, "but their huts and cornfields must remain, the destruction

[82] Ibid., 84.

[83] Copy of a Speech delivered to the head Men & Warriors of the Creek Nation at the Treaty held on the River Ogeechee, June 17, 1777, in North Carolina State Archives, Treasurer's and Comptroller's Records. *Indian Affairs and Lands* (box 1), Cherokee Nation, 1739–1791, reprinted in *Revolution and Confederation*, 221–3.

[84] White, *Middle Ground*, 384, 395.

[85] In 1777, in an effort to halt Osage depredations, Lieutenant Governor Athanase de Mézières proposed striking the Indian villages in late August or early September, when the people returned home to harvest their gardens; Herbert E. Bolton, ed., *Athanase de Mézières and the Louisiana–Texas Frontier, 1768–1780*, 2 vols. (Cleveland: Clark, 1914), vol. 2: 143–7, cited in Gilbert C. Din and A. P. Nasatir, *The Imperial Osages: Spanish–Indian Diplomacy in the Mississippi Valley* (Norman: University of Oklahoma Press, 1983), 109. In their wars with the Chickasaws earlier in the century, the French tried to enlist Choctaw allies to cut down Chickasaw corn in early August "because they could do a great deal more damage to it by finding it in the milk than when it was more mature." *MPA, FD*, vol. 4: 202.

whereof greatly affects their old men, their women, and their children." American troops and militia tramped through the Susquehanna, the Allegheny, the Scioto, Miami, and Tennessee valleys, leaving smoking ruins and burned cornfields behind them.[86] As John Shy has pointed out, colonial military forces were used less often for protection of settlements than for exacting retribution and retaliation.[87]

American soldiers and militia matched and sometimes exceeded their Indian adversaries in the use of terror tactics. George Rogers Clark informed Fernando dc Lcyba, lieutenant governor of Spanish Illinois in November 1778, that "the Absolute orders of Congress to the Army now in Indian Country is to Shew no mercy to those that have been at war against the States." Clark believed no punishment was too great for Indians and those who fought alongside them. He declared that "to excel them in barbarity was and is the only way to make war upon Indians and gain a name among them," and carried his policy into grisly effect at Vincennes by binding and tomahawking Indian prisoners within sight of the besieged garrison.[88] William Henry Drayton and Andrew Williamson of South Carolina advocated that captured Indians become the slaves of the captors but the legislature refused, fearing Indian retaliation for such a precedent. Since Indian prisoners brought no reward, soldiers killed them for their scalps. Captain William Moore's contingent captured three Cherokees in their campaign against the Middle towns in 1776. Moore argued that the prisoners should be kept under guard until Congress approved their sale, but he was obliged to give in to the demands of his men since "the Greater Part swore Bloodily that if they were not Sold for Slaves upon the Spot, they would kill

---

[86] *Frontier Advance*, 311; *Penn. Archives*, 1st series, vol. 6: 614; cf. James H. O'Donnell, III, "Frontier Warfare and the American Victory," in John Fehrling, ed., *The World Turned Upside Down: The American Victory in the War of Independence* (Westport, Conn.: Greenwood, 1988), 119; Namias, ed., *Narrative of the Life of Mary Jemison*, 28–9; Samuel Cole Williams, ed., *Adair's History of the American Indians* (New York: Promontory Press reprint of 1930 ed.), 437. On the significance of corn, see, for example, John Witthoft, "Green Corn Ceremonialism in the Eastern Woodlands," *Occasional Contributions from the Museum of Anthropology of the University of Michigan* 13 (1949). For the Cherokees: Thomas Hatley, "Cherokee Women Farmers Hold Their Ground," in Robert D. Mitchell, ed., *Appalachian Frontiers: Settlement, Society, and Development in the Preindustrial Era* (Lexington: University Press of Kentucky, 1991), 38–9; on the Iroquois: William N. Fenton, ed., *Parker on the Iroquois: Iroquois Uses of Maize and Other Food Plants; The Code of Handsome Lake, the Seneca Prophet; the Constitution of the Five Nations* (Syracuse, N.Y.: Syracuse University Press, 1968), book 1. For an overview of the rich agricultural base of eastern woodland life at time of contact, see R. Douglas Hurt, *Indian Agriculture in America* (Lawrence: University of Kansas Press, 1987), ch. 3.

[87] John Shy, *A People Numerous and Armed: Reflections on the Military Struggle of American Independence* (New York: Oxford University Press, 1976), 236.

[88] Lawrence Kinnaird, ed., "Clark–Leyba Papers," *American Historical Review* 41 (1935), 100–1; Milo M. Quaife, ed., *The Conquest of the Illinois* (Chicago: Donnelley 1920), 148–9, 167–9; James, ed., *George Rogers Clark Papers, 1771–1781*, 144, 167, 189; HMC, *Report on the Manuscripts of Mrs. Stopford-Sackville*, 2 vols. (London: His Majesty's Stationary Office, 1910), vol. 2: 234; *MPHC*, vol. 9: 501–2; Barnhart, ed., *Henry Hamilton and George Rogers Clark*, 182–3; *Collections of the Illinois Historical Society* 1 (1903), 262, 282, 405.

and Scalp them Immediately." South Carolina paid £75 for male scalps; Pennsylvania offered $1,000 for every Indian scalp. Kentucky militia who invaded Shawnee villages dug up graves to scalp corpses.[89]

Barely had the Cherokees launched their attacks on the backcountry settlements than the colonists carried fire and sword to the Indians' towns and villages, bringing the nation to its knees. As usual, the war in Cherokee country revolved around corn. "Make smooth work as you go," William Henry Drayton advised the troops. "Cut up every Indian cornfield, and burn every Indian town."[90] In 1776 General Griffith Rutherford attacked the Cherokee Middle settlements from North Carolina and destroyed thirty-six towns, along with cornfields and livestock. At one town, William Moore's men burned "Corn, Pumpkins, Beans, peas, & Other Trifling things, Of which We found Abundance in Every house." Colonel Andrew Williamson attacked the Lower towns with a thousand men from South Carolina, then joined forces with Rutherford and spent two weeks laying waste the Cherokee Middle settlements. Colonel William Christian invaded the Overhill towns from Virginia, driving the people into the mountains and burning their food supplies. American soldiers destroyed "curious buildings, great apple trees, and whiteman-like improvements" as well as "vast quantities of corn, and houses beyond our numbering."[91]

In April 1779, Evan Shelby invaded Chickamauga Cherokee country. The damage inflicted, according to Thomas Jefferson, included "killing about half a dozen men, burning 11 towns, 20,000 bushels of corn . . . and taking as many goods as sold for twenty-five thousand pounds." That summer, British agent Alexander Cameron was poised to raise a Cherokee force "as soon as our corn in the nation would be hard enough to be converted into flour," but in the

---

[89] Robert Wilson Gibbes, ed., *Documentary History of the American Revolution*, 3 vols. (New York: Appleton, 1853–7), vol. 2: 29; C.O. 5/77: 121; Rachel N. Klein, "Frontier Planters and the American Revolution: The South Carolina Backcountry, 1775–1782," in Hoffman, Tate, and Albert, eds., *Uncivil War*, 67; William Moore to Brig. Gen. Rutherford, Nov. 18, 1776, Rutherford Papers, in the Southern Historical Collection of the Manuscripts Dept., University of North Carolina, Chapel Hill, SHC 2188; *Penn. Archives*, lst series, vol. 8: 167; *American Archives*, 5th series, vol. 3: 32; Calloway, "'We Have Always Been the Frontier,'" 43.

[90] Gibbes, ed., *Documentary History of the American Revolution*, vol. 2: 29.

[91] O'Donnell, *Southern Indians in the American Revolution*, 45–8; idem, *The Cherokees of North Carolina in the American Revolution* (Raleigh, N.C.: Department of Cultural Resources, 1976); idem, "The Virginia Expedition against the Overhill Cherokees, 1776," *East Tennessee Historical Society* 39 (1967), 13–25; Robert L. Ganyard, "Threat from the West: North Carolina and the Cherokee, 1776–1778," *North Carolina Historical Review* 45 (1968), 47–66; *North Carolina Colonial Records*, vol. 10: 745–8, 751–2; 837–9, 844–7, 860–1, 881–5, 895–8; vol. 11: 346, 351–2; "Reports of Colonels Christian and Lewis During the Cherokee Expedition, 1776," *Virginia Magazine of History and Biography* 17 (1909), 52–64; J. G. de Roulhac Hamilton, ed., "Revolutionary Diary of William Lenoir," *Journal of Southern History* 6 (1940), 247–57; Draper Mss. 12S200–1; 28S13–21, 69–75; 30S66–76; 31S170–1; 1U45–8; 3VV152–210. J. G. M. Ramsey, *The Annals of Tennessee* (Charleston, S.C.: Russell, 1853), contains detailed accounts of the Cherokee campaigns. Quotes: William Moore to Brig. Gen. Rutherford, Nov. 18, 1776. in the Southern Historical Collection of the Manuscripts Dept., University of North Carolina, Chapel Hill, SHC 2188; Draper Mss. 1U47–8.

meantime Andrew Williamson and seven hundred cavalrymen invaded Cherokee country. The Cherokees promptly dispatched two chiefs "to treat for peace and save their corn." Williamson agreed to spare the corn only if the Cherokees handed over Cameron; the Cherokees refused, and Williamson burned their houses and cut down their corn. The Cherokees were reduced to "living upon nuts and whatever they can get besides."[92] Corn concerned all the combatants in this war: Shelby's expedition against the Chickamauga towns and crops was timed so that the militia could get home to their own crops for the summer harvest.[93]

In December 1780, Arthur Campbell burned "upwards of one thousand Houses, and not less than fifty thousand Bushels of Corn" among the Overhill Cherokees. John Sevier burned fifteen Middle Cherokee towns in 1781, and the following summer and fall destroyed new Lower Cherokee towns on the Coosa River. Sevier's son, who accompanied him, recalled in his old age the rampage through the towns on the Hiawasse River and Chickamauga Creek in fall 1782: "We destroyed their towns, stock, corn, & everything they had to support on." American armies marching through Cherokee country in pursuit of Chickamauga raiders did not always distinguish between Cherokee friends and Cherokee foes, thereby swelling Dragging Canoe's ranks with new recruits. British reports claimed Cherokee women and children were butchered in cold blood and burned alive.[94] Changing land-use practices and an altered landscape increased Cherokee vulnerability as villages no longer enjoyed forest cover, and as open fields provided easy avenues for cavalry attacks. Andrew Pickens's South Carolina militia, riding down on such a village in 1781 and wielding specially smithed short swords, hacked to death the defenseless occupants as they fled on foot across the open spaces that now fringed their town.[95] A Cherokee headman summed up the cost to his people of supporting the British against "the madmen of Virginia": "I . . . have lost in different engagements six hundred warriors, my towns have been thrice destroyed and my corn fields laid waste by the enemy."[96]

Some Iroquois towns in the Mohawk and Susquehanna valleys fell victim to

---

[92] *North Carolina State Records*, vol. 14: 243–8; *PCC*, reel 85, item 71, vol. 1: 242; Samuel Cole Williams, *Tennessee During the Revolutionary War* (Nashville, 1944; reprinted Knoxville: University of Tennessee Press, 1974), 91–9; John P. Brown, *Old Frontiers: The Story of the Cherokee Indians from the Earliest Times to the Date of Their Removal to the West, 1838* (Kingsport, Tenn.: Southern Publishers 1938), 175; *DAR*, vol. 17: 232–3.

[93] *North Carolina State Records*, vol. 14: 245.

[94] Major James Sevier to L. C. Draper, Aug. 19, 1839, Tennessee State Library and Archives, John Sevier Papers, box 1, folder 1; and Tennessee Historical Society, misc. files, reel 7, box 14, S-39; *PCC*, roll 85, item 71, vol. 1: 45, 241–2; *DAR*, vol. 17: 269; vol. 21: 122; C.O. 5/82: 287–8, 343; Draper Mss. 9DD24; 30S14–80; *Virginia State Papers*, vol. 1: 434–7; vol. 2: 24; Brown, *Old Frontiers*, 195–6.

[95] M. Thomas Hatley, "The Three Lives of Keowee: Loss and Recovery in Eighteenth-Century Cherokee Villages," in Peter H. Wood, Gregory A. Waselkov, and M. Thomas Hatley, eds., *Powhatan's Mantle: Indians in the Colonial Southeast* (Lincoln: University of Nebraska Press, 1989), 241.

[96] Carleton Papers, PRO 30/55/60, No. 6742: 4–6; C.O. 5/82: 349–50.

American attack or Iroquois vengeance in the early years of the war. Unable to mount effective defenses against Iroquois raids on the frontier, George Washington in 1779 determined "to carry the war into the Heart of the Country of the six nations; to cut off their settlements, destroy their next Year's crops, and do them every other mischief of which time and circumstances will permit." "It will be essential," said Washington, "to ruin their crops now in the ground and prevent them planting more."[97] While British General Frederick Haldimand assured Onondaga and Cayuga delegates to Quebec that they need have no fear of a rebel invasion, the Americans were poised to carry fire and sword to Iroquois longhouses.[98]

That spring, Colonel Goose Van Schaick marched against the Onondaga settlements, laying waste their towns and crops, slaughtering their cattle and horses, and carrying off thirty-three prisoners. In the fall, General John Sullivan led his famous expedition into Iroquois country on a campaign of destruction that burned forty towns, an estimated 160,000 bushels of corn, and "a vast quantity of vegetables of every kind." Meanwhile, Daniel Brodhead and six hundred men battered at the western door of Iroquoia, burning and plundering their way through Seneca and Munsee towns on the Allegheny. As Iroquois resistance melted before them, American soldiers and officers marveled at the well-built towns, extensive crops of corn, beans, and squash, and beautiful orchards of apple and peach trees. Mary Jemison said the Senecas had a good corn crop that year and had set some by for the winter. The Americans found some of the houses filled with corn hanging up to dry. "The Quantity of Corn in the towns is far beyond what any body has imagined," noted one of the army's physicians. Several officers acknowledged that without the food found in the Iroquois towns the campaign would have had to be abandoned. At town after town soldiers spent whole days destroying cornfields and cutting down fruit trees. At the Seneca capital at Genesee the troops burned 128 large houses and systematically burned crops, orchards, and food supplies. Returning to their villages, the Senecas found "there was not a mouthful of any kind of sustenance left, not even enough to keep a child one day from perishing with hunger." Some soldiers plundered graves for burial items; others skinned bodies "from the hips down for bootlegs."[99] By the end of the year, the Mohawk,

[97] *Writings of Washington*, vol. 14: 199; vol. 15: 189–93.
[98] *NYCD*, vol. 8: 777; NAC, C-1223, vol. 12: 14.
[99] Almon *Remembrancer* 1779, pt. 2: 273–4; 1780, pt. 1: 152–8; Haldimand Papers, 21774: 50; Frederick Cook, ed., *Journals of the Military Expedition of Major General John Sullivan against the Six Nations* (Auburn, N.Y.: Knapp, Peck, Thomson, 1887), 6, 8–9, 47, 58–61, 73–7, 91, 96, 99, 106, 112–13, 142–3, 151, 155–60, 187, 189, 206, 218, 229, 236, 272, 281, 299–303; *Writings of Washington*, vol. 16: 348, 478, 480, 492–3; Draper Mss., 1AA39; *Frontier Retreat*, 56–66; *Penn Archives*, 1st series, vol. 7: 709, 721–4; vol. 12: 155–8; Craig, ed., *Olden Time*, vol. 2: 308–17; Namias, ed., *Narrative of the Life of Mary Jemison*, 104–5. See also Arthur C. Parker, "The Indian Interpretation of the Sullivan–Clinton Campaign," *Rochester Historical Society Publication Fund Series* 8 (1929), 45–59.

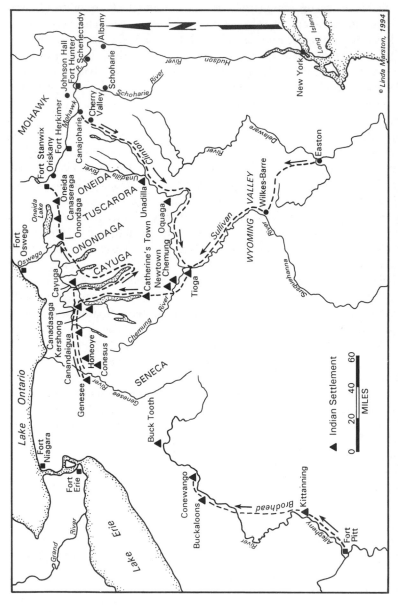

Map 3. The Sullivan–Clinton–Brodhead invasions of Iroquoia, 1779. Adapted from Barbara Graymont, *The Iroquois in the American Revolution* (Syracuse, N.Y.: Syracuse University Press, 1972), p. 195, and Carl Waldman, *Atlas of the North American Indian* (New York: Facts on File, 1985), p. 112.

Onondaga, and Cayuga towns had been destroyed or abandoned; Iroquois towns on the upper Susquehanna lay in ruins, and all but two of the larger Seneca towns had been destroyed.[100] The Iroquois pulled back and sustained minimal casualties, but an Onondaga chief later claimed that when the Americans attacked his town, "they put to death all the Women and Children, excepting some of the Young Women, whom they carried away for the use of their Soldiers & were afterwards put to death in a more shameful manner."[101] Members of the Clinton – Sullivan expeditions also looted and destroyed Iroquois false-face masks.[102]

Deprived of food and shelter, Iroquois women and children faced starvation as one of the coldest winters on record gripped North America. Refugees fled to British posts for support, and thousands of Indian men, women, and children huddled in miserable shelters around Fort Niagara.[103] Fleeing retaliation from Iroquois relatives and British enemies who burned their villages in 1780, many Oneidas abandoned their villages and sought protection near Schenectady, where, living in wretched refugee camps, they endured the prejudice of the American garrison.[104]

Meanwhile, Shawnee Indian villages suffered similar assaults as American commanders and Kentucky militia endeavored to carry out governor of Virginia Thomas Jefferson's wishes that they be driven from their lands or exterminated.[105] In May and June 1779, with the Shawnees badly weakened by recent out-migrations, John Bowman led an inglorious campaign from Kentucky against the principal town of Chillicothe. A handful of warriors repelled and harassed the attackers, but chief Black Fish suffered a mortal wound. A severe winter followed, and Shawnee emissaries urged the British to provide the support they had promised.[106]

When George Rogers Clark invaded their country in the summer of 1780, the Shawnees burned Chillicothe themselves rather than let it fall to the enemy. Luring the Americans onto ground of their own choosing, they fought a full-

---

[100] Wallace, *Death and Rebirth of the Seneca*, 144.
[101] Haldimand Papers, 21762: 238
[102] William N. Fenton, *The False Faces of the Iroquois* (Norman: University of Oklahoma Press, 1987), 81.
[103] *Frontier Retreat*, 137–8, 141–2, 159; Haldimand Papers, 21760: 220, 244; 21765: 140–1; 21770: 242–6; *MPHC*, vol. 19 (1891), 461.
[104] Graymont, *The Iroquois in the American Revolution*, 242–4; Walter Pilkington, ed., *The Journals of Samuel Kirkland* (Clinton, N.Y.: Hamilton College, 1980), 121; Francois Jean de Chastellux, *Travels in North-America; in the Years 1780, 1781 and 1782*, 2 vols. (London: G. G. J. and J. Robinson, 1787), vol. 1: 401–3; Draper Mss. 16S24–5; 11U124, 136; Penrose, comp., *Indian Affairs Papers: American Revolution*, 124, 265–6, 269–70. For assaults on Oneida villages, see Haldimand Papers, 21764: 232–3; 21767: 104, 125, 129.
[105] Calloway, "'We Have Always Been the Frontier,'" 43–4.
[106] Draper Mss. 5D1–20, 27, 49J90; Haldimand Papers, 21757: 304–5; 21760: 147; 21782: 301–3; "Bowman's Expedition against Chillicothe, May-June 1779," *Ohio Archaeological and Historical Publications* 19 (1910), 446–59; "Bowman's Campaign of 1779," ibid. 22 (1913), 502–19.

scale battle at Piqua on the Mad River until Clark turned his artillery on the village council house, where many Shawnees had taken refuge. Clark described the town as "composed of well built cabins located along the river, each surrounded by a strip of corn." His men spent two days burning cornfields, and plundered Shawnee graves for burial goods and scalps. The inhabitants of Piqua withdrew and rebuilt their town on the Great Miami River. Shawnee losses were slight, but the destruction of their corn hit them hard, "on account of our Women and Children who are left now destitute of Shelter in the Woods or Food to subsist upon." Captive Mary Erskine said the Shawnees lived the whole winter on meat. Refugees filtered into Detroit in search of food and shelter from the British, just as Iroquois refugees fled to Niagara after Sullivan's expedition the year before.[107] The British, stretched to the limit, discouraged Indians from congregating at Detroit and sent out war parties as a means of relieving the pressure on the king's stores.[108]

Two years later, Clark was back in Shawnee country, seeking revenge for the disaster at Blue Licks, where the Indians ambushed and defeated the Kentucky militia. According to Daniel Boone, who accompanied the expedition, Clark burned five villages, "entirely destroyed their corn and other fruits, and spread desolation through their country." Most of the warriors were absent when Clark attacked, and old men and women marched out to meet the invaders, together with "every man . . . who was able to crawl." Reports of atrocities by "the white Savages Virginians" flew through Indian country, alarming the tribes at a time when they were being restrained from going to war by British allies in anticipation of a final peace settlement. The "perfidious Cruel Rebels," said Tioguando of the Onondagas, no doubt recalling his own people's experiences in 1779, "have come like Thieves in the Night, when the Shawanese Warriors were out at their hunting Grounds, surrounded one of their Towns and murdered all the Women and Children." In fact, the Shawnees refused to be drawn into open battle and suffered minimal losses.[109] That winter, the Shawnees congregated on the headwaters of the Great Miami and Mad rivers

---

[107] James, ed. *George Rogers Clark Papers, 1771–1781*, cxxxix–cxli, 451–3, 476–84; Boyd, *Papers of Thomas Jefferson*, vol. 3: 560–1, 670; William A. Galloway, *Old Chillicothe* (Xenia, Ohio: Buckeye 1934), 67–8; Draper Mss. 8J136–40, 21–12, 265; 11J24; 26D101; 26J3–5; Haldimand Papers, 21781: 75–7; 21782: 383; *MPHC*, vol. 10 (1886), 418–23; John H. Moore, "A Captive of the Shawnees, 1779–1784," *West Virginia History* 23 (1962), 291. The main reports of the expedition are compiled in J. Martin West, ed., *Clark's Shawnee Campaign of 1780: Contemporary Accounts* (Springfield, Ohio: Clark County Historical Society, 1975).

[108] Haldimand Papers, 21765: 34–5; 21774: 7; Claus Papers, NAC, MG 19 Fl 3: 45–7; *MPHC*, vol. 10 (1886), 423, 343; vol. 19 (1891), 461.

[109] Draper Mss. 8J320–2, 11J24, 11S160–2, 1AA275–7; Claus Papers, vol. 3: 189–90; C.O. 5/109: 49; C.O. 42/15: 381; Haldimand Papers, 21717: 158; 21775: 49; 21756: 88, 91, 93–5, 125–8, 132, 135; 21762: 238; 21763: 1; 21775: 49; 21779: 109–10; 21781: 88; "Journal of Daniel Boone," *Ohio Archaeological and Historical Publications* 13 (1904), 276; *Virginia State Papers* 3 (1883), 381–2.

around Maquachake, Girty's Town, Blue Jacket's Town, and Wapatomica, the only towns Clark had not attacked. There were eight invasions of Shawnee settlements between 1774 and 1794. Chillicothe was attacked four times between 1779 and 1790, though the Shawnees kept rebuilding it with the same name in different locations.[110]

American soldiers were impressed by the cornucopia they destroyed in Indian fields and villages; by eighteenth-century frontier standards, Indian communities were rich in agricultural foodstuffs when not disrupted by the ravages of war. Moreover, as postwar Oneida claims for compensation demonstrate, many Indian towns offered material comforts that were the envy of frontier whites.[111] American frontiersmen were often eager to join campaigns into Indian country, and anxious to seize fertile Indian lands once the war was over. William Moore's contingent of ninety-seven men netted £1,100 from the sale of plunder and slaves taken in their expedition against the Cherokees in 1776, and were eager to go again.[112]

In the East, the character and social meaning of the Revolutionary War often were transformed from a voluntary struggle to one in which, as men deserted or failed to reenlist, American conscripts, substitutes, and the permanent poor battled British troops and Hessian mercenaries in a conflict between armies composed of "society's losers." Some New Englanders even tried to hire Indians to take their places in the patriot army.[113] In Indian country the war of the Revolution remained a communitywide effort producing common suffering. In some societies it was not unusual for Indian women to accompany their men on expeditions, but in this war whole communities turned out on occasion to resist American assaults on their villages.[114] Indian leaders died and suffered along with their people. Pluggy was killed in an attack on McClelland's fort in 1776; White Eyes and Cornstalk fell to American treachery; Emistisiguo of the Creeks died fighting at the siege of Savannah in 1782, and the Wyandot Half King lost

---

[110] Galloway, *Old Chillicothe*, 43; "General Harmar's Daily Log," *Ohio Archaeological and Historical Quarterly*, vol. 20: 94. For the location of these Shawnee towns see Helen H. Tanner, *Atlas of Great Lakes Indian History* (Norman: University of Oklahoma Press, 1987), 80, map 16.

[111] Massachusetts Historical Society, Boston, Timothy Pickering Papers, reel 62: 157–74.

[112] *PCC*, reel 85, item 71, vol. 1: 242; William Moore to Brig. Gen. Rutherford, Nov. 18, 1776, Rutherford Papers, in the Southern Historical Collection of the Manuscripts Dept., University of North Carolina, Chapel Hill, SHC 2188.

[113] Robert Gross, *The Minutemen and Their World* (New York: Hill Wang 1976), 147–53; John S. Pancake, *This Destructive War: The British Campaign in the Carolinas 1780–1782* (University: University of Alabama Press, 1985), 45–6, 50, 55; Blodgett, *Samson Occom*, 167. Though the British employed the press system twice during the Revolution, in 1778 and 1779, the majority of British soldiers were victims not of press gangs "but of incipient industrialization," forced into the ranks by new technology and demographic changes. Sylvia R. Frey, *The British Soldier in America: A Social History of Military Life in the Revolutionary Period* (Austin: University of Texas Press, 1981), ch. 1, esp. 4–7.

[114] Draper Mss. 1AA 276–7.

two sons in the war.[115] At the war's end, in council with the British at Detroit in May 1782, the Delaware chief Silver Heels voiced what must have been a sentiment widely held in Indian country: "We Indians are the only Sufferers this War, as we day by day loose our people while you are quietly in your Fort."[116]

## The war on the Indians' home front

Even when the war was not fought on the Indians' home ground, it produced reverberations in Indian communities. News of battles lost and won spread far and wide through Indian villages, often faster than British and American agents could convey or contain it. Rebels and redcoats regularly attributed news adverse to their cause as the false singing of "bad birds."[117] News of Henry Hamilton's capture by George Rogers Clark in 1779 reached Wabasha and the Sioux as they were on route to fight for the British, and stopped them short at Prairie du Chien.[118] Likewise, news of Clark's attack on the Shawnee villages in 1782 reached the Indians at Detroit and Niagara before the British had it.[119] British attempts to suppress news of Burgoyne's defeat and the Peace of Paris had no chance of success.

Whether warriors fought on their own ground or in some distant campaign, communities suffered from their absence. Men who fell in battle were not only warriors; they were "part-time soldiers" who were also husbands, fathers, sons, and providers. Warriors who were off fighting could not hunt or clear fields; women who were forced to flee when invasion threatened could not plant and harvest. Indians still tried to wage war with the seasons: warriors preferred to wait until their corn was ripe before they took up the hatchet, and according to one observer "quit going to war" when hunting season came.[120] But war now dominated the activities of the community and placed tremendous demands on the people's energy at the expense of normal economic and social practices. Even before Sullivan's campaign, there were food shortages in Iroquois longhouses. British Indian agent John Butler reported in September 1778, "As the Young Men were already either out at War, or ready to go with me, they had nothing to subsist upon but the remains of last Years Corn which was near expended, their hunting being neglected." A month later the Mohawks were getting sick from eating nothing but salt meat. At a time when the need for food

[115] Draper Mss. 2D122; H.M.C., *Report on American Mss.*, vol. 3: 157; O'Donnell, *Southern Indians*, 123; White, *Middle Ground*, 436.
[116] NAC, C-1223, vol. 13: 102.
[117] Morgan Letterbook, vol. 2: 9; Henry Hamilton, "Drawings of North American Scenes and American Indians, 1769–1778," Houghton Library, Harvard, pf. MS Eng. 509.2.
[118] Haldimand Papers, 21756: 22; *MPHC*, vol. 9: 384; *WHC*, vol. 11: 132, 134.
[119] Haldimand Papers, 21756: 88, 94, 132; C.O. 42/15: 381.
[120] White, *Middle Ground*, 378; Draper Mss. 2AA70; *Revolution on the Upper Ohio*, 190.

increased greatly, Indians could not cultivate the usual quantities of corn and vegetables, and what they did grow was often destroyed before it could be harvested.[121]

Crops also suffered from natural causes in time of war. The late 1770s *crops suffered* marked the beginning of a period of "sporadically poor crops" among southeastern tribes. Partial failure of the Creek corn crop in 1776 produced near famine at a time when the influx of Cherokee refugees placed additional demands on food supplies , and there was "an absolute Famine" in the Creek nation in July 1778. Choctaw crops failed in 1782, increasing the people's reliance on deer hunting.[122] A bushel of corn sold for $8 in the Wyandot towns in the winter of 1781–2, and Moravian Indians in exile around Sandusky had nothing to eat but wild potatoes and the meat of their dead cattle. As the famine deepened, many Moravian Delawares returned to their homes on the Tuscarawas in search of food, where they fell victim to American frontiersmen. Famine returned to the Ohio Valley in 1784.[123] Hunting became vital to group survival but fewer hunters were available, fighting scared away game, and hunting territories could be perilous places in time of war. There was never enough game to support the unusually large concentrations of Indians at refugee centers like Niagara, Sandusky, and Detroit.

The war severed trade routes and cut off Indian peoples from goods on *cut off trade* which they had become dependent. Indians as far from the conflict as the southern plains felt its repercussions in the disrupted flow of trade goods into the area.[124] With normal subsistence and commercial activities thrown out of *reliance on Euro allies* joint, Indian communities became increasingly dependent on British, American, or Spanish allies to provide them with food, clothing, and trade. Meslamonehonqua, a Miami, voiced the views of Indian women on the situation in conference with Major De Peyster at Detroit in September 1781:

> Father!
> I am Deputized by the Women of our Villages, to pray you to send them Ammunition for to Support their families, as they had consented with a good heart that their sons enter into your cause against the Virginians, they therefore expect you will take care of them and [their] Children.[125]

---

[121] Haldimand Papers, 21765: 34–5, 21774: 7, 115–16, and Peter C. Mancall, "The Revolutionary War and the Indians of the Upper Susquehanna Valley," *American Indian Culture and Research Journal* 12, no. 1 (1988), 39–57. NAC, Claus Papers, vol. 25: 40.

[122] *DAR*, vol. 15: 96, 184; vol. 17: 233; Martha Condray Searcy, *The Georgia–Florida Contest in the American Revolution, 1776–1778* (University: University of Alabama Press, 1985), 110; C.O. 5/558: 270, 276; White, *Roots of Dependency*, 28–9, 98.

[123] Draper Mss. 5D121; White, *Middle Ground*, 487, n. 27; Schweintz, *Life of David Zeisberger*, 533.

[124] Elizabeth A. H. John, *Storms Brewed in Other Men's Worlds: The Confrontation of Indians, Spanish, and French in the Southwest, 1540–1795* (Lincoln: University of Nebraska Press, 1981), 590–1.

[125] NAC, C-1223, vol. 13: 63.

Rival powers waged economic warfare to compel Indian allegiance, and harsh economic realities increasingly curtailed the tribes' freedom of action and governed their decisions.[126]

Tribes that supported the Americans or remained neutral suffered as much as those that fought on the side of the British. Two years into the war, Tuscaroras who had remained in their North Carolina homelands after the rest of their people had migrated north to Iroquoia were in such dire straits they petitioned the colonial assembly for relief.[127] In the spring of 1782, Cherokees who remained friendly to the Americans were "in a deplorable situation, being naked & defenceless for want of goods and ammunition," besides being caught between Tories and Americans who assumed they were hostile.[128] In December a group of Cherokees en route to Richmond elicited the sympathy of William Christian, one of the generals who had carried devastation to their towns in the summer of 1776:

> The miseries of those people from what I see and hear seem to exceed description; here are men, women & children almost naked; I see very little to cover either sex but some old bear skins, and we are told that the bulk of the nation are in the same naked situation. But this is not the greatest of their evils; their crops this year have been worse than ever was known, so that their corn & potatoes, it is supposed will be all done before April; and many are already out, particularly widows and fatherless children, who have no men nearly connected with them.[129]

The next month the Cherokee chief Oconostota begged Colonel Joseph Martin to take care of the Cherokees and provide them with trade at low prices.[130]

Disease took an additional toll, sometimes carrying off key leaders at critical times. An epidemic swept away many Schoharie Mohawks in 1775; another appears to have been present in Shawnee villages in 1776. Smallpox raged at Onondaga in the winter of 1776–7, struck Indians wintering near Michilimackinac in 1777, was killing Creeks and Cherokees in the fall of 1779 and the spring of 1780, and struck the Cherokees again in 1783. It visited the Oneida refugees at Schenectady in December 1780 and hit the Genesee Senecas the following winter. Smallpox reduced the Wyandots to a hundred warriors by 1781. Cold and disease killed three hundred Indians in the refugee camps at Niagara in the winter of 1779–80.[131] While redcoats and rebels killed each other by the hundreds

*disease*

---

[126] *DAR*, vol. 15: 67.
[127] Richard Caswell to North Carolina General Assembly, Dec. 13, 1777, Richard Caswell Papers, 1777–1790, Duke University, Perkins Library.
[128] Draper Mss. 11S77–83.
[129] Draper Mss. 11S10.
[130] Draper Mss. 12S10.
[131] Stone, *Life of Joseph Brant*, vol. 1: 104 (Schoharie Mohawks); Ernest H. Howerton, "Logan, the Shawnee Indian Capital of West Virginia, 1760–1780," *West Virginia History* 16 (July 1955), 325

on the eastern seaboard, a huge smallpox pandemic slaughtered Indian people by the thousands in western America. Between 1779 and 1782 the contagion, which also ravaged central Mexico and the Guatemalan highlands, traveled north across the Rockies and the plains, then spread into the forests of eastern Canada. Hudson's Bay Company employees gathered beaver robes from the corpses of their customers around the bay.[132] The uncertainties and disruptions of war produced plummeting birth rates in some white communities, and it would be unusual if falling birth rates did not also contribute to overall decline in Indian population in these years.[133]

The revolutionary era intensified political changes in Indian communities. As in colonial society, voices of moderation were often drowned out by the clamor of the militants. Endemic warfare and outside influences continued the elevation of war chiefs, who traditionally exercised only temporary authority, over the village chiefs who looked after the concerns of the community in normal circumstances. The abnormal was now normal, and war captains like Pipe and White Eyes of the Delawares, Mohawk Joseph Brant, and Dragging Canoe among the Cherokees spoke with an increasingly loud voice in their nation's councils. Tenhoghskweaghta, an Onondaga chief, explained: "Times are altered with us Indians. Formerly the Warriors were governed by the wisdom of their uncles the Sachems but now they take their own way & dispose of themselves without consulting their uncles the Sachems – while we wish for peace and they for war." Oneida chiefs lamented, "We Sachems have nothing to say to the Warriors. We have given them up for the field. They must act as they think wise."[134] War and disease aggravated the situation. Cha-ha, a Wea war chief, told Henry Hamilton in a council at Detroit in 1778, "I am a War Chief, but speak on Wampum that came from our Village Chiefs or those remaining of

(Shawnee); *PCC*, reel 73, item 153, vol. 3: 59–60; reel 173: 551–4; Wallace, *Death and Rebirth of the Seneca*, 195 (Onondaga, Genesee, and Niagara); *DAR*, vol. 17: 233; and Brown, *Old Frontiers*, 182n (Cherokees); Russell Thornton, *The Cherokees: A Population History* (Lincoln: University of Nebraska Press, 1990), 33; Wood, "The Changing Population of the Colonial South," 65 (Cherokees in 1783); HMC, *Report on American Mss.*, vol. 2: 96, 104 (Georgia); *Frontier Retreat*, 189 (Conewago and Niagara); Armour and Widder, *At The Crossroads*, 62 (Michilimackinac); White, *Middle Ground*, 436 (Wyandots).

[132] E. E. Rich, ed., *Cumberland and Hudson House Journals, 1775–82: Second Series, 1779–82* (London: Hudson's Bay Record Society, 1954), 224; Richard Glover, ed., *David Thompson's Narrative, 1784–1812* (Toronto: Champlain Society, 1962), 234–8, 245–6; Arthur J. Ray, *Indians in the Fur Trade: Their Role as Hunters, Trappers and Middlemen in the Lands Southeast of Hudson Bay, 1660–1870* (University of Toronto Press, 1974), 105–8; W. George Lovell, *Conquest and Survival: A Historical Geography of the Cuchumatan Highlands, 1500–1821* (Montreal: McGill-Queens University Press, 1992), 154–7.

[133] Gross, *Minutemen and Their World*, 143.

[134] Weslager, *Delawares*, 291–2; Graymont, *Iroquois in the American Revolution*, 23; Speech of Tenhoghskweaghta at the Johnstown conference, March 10, 1778, Schuyler Papers, NYPL, reel 7, box 14, reprinted in *Revolution and Confederation*, 67; Gates Papers, vol. 6: 191; *Remembrancer*, 1778: 217.

them, for you know the loss we have met with."[135] New leaders like Pluggy and Dragging Canoe attracted followings that cut across village, tribal, and kinship ties. Older chiefs complained increasingly that they could not control their young men – or as was often the case in the polyglot communities created by the Revolution, control somebody else's young men.

The interference of outsiders further complicated tribal politics and undermined traditional patterns of leadership as British, Americans, and Spaniards cultivated client chiefs. Medals, uniforms and other tangible signs of authority added to a chosen leader's prestige, and the practice of handing out commissions was so common that it became standard practice to identify Choctaw and Chickasaw leaders as "great medal," "small medal," and "gorget" chiefs. Access to guns and gifts became important criteria of leadership and a key to securing the voluntary obedience that underlay so much of Indian political relations. Daniel Brodhead complained that the Indian chiefs appointed by the British commander at Detroit were "clothed in the most elegant manner," whereas chiefs appointed by Congress went naked and were scorned by the Indians. A Seneca chief warned the British he would be unable to exert any authority over his warriors unless they provided him with goods to distribute to them.[136]

The British elevated Mohawk Joseph Brant, protégé of Sir William Johnson and friend of the Prince of Wales, to a position in which he exerted tremendous influence in Indian councils during and after the Revolution.[137] Americans and British alike tried to turn Joseph Louis Gill of the Abenakis at Odanak into a client chief.[138] The Americans interfered with traditional succession among the Delawares in favor of pro-American individuals and exerted their influence in the choice of a successor to White Eyes.[139] Among the Creeks, Alexander McGillivray, who was descended from the influential Wind Clan on his mother's side (and from the Scottish Clan Chattan – the Clan of the Cat – on his father's side) owed much of his growing power to British connections.[140] The British in Saint Augustine courted the Seminole chief Cowkeeper as the key figure in securing the allegiance of Indians in East Florida.[141]

[135] "Letters from the Canadian Archives," *Collections of the Illinois Historical Society* 1 (1903), 321.
[136] LC, C.O. 5/81: 111; *DAR*, vol. 15: 153–7; Draper Mss. 3H52; Haldimand Papers, 21783: 276–9. For information on Choctaw "medal chiefs" see White, *Roots of Dependency*, chs. 2–3; see also White, *Middle Ground*, esp. 322, 403–6.
[137] Haldimand Papers, 21717: 39–40. On Brant, see Isabel Thompson Kelsay, *Joseph Brant, 1743–1807: Man of Two Worlds* (Syracuse, N.Y.: Syracuse University Press, 1984).
[138] See ch. 2, this volume.
[139] Weslager, *Delawares*, 298, 324, n. 21; *Frontier Retreat*, 376, 419–20, n. 3; *Frontier Advance*, 194.
[140] Michael D. Green, "Alexander McGillivray," in R. David Edmunds, ed., *American Indian Leaders: Studies in Diversity* (Lincoln: University of Nebraska Press, 1980), 41–63; John Walton Caughey, *McGillivray of the Creeks* (Norman: University of Oklahoma Press, 1938); Edward J. Cashin, *Lachlan McGillivray, Indian Trader: The Shaping of the Southern Colonial Frontier* (Athens: University of Georgia Press, 1992), chs. 1 and 3.
[141] See this volume, ch. 9.

In addition, at a time when non-Indians in London and Philadelphia, Detroit and Fort Pitt, Saint Augustine and Pensacola, were making decisions that reverberated through Indian country, non-Indians who lived in Indian country played a growing role in Indian councils. Men like Simon Girty, Matthew Elliott, and Alexander McKee among the Ohio tribes, Alexander Cameron among the Cherokees, and James Colbert among the Chickasaws, lived in Indian communities but maintained important connections elsewhere. They functioned as influential intermediaries, interpreters, leaders of expeditions, and conduits of supply and support.[142] Loyalist officers and British Indian agents often accompanied and sometimes replaced Indian war chiefs on campaign. The end of the war did not end the presence or the influence of British trader agents, and in the south, British companies continued their lucrative Indian trade with the grudging blessing of the Spanish authorities.[143]

Migrations increased dramatically in the revolutionary era. Seasonal movements for social or subsistence purposes now gave way to flight from the horrors of war. Some groups migrated rather than be caught up in the fighting.[144] Communities splintered and reassembled, sometimes amalgamating with other communities beyond the reach of American armies.[145] Refugees flooded into Niagara, Schenectady, Detroit, Saint Louis, Saint Augustine, and Pensacola; Iroquois Loyalists moved to new homes on the Grand River in Ontario.[146] Hundreds of refugee Indians drifted west of the Mississippi and requested permission to settle in Spanish territory. Spanish officials at Saint Louis complained that visiting Indians ate them out of house and home and did not even allow them time to sleep.[147] Migrations produced chain reactions far across Indian country. Displaced peoples from the eastern woodlands pushed into the hunting territories of Osages and Pawnees, who then pressured the ranges of the Comanches, who in turn pushed against Apaches and the northern frontier of Spanish settlement.[148] Leaving familiar sites took an emotional as well as an economic toll.

[142] Haldimand Papers, 21767: 73 (McKee); Reginald Horsman, *Matthew Elliott, British Indian Agent* (Detroit, Mich.: Wayne State University Press, 1964); Colin G. Calloway, "Simon Girty: Interpreter and Intermediary," in James A. Clifton, ed., *Being and Becoming Indian: Biographical Studies of North American Frontiers* (Chicago: Dorsey, 1989), 38–58; C.O. 5/82: 114; *PCC*, reel 104, item 78, vol. 24: 435, 440–3.

[143] William S. Coker and Thomas D. Watson, *Indian Traders of the Southeastern Spanish Borderlands: Panton, Leslie and Company and John Forbes and Company, 1783–1847* (Pensacola: University Presses of Florida, 1986).

[144] E.g., "Diary of Mrs Elizabeth Trist, 1783–85," 19, in the Southern Historical Collections of the manuscript department, University of North Carolina, Chapel Hill.

[145] Calloway, "'We Have Always Been the Frontier,'" 44–5; Helen Hornbeck Tanner, "The Glaize in 1792: A Composite Indian Community," *Ethnohistory* 25 (1978) 15–39; *DAR*, vol. 14: 94, 115, 194.

[146] Carleton Papers, reel 17, no. 6742: 18, 23; no. 6476: 3; *DAR*, vol. 14: 35; vol. 17: 181–2; Charles M. Johnston, ed., *Valley of the Six Nations: A Collection of Documents on the Indian Lands of the Grand River* (Toronto: Champlain Society, 1964).

[147] *Spain in the Mississippi Valley*, vol. 2, pt. 1: 298; Nasatir, "Anglo-Spanish Frontier," 291–358.

[148] John, *Storms Brewed in Other Men's Worlds*, 590–1.

Nor were Indian people the only migrants in Indian country. Micmacs in Nova Scotia suffered from the inroads of Loyalist settlers fleeing the Revolution to the south; Loyalists poured into West Florida, sometimes via Upper Creek villages; English settlers from Natchez who rebelled against Spanish rule in 1781 fled reprisals and took refuge in Chickasaw country.[149]

Escalating warfare and its concomitant economic disruption reached even into ritual and ceremonial life. Eastern woodland Indians followed a social and ceremonial calendar tied to the rhythm of the seasons. Traditional warfare could be waged when the season was appropriate, and in 1778 the Creeks frustrated the British by refusing to take the warpath until after the Green Corn Ceremony.[150] But the endemic warfare of the Revolution threw many traditional religious practices and sacred observances into disarray. Not only did the ancient unity of the Iroquois League crumble, but many of the ceremonial forms that expressed that unity were transformed or lost altogether. Preparatory war rituals were neglected or imperfectly performed. The Cayuga leader Kingageghta lamented in 1789 that a "Great Part of our ancient Customs & Ceremonies have, thro' the Loss of Many of our principal men during the War, been neglected & forgotten, so that we cannot go through the whole with our ancient Propriety."[151] The traditional Cherokee year was divided into two seasons, with the winter reserved for war, and returning warriors underwent ritual purification before reentering normal village life. Now war was a year-round activity, and Chickamauga communities existed on a permanent war footing. In addition, the Cherokees' six major religious festivals of the year became telescoped into one – the Green Corn Festival. Cherokees remembered the 1780s as marking the end of the old ways.[152] The loss of sacred power threatened the Indians' struggle for independence and, according to historian Gregory Dowd, Indian resistance movements of the revolutionary and postrevolutionary era drew strength from the recognition that they "could and must take hold of their destiny by regaining sacred power." Indians in the new republic sought to recover through ritual, as well as through war and politics, some of what had been lost.[153]

New religious practices also suffered, and missionary work was disrupted. Christian Mohawks devoted less time to their observances because war occupied

---

[149] Ruth Holmes Whitehead, ed., *The Old Man Told Us: Excerpts from Micmac History, 1500–1900* (Halifax, N.S.: Nimbus, 1991), 77; Usner, *Indians, Settlers, and Slaves*, 112; *Spain in the Mississippi Valley*, vol. 3, pt. 2: xi–xii, 15, 32–33, 60.

[150] *DAR*, vol. 15: 180; C.O. 5/79: 184; 80: 23.

[151] Graymont, *Iroquois in the American Revolution*, 224; Kingageghta to Col. Johnson, 25 Jan. 1780, quoted in Jones, *License for Empire*, 131.

[152] Gearing, "Priests and Warriors," 47, 49, 74, 104; cf. Dowd, *Spirited Resistance*, 10: "The warlike state of man [was] an unnatural state that had been ritually prepared."

[153] Dowd, *Spirited Resistance*, 27. Cf. Joel W. Martin, *Sacred Revolt: The Muskogees' Struggle for a New World* (Boston: Beacon, 1991).

their attention. John Stuart, the Anglican minister at Fort Hunter, was arrested by the Americans and confined at Schenectady. Most of the Mohawks' prayer books were destroyed, and the war interrupted the translation of the gospels on which Stuart and Brant had been collaborating. Joseph Fowler, a Montauk from Long Island, found he could no longer be paid to teach Indian students reading, writing, and religion because "the unhappy War put a stop to everything of that Nature."[154] In the Muskingum Valley, nine years of missionary work and three model communities were ruined when the Moravians and their Delaware converts were forced to abandon Schönbrunn, Salem, and Gnadenhütten, and make a grueling trek north to Sandusky, which they did "as if in a dream so as to hardly know our senses."[155]

As more and more Indians joined in the British war effort, the number of warriors arrayed against the Americans became impressive, and the Indians won some notable victories. In 1780, a British–Indian expedition invaded Kentucky and returned to Detroit with a horde of captives.[156] In 1782 alone the Indians routed William Crawford's expedition against Sandusky, and the Delawares exacted grim retribution on Crawford for the slaughter of their relatives at Gnadenhütten. They also routed the Kentucky militia at Blue Licks, and Kayashuta burned Hannastown, Pennsylvania, to the ground.[157] "Indians appear to attack our frontiers in all quarters," wrote an American in Philadelphia in the summer of 1782.[158] Surveying the semicontinental scale of the anti-American alliance during the Revolution, Gregory Dowd has called it "the largest, most unified Native American effort the continent would ever see."[159] As early as February 1777, Lord George Germain wrote that "all the Indians upon the Continent are united in a solemn League to oppose any encroachments upon their hunting Grounds, and in support of His Majesty's Government."[160]

But Germain was in Whitehall, far from Indian country, where the cost of multitribal unity was often intratribal disunity. As Richard White has observed

[154] *Annual Report* of the Society for the Propagation of the Gospel (London), 1781: 41; 1782: 45; *Journals of the Proceedings of the Society for the Propagation of the Gospel* 25 (1787), 26; *The Book of Common Prayer . . . A New Edition, to which is added the Gospel According to St. Mark, Translated into the Mohawk Language, by Captn. Joseph Brant* (London, 1787), i–ii (all of the above are in the archives department of the United Society for the Propagation of the Gospel, London). PCC, reel 54, vol. 3: 137.
[155] Earl P. Olmstead, *Blackcoats Among the Delawares: David Zeisberger on the Ohio Frontier* (Kent, Ohio: Kent State University Press, 1991), ch. 2, esp. 37–9; Heckewelder, *Narrative of the Mission of the United Brethren*, 232–80.
[156] *Official Letters of the Governors of the State of Virginia* 3 (1929), 357–8.
[157] White, *Middle Ground*, 407; Haldimand Papers, 21762: 80; James B. Richardson and Kirke C. Wilson, "Hannas Town and Charles Foreman: The Historical and Archaeological Record, 1770–1806," *Western Pennsylvania Historical Magazine* 59 (1976), 164–9.
[158] Draper Mss. 2AA64.
[159] Dowd, *Spirited Resistance*, 46, 49, 59–61.
[160] Germain to Governor Peter Chester, Feb. 7, 1777, Mississippi Department of Archives and History, Jackson, RG 25, English Provincial Records, vol. 14

in reference to the Choctaws during the colonial wars earlier in the century, what outsiders perceived as factionalism could have proved an asset in frontier diplomacy, enabling different parties to cultivate relations with different powers and prevent domination by any one.[161] The Seven Nations of Canada practiced this strategy with some success in the Revolution, as did Chickasaws, Potawatomis, and others on the peripheries of the war. But it was a dangerous game, and for Indian people living in frontier war zones, divided councils all too often brought only disaster. By the end of the Revolution, Indian country was pockmarked with ruined villages from the Mohawk Valley to the Tennessee. Indian people who survived the war faced an uncertain future as they set about rebuilding war-torn lives. Many of them also had bitter scores to settle with fellow Indians as well as with white adversaries.

[161] White, *Roots of Dependency*, 64.

# 2

# *Odanak:*
# *Abenaki ambiguity in the North*

The Revolution tolerated few neutrals. In time and in general, most Indian peoples came around to siding with the British, but in individual communities the situation was always more complex. A struggle that split non-Indian communities throughout the colonies generated similar repercussions in communities in Indian country, but not necessarily for the same reasons. The Abenakis at Odanak in Quebec had ties to other Indian communities in New England and Canada, and, via the Seven Nations confederacy, to the Iroquois in New York. They also occupied a key location on the Saint Lawrence River, which placed the community in a tug-of-war between the British in Quebec and the Americans in northern New England, both of whom regarded them with suspicion. The people of Odanak lacked consensus about what course to pursue in the Revolution, and Abenakis served in small-scale operations on both sides during the war. But beneath the surface confusion and ambivalence, all Abenakis at all times shared the goal of preserving their community and keeping the war at arm's length. All they disagreed on was the means to that end. Neutrality was a perilous strategy, more likely to make the village a target than a haven when British and Americans alike adhered to the notion that if Indians were not fighting for you they would fight against you. Many Abenakis opted instead for limited and sometimes equivocal involvement in the conflict. The family-band structure of Abenaki society meant that different people could espouse different allegiances without tearing the community apart. Individual participation on both sides, though limited and part of no master strategy, also allowed flexibility as the fortunes of war shifted. The Revolution would not leave the Abenakis alone, but they could divert it into less destructive channels.

Odanak, or Saint Francis, emerged as a mission village and refugee center in Quebec during the previous century. The mission of Saint François-de-Sales on the Chaudière River was established in 1683. In 1700 Father Jacques Bigot moved the mission to the Saint Francis River, where some Sokokis and other Abenakis had already settled. During the French and Indian wars, Sokokis, Cowasucks, Pennacooks, and other Abenaki peoples driven from Vermont, New Hampshire, and Maine migrated to the northern reaches of their homelands and took refuge in the mission village. Odanak became a center of Abenaki resistance to English expansion in the eighteenth century and earned the enduring enmity of New England settlers. In 1759, Robert Rogers's New Hampshire rangers burned the village and claimed to have destroyed it, but the community survived, revived, and adjusted to the new military and political dominance of the British.[1]

After the conquest of New France, a contingent of British troops occupied Odanak, watching over the Abenakis in a tense period of readjustment. The Abenakis and other nations on the Saint Lawrence sent wampum belts to the western tribes urging them to desist from rash actions and to hold fast the chain of friendship with their new king. Abenaki chief Joseph Louis Gill assured General Frederick Haldimand that the Abenakis at Odanak had nothing but peaceful intentions.[2]

The British Indian Department endeavored to centralize relations at Odanak in an effort to keep tabs on the Abenakis. The British regularly referred to all western Abenakis as "Saint Francis Indians," a practice both they and the Americans continued through the Revolution. Sir William Johnson urged the Abenakis "to collect your people together on one Village, apply yourselves to your hunting, planting and Trade, and leave off Rambling about through the Country." Many Abenakis reassembled at Odanak, built a new church to replace the one burned by Rogers, and requested help in supporting their priest.[3]

However, cut off from customary French gifts, and with the fur trade in the Saint Lawrence Valley in serious decline, Abenakis at Odanak found they had to hunt far and wide in search of sustenance. Meanwhile, settlers who flooded north into Abenaki country after the Seven Years' War presented Abenaki people with new neighbors and new ecological challenges. Clashes with English settlers and hunters escalated. The Abenaki way of life that involved family bands dispersing over wide areas had worked well as a subsistence pattern for countless generations, and had served as a strategy for keeping casualties low during the colonial wars with the English. Abenakis responded to the new situation in the old way. Many families appear to have pulled back farther into their territory, and most seem to have preferred to continue avoiding direct involvement with the British.[4]

[1] Gordon Day, *The Identity of the St. Francis Indians* (Ottawa: National Museums of Canada, 1981); Colin G. Calloway, *The Western Abenakis of Vermont, 1600–1800: War, Migration, and the Survival of an Indian People* (Norman: University of Oklahoma Press, 1990), 87–8, 175–9, 189–92, 197–203.

[2] Calloway, *Western Abenakis of Vermont*, 191–2; Thomas M. Charland, Les *Abénakis d'Odanak: Histoire des Abénakis d'Odanak, 1675–1937* (Montreal: Editions du Levrier, 1964), 132, 134; *NYCD*, vol. 7: 544–5.

[3] Calloway, *Western Abenakis of Vermont*, 197; *Johnson Papers*, vol. 10: 412–14; vol. 12: 569–71.

[4] Calloway, *Western Abenakis of Vermont*, 183–9, 192–7; Mass. Archives, vol. 27: 338; vol. 33: 427–8, 575–8.

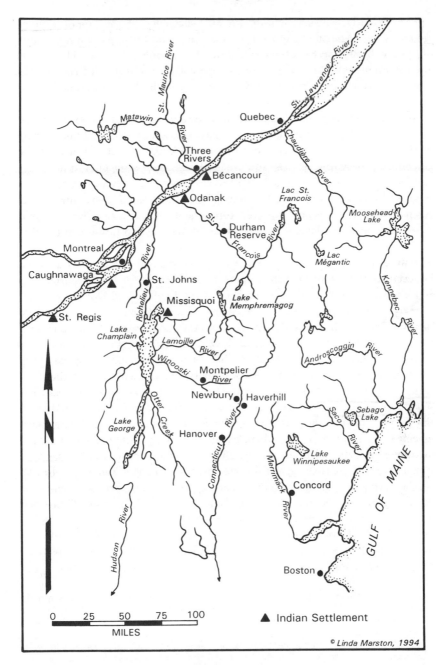

Map 4. Odanak and Abenaki country during the Revolution.

Consequently, the competition for the allegiance of the "Saint Francis Abenakis" at the beginning of the Revolution embraced not only the inhabitants of Odanak itself – perhaps four or five hundred people – but also other bands and communities that had ties to the mission village. For historians delving into Abenaki experiences during the revolutionary era, the light is best at Odanak because the British focused their attention on that community and kept records. Nevertheless, the light at Odanak can blind us to what was happening elsewhere in Abenaki country. The British tried to make Odanak the center of the Abenaki world, but in reality they were operating on the edges of that world. On Lake Champlain, the village at Missisquoi had served as a center of Abenaki independence throughout the French and Indian wars and continued to function as the core community for Abenaki bands in the Champlain Valley. Many other Abenaki families remained scattered throughout northern New England and southern Quebec. Colonel Timothy Bedel of New Hampshire estimated that the Saint Francis Abenakis could muster two hundred warriors; Henry Tufts, who lived with the Indians in the early 1770s, estimated that as many as seven hundred Abenakis inhabited the remote region between lakes Memphremagog and Umbagog on the borders of northern New England and Quebec.[5]

Like many Indian peoples, most Abenakis desired neutrality in a struggle that was not of their making and not in their interests. Like neighboring Canadian *habitants*, they had no great love for Britons or "Bostonians."[6] Early reports from Canada indicated that the Saint Francis Abenakis, Caughnawagas, and other tribes of the Seven Nations of Canada, who could muster two thousand men, were determined to remain neutral and "refuse to take up arms on either side." Lewis, a Caughnawaga chief who scouted for the American general Jacob Bayley, reported that the governor of Canada had sent French-speaking officers to enlist the support of the Abenakis at Odanak and their neighbors by a mixture of threats and inducements. But the Indians made it clear that they would take the offensive against no one and resist anyone, Yankees or British regulars, who came to attack them. According to Lewis, the officers tried to get the young men to take up arms by pressing coins into their hands, "but when the Chiefs knew it, they took the money from them & returned it to the Officers, and told the young men if they offered to engage, they would put them to death."[7] Such an extreme assertion of authority seems unlikely in Abenaki society, and Lewis clearly was speaking for an American audience, but

[5] Day, *Identity of the St. Francis Indians*, 54; Edmund Pearson, ed., *Henry Tufts: The Autobiography of a Criminal* (New York: Duffield, 1930); Gordon Day, "Henry Tufts as a Source on the Eighteenth Century Abenakis," *Ethnohistory* 21 (1974), 189–97; "Report of Col. Bedel," Vermont State Archives, Stevens Papers, vol. 3: 81–2.

[6] S. F. Wise, "The American Revolution and Indian History," in John S. Moir, ed., *Character and Circumstance: Essays in Honor of Donald Grant Creighton* (Toronto: Macmillan, 1970), 195.

[7] *American Archives*, 4th series, vol. 2: 1734–5, vol. 3: 339–400; *PCC*, reel 172, item 153, vol. 1: 75; *New Hampshire State Papers* [hereafter *NHSP*], vol. 8 (1874), 311; Mass. Archives, vol. 144: 323.

the desire of the Indians on the Saint Lawrence for neutrality was evident. The presence of some Abenakis from Odanak at Dartmouth College in New Hampshire when the war broke out added to the Indians' reluctance to go to war.[8]

Unfortunately, neutrality was not an option. The American invasion of Canada placed Odanak in the direct line of fire and demanded some early decisions. Abenaki decisions were as often as not pro-American. According to an Abenaki woman on the Androscoggin River, the competition of agents and messages was so intense that the men in her band could not hunt, eat, or sleep. Though ignorant of the issues of the conflict – "O, strange *Englishmen* kill one another. I think the world is coming to an end" – she knew where her allegiance lay. "Why should we fight for t'other country, for we never see t'other country; our hunting is in this country." Some of the settlers were alarmed to see the Indians wearing paint for the first time.[9]

Some Abenakis took the crown's part in the early fighting: Governor Guy Carleton sent a contingent of warriors to the unsuccessful defense of Saint Johns in 1775, and Abenakis may have helped defend Quebec the same year.[10] But the British mainly employed Abenakis on scouting duties, and even then suspected them of carrying news to the rebels. They had reason to be suspicious; the Americans were quick to tap Abenaki ambivalence toward the British.

In August 1775 a chief named Swashan and "four other Indians of the Saint Francois tribe," arrived at George Washington's camp in Cambridge, offered "their service in the cause of American liberty," and remained throughout the siege of Boston. Swashan said he would bring half his tribe if they were wanted. The Massachusetts House of Representatives appointed a committee to confer with the chief, "who appears as an Ambassador from that Tribe." Swashan portrayed the Abenakis as making their own decisions, unintimidated by British threats. New Englanders, for whom the colonial wars and the propaganda they generated were not-too-distant memories, retained lingering images of black-robed priests inciting Abenaki warriors to war. But if Jesuit influence was ever significant in Abenaki villages in previous conflicts, it was evidently lacking in this one, as revealed by the committee's interrogation:

---

[8] *American Archives*, 4th series, vol. 2: 1595; Otis G. Hammond, ed., *Letters and Papers of Major-General John Sullivan*, 3 vols. (Concord: New Hampshire Historical Society, 1930–9), vol. 1: 287.

[9] *American Archives*, 4th series, vol. 2: 621.

[10] Day, *Identity of the St. Francis Indians*, 53; Charland, *Histoire des Abénakis d'Odanak*, 10; Leonard A. Auger, "St. Francis Through the Years," *Vermont History* 27 (1959), 292–5. Joseph P. A. Maurault, *Histoire des Abénakis depuis 1605 jusqu'à nos jours* (Sorel, Quebec: L'atelier typographique de la Gazette de Sorel 1866), 586–8, recounted a mid-nineteenth-century story that Abenakis assisted Carleton in defending Quebec, but Paul Lawrence Stevens finds no corroborating evidence and concludes that the story was a self-serving fiction, created later to make life easier for Abenakis living in British Canada. Stevens, "His Majesty's 'Savage' Allies: British Policy and the Northern Indians during the Revolutionary War. The Carleton Years, 1774–1778," Ph.d. diss., SUNY Buffalo, 1984, 511, 2036, n. 20.

*Q:* Have you a *French* Priest in your Tribe?
*A:* Yes.
*Q:* Has he given you any Advice with Regard to this Dispute?
*A:* Our Priest is no Warriour, and does not concern himself about it.[11]

Abenakis from Odanak as well as from Penobscot also guided Benedict Arnold's army up the Kennebec River through the Maine Wilderness in the fall of 1775 and served in the American campaign against Quebec.[12] In council with Arnold in June 1776, delegates from Odanak, Caughnawaga (Kahnawake), and Lake of Two Mountains rejected the hatchet they had received from Governor Carleton the year before and resolved to remain neutral. The next month Odanak spokesmen declared they were ready to assist the Americans, and in August the Continental Congress employed "One Mr. Gilman . . . to go to the *Saint Francois Indians* and engage as many of them as he can."[13]

In September, General Philip Schuyler ordered Colonel Timothy Bedel to take measures to bring into the settlements on the upper Connecticut Indian families who had left Canada and were living in the woods. General Jacob Bayley sent messengers to the Indians' hunting grounds, informing them that, contrary to what the British might have told them, the Americans were willing and able to provide them with all the trade they needed at Coos on the upper Connecticut. The American plan was to attract the Abenakis as a protective buffer for, as Bedel said, "if the Indians Trade with us we need no Soldiers."[14] Abenakis who came into the American settlements requested that a blockhouse be built "on Connecticut River near the Canada Line where they would make their abode until this dispute is ended."[15] The Marquis de Lafayette supported the idea of building a fort on the upper Connecticut, but the primary defense of the northern frontier came to rest on militia and Abenakis.[16]

[11] *Writings of Washington*, vol. 3: 423–4, 437; Mass. Archives, vol. 29: 500–1; vol. 144: 326–9; J. Almon, *The Remembrancer* (London: Author, 1775–84), 1775: 251; *Journals of the House of Representatives of Massachusetts*, vol. 51, pt. 1: 35, 80–1; "The Catholic Indians and the American Revolution," *American Catholic Historical Researches*, new series, 4 (1908), 195–8.

[12] John Joseph Henry, *Account of Arnold's Campaign Against Quebec* (Albany: Munsell, 1887), 31–2, 74–5; William Allen, comp., "A Journal of the Expedition to Quebec in 1775," *Collections of the Maine Historical Society*, lst series, 1 (1831) 394, 397.

[13] *PCC*, reel 172, vol. 2: 206; *NHSP*, vol. 8: 311; *Collections of the Maine Historical Society*, 2d series, 24 (1916) 193–5; *American Archives*, 5th series, vol. 1: 837.

[14] Vermont State Archives, Montpelier, Stevens Papers, vol. 2: 395–7; *NHSP*, vol. 8: 405; Abby Hemenway, ed. *The Vermont Historical Gazeteer*, 5 vols. (Burlington: Hemenway 1868–91), vol. 2: 936.

[15] Bedel to Schuyler, Feb. 16, 1777, New Hampshire Historical Society, Bedel Papers, folder 1; *NHSP*, vol. 17: 128–30; Vermont State Archives, Stevens Papers, vol. 3: 76.

[16] Stanley J. Idzerda et. al, eds., *LaFafayette in the Age of the American Revolution: Selected Letters and Papers, 1776–1790*, 5 vols. (Ithaca, N.Y.: Cornell University Press, 1977–83), vol. 1: 359, 370; Lafayette to Bedel, March 16, 1778, Bedel Papers, folder 2; *NHSP*, vol. 17: 223; Colin G. Calloway, "Sentinels of the Revolution: Bedel's New Hampshire Rangers and the Abenakis on the Upper Connecticut," *Historical New Hampshire* 4 (1990), 271–95.

British troops occupied Odanak, treated the inhabitants "extremely ill" and pressured them to take up arms. They issued the Abenakis with hunting passes and forbade them to go near the Connecticut River "on pain of death." "Indian officers from different tribes" came to Odanak to recruit warriors but met with no success. According to one group of Abenakis who ignored the British restrictions and went to Coos, General Carleton refused to let them buy blankets or ammunition unless they took up arms for the crown.[17]

In June 1777, Bedel reported to Schuyler from Haverhill, New Hampshire, that "the Indians who come here are very Peaceable and I am satisfied there is no danger of them Joining the British Troops."[18] By September as many as forty-five Abenaki families were reported to be in the region around Lake Memphremagog, with the intention of settling on the upper Connecticut. This would appear to indicate a mass exodus from Odanak. If we estimate an Abenaki family at five persons, the exodus of some 225 people would have emptied Odanak of almost half of its population. However, if the families in question were extended family bands, which is more likely, they would contain something in the region of fifteen people, which gives a total of around seven hundred – more than the total population of Odanak but exactly the estimate Henry Tufts gave of Abenakis living in the Lake Memphremagog area several years *before* the Revolution. Tufts was a liar, a counterfeiter, a bigamist, a thief, a cheat, and a fraud, who peddled alcohol to his Abenaki healers in order to extract from them medical secrets that he later used to masquerade as a physician in the colonies. But his observations on the Abenakis seem accurate. What the British in Quebec and the Americans in northern New England interpreted as an exodus from Odanak may in fact have been nothing of the sort. Rather, hundreds of Abenakis in the large stretch of territory between Coos and Odanak moved freely and maintained close ties to both places. Coos, "the place of the pines," was an area of strategic importance, economic abundance, and spiritual significance, and had been the site of an Abenaki community for generations. The French had established a mission there for the inhabitants before 1713, and Abenakis remained in the area throughout the long contests for empire that transformed the Connecticut Valley into a war zone. Even after settlers occupied the area, Abenakis continued to follow well-trodden paths and long-established patterns of seasonal movement between Odanak and the upper Connecticut. The Revolution did not produce these movements and, despite British efforts, it did not bring them to a halt. Bedel dispatched runners to the Abenakis, offering them assistance on their journey and supplies on their arrival. Most of them probably remained in the remote areas around Memphremagog and tried

---

[17] Bedel to Schuyler, Feb. 16 and Feb. 24, 1777, Bedel Papers, folder 1; Stevens Papers, vol. 3: 75, 81; *NHSP*, vol. 17: 128.

[18] Bedel to Schuyler, June 22, 1777, Bedel Papers, folder 1; *NHSP*, vol. 17: 133.

to keep out of the conflict; but some warriors, many with their families, accepted Bedel's offer, settled around Haverhill at the great meadows of the lower Coos, and enlisted as scouts. Less than twenty years after Rogers's Rangers burned Odanak, Abenakis and New Hampshire rangers were serving together on the upper Connecticut.[19]

The British coerced warriors from Odanak, from the neighboring Abenaki mission village of Bécancour, and from Caughnawaga, Saint Regis (Akwesasne), and Lake of the Two Mountains (Oka) into joining Burgoyne's campaign in 1777. About four hundred Indians from the towns had joined Burgoyne's army by June but, Carleton cautioned Germain with a professional soldier's frustration, "there is always an uncertainty as to the force of the Indians, parties continually leaving them and returning as their humour leads them." More of the "domiciled Indians of Canada" returned home during the summer, giving Carleton a variety of excuses, "which considering that these people are never to be prevailed upon by compulsory means I did not enter into."[20] The disastrous campaign only reinforced Canadian Indians' reluctance to support the British, and the death of Lieutenant Wright, the British officer at Odanak, at the Battle of Bennington, compounded Abenaki discontent with British policies. Many Abenakis at Odanak now took an increasingly anti-British stance. As early as October 4, 1777, General Horatio Gates, with more optimism than the situation warranted, called on Bedel to bring to Saratoga "all the Saint Francis Indians who have lately come to Co'hos, with all those, who from Friendship to You, and Affection to Our Noble Cause, are ready to Step forth at this important Crisis, to put a finishing Stroke to this Campaign."[21]

Abenaki involvement in the war was to be less dramatic, however. The community at Odanak split: one party favored King George; the other leaned toward the Americans and seems to have grouped behind Joseph Louis Gill, "the White Chief of the Saint Francis Abenakis" who was the son of two adopted English captives. Odanak quickly emerged as a conduit for the dissemination of war news, and uncertainty and divisions within the community made it accessible to emissaries from both sides. In addition, the village lay across the river from, and had close ties with, a village of French Canadians. Indians and French Canadians beat a regular path between Odanak and the upper

[19] Vermont State Archives, Stevens Papers, vol. 3: 667, 851; Collections of the New-York Historical Society 12 (1879): 189–90; "Timothy Bedel's Account with the Commissioners of Indian Affairs, 8 Jan. 1777–18 Jan. 1778," in Schuyler Papers, NYPL, box 14; Bedel Papers, folder 1; Calloway, "Sentinels of the Revolution." On Coos see Calloway, Western Abenakis of Vermont, 12, 46–8, 83–4, 188.

[20] DAR, vol. 14: 121, 187; C.O. 42/36: 172; 37: 86. Lawrence Ostola, "The Seven Nations of Canada and the American Revolution, 1774–1783," M. A. thesis, University of Montreal, 1989, ch. 4.

[21] Stevens, "His Majesty's 'Savage' Allies," 1012, 1021, 1356–60, 1384, 1444; Horatio Gates Papers, 1726–1828 (20 reels, New York: Microfilming Corporation of America, 1978), vol. 5: 87.

Connecticut, following the old Indian route via the Saint Francis River and Lake Memphremagog. Gill passed freely back and forth between Odanak and the rebel settlements in the upper Connecticut Valley, and seems to have operated as an American agent in the early years of the war. His brother-in-law, Annance, apparently went over to the Americans, whereas Joseph Traversy, a Canadian from the village across the river, was an active rebel collaborator.[22]

In an effort to halt the traffic, the British sent a Canadian officer, Hertel de Rouville, to occupy the French Canadian village in the fall of 1777. Abenakis came to smoke with Rouville often, but Gill and others continued to penetrate the British cordon with ease.[23] Late in November, Colonel John Campbell took charge of Indian affairs and appointed Lieutenant Wills Crofts of the Thirty-fourth Regiment to take up permanent residence at Odanak.[24] Campbell paid particular attention to Gill and tried to reunite the community. In addition to stationing Crofts and Rouville in the area, he sent his deputy, Alexander Fraser, to arrange Indian expeditions and patrols along the Saint Francis River. Nevertheless, rebel emissaries and messages continued to turn up in Odanak. That same November, Abenaki delegates from Odanak accompanied pro-American Oneidas at a daylong council with United States Indian commissioners.[25] The Abenakis were keeping the paths to Odanak open to all comers.

The Americans could point to few concrete benefits in supporting their cause, however. By the winter of 1777–8 the Abenakis who had relocated on the upper Connecticut were in dire straits, and Timothy Bedel sent letter after letter to his superiors requesting clothing for his naked Indians.[26] In May 1778 a "committee from the Micmac & Saint Francois Indians" visited Bedel at Haverhill, asking what was to be done for them. They seemed uneasy and dispersed to go hunting while they waited for an answer.[27]

The next month, Bedel sent Schuyler a list of twenty Saint Francis Indians in his service, one of whom was Swashan, the warrior who had been with Washington at Boston. Five of the warriors had their families with them and there were fourteen children in the group.[28] The Abenaki exodus from Canada was not yet over. In July Bedel met with a chief from Sartigan on the Chaudière River who declared that his people – one hundred families, he said – had

---

[22] John C. Huden, "The White Chief of the St. Francis Abenakis," *Vermont History* 24 (1956), 207, 337–8; Stevens, "His Majesty's 'Savage' Allies," 649.
[23] Huden, "White Chief of the St. Francis Abenakis," 337–8; Gates Papers, vol. 5: 468, 871, vol. 6: 689; Stevens, "His Majesty's 'Savage' Allies," 1459.
[24] Stevens, "His Majesty's 'Savage' Allies," 1444–6.
[25] Stevens, "His Majesty's 'Savage' Allies," 1470, 1536; Haldimand Papers, 21777: 15–21, 63–6.
[26] Calloway, "Sentinels of the Revolution," 282–4; Bedel Papers, folder 1; Gates Papers, vol. 6: 689.
[27] Bedel to Lafayette and Bedel to Gates, 14 May 1778, Bedel Papers, folder 2; *NHSP*, vol. 17: 227–8.
[28] "List of St. Francis Indians," June 5, 1778, Schuyler Papers, reel 7, box 14.

abandoned their village and were moving south to the Androscoggin River, never to return to Canada, after Governor Carleton had threatened to burn their village if they allowed any more rebel scouts to infiltrate the area.[29]

In August Gill was back in Haverhill, having been chased out of Odanak by the arrival of British and Hessian troops under Captain Alexander Fraser, who made "great Threats." "The Chief from Saint Francis" wanted to know what the Americans intended to do for his people "as he says we have a great number of Friends that way."[30]

At Odanak, Crofts found his job of keeping tabs on comings and goings increasingly exasperating as the mood in the village swung toward the rebels. The German troops stationed at the French Canadian village across the river may have kept rebel sympathizers in awe, and they certainly produced tensions with that community, but they exerted no control over the Abenakis.[31] Despite Crofts's efforts to prevent it, most of the Abenakis went hunting in September. He sent messengers to call them back but expected that some would return only to go out again; he wrote, "Others I am pretty confidant will not pay any attention to it." Moreover, he sensed that the Loyalist faction at Odanak was losing ground to a younger generation of rebel sympathizers behind Gill:

*problems controlling Abenakis movement*

> I fear there has been some person abusing the ears of the Indians, for the old people who have shewn the greatest steadiness begin to be a little alarmed, and have intimated that should our affairs turn out contrary to their expectations, their only security will be in quitting this Village, and attaching themselves to some other in the upper Country.

Some of the opposition party went so far as to threaten the British with retribution if anything happened to Gill. In October 1778, Traversy brought word to the Americans that the fifty Hessians sent to guard Odanak had been deemed unreliable and replaced by forty British regulars, and that only four Indians at Odanak were against the Americans. Frederick Haldimand summed up the situation at Odanak, telling the home government that the Abenakis "are lately become very ungovernable and 'tis feared attached to the rebels."[32]

Gill told Bedel in November that the Abenakis of Odanak were "all willing to Join the United States." Jacob Bayley described Gill as "a man of excellent understanding" who had given the Americans "the most Exact Account of Affairs," and had "been the means of keeping the Saint Francois Indians from taking Arms against Us," even though his attachment to the rebel cause had

---

[29] Bedel to Gates, July 15, 1778, Bedel Papers, folder 2; Gates Papers, vol. 7: 1246–7, 1284–5; *NHSP*, vol. 17: 241–3.

[30] Bedel to Gates, Aug. 25, 1778, Bedel Papers, folder 2; Gates Papers, vol. 8: 15–16, 18; *NHSP*, vol. 17: 265.

[31] Stevens, "His Majesty's 'Savage' Allies," 838; *Journals of the House of Representatives of Massachusetts*, vol. 51, pt. 1: 81; Haldimand Papers, 21867.

[32] Haldimand Papers, 21777: 34–5; *NHSP*, vol. 17: 276–7; *DAR*, vol. 15: 221.

forced him to leave his home and family.[33] Before the end of the year, Gill and "the faithful Traversie" were off on another mission to Canada, and did not return until March.[34]

In January 1779, according to Bedel, Indians from Canada were coming south with news every day.[35] Nevertheless, all was not well that winter with the Abenakis who had resettled on the Connecticut. Bedel reported that he had "upwards of 30 Families of Indians" at Haverhill who were almost naked. Tired of waiting, they dispersed into the woods to hunt. A group of Abenakis from Odanak who left their hunting grounds and, defying British orders, went down to the rebel settlements to trade, returned in February 1779 with word that the Abenakis they met there were very poor and discontented. They said Abenakis on the Connecticut promised to return home in the spring if they could be certain of a good welcome.[36]

The news from the south may have increased the crown party's following at Odanak. In May they requested Governor Haldimand's permission to send a war party of twenty or twenty-five men to Coos "to put that country in confusion."[37] Crofts dispatched scouting parties to the Connecticut River to ascertain the truth of reports that the enemy were making preparations for an invasion.[38] Even so, the British remained concerned about the loyalties of the Odanak Abenakis. In July, Colonel Campbell delivered a formal reprimand in Montreal to a group of Hurons from Lorette and Abenakis from Odanak who had been intercepted carrying belts and messages to other villages in Canada. The Hurons said that more than half their tribe were in the rebel interest and that they hoped the Abenakis were similarly disposed. The British felt sure the Canadians had been "tampering" with these Indians.[39]

War disrupted peacetime patterns of subsistence, and British attempts to regulate Abenaki hunting aggravated the situation. Abenakis who remained at Odanak and loyal to the crown fared little better than their relatives on the Connecticut. When the time for their fall hunt arrived, the Abenakis at Odanak, along with some from Bécancour, gathered to ask Crofts if the British intended to employ them. If not, they wanted permission to go hunting so they could repay some of their debts. Crofts asked them to wait a little longer but complained

[33] Bedel to George Washington, Nov. 5, 1778, Bedel Papers, folder 2; *NHSP*, vol. 17: 281; Gates Papers, vol. 8: 521, 718–19.

[34] Gates to Bedel, Dec. 22, 1778, Bedel Papers, folder 2; *NHSP*, vol. 17: 290, 328.

[35] *NHSP*, vol. 17: 312.

[36] Gates Papers, vol. 8: 1005–6, 1018; Bedel to Schuyler, Jan. 11, 1779, Bedel Papers, folder 2; *NHSP*, vol. 17: 311–12; Haldimand Papers, 21777: 67–8.

[37] Haldimand Papers, 21777: 107–8.

[38] Haldimand Papers, 21777: 109, 117, 137–8. The reports of American activities were accurate, but the preparations were merely to create a diversion for General John Sullivan's campaign against the Iroquois that summer.

[39] NAC, Claus Papers, vol. 26: 100–1.

that they placed unreasonable demands on him now that they had a pretext. "Tho they are really wretchedly off in point of provision, I do not believe Victualing would be sufficient to detain them, was it not for the addition I am obliged frequently to make of a few Bottles of rum, in which they seem to place their whole Delight." He also suspected there was a rebel Indian concealed close by.[40]

The United States meanwhile intensified its efforts to secure Abenaki allegiance. John Wheelock, the new president of Dartmouth College, urged Congress to support his school as a means of retaining the loyalty of key Odanak and Caughnawaga families who sent their sons there.[41] George Washington endorsed a recommendation that Joseph Louis Gill be granted a commission. Other northern chiefs had been granted continental commissions, and Gill thought himself entitled to the rank of major, "having been a long time a Captain." In April, Congress granted Gill his commission and provided that all Abenakis who were willing to join the service of the United States "be collected & formed into a Company or Companies under the Command of the said Joseph Louis Gill & receive while in Service the like pay Subsistence & Rations with the officers & Soldiers of the Continental Army."[42] Meanwhile, Swashan and the other Abenakis in Caughnawaga captain John Vincent's company of Indian rangers enlisted for another year of service on the upper Connecticut.[43]

But Odanak remained volatile and unpredictable. The following autumn, Gill took an oath of allegiance to King George. According to the British, he returned from the colonies "full of Contrition for his past Conduct and Professions of Loyalty for the time to Come." Governor Haldimand intended "Soon to prove his Fidelity."[44]

In February 1780, Captain Alexander Fraser of the British Indian Department visited Odanak to report on conditions there and cultivate a good understanding with Gill.[45] He found the place a hotbed of politics and intrigue. Meeting with Gill in an effort to root out the cause of the trouble, Fraser reminded the chief that here was his chance to prove himself a loyal subject. Since the Abenakis were known for their bravery and fidelity, and the problem could not possibly be lack of attention by the government, Fraser concluded that "the present

[40] Haldimand Papers, 21777: 168.
[41] *PCC*, reel 52, item 41, vol. 10: 423–4. Most of the Indian students at Dartmouth during the Revolution came from Odanak and Caughnawaga: "List of Indians in the Indian Charity School," typescript, Stockbridge Town Library, Historical Room, "Stockbridge Indians" box.
[42] *Writings of Washington*, vol. 17: 68–9, 82–3; *PCC*, reel 170, item 152, vol. 8: 159; reel 159, item 147, vol. 4: 301; reel 24, item 14: 327; Washington C. Ford and Gaillard Hunt, eds., *Journals of the Continental Congress, 1774–1789*, 34 vols. (Washington: Government Printing Office, 1904–37), vol. 15 (1779): 1263; vol. 16 (1780): 334–5; Paul H. Smith, ed., *Letters of Delegates to Congress, 1774–1789* (Washington: Library of Congress, 1976–) vol. 15: 33.
[43] Frederic P. Wells, *History of Newbury, Vermont* (St. Johnsbury: Caledonian, 1902), 409.
[44] Haldimand Papers, 21777: 250; 21773: 159.
[45] Fraser's account of his visit and interview with Gill is in Haldimand Papers, 21772: 2–4.

despicable state . . . must be the effect of evil councils which divided them or a want of wisdom in their Chiefs." Gill agreed that the problem lay with the chiefs, but since Abenaki leadership traditionally rested on voluntary obedience, *he* felt the trouble was that the chiefs were too overbearing in their behavior toward the warriors. ("They are the very opposite of that," editorialized Fraser in his report.) Continuing the British practice of interfering in Abenaki chief making, Fraser suggested making Gill chief, "provided he would undertake to unite the Village, and conduct them in a loyal and useful manner." Fearing that such a move might excite jealousy, however, he advocated putting Gill's son, Antoine, in the position. Gill agreed, pointing out that his son had more right to it anyway, being descended from a chief himself. Gill's first wife was an Abenaki woman named Marie Jeanne, whom captive Susanna Johnson said was the daughter of "the grand sachem."[46] Fraser assured him that his son would be appointed chief, but demanded that the family first prove its loyalty to the crown by striking a blow against the rebels. He dismissed Gill's protests that only British threats had caused his defection in the first place, and warned him that he should not try to deceive the governor "by such shallow Artifices." Haldimand had pardoned his errors, but Gill had to give proof of his change of heart. If he gave any hint in the future of conniving with rebel scouts, the British would burn the village and drive his family into exile.

So Gill accepted the role of compliant yet valuable client chief. He admitted that "he had been a very bad Subject," but hoped to convince the world he was a good one. Exaggerating his influence, he said he would "immediately take measures to bring back all the Abenakis that are amongst the Rebels & he was sure he coud do it, and he would also be responsible for their future good behaviour." He said he was eager for the chance for his family to prove their mettle, but preferred to wait until the snow had a crust on it, which would make any undertaking less hazardous.

Fraser found the Abenakis at Odanak "apparently well disposed," but there were only sixty of them at home, probably the Loyalist element since they declared they were ready "to march out at a moment's warning" on Haldimand's orders. Fraser ordered them to stay put until they heard that the governor needed their services. He also investigated rumors that an Abenaki chief had died following a scuffle with Crofts. Crofts denied the reports, saying that the Indian was drunk and all he had done was push him away. Fraser concluded

[46] Alvin H. Morrison, "Dawnland Directors: Status and Role of Seventeenth-Century Wabanaki Sagamores," in William Cowan, ed., *Papers of the Seventh Algonquian Conference* (Ottawa: Carleton University Press, 1976), 1–19. In 1768, the Abenakis of Odanak brought two new chiefs to Sir William Johnson "for approval." *Johnson Papers*, vol. 12: 841–2. "Captivity of Mrs. Johnson," in *Indian Narratives* (Claremont, N.H.: Tracy, 1854), 158–9. Marie-Jeanne gave Gill two or three children. Antoine was the only one of Gill's family to survive Rogers' raid and the subsequent captivity. In 1763 Gill married the daughter of a French militia captain, Antoine Gamelin. She bore him six sons and two daughters.

that the chief "died of a Complaint on his Lungs under which he had lingered a long while before." But the British were taking no chances in a pressure cooker like Odanak: Crofts was removed from command and sent to Saint Johns to await further orders. Crofts, who spoke no Abenaki, had frequently been frustrated in his attempts to keep track of movements in and out of the village, and to distinguish between Abenakis from Odanak and those who had moved to Coos and elsewhere. Despite his vigilance and his diligence in issuing passes, he complained, "You know perfectly well that when Indians go out hunting there is no preventing them going where they please." Crofts had acquired considerable knowledge about the Odanak Abenakis, but Fraser doubted if he would be much use elsewhere, as he would have to learn it all anew in another community. Luc Schmid, a captain in the Yamaska militia, took over at Odanak.[47]

Haldimand made it clear that, in the event of a rebel attack, "he expected every Abenaki would distinguish himself," and "listen to nothing but the words that came from their Father['s] mouth." But he decided not to employ the Abenakis assembled at Odanak other than as scouts and messengers. To save on provisions, he gave orders that they be allowed to disperse to their hunting grounds.[48] The governor attached little weight to Gill's excuses, but as the chief had promised to mend his ways, Haldimand was willing to believe his professions were sincere, or "at least Act with Him as if He thinks it."[49] The layers of deception multiplied.

In an apparent effort to prove his newfound loyalty, Gill went on a secret mission to the upper Connecticut with ten warriors and captured American general Benjamin Whitcomb. But Whitcomb escaped on the way back to Odanak, reinforcing British suspicions that their new ally was playing both ends against the middle. In fact, the reasons for Gill's action are clearly explained in a document written in French and in the consistent strategy of the Abenakis. Luc Schmid learned that Gill allowed Whitcomb to escape on the assurance that if the Bostonians invaded Canada again they would not burn Odanak. The memory of Rogers's raid, in which he had lost a wife and children, was vivid in Gill's memory. He volunteered to go on the mission to safeguard Odanak, and he allowed the mission to fail in order to safeguard Odanak. Lest he burn his bridges with the British, he brought in another prisoner taken in the raid.[50]

Four months after his first visit in February 1780, Fraser returned to Odanak to investigate reports of drunken disorder in the village. The illegal traffic of liquor in large quantities prompted the chiefs and the women to request Schmid

[47] Haldimand Papers, 21772: 6–7, 12; 21773: 173–5; 21777: 269–70.
[48] Haldimand Papers, 21773: 183, 185; 21777: 271.
[49] Haldimand Papers, 21773: 175.
[50] Huden, "White Chief," 343–4; Haldimand Papers, 21777: 364–5; Ostola, "Seven Nations of Canada," 135.

to stop the sale of rum to them, "otherwise their families would perish for want of food and cloathing as they neglected their hunting & every thing else." Gill's wife, "a woman of veracity," said that both rum and wine were available in the village and that a hundred bottles had been consumed in her house alone over the course of the winter. Fraser reported that disorders in the village had been so great "that the service of those Indians was almost lost by it," but that things were now under control and he hoped there would be no repetition.[51]

Odanak ended the war as it had begun it: as both a channel for rebel intelligence and a source of scouting parties for the British.[52] On the upper Connecticut, Captain John Vincent's company of Indian rangers continued in service with the Americans until at least 1781. Bayley's muster roll in May listed seventeen, but the general told Washington that "a much larger number has been here at times but are not steady and though I do not think they have ever done us any damage but are rambling in the woods those inserted have been serviceable as scouts &c." He reckoned he had supported about fifty Abenakis from Odanak from November 1778 to February 1781 when they were in from hunting, which was about half the time.[53]

Luc Schmid continued to send out scouting parties from Odanak to Coos, although he acknowledged that their purpose was as much to keep the other Abenakis at home in anticipation of being employed as to gather useful news. He described the "grand chef" at Odanak as "un Homme Zèle pour le Service, meritant quelque attention," and was careful to secure his approval for such expeditions. In the late spring of 1782, Abenakis scouting in Vermont overtook and captured several American officers who had escaped from Montreal, took another prisoner from the Coos region, and set fire to an abandoned blockhouse.[54] Despite such successes, the Abenakis at Odanak resented the restraints placed upon them by the British. By July 1782 they were "very impatient to have Liberty to Goe to their Different occupations."[55]

Those "different occupations" involved, for some, routine movement between Odanak and Lake Memphremagog. In the wake of the Revolution, Odanak continued, as it had for generations, to accommodate a variety of bands hunting over a wide area of northern New England and southern Quebec. Abenaki opposition to settlement around the north end of Lake Champlain in the late 1780s was attributed to "Saint Francis Indians," even though it more probably was the work of Missisquoi Abenakis who lived in the area but maintained ties

[51] Haldimand Papers, 21772: 46–50.
[52] Haldimand Papers, 21772: 62; 21774: 242; Huden, "White Chief," 345–6.
[53] Wells, *History of Newbury*, 400, 409; "Colonel Thomas Johnson's Letters and Documents," in *The Upper Connecticut: Narratives of Its Settlement and Its Part in the American Revolution*, 2 vols. (Montpelier: Vermont Historical Society, 1943), vol. 2: 94–5.
[54] Haldimand Papers, 21797: 122, 135, 163, 165, 169; 21865: 139.
[55] Haldimand Papers, 21772: 150.

with Odanak.[56] An Abenaki oral tradition recalls that Swashan, the chief who served with Washington and with the Indian rangers on the upper Connecticut, and who was identified by the Americans as a "Saint Francis Indian," was back at Missisquoi after the Revolution.[57] Travelers met "Saint Francis Indians" on the shores of Lake Memphremagog in the 1780s and 1790s, and scattered family bands of Abenakis remained in the extensive territory between Coos and Odanak.[58] In the 1790s, Abenakis from Odanak petitioned the British for additional lands in Durham township, in recognition of their services during the Revolution and to help accommodate an influx of families after the war.[59] Some of these people may have been new arrivals; others probably were returning to the village now that the Revolution, and the divisions it generated, was over.

Why was Odanak such a political hotbed during the Revolution? Alexander Fraser said it was even worse than Caughnawaga, which was saying something.[60] The written sources do not reveal a clear picture of the factional lines within the community, but what we know of Odanak and its place in Abenaki history helps to explain why, for the British in particular, the village proved such a headache.

Odanak occupied a key frontier situation. The Saint Francis River–Lake Memphremagog–upper Connecticut route was a well-traveled highway, and spies, scouts, messengers, and envoys made their way in, out, and through Odanak. The British lacked a clear sense of the actual composition and character of the community, and were not always able to distinguish between residents and visitors. The neighboring village of French Canadians were even more suspect than Abenakis in British eyes. Both communities may well have entertained hopes of a return of the French, and the close connections between the Abenakis and their French-speaking neighbors worried and frustrated the British. Joseph Traversy was able to come and go with ease among both communities, and a glance at the names of the Abenakis who served with Jacob Bayley on the upper Connecticut illustrates the interconnectedness of Abenakis and French: John Sabattis, Joseph Sabattist, John Battist, Louis, Francis, Benedic, and Lazelle.[61]

Nor were Abenaki relations with their American neighbors consistently hostile. Despite the French and Indian wars that cast such a long shadow over

[56] Calloway, *Western Abenakis*, 226–30.
[57] Addendum to the Petition for Federal Recognition as an American Indian Tribe, submitted to the Bureau of Indian Affairs by the Abenaki Nation of Vermont (unpublished mss., 1986), 69–73.
[58] Calloway, *Western Abenakis*, 231.
[59] Day, *Identity of the St. Francis Indians*, 6–61; Calloway, *Western Abenakis*, 233; NAC, Lower Canada Land Papers, reel C-2559, vol. 172: 83659–728.
[60] Haldimand Papers, 21772: 2–4.
[61] "List of St. Francis Indians," June 5, 1778, Schuyler Papers, reel 7, box 14; Wells, *History of Newbury*, 409.

northern New England's history, colonists and Indians there had shared long periods of peaceful, if cautious, coexistence.[62] The settlers who rushed into Abenaki country after the French defeat in 1760 brought dispossession and hardship for the Abenakis, but they also mingled with them in remote frontier communities.[63] Confronted with a choice between British redcoats, their foes during the colonial wars, and American colonists, many of whom they had come to know as individual neighbors, Abenakis sometimes chose the latter. With Abenaki bands moving back and forth between Odanak and northern New England, these local and individual relationships often proved more influential than British tactics of coercion when the Revolution initiated renewed competition for Abenaki allegiance.

The nature of Abenaki society frustrated British efforts to try and control politics at Odanak and to muster Abenaki allies. The British Indian Department's efforts to center its control of all Abenaki bands at Odanak and to deal with chiefs it recognized ignored the social, political, economic, and geographic realities of Abenaki life. Joseph Louis Gill may well appear more important in British documents than he was in Abenaki country. Most Abenakis ignored the British efforts and carried on their dispersed and mobile lifestyle.[64] When the Revolution broke out, the British tightened up on their efforts to control the Abenakis via Odanak, and the Abenakis had to work harder to ignore those efforts. Odanak had emerged, endured, and survived as a composite community, and it maintained ties with other communities. Whether the forty-five families who moved to Lake Memphremagog represented an exodus of rebel sympathizers or hunting bands pursuing familiar patterns of movement, the ties that existed between Abenaki families who remained at Odanak during the Revolution and those who inhabited the region around the upper Connecticut rendered it unlikely that warriors from Odanak would volunteer for campaigns against the New England frontier. They expressed their willingness to do so on occasion, but then so did Joseph Louis Gill, and little came of these expeditions. Abenakis promised to watch the woods, but Abenakis from Odanak who were out as scouts and rangers for the British consistently avoided coming into conflict with Abenakis who were scouting for the Americans at Haverhill. "Watching the woods" was an ideal strategy for people who wanted to give the appearance of commitment but whose main concern was to keep the war away from their homes and families.

As the Revolution entered its closing years, many Abenakis at Odanak, and Joseph Louis Gill in particular, gave indications of newfound devotion to the

---

[62] Colin G. Calloway, ed., *Dawnland Encounters: Indians and Europeans in Northern New England* (Hanover, N.H.: University Press of New England, 1991).
[63] Day, *Identity of the St. Francis Indians*, 52.
[64] Calloway, *Western Abenakis*, 190–2, 197–202.

British. The redcoats suspected them of double-dealing, and perhaps with good reason; after all, the Abenakis knew all too well the consequences of putting all their eggs in one basket, having been left high and dry by the defeat of their French allies in 1760. Pro-British sentiment at Odanak actually seemed to increase as the British lost the war. From the Abenaki point of view, whether the American colonies won or lost was probably of less importance than whether an American invasion of Canada succeeded. For years, Indian messengers from Canada told American commanders that their people were waiting expectantly for another invasion.[65] For Abenakis, the threat such an invasion posed to their village was more important than its impact on the course of the war. By the time Joseph Louis Gill took his oath of loyalty to King George, the Abenakis must have sensed that no invasion was coming. Their need to operate a "play-off system" between two powers decreased and they proceeded to mend their diplomatic fences with the British. Whatever the result of the American struggle for independence, Odanak still would have to live with – and in – the reality of a British Canada. Abenakis might continue covertly to assist the rebels, but they also had to put by some insurance for when the war was over. Having done so, they were able to request a grant of lands in subsequent years in recognition of their services.

The support lent to the American cause by many Abenakis in Vermont and New Hampshire could have entitled them to claim special protection from the newly independent states and the new republic. However, the expulsion of Stockbridge and Oneida Indians from their homelands in the wake of the American victory they had helped to achieve proved the futility of that strategy.[66] Americans knew that some Abenakis from Missisquoi had served the United States during the Revolution, but that did nothing to stem the postwar land grabbing of Ethan and Ira Allen in Vermont.[67] In New Hampshire, Timothy Bedel at one point recommended that land be set aside for the friendly Indians around Coos who had served in the American cause, but that did not stop his son from acquiring a huge swath of Abenaki territory in northern New Hampshire in 1798 in defiance of federal law.[68] In the uncertain times following the Revolution, the best way for the Abenakis to survive the future was as they had survived in the past.

Colonel John Allan, the American agent to the Indians of Maine and Nova Scotia during the Revolution, writing in 1793, described a situation of persistent intertribal fluidity and mobility in northern New England and eastern Canada

---

[65] For example: Gates Papers, vol. 8: 15–16; *NHSP*, vol. 17: 242–4, 265.
[66] See this volume, ch. 3.
[67] Major Clement Gosselin to Ira Allen, Aug. 18, 1786, Vermont State Archives, Stevens Papers, Misc. Correspondence, 1780–9; Calloway, *Western Abenakis*, 221–31.
[68] Calloway, "Sentinels of the Revolution," 294–5; Peter Shea, "A New and Accurate Map of Philip's Grant," *Vermont History* 53 (1985), 36–42.

that was central to the Abenaki way of life, and which the British were never able to fully appreciate or regulate:

> A correspondence & intercourse have been open'd a long time, thro' the several tribes, Viz, from Penobscot Saint Francis in Canada & the whole of the Mickmac Country as far as Chaleurs. During the last French war the Indians being called in from different parts for the defence of Louisburg, Canada &c, an acquaintance became more General, & I can assert from authority, that an Indian can hardly be found past 30 years of age but is acquaint'd and known within this circle. The very easy conveyence by the Lakes, rivers and Streams so Interspersed in this Country, they can easy take their women children & baggage, where ever their Interest, Curiosity, or caprice may lead them, & their natural propensity for roving is such that you will see families in the course of a year go thro' the greatest part of this extent. This of course brings on a nearer Connection by Inter marriages which is now become universal, particular as far as Merrimichi & Saint Francis, so much that I well know that numbers which I had in the War are now residents in Canada & other distant parts, and many from thence are now Living at St Johns, Penobscot & Passamaquoddy.[69]

The apparent complexity and contradictions of Odanak's role in the Revolution assume greater clarity and consistency if that role is viewed as one phase in a continuing Abenaki struggle to maintain their lands and independence against all comers, if necessary by dealing with them all. Confronted with British military and economic strength, some Abenakis advocated and pursued policies amenable to the crown. Others cast their lot with the Americans. Joseph Louis Gill assured first the Americans and then the British that Abenaki support was certain, Abenaki action a possibility. To British and Americans, such behavior appeared duplicitous, but the central objective of Abenaki strategy remained unchanged.

Like other Indian communities along the Saint Lawrence, Odanak played no great role in the war of the Revolution. At the end of the war, a British officer estimated that Britain had had the support of no more than two hundred warriors from the various Abenaki groups along the Saint Lawrence.[70] The Abenakis fought no major actions, and their ambiguous stance frustrated Britons and Americans alike. But by successfully keeping the Revolution at arm's length, they avoided devastating losses. Unlike their parents during the Seven Years' War and unlike their contemporaries in New York, the Ohio Valley, and the

---

[69] "Col. Allan's Report on the Indian Tribes in 1793," in Frederic Kidder, ed., *Military Operations in Eastern Maine and Nova Scotia during the Revolution, Chiefly Compiled from the Journals and Letters of Colonel John Allan* (Albany, N.Y.: Munsell, 1867), 307–8,

[70] "An Estimate of the Indian Nations employed by the British in the Revolutionary War," *Collections of the Massachusetts Historical Society*, lst series, 10 (1809), 123; cf. Wise, "American Revolution and Indian History," 196.

Smoky Mountains, the Abenakis did not have to endure the burning of their homes and the destruction of their crops. British threats to burn Odanak remained just threats so long as some Abenakis gave evidence of loyalty to the crown. Odanak survived the Revolution, politically divided but physically intact. In a conflict that tolerated no neutrals, internal turmoil was a small price to pay for group survival.

# 3

# *Stockbridge: the New England patriots*

On a cold January night in 1778, Albigence Waldo, a homesick Connecticut surgeon serving with Washington's army at Valley Forge, was called to minister to a dying soldier. The man expired before Waldo reached the hut where he lay, but his passing prompted the doctor to reflect on life, death, and the human condition:

> There the poor fellow lies not Superior now to a clod of earth – his Mouth wide open – his Eyes staring. Was he affrighted at the scene of Death – or the consequences of it? . . . What a frail – dying creature is Man. We are Certainly not made for this world – daily evidences demonstrate the contrary.[1]

Such thoughts in the midst of war and in face of death may not be unusual, but in this case the fallen comrade in arms, dying in a place that has become symbolic of America's struggle for freedom, was an Indian.

Ever since the Declaration of Independence denounced the Indians as "savage" allies of a tyrannical monarch, those who fought with, rather than against, the Americans have tended to be forgotten.[2] The Oneidas, Tuscaroras, and several tribes in Maine and Nova Scotia lent their support to the American war effort, as did Indian towns in southern and central New England. No Indian community gave the patriot cause more dedicated service than the town of Stockbridge, Massachusetts, a composite community of Mahican, Housatonic, and Wappinger peoples from the Hudson Valley and western Massachusetts. The Stockbridge experience vividly illustrates that though Indian people laid down their lives in the cause of freedom, they could not enjoy the benefits of freedom once it was won.

---

[1] Hugh F. Rankin, ed., *Narratives of the American Revolution* (Chicago: Donnelley, 1976), 201–2.
[2] An exception is Barbara Graymont, "The Oneidas and the American Revolution," in Jack Campisi and Laurence M. Hauptman, *The Oneida Indian Experience: Two Perspectives* (Syracuse, N.Y.: Syracuse University Press, 1988), 31–44. See also Russell Lawrence Barsh, "Native American Loyalists and Patriots: Reflections on the American Revolution in Native American History," *Indian Historian* 10 (Summer 1977), 9–19.

According to a native account, the Mahican or Muhheakunnuk nation were formidable before the *Chuckopek* or white people came to their country: "Before they begun to decay, our forefathers informed us, that Muhheakunnuk nation could then raise about one thousand warriors."[3] But ever since the Dutch established trading posts on the Hudson River early in the seventeenth century, the Mahicans had endured devastating new forces. Recurrent warfare with the neighboring Mohawks and epidemics of new diseases cut Mahican numbers from an estimated four thousand to a mere five hundred by 1700. Some Mahicans migrated north and east, amalgamating with Abenaki communities; others migrated to the upper Susquehanna and the Midwest; many moved to the territory of the related Housatonics, who had been all but exterminated by smallpox.[4]

English colonists bought up most of southwestern Massachusetts in the first half of the eighteenth century, and the Mahicans and Housatonics were reduced to living in four villages. There, they attracted the attention of English missionaries. In 1734, Timothy Woodbridge and Yale scholar John Sergeant began to visit the two main villages and to cultivate potential leaders for the church. Weighing their people's chances of survival in an alien world that threatened to engulf them, two hereditary leaders, Konkapot and Umpachenee, accepted the mission, and the Mahicans embarked on a new path. Two years later, the town of Stockbridge was laid out as an Indian mission, the last of the "praying towns" to be established in Massachusetts. The English had definite military and political motives in creating the mission: Stockbridge lay astride a principal warpath from Canada, and the Protestant religion was seen as a key means of securing the Indians' allegiance against the Catholic French and their allies. Ninety Indian people took up residence there. While Sergeant instructed them in Christianity, Woodbridge taught their children the English language, although church services continued to be held in Mahican. Sergeant introduced four English families into the town, ostensibly to help promote the Indians' education and provide a model of "civilization." Wappinger and other Indians joined the community, and in 1740 the Mahicans moved the "fireplace" of their nation from the Hudson River to Stockbridge. Stockbridge was "certainly the

---

[3] "Extract from an Indian History," *Massachusetts Historical Collections*, 1st series, 9 (1809), 102.
[4] Ted J. Brasser, "Mahican," in Bruce G. Trigger, ed., *Handbook of North American Indians, Vol. 15: The Northeast* (Washington, D.C.: Smithsonian Institution Press, 1978), 198–212; idem, *Riding on the Frontier's Crest* (Ottawa: National Museums of Man, Publications in Ethnology, no. 13, 1974), 23–31, 65–70; Bruce G. Trigger, "The Mohawk–Mahican War (1624–8): The Establishment of a Pattern," *Canadian Historical Review* 52 (1971), 276–86; Laurence M. Hauptman, "The Dispersal of the River Indians: Frontier Expansion and Indian Dispossession in the Hudson Valley," in Hauptman and Jack Campisi, eds., *Neighbors and Intruders: An Ethnohistorical Exploration of the Indians of Hudson's River* (Ottawa: National Museum of Man, 1978), 244–60. A Stockbridge account of their early history and decline is given in "Speech of John W. Quinney," *WHC*, vol. 4 (1859), 314–20, esp. 318.

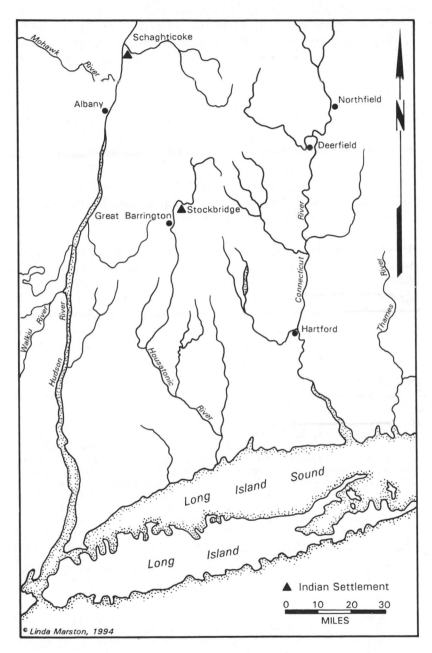

Map 5. The Stockbridge mission town in western Massachusetts.

most impressive Indian settlement in New England" by the time of the Revolution. However, the experimental community hardly fit the Puritan model of a "peaceable kingdom." As the English population grew, the newcomers crowded the Indians out, and the town became divided into Indian and English neighborhoods.[5]

Indians from Stockbridge served with the British in the French and Indian wars, notably with Robert Rogers' Rangers, and in Pontiac's War.[6] The Wappingers served in the Seven Years' War, after having moved their families (more than two hundred people) to Stockbridge, but they returned from the war to find New York landlords had taken over their land, and most of the tribe merged with the Stockbridge community.[7] The Wappinger chief Daniel Nimham complained about the encroachments made by settlers on land in western Massachusetts claimed by his people. However, in the 1760s he made common cause with small farmers squatting on the lands against the powerful Philipse family and other Hudson Valley manor lords who demanded rents from anyone living on the lands they claimed. In 1762 Nimham lodged a formal complaint against the Philipse family heirs in an effort to regain his people's land. He was granted a hearing in New York City in 1765 but was unable to find a lawyer to represent him, and his case was promptly thrown out. The next year, he traveled to London and presented his case to the Lords of Trade, who ordered New York to reconsider his cause, but Sir William Johnson declined to support Nimham, and the New York Council once more threw out the Wappinger petition. Like the small farmers known as "rent rioters" who called themselves "Sons of Liberty," Nimham and his people had real grievances against the area's landed aristocracy and their political supporters, and had real reasons for

[5] Rev. Jonathan Edwards, "Letter Relating to the Indian School at Stockbridge," *Massachusetts Historical Collections*, series 1, 10 (1809), 142–54; W. DeLoss Love, *Samson Occom and the Christian Indians of New England* (Boston: Pilgrim, 1899), 236; James Axtell, *The Invasion Within: The Contest of Cultures in Colonial North America* (New York: Oxford University Press, 1985), 196–204; Brasser, *Riding on the Frontier's Crest*, 34, 39–40; William Kellaway, *The New England Company, 1649–1776: Missionary Society to the American Indians* (New York: Barnes & Noble, 1962), 270–6; Mass. Archives, vol. 32: 258–61; Lion G. Miles, "Indian Landownership in Colonial Stockbridge, Massachusetts, 1739–1818," unpublished manuscript, Stockbridge Town Library, Historical Room, 48 et passim. A revised version of Miles's work has recently been published as "The Red Man Dispossessed: The Williams Family and the Alienation of Indian Land in Stockbridge, Massachusetts, 1736–1818," *New England Quarterly* 47 (1994), 46–76. For an account of the Mahican decision to accept the mission and its subsequent history, see Patrick Frazier, *The Mohicans of Stockbridge* (Lincoln: University of Nebraska Press, 1992), esp. chs. 1–4.

[6] Mass. Archives, vol. 32: 594–6; vol. 33: 210–11; Frazier, *Mohicans of Stockbridge*, chs. 9–10; Colin G. Calloway, *The Western Abenakis of Vermont: War Migration, and the Survival of an Indian People, 1600–1800* (Norman: University of Oklahoma Press, 1990), 175–8, 189–90; *Journals of Major Robert Rogers* (London, 1765), 26, 136; *Johnson Papers*, vol. 9: 912–13; vol. 12: 273.

[7] Brasser, *Riding on the Frontier's Crest*, 36.

fighting against the crown. For Indians and whites, the Revolution offered an opportunity to settle some old scores.[8]

The end of the French and Indian wars unleashed a flood of settlers into western Massachusetts. The Massachusetts government now had little reason to protect the interests of an Indian community it no longer needed as a buffer on its frontier. Led by Elijah Williams, a new generation of immigrants set about gaining control of the town government and excluding the Indians from town meetings. In May 1763, John Konkapot complained to the Massachusetts authorities that "Williams and a party he has made in the Town are endeavouring not only To get all the power but our Lands too into their hands." A committee appointed to investigate affairs at Stockbridge found that the traditional division of three Indian and two English selectmen had now changed to two and three, and the new English majority frequently conducted meetings without notifying the Indians. Although the center of the town remained Indian, surrounding lands continued to slip into English hands, until the Indians owned only a fraction of their original acreage. Alcohol, accumulated debts, and unscrupulous traders combined to erode Stockbridge holdings. Land transfers increased dramatically after 1765, when the General Court of Massachusetts declared that Indian lands could be used for payment of debts.[9] Viewing the rapid loss of Stockbridge Indian land and the increasing pressures upon them, the investigating committee predicted "that unless some special care be taken to guard the Indian Interest, they will in a short time become a very insignificant People."[10]

Special care was not forthcoming. In 1773, after the Indians had been obliged to sell their remaining common land in west Stockbridge, they sent a complaint to the General Court of Massachusetts. They were, they said, in "the Utmost Dificulty & Distress by Reason of the Traders who have setled Among & Near

[8]  Robert S. Grumet, "The Nimhams of the Colonial Hudson Valley, 1667–1783," *Hudson Valley Regional Review* 9 (Sept. 1992), 80–101, gathers the available information on the Nimhams, including Daniel's struggle against the Philipse family. Oscar Handlin and Irving Mark, eds., "Chief Daniel Nimham *v.* Roger Morris, Beverley Robinson, and Philip Philipse – An Indian Land Case in Colonial New York, 1765–1767," *Ethnohistory* 11 (1964), 193–246; Georgiana C. Nammack, *Fraud, Politics, and the Dispossession of the Indians: The Iroquois Land Frontier in the Colonial Period* (Norman: University of Oklahoma Press, 1969), ch. 5; Sung Bok Kim, *Landlord and Tenant in Colonial New York: Manorial Society, 1664–1775* (Chapel Hill: University of North Carolina Press, 1978), ch. 8. Mass. Archives, vol. 118: 202; Frazier, *Mohicans of Stockbridge*, chs. 12–13.

[9]  Mass. Archives, vol. 32: 61–4, 72–3, 76–8; vol. 33: 115–17, 210–11, 249–52, 265–8, 279–80, 287–8, 311–13; Miles, "Indian Landownership in Colonial Stockbridge," 25, 36–44, et passim. The Stockbridge Town Library Historical Room's "Stockbridge Indians" box contains about twenty original manuscript deeds (1738–86) with accompanying survey documentation, conveying lands from Indian proprietors to English settlers. See also Indian Proprietors Records, 1749–90, Stockbridge Town Hall.

[10]  Mass. Archives, vol. 33: 288.

us as well as other Designing People who aim at Geting Away All that The Indians are possessed of." The Court responded by ordering that no person could take legal action against the Stockbridge Indians for any debt or payment of more than 35 shillings, but it was too late.[11] Three years later the Stockbridge Indians submitted a petition to the Massachusetts House of Representatives, "praying for Reasons therein mentioned, that a Law may be passed to prevent their being sued for Debts for the Term of two Years, and that Tavern-Keepers may be restrained from selling them spiritous Liquors."[12]

On the eve of the Revolution, Indian people at Stockbridge were selling land to pay off debts and to support themselves in old age and illness.[13] As late as 1763, Indians owned more than 75 percent of the town's land, much of it still held in common; but by the end of 1774 they had given up most of it, retaining perhaps no more than 6 percent of the original. There were now more than fifty white families in Stockbridge who owned virtually all of the western part of the township. While men like Elijah Williams had grown wealthy in the process, the Indians had become ghettoized on about twelve hundred acres. In 1774 the district of West Stockbridge was separated from the town and incorporated. Timothy Woodbridge, who was "looked upon as the Patron of the Indians," died the same year.[14]

Native tradition and resident missionaries agreed that the Mahicans were held in veneration by western tribes like the Delawares and Shawnees, and the Stockbridge–Delaware connection evidently remained strong. But the Indians at Stockbridge were now a shadow of their former selves. The Rev. John Sergeant said they numbered about two hundred, while another five hundred or so, dispersed and living mainly in New York, "consider Stockbridge as their capital."[15] Ted J. Brasser estimated that, in addition to perhaps a hundred Mahicans scattered through the Hudson Valley and an unknown number in Pennsylvania, Ohio, and Indiana, the Stockbridge population stood at about three hundred in 1774, a figure that included Wappinger, Nipmuck, and Tunxis

[11] Mass. Archives, vol. 33: 574, 591–2; Miles, "Indian Landownership," 45.

[12] *Journals of the House of Representatives of Massachusetts* 51, pt. 2 (1775–6), 224 (the date of the petition is misprinted as 1777 in the *Journal*).

[13] Mass Archives, vol. 33: 543–6, 565–6.

[14] Miles, "Indian Landownership," 29–30, 45; Mass. Archives, vol. 33; 277; Daniel Mandell, "Native Persistence in an Anglo-American Commonwealth: Eighteenth Century Massachusetts," paper presented at the annual meeting of the American Historical Association, 1992.

[15] "Extract from an Indian History," 102; *PCC*, reel 93, item 78, vol. 5: 57–8; "Journal of John Sergeant [Jr.], Missionary to the Stockbridge Indians from the Society in Scotland for Propagating Christian Knowledge, from January 1804 to July 1824," manuscript and typed copy, Dartmouth College, Baker Library Special Collection, typescript p. 22; "Rev. John Ettwein's Notes of Travel from the North Branch of the Beaver River, Pennsylvania, 1772," *Pennsylvania Magazine of History and Biography* 25 (1901), 213; *American Archives* 5th series, vol. 1: 903; Harold Blodgett, *Samson Occom* (Hanover, N.H.: Dartmouth College Publications, 1935) 162; Frazier, *Mohicans of Stockbridge*, 176.

Indians who had joined the community. Meanwhile, the non-Indian population of Stockbridge was edging toward a thousand.[16]

Stockbridge continued to adjust to change on the eve of the Revolution. According to local tradition, the aged sachem at Stockbridge, Benjamin Kokewenaunaut, known as King Benjamin, resigned his office in 1771 and asked his people to choose a successor. The new sachem was Solomon Unhaunauwaunnutt or Uhhaunauwaunmut. Hereditary leadership remained with a small group of related families who were able to strengthen their positions through membership in church committees and town government.[17] Descent and inheritance continued to be matrilineal but residence patterns were no longer matrilocal. Single families now inhabited frame houses and log cabins, and the church took over the communal function of the chief's longhouse.[18] Several Stockbridge Indians had left the town and were enrolled at Dartmouth College on the eve of the Revolution; a total of eight of them would attend the school between 1771 and 1780.[19]

The Great Awakening had repercussions in the community. Rev. Dr. Stephen West, who served at the Indian mission from 1758–75, wrote to the Rev. Samuel Kirkland in 1773 that "the hand of God" was "remarkably visible" in the community, and that "the awakening increases daily, & faster than ever."[20] In addition, there was "more or less distinction between the natives and the English" in the church. In 1775, West committed the Indian portion of the congregation to John Sergeant, Jr., the son of the first minister, who had been teaching the Indian children for several years. The "Indian town" now had separate ministers for its Indian and English congregations.[21]

Neighboring Indians suffered similar experiences of dispossession, pressure from surrounding settlers, and loss of political control.[22] In 1774 Indians from seven praying towns – Charlestown, Groton, Stonington, Niantic, Farmington, Montauk, and Mohegan – removed to Brothertown, New York, because they

---

[16] Brasser, *Riding on the Frontier's Crest*, 36; Miles, "Indian Landownership," 25; Frazier, *Mohicans of Stockbridge*, 176.

[17] The names of the Indians who served as selectmen and in other positions are recorded in the Stockbridge Town Book, 1760–1825, Stockbridge Town Hall. Electa F. Jones, *Stockbridge, Past and Present; or, records of an old mission station* (Springfield Mass.: Bowles, 1854), 28, 75–6; Brasser, *Riding on the Frontier's Crest*, 39. Daniel R. Mandell, "Change and Continuity in a Native American Community: Eighteenth Century Stockbridge," M.A. thesis, University of Virginia, 1982, provides a list of Stockbridge selectmen, 1739–84, in the appendix.

[18] Brasser, *Riding on the Frontier's Crest*, 40.

[19] James Dow McCallum, ed., *Letters of Eleazar Wheelock's Indians*, (Hanover, N.H.: Dartmouth College Publications, 1932), 296–7; see also "List of Indians in the Charity School," typescript, Stockbridge Town Library, "Stockbridge Indians" box.

[20] Stephen West to Samuel Kirkland, June 25, 1773, Correspondence of Samuel Kirkland, Hamilton College, Clinton, N.Y., 42d.

[21] Love, *Samson Occom*, 236; Kellaway, *New England Company*, 276.

[22] Cf. Daniel Mandell, "'To Live More Like My Christian English Neighbors': Natick Indians in the Eighteenth Century," *William and Mary Quarterly* 48 (1991), 552–79.

no longer had enough land to live on in New England. The outbreak of the Revolution drove them back, however, and most took refuge at Stockbridge. They requested that Connecticut provide them with a teacher "as we Shall reside in the neighborhood of Stockbridge till these troubles be over."[23]

By the time of the Revolution, therefore, the Indian community had had a long and varied contact with the surrounding non-Indian population. Stockbridge had become an Indian and English township, in which town offices were shared but where the newcomers steadily deprived the original native inhabitants of their land base. The Indians were now under additional pressure from the influx of returning Christian Indians from Brothertown. As Patrick Frazier points out, the revolutionary struggle that gave birth to a new nation coincided with the Stockbridge Mahicans' struggle to survive as a nation.[24]

Stockbridge Indians volunteered as minutemen even before the outbreak of the Revolution. Thirty-five men enlisted in Captain William Goodrich's company, with Jehoiackim Mtohksin (Metoxin) as second lieutenant; others appear to have formed their own company of minutemen.[25] In February 1775 the Massachusetts Provincial Congress sent the Stockbridge Indians a message of friendship and promised a blanket and a red ribbon to every warrior who joined the service. In March the Continental Congress accepted the services the Stockbridges offered and enlisted them as minutemen, assuring them they were fighting in the common cause. Captain Solomon Uhhaunauwaunmut requested that his men be allowed to fight Indian fashion rather than train like English soldiers.[26]

Seventeen Stockbridge Indians enlisted in the Provincial army and joined Washington's troops at Cambridge in the spring of 1775. Local merchants provisioned them "on their way to ye Armie," and their arrival attracted the interest of diarists in both camps.[27] One informed General Seth Pomeroy that the Stockbridges might "be of great Service should the King's Troops march out of Boston," and believed rather unrealistically that they could also call on an additional five hundred Mohawks.[28] The Indians brought their women and

[23] Brothertown Records, 1774–1804, Hamilton College Library, Clinton, N.Y., 1–2; Love, *Samson Occom*, 222, 240–1; Connecticut State Library, Hartford, Connecticut Archives, Indian Series I, vol. 2: 193, 226, 308.

[24] Frazier, *Mohicans of Stockbridge*, 193.

[25] Sarah Cabot Sedgwick and Christina Sedgwick Marquand, *Stockbridge, 1739–1939: A Chronicle* (Great Barrington, Mass.: Berkshire Courier, 1939), 138; Love, *Samson Occom*, 222; Deirdre Almeida, "The Stockbridge Indians in the American Revolution," *Historical Journal of Western Massachusetts* 4 (Fall 1975), 36. Frazier, *Mohicans of Stockbridge*, chs. 16–18, provides a narrative of Stockbridge participation in the Revolutionary War.

[26] *American Archives*, 4th series, vol. 1: 1347; 5th series, vol. 2: 315–16, 476.

[27] Stephen Noble: Bill to Massachusetts for Feeding Stockbridge Indian Troops, Dec. 26 1775, Boston public Library, Ms. G 38.16; [Joseph Merriam] Diary of an (unknown) soldier at Cambridge, 1775. Boston Public Library, Ms. Ch. B. 12. 72; *Diary of Frederick Mackenzie*, 2 vols. (Cambridge, Mass.: Harvard University Press, 1930), vol. 1: 32.

[28] Thomas Allen to Gen. Seth Pomeroy, May 9, 1775, Boston Public Library, Ms. Ch. E. 7.32; *Remembrancer*, 1775: 66.

children along with them, and asked their allies to curtail the amount of liquor available to them so "that we may get so much as will be good for us and no more." Acknowledging their "aptness to drink spiritous liquors to excess when we are under temptation," they wanted to avoid rendering themselves "unfit for usefulness and service to our fellow-men, and also disagreeable to those that have anything to do with us."[29]

According to the English New England Company, which saw its charges slipping away, the Stockbridge Indians had been brought to Boston when the British naval vessels were there "on purpose to insult them, and were taught, by turning up their backsides, to express their defiance of them."[30] The Stockbridge presence in the patriot army gave the British the excuse they needed for employing Indian support elsewhere. General Gage, writing from Boston to southern Indian Department superintendent John Stuart in September 1775, declared, "The Rebells have themselves open'd the Door; they have brought down all the Savages they could against us here, who with their Rifle men are continually firing on our advanced Sentries."[31]

Initially, the Stockbridges' most important services were diplomatic rather than military. In April, Captain Solomon, "after sitting near two days in Council," responded to a message sent him by Congress. "I am sorry to hear of this great quarrel between you and Old *England*," he said. "It appears that blood must be shed to end this quarrel. We never till this day understood the foundation of this quarrel between you and the Country you came from." He offered "to take a run to the Westward, and feel the minds of my *Indian* brothers, the *Six Nations*," arguing that he could do the American cause more good as an ambassador to the Iroquois than by marching off immediately to Boston.[32] In a rather insidious attempt to engage the Indians in the fighting, Massachusetts invited the Stockbridges to send "any of your warriors who wish to see what our army is doing."[33] That spring Abraham Nimham and two other Stockbridges went as emissaries to the tribes around Montreal, carrying a message from Ethan Allen, and a speech of their own urging neutrality. British regulars arrested the messengers and took them to Montreal, where they were sentenced to be hanged. The Caughnawagas protested angrily and the Stockbridges were released. Returning to Caughnawaga, they delivered their speech: "Now I think

[29] *American Archives*, 4th series, vol, 2: 1049; Stockbridge Indians to Joseph Warren, June 21, 1775, American Antiquarian Society, U.S. Revolution Collection.
[30] Quoted in Kellaway, *New England Company*, 280.
[31] *DAR*, vol. 11: 56; LC, C.O. 5/76: 195; Clements Library, Clinton Papers, vol. 11: 8.
[32] *American Archives*, 4th series, vol. 2: 315–16; Mass. Archives, vol. 33: 629–30. Unhaunauwaunnutt petitioned and received compensation "for Services performed in consequence of a Letter he received from the Provincial Congress." *Journal of the House of Representatives of Massachusetts* 51, pt. 1: 122; *Acts and Resolves of the Province of Massachusetts Bay* 19 (1775–6), 89.
[33] LC, Force Transcripts, Massachusetts Committees, reel 20, item 81: 4; Mass. Archives, vol. 144: 309–10.

'tis the best way for you and I to sit down, and smoak our Pipes, under the Shade of our great Tree, and have our Ears open and see our Brethren fight." The Caughnawagas agreed.[34]

At the Treaty of Albany, held with the Six Nations in August and September 1775, Captain Solomon assured the American commissioners of his people's commitment to the patriot cause: "Wherever you go we will be by your Side Our Bones shall lay with yours. We are determined never to be at peace with the Red Coats while they are at Variance with you. . . . If we are conquered our Lands go with yours, but if we are victorious we hope you will help us to recover our just Rights."[35] The Mohawks warned the Stockbridges against taking up the hatchet, but the Stockbridges asserted their independence and ignored the Mohawks' advice. "If any ill Consequences should follow, you must conclude you have brought it on yourselves, and that it is your own fault," responded the Mohawks.[36]

The Indian commissioners for the northern department recommended that Indian companies be raised, and addressed the arrangements for raising the Stockbridge company. One of the commissioners, Timothy Edwards, who lived at Stockbridge, was to work with the town committee and appoint suitable white men as officers for the Stockbridge company.[37] The Continental Congress hesitated to employ the Indians, and at one point ordered that arrangements for raising them be terminated, which caused the Stockbridges some uneasiness. But finally, on August 2, 1776, Congress authorized Washington to employ the Stockbridges if he thought proper, and to engage them either with his or the northern army, or both.[38] The Stockbridges were issued with red and blue caps to distinguish them from enemy Indians.[39]

In the fall, two Stockbridge Mahicans, in the pay of the Americans, went as delegates to the Delawares and Shawnees at the treaty council being held at Fort Pitt. In doing so, they were employing long-standing diplomatic avenues and continuing what was apparently a traditional Mahican role in dealing with the tribes of the Ohio and Great Lakes country. "It was the business of our fathers," said Hendrick Aupaumut, "to go around the towns of these nations to renew the agreements between them and tell them many things which they

[34] *American Archives*, 4th series, vol. 2: 714, 1002–3, 1060–1; *Minutes of the Albany Committee of Correspondence*, vol. 1: 129–32; *DAR*, vol. 9: 142–3; *PCC*, reel 172, item 153, vol. 1: 176.

[35] *PCC*, reel 144, item 134: 43; *NYCD*, vol. 8: 626.

[36] "Abraham's reply to the Stockbridge Indians" [in council at Johnstown, May 21–6, 1776], NYPL, Schuyler Papers, reel 7, box 13.

[37] "At a meeting of the Commissioners for transacting Indian Affairs for the Northern Department held at Albany, 13 June 1776," Schuyler Papers, reel 7, box 13.

[38] *PCC*, reel 23, item 12A, vol. 1: 196; vol. 2: 14; reel 166, item 152, vol. 2: 313–16; Washington C. Ford and Gaillard Hunt, eds., *Journals of the Continental Congress, 1774–1789*, 34 vols. (Washington: Government Printing Office, 1904–37), vol. 5 (1776): 627, 473; *American Archives*, 5th series, vol. 1: 676, 725.

[39] *PCC*, reel 166, item 152, vol. 2: 363; *American Archives*, 5th series, vol. 2: 476.

discover among the white people in the east, &c."⁴⁰ "I am not come here for nothing," declared the Stockbridge speaker. "I am come to see you, & tell you what has been done in our quarter." He proceeded to relate how the king of England, "who formerly called us his Children," now "abused us, sold us, & gave our Lands to those who would conquer us." While the Shawnees and Delawares, the supposed terrors of the Ohio frontier, clung to a precarious neutrality, the Christian Stockbridges preached war and presented the western tribes with a war belt and tomahawk:

> When I maturely considered & fully understood what this Great King was going to do to us, & what Business he had sent his Warriors on to this Big Island, I put him aside, I denied his authority, fire rose in my face, I took up my Hatchet, . . . I now bring it to you: my friends must take hold of it, & rise up against the Red Coats that they may not do as they please with this Big Island; they began this mischief, they have got proud & haughty, let us humble them; my Tomahawk is sharp and already stained with their Blood.

Rather than be drawn into war, the Delawares invited the Mahicans to remove from the overcrowded and war-torn east and settle in Delaware country.⁴¹

John Sergeant summed up his charges' services in a November memorial to Congress:

> Far from desiring to remain neuter in the dispute between *Great-Britain* and *America*, they have made themselves acquainted with the merits of the controversy, and have taken an active part in our favor, inlisting [*sic*] their young men in our Army, while their counsellors and sachems have carefully sent belts of wampum by their messengers to the *Six Nations*, to the *Canada Indians*, and to the *Shauwanese*, on the *Ohio*, addressing them in such terms as they judged would have the greatest tendency to attach them to the interests of the *United States*.

Sergeant's purpose was to secure congressional assistance now that his stipend from England had been cut off, and he naturally stressed the importance of the Stockbridge contribution and his own role as the crucial link with the community. Congress evidently was unimpressed and unwilling to assume financial

---

⁴⁰ *American Archives*, 5th series, vol. 2: 87; B. H. Coates, ed., "Narrative of an Embassy to the Western Indians from the original manuscript of Hendrick Aupaumut," *Memoirs of the Historical Society of Pennsylvania*, vol. 2, pt. 1 (1827), 77–8; also *American Archives*, 5th series, vol. 1: 903.

⁴¹ "Speech of 2 Mahicans from Stockbridge to the Delawares & Shawnees at the Fort Pitt Council, Oct.–Nov. 1776, and White Eyes' speech," Nov. 5, 1776, George Morgan Letterbook, 1776, Pennsylvania Historical and Museum Commission, 37–8, 47; also in Francis Jennings, William N. Fenton, et al., eds., *Iroquois Indians: A Documentary History of the Diplomacy of the Six Nations and Their League*, 50 reels (Woodbridge, Conn.; Research Publications, 1985), reel 32, reprinted in *Revolution and Confederation*, 136–7, 141–2.

responsibility for the mission now that the New England Company had withdrawn its support.[42]

As the war progressed, Stockbridge warriors served in New York, New Jersey, and Canada.[43] They earned a reputation for zealous service in the patriot cause.[44] Captain Ezra Whitney's Stockbridge company served with the garrison at Ticonderoga, and several Stockbridges fell into British hands along with other sailors from Benedict Arnold's fleet after the defeat at Valcour Bay in 1776. When Carleton's Indian allies found the Stockbridges in irons, the British expected they would want to kill them. Instead, Carleton's warriors treated the Stockbridges kindly and arranged for their release. It was reported that they made a private agreement to return to Canada if the Stockbridges would also return home, so that Indians could avoid killing Indians in a white man's war.[45] Stockbridge Indians reenlisted in 1777 and served with Horatio Gates's army against Burgoyne in the operations around Saratoga, although most of the warriors returned home to help with the harvest before the British general surrendered.[46]

Meanwhile, Abraham Nimham traveled to Philadelphia to petition Congress that he and his companions be employed and supplied with clothing while on service. Congress assigned them to Gates's army and paid them $200.[47] Once with Gates's army, Nimham asked the general to discharge Stockbridge Indians who had enlisted in different regiments in the Continental Army and allow them all to serve in one company. "Do not think that I want get these Indians away from their Soldiering," Nimham told Gates, "but we want be together always & we will always ready to go any where you wanted us to go long as this war stands &c."[48]

The Stockbridges served with Gates's army at White Plains in the summer of 1778 as the British and Americans sparred around New York City. On August 31, the Stockbridge contingent was cut to pieces in a vicious skirmish at Kingsbridge or Indian Field, in what is now Van Cortlandt Park in the north Bronx. Caught front and rear by the British cavalry and infantry, they fought

[42] *American Archives*, 5th series, vol. 3: 868–9; Ford and Hunt, eds., *Journals of the Continental Congress* 6 (1776): 984. In fact, the New England Company did make a payment to Sergeant as late as May 1783, in spite of its earlier resolutions to suspend support of missionaries and schoolteachers in America. Kellaway, *New England Company*, 277–8.

[43] *American Archives*, 4th series, vol. 4: 1481; 5th series, vol. 1: 189; vol. 2: 1120.

[44] *PCC*, reel 55, item 42, vol. 5: 451; Ford and Hunt, eds., *Journals of the Continental Congress*, vol. 9 (1777): 840; *Horatio Gates Papers, 1726–1828* (New York: Microfilming Corporation of America, 1978), vol. 6: 720.

[45] Paul L. Stevens, "His Majesty's 'Savage' Allies," Ph.D. dissertation SUNY Buffalo, 1984, 807, 2136–7, n. 31.

[46] Walter Hill Crockett, *Vermont: The Green Mountain State*, 5 vols. (New York: Century History, 1921), vol. 2: 122; Frazier, *Mohicans of Stockbridge*, 215.

[47] *PCC*, reel 55, item 42, vol. 5: 451; Ford and Hunt, eds., *Journals of the Continental Congress*, vol. 9 (1777): 840.

[48] *Gates Papers*, vol. 6: 720.

gallantly, even pulling riders from their horses, but the ambush was a disaster for Stockbridge. "They fell into our hands completely," recalled a Loyalist officer of the Queen's Rangers. Daniel Nimham, who had joined his son Abraham's command, was reported to have called on his people to fly, "that he himself was old, and would die there." "No Indians, especially, received quarter, including their chief called Nimham and his son, save for a few," a Hessian officer noted in his diary. "The chief, his son, and the common warriors were killed on the spot," reported another. Estimates of the Indian casualties ranged from nineteen missing to almost forty killed "or desperately wounded."[49] A list of Stockbridge Indians killed in battle, subsequently submitted to Congress, gave the names of seventeen dead, besides a number of others who died of illnesses sustained while on campaign.[50]

After the skirmish, Lieutenant General Johann Von Ewald of the Schleswig Jäger Corps went over the field and examined the dead Indians, whose "strong, well built, and healthy bodies" stood out from those of the Europeans, "with whom they lay mingled on the ground." Ewald's description of the fallen Stockbridge warriors, indicates a substantial degree of traditional cultural survival after almost half a century of mission life (Fig. 2):

> Their costume was a shirt of coarse linen down to the knees, long trousers also of linen down to the feet, on which they wore shoes of deerskin, and the head was covered with a hat made of bast.[51] Their weapons were a rifle or musket, a quiver with some twenty arrows, and a short battle-axe which they know how to throw very skillfully. Through the nose and in the ears they wore rings, and on their heads only the hair of the crown remained standing in a circle the size of a dollar-piece, the remainder being shaved off bare. They pull out with pincers all the hairs of the beard, as well as those on all other parts of the body.[52]

[49] J. G. Simcoe, *Simcoe's Military Journal: A History of the Operations of a Partisan Corps, called The Queen's Rangers* (New York: Bartlett & Welford, 1844), 81, 85–6; James J. Talman, ed., *Loyalist Narratives from Upper Canada* (Toronto: Champlain Society, 1946), 165; Duke University, Perkins Library, Thomas Stinson Jarvis Papers: "Sketches of the Military and Civil Life of Stephen Jarvis . . . 1775–1828," 14; Bernard A Uhlendorf, trans. and ed., *Revolution in America: Confidential Letters and Journals, 1776–1784 of Adjutant General Baurmeister of the Hessian Forces* (Westport, Conn.: Greenwood, 1973 reprint), 205; Joseph P. Tustin, ed., *Diary of the American War, A Hessian Journal: Captain Johann Ewald, Field Jager Corps* (New Haven, Conn: Yale University Press, 1979), 145; Hugh Hastings, ed., *Public Papers of Governor George Clinton*, 10 vols. (Albany: State of New York, 1899–1914), vol. 3: 726–7; Thomas F. De Voe, "The Massacre of the Stockbridge Indians, 1778," *Magazine of American History* 5 (1880), 187–95; Frazier, *Mohicans of Stockbridge*, 221–4. Abraham Nimham was actually the commander of the Stockbridge contingent; his father joined the command prior to the battle. Thanks to Robert Grumet for this.

[50] Massachusetts Historical Society, Timothy Pickering Papers, reel 62: 167. Frazier, *Mohicans of Stockbridge*, 223–5, discusses Stockbridge casualties in the battle and the war.

[51] Matting or cordage made of the inner bark of basswood.

[52] Tustin, trans. and ed., *Hessian Journal*, 145.

Figure 2. Sketch of a Stockbridge Indian serving with the American army. From Joseph P. Tustin, trans. and ed., *Diary of the American War: A Hessian Journal, by Captain Johann Ewald, Field Jager Corps.* (New Haven, Conn.: Yale University Press, 1979). By permission of Yale University Press.

The surviving Stockbridge soldiers requested blankets, coats and money, and returned home, but they remained in dire straits. They petitioned the General Court of Massachusetts for assistance for five widows of men killed in the August battle, "who were without help from their Husbands, who at this season of the year provided for their families by hunting." While the town of Stockbridge met its quotas of food and clothing for the war effort, the Indians complained that "by this War we cant find Cloathing as we use[d] to." John Sergeant echoed their request and in January 1779 Massachusetts directed the Board of War to furnish the minister with twenty blankets for the Stockbridges, "five of which he is to deliver as a donation to five widows of the said tribe, whose husbands were lately slain by the enemy near White Plains"; the rest Sergeant was to distribute to those in greatest need.[53] A year later, however, the people were still suffering: Joseph Shauquethqueat and other Stockbridges sent a petition to the Massachusetts House of Representatives, "praying that some Way be provided by which they may be enabled to procure Cloathing."[54]

Despite the slaughter of their warriors at Kingsbridge, and despite persistent hardships at home, thirty-two Stockbridges volunteered to take part in John Sullivan's expedition against the Iroquois later that year. Washington authorized their employment, although he stipulated they were not to receive more than a private's pay except where it was necessary to distinguish the chief by "some little pecuniary."[55]

With Abraham Nimham dead, Washington promoted Hendrick Aupaumut to be captain of the survivors. In 1780, Aupaumut and thirty warriors served in Washington's army. Aupaumut had enlisted in the Stockbridge company in 1775 at eighteen years of age. He consistently supported the American cause during the Revolution, acted as a peace ambassador from the United States to the western tribes in the 1790s, and opposed Tecumseh's Indian confederacy in the first decade of the nineteenth century.[56]

Writing to Congress in September 1780, Washington reported that twenty Stockbridges had been serving as volunteers since the beginning of July. They had generally been attached to the light infantry "& have conducted themselves with great propriety and fidelity." Seeing no immediate prospect of action, the

[53] Mass. Archives, vol. 144: 413–14; "List of Articles sent to Distressed Stockbridge Indians," *American Archives*, 5th series, vol. 3: 443; *Journals of the House of Representatives of Massachusetts* 53, pt. 1 (June 16, 1777); *Acts and Resolves of the Province of Massachusetts Bay* 20 (1777–8), 35, 549.
[54] *Journals of the House of Representatives of Massachusetts*, vol. 54: 90, 93.
[55] *Writings of Washington*, vol. 15: 286–7, 367–8; vol. 20: 44–5; *PCC*, reel 170, item 152, vol. 9: 165–6.
[56] Massachusetts Historical Society, Pickering Papers, reel 62: 167A; Jeanne and James P. Ronda, " 'As They Were Faithful': Chief Hendrick Aupaumut and the Struggle for Stockbridge Survival, 1757–1830," *American Indian Culture and Research Journal* 3 (1979), 43–55; Coates, ed., "Embassy to the Western Indians."

Indians wanted to return home and requested some financial compensation for the time they had been with the army. Washington thought it best to gratify their wishes as he had no clothing to give them.[57] The United States's inability to supply its Indian allies with clothing also limited its ability to exploit the Stockbridges' traditional influence among other tribes. By 1781 the patience and neutrality of the Delawares was finally snapping, and Daniel Brodhead, commanding at Fort Pitt, hoped that sending a few Stockbridges there "would make a material change in the Councils of the Western Tribes." But since the Americans' failure to supply the Delawares had been a material factor in the loss of Delaware allegiance, Brodhead cautioned that the Stockbridge emissaries "ought to come in good Clothing."[58]

As the war drew to its close, the Stockbridges continued to offer their services. But Washington now politely declined, saying their help was not needed, but complaining in private that "their services never compensated the expense."[59] In mid-1782, Joseph Chew, the British secretary for Indian Affairs, received word that the Stockbridges were back home and that if the British sent them a message forgiving their past behavior, they would "remain at home, attend to their own affairs, and have nothing more to do with the Rebels notwithstanding Mr. Kirkland's endeavours to keep them in their service."[60]

The victory they had fought and bled for brought little benefit to the Stockbridge Indians. The home community had suffered considerable hardship during the war years. Impoverished widows, left with their husbands' debts, continued to sell off lands even as Stockbridge men were away fighting for the American cause.[61] Not only did the Stockbridges lose leaders in battle, but Solomon Uhhaunauwaunmut died in February 1777. The government then is said to have devolved on Joseph Quanaukaunt or Quinney, who shared it with Hendrick Aupaumut and councilors Peter Pauquanaupeet and John Konkapot, both Dartmouth graduates.[62] Moreover, whites had taken over the local government by the end of the Revolution. The town records, which had previously listed Indian and white selectmen alike by name only, in 1783 identified Hendrick Aupaumut and Johaickim Naunauphtook as "Indian Selectmen," indicative that Indian participation was declining. There were no Indian selectmen by 1784.[63]

Education of the Stockbridge children continued during the war – Daniel Simon, a Narragansett Indian and Dartmouth graduate, was teaching there in 1778 with classes of between thirty and fifty students, and John Konkapot

[57] *Writings of Washington*, vol. 20: 44–5; *PCC*, reel 170, item 152, vol. 9: 165–6.
[58] *PCC*, 92, item 78, vol. 4: 133.
[59] *PCC*, reel 50, item 41, vol. 4: 422; *Writings of Washington*, vol. 23: 75, 80–1.
[60] HMC, *Report on American Manuscripts*, vol. 3: 9.
[61] Mass. Archives, vol. 144: 460–1.
[62] Jones, *Stockbridge, Past and Present*, 28, 75; Love, *Samson Occom*, 239; Brasser, "Mahican," 209.
[63] Stockbridge Town Book, 1760–1825, Stockbridge Town Hall, 164.

taught there after he returned from the war – but funds were short and Konkapot was obliged to petition the Massachusetts government for pay.[64] Many of the young men did not return from the war, and "idleness and intemperance increased" among the survivors.[65] A large proportion of widows and orphans were left without support, and marriage outside the community presumably increased, although the Stockbridges were said to be "mostly pure" in 1796.[66]

Encroachments on Stockbridge land continued, and the people were reduced to petitioning their former allies for land and relief. Congress referred the Stockbridges' petition to the legislature of New York. In February 1782, Stockbridges addressed petitions to the governments of both New York and Vermont, reminding them that they had seen their lands slip away from them without payment, and requesting grants of land in reward for their services in the war. The Stockbridge claims encompassed land from the Hudson River, Wood Creek, and Lake Champlain to the mouth of Otter Creek, which, they pointed out, they had never sold or given to New York. Joseph Shauquethqucat reminded his "Brothers of the Great Green Mountains" that "We and our fathers were once the rightful possessor of all your Country," but had diminished in numbers "until we are become very small." In a second petition in March 1782, the Stockbridges said Vermont first offered them a tract of land west of Ticonderoga which, it turned out, Vermont did not own; then offered them a township near Canada; and finally refused to give them any land at all. The Stockbridges did not believe they could be treated that way by people for whom they had fought and suffered. They subsequently sold their Vermont claim grant to Isaac Marsh, a tavern keeper from Stockbridge, who founded the town of Marshfield.[67]

When relief came, it came from fellow Indian patriots. In 1783 Stockbridge chiefs accepted an offer of land from the Oneidas, who also had suffered heavily during the war for their commitment to the patriot cause. Close connections seem to have developed between the two tribes: when Oneidas moved from their country to take refuge near Albany in 1780, some went to "the vicinity of Stockbridge." When the Brothertown Indians returned to Oneida country in 1783, several Stockbridge chiefs accompanied them. The Stockbridges held

[64] McCallum, ed., *Letters of Eleazar Wheelock's Indians*, 224; "Petition of John Konkapot," June 7, 1781, LC, Force Manuscripts, Massachusetts Committees, reel 20, item 81.5; Mass. Archives, vol. 144: 476.

[65] *Massachusetts Historical Collections*, 1st series, 4 (1795), 69. A list of Stockbridge warriors killed in battle during the Revolution is given in Massachusetts Historical Society, Pickering Papers, reel 62: 167.

[66] Love, *Samson Occom*, 238; *Massachusetts Historical Collections*, 1st series, 5 (1798), 13.

[67] Vermont State Archives, Manuscript Vermont State Papers, vol. 22: 26–7; E. P. Walton, ed., *Records of the Governor and Council of the State of Vermont*, 8 vols. (Montpelier: Poland, 1813–80), vol. 2: 127–8; vol. 3: 180, 200; vol. 5: 82; *PCC*, reel 24, item 16: 144; reel 37, item 30: 355; reel 50, item 41, vol. 4: 435; reel 73, item 59, vol. 3: 211–12; Frazier, *Mohicans of Stockbridge*, 234–7; Verne R. Hudson, "The Naming of Marshfield, Vermont," *Vermont History* 23 (1955), 56–7.

council with the Oneidas, received the promise of a tract of land six miles square, and returned home to prepare their people to move.[68] In a petition to the Massachusetts government, they declared:

> In this late War we have suffered much, our Blood has been spilled with yours and many of our Young Men have fallen by the Side of your Warriors, almost all those Places where your Warriors have left their Bones, there our Bones are seen also. Now we who remain are become very poor. Now Brothers. We will let you know we have been invited by our Brothers the Oniadas, to go and live with them. We have accepted their invitation.

They asked Massachusetts to appoint "a few of our Neighbors, whom we believe to be our Friends to have Power to take Care of the little Interest of Land we have in this Town" and to examine all their past land sales to white people to make sure "that we hant been cheated."[69] Tunxis "& other poor Indians formerly of Connecticut," who had gone to Oneida in 1774 and been driven away by the Revolution "to sojourn where they could find a Place" among the Stockbridges, also requested assistance from the Connecticut General Assembly to return to Oneida. There, "instead of being further burdensome, we hope to be of some advantage to the United States."[70]

George Washington furnished the Stockbridges with a certificate attesting that during the war "the aforesaid Muhheekunnuk Tribe of Indians have remained firmly attached to us and have fought and bled by our side; That we consider them as friends and Brothers," and recommending the Indian and non-Indian inhabitants of the western country to treat them as friends and subjects of the United States.[71] Most of the young men went out to the Oneida country in the spring of 1784 to plant and make other preparations for the women and children to follow; the majority of the Stockbridges had migrated west to their new lands by 1785.[72] About forty people, mainly of the Konkapot and Mtohksin families, stayed behind until the spring of 1788, leaving after Shay's Rebellion brought additional disruption in western Massachusetts. Stockbridge-style decorated splint baskets continued to be made there in the years after the Revolution, but most of the Stockbridge people were gone.[73]

---

[68] Love, *Samson Occom*, 244–5.
[69] Copy of a petition from Stockbridge Indians, Sept. 2, 1783, Stockbridge Library Historical Room, "Stockbridge Indians" box, m.73–130 (1).
[70] Connecticut State Archives, Hartford. Connecticut Archives: Indian Series 1, vol. 2: 227a.
[71] *Writings of Washington*, vol. 27: 53; see also "Proclamation by George Washington, July 1783," Connecticut Historical Society, Hartford, microfilm 80010: 266.
[72] Kirkland to James Bowdoin, March 10, 1784, Samuel Kirkland Papers, Hamilton College, 85c.
[73] Brasser, *Riding on the Frontier's Crest*, 40; Frazier, *Mohicans of Stockbridge*, 243; Ann McMullen, "Native Basketry, Basketry Styles, and Changing Group Identity in Southern New England," *Annual Proceedings* of the Dublin Seminar for New England Folklife, 1991 (Boston University, 1994), 84.

The Revolution inflicted the coup de grâce on the Indian town at Stockbridge. The last Indian land in West Stockbridge was sold in 1783; the last Indian proprietors' meeting was held in Stockbridge in February 1785. Only a handful of people remained, engulfed by a soaring non-Indian population. The population of Berkshire County reached almost twenty-five thousand by the end of the Revolution, that of the town passed thirteen hundred by 1790. In 1809 the Indians granted to Dr. Oliver Partridge, for $10 in services rendered, the Indian burial ground, on condition that "the bones of our Ancestors may lie there undisturbed."[74]

The main thread of the Stockbridge story in the revolutionary era now shifted to New Stockbridge in New York and became closely entwined with that of the Oneidas. Samuel Kirkland said in 1784 that the Oneidas expected more than a thousand Indians to move to their country in the course of the next two years.[75] By the time the Mohegan preacher Samson Occom arrived in New Stockbridge in 1787, "there was a vast concourse of People of many Nations" there, speaking as many as ten different languages.[76] Kirkland and Occom both found New Stockbridge to be an orderly and pious community, and contrasted it with Oneida. Writing to his wife in 1785, Kirkland feared his Oneida charges had sunk to new lows, whereas their New Stockbridge neighbors displayed "order, sobriety, love & kindness."[77]

Kirkland's comments may have been more than just self-serving missionary declarations. The Stockbridges seem to have made every effort to recreate "a stable community, modeled after a regular rural American village." War and migration had taken a heavy toll on the Stockbridge community, but it does seem that they were able to avoid, for a time at least, some of the extreme manifestations of dysfunctionalism apparent in other displaced communities. Membership in a church community, combined with the continuing influence of hereditary leaders and the principal women, helped to keep the people together. The hereditary leaders and women tended to be most active in the church and so, as Ted Brasser observes, their influence "reached the people both through the traditional channels of lineage and clan, as well as through the church and its related organizations."[78]

After the war, the United States dictated treaties to tribes that had sided with the British, exacting huge land cessions as the price of peace. The government assured its former Indian allies that *their* lands would be protected, but this proved not to be the case. The country of the Oneidas, to which most

[74] Miles, "Indian Landownership," 25, 47; Frazier, *Mohicans of Stockbridge*, 238. The burial ground now lies at the edge of a golf course.
[75] Love, *Samson Occom*, 244; Kirkland to Bowdoin, March 10, 1784, Kirkland Papers, 85c.
[76] Blodgett, *Samson Occom*, 195.
[77] Samuel Kirkland to Jerusha Kirkland, Sept. 10, 1785, Kirkland Papers, 97b.
[78] Brasser, *Riding on the Frontier's Crest*, 41, 45–6.

Stockbridges had moved, was soon up for grabs as the federal and state governments, local settlers, and a variety of private companies and land speculators competed to get control of the lands of their former allies.[79]

At the treaty conference held at Fort Herkimer in June 1785 between the state of New York and the Oneidas and Tuscaroras, the Oneida sachem Good Peter asked Governor Clinton to help "our younger Brethren," the Stockbridges: "They have Claims to the Eastward, altho' their Lands are all gone, & they know not how."[80] In 1785 four Stockbridge chiefs visited Congress, but Congress passed the buck to Massachusetts and dismissed the chiefs with "some presents, covering according to the indian custom, the bones of those who have been killed in the war with shrouds, blankets or cloathing to be delivered to the widows or families of the deceased; the amount of the whole not to exceed 100 dollars."[81] In that year the Stockbridge population at New Stockbridge numbered 450.[82]

Two years later, after a harvest failure in which the Indians' wheat was "blasted," and frost killed their corn and bean crops, Samson Occom, David Fowler of Brothertown, and Peter Pauquanaupeet of New Stockbridge embarked on a fundraising tour. "The late unhappy wars have Stript us almost Naked of every thing," they said, "our Temporal enjoyments are greatly lessened, our Numbers vastly diminished, by being warmly engaged in favour of the United States Tho' we had no immediate Business with it. . . . we are truly like the man that fell among Thieves, that was Stript, wounded and left for dead in the high way."[83]

New York land speculator John Livingston cited the Stockbridge experience as a warning of what the Oneidas could expect: "You see how the Stockbridge Indians are served," he told them in 1788. "They have lost their Lands and are obliged to beat Sticks along the Rivers into Brooms."[84] At the Treaty of Fort Schuyler in September 1788, the Oneidas, while ceding lands of their own to New York, stipulated that their neighbors at Brothertown and New Stockbridge were to enjoy their settlements forever.[85]

The Oneidas, Tuscaroras, and Stockbridges continued for years to petition Congress for compensation for the losses they had sustained while serving in

[79] J. David Lehman, "The End of the Iroquois Mystique: The Oneida Land Cession Treaties of the 1780s," *William and Mary Quarterly* 3d series, 48 (1990), 524–47.

[80] Franklin B. Hough, ed., *Proceedings of the Commissioners of Indian Affairs Appointed by Law for the Extinguishment of Indian Titles in the State of New York* (Albany, N.Y.: Munsell, 1861), 93.

[81] Ford and Hunt, eds., *Journals of the Continental Congress*, vol. 29 (1785): 688–9.

[82] Love, *Samson Occom*, 245. Cf. a population estimate compiled from information supplied by Iroquois chiefs at the Treaty of Canandaigua in 1794, which gave the number of Stockbridge Indians living in Oneida country as 315; Pickering Papers, reel 62: 250.

[83] Quoted in Love, *Samson Occom*, 276.

[84] Hough, ed., *Proceedings of the Commissioners*, 147.

[85] Love, *Samson Occom*, 245; *Revolution and Confederation*, 472–5.

the patriot cause, and urged the United States to honor promises made to them at the end of the war. They submitted statements of their services as well as itemized lists of their losses, and requested financial assistance in rebuilding churches and sawmills. In 1792, for example, Hendrick Aupaumut requested from Congress a yoke of oxen, a yoke of steers, an ox cart, a plow, a harrow, three chains, and a grindstone, estimated at $120, for the Stockbridge community in compensation for their "steady attachment & suffering in the cause of the U States"; a further $80 for the poor families, widows, and children; and an additional $142 for himself in payment for his services in carrying a message of peace to the western Indians.[86]

Aupaumut undertook his peace embassy at a time when claims for past grievances and services remained unsettled. Recalling his speeches to the western tribes he declared:

> In all my arguments with these Indians, I have as it were oblige to say nothing with regard to the conduct of Yorkers, how they cheat my fathers, how they taken our lands Unjustly, and how my fathers were groaning as it were in their graves, in loseing their lands for nothing, although they were faithful friends to the Whites; and how the white people artfully got their Deeds confirm in their Laws, &c. I say had I mention these things to the Indians, it would agravate their prejudices against all white people, &c.[87]

The small amount of compensation that the Stockbridges did receive caused resentment among the Oneidas and fueled growing divisions among the Stockbridges themselves. In 1792, Congress granted the Oneidas an annuity of $148, but granted $200 (the amount requested by Aupaumut) to the Stockbridges. Samuel Kirkland said the Oneidas were mortified to receive less money than the Stockbridges "whom they consider a small & unimportant people." Moreover, there was "much disputing & ill blood" among the Stockbridges themselves about how the money should be divided. Since Samson Occom arrived at New Stockbridge as minister in 1787, there had been religious divisions among the people. John Konkapot and one party preferred their old pastor, John Sergeant; Aupaumut and the other party supported Occom. Rival churches formed, mirroring the emergence of what Brasser terms "White-oriented" and "Indian-oriented" factions. According to Kirkland, Occom's faction tried to control the money and keep everyone else in the dark, but the rest of the people stepped in and put the money into the hands of "their proper chiefs." Aupaumut had changed considerably since he returned from the West, noted Kirkland: he was

---

[86] Massachusetts Historical Society, Pickering Papers, vol. 62: 32–33A, 174, 197, 237, 248, et passim; also Kirkland Papers, 148 (May 1792 file).

[87] Coates, ed., "Embassy to the Western Indians," 128. The original narrative of Aupaumut's embassy is in Pickering Papers, reel 59.

now much less friendly and had taken to drink. Kirkland suspected he had fallen under the influence of Joseph Brant during his trip.[88] Divisions in the community reached such a point that Peter Pauquanaupeet seems to have been poisoned by members of an opposing faction.[89]

Others in the community continued to seek what was due to them for their efforts in the Revolution. In May 1794, Abraham Konkapot, Isaac Wanaumpey, and Andrew Waumauhewey or Mavwehv petitioned Massachusetts for "our just wages." Nimham had taken the three soldiers out of their original company on Washington's orders, and they had served under their chief until he was killed in the battle near White Plains. After the war, they had applied for their pay before they left Stockbridge, "but to our great surprise found we were returned deserters." Only after much trouble and expense were they able to obtain a certificate "that we were honest men."[90]

*treaty (1795)*

In 1795 the United States concluded a treaty with the Oneidas, Tuscaroras, and Stockbridges. The Indians dropped their claims in return for a sawmill and a gristmill, training in use of both, $1,000 to build a church at Oneida, and $5,000 to be distributed among the Oneidas "as well as some very few meritorious persons of the Stockbridge Indians." Payment of the $5,000, said the Americans, should convince the Indians of how much the United States had done for them and that the tribes had done the right thing in supporting the American cause. "Remember, they have paid all your demands, when many thousands of your white Brethren, who lost all their property in the same War, have not received anything in return," said one of the commissioners.[91]

*cont'd pressure of Indian lands in NY*

But the pressure on Indian lands in New York continued unabated. In 1818, John Mtohksin led about seventy-five Stockbridges west to new homes on the White River in Indiana. From there they continued to petition the government for protection, reminding President Monroe in 1819 that they had sent their warriors "to join your great chief, Washington, to aid him in driving back into the sea the unnatural monsters who had come up from thence to devour you, and ravage the land which we a long time before granted to your fathers to live on."[92] The United States in 1819 had little interest in remembering the sacrifices made by a small tribe in helping to secure the Revolution. In 1822, another

---

[88] Kirkland to Timothy Pickering, May 31, 1792 and June 5, 1792, Kirkland Papers, 148j, 149a, also Pickering Papers, reel 62: 45–8; Brasser, *Riding on the Frontier's Crest*, 41.

[89] McCallum, *Letters of Wheelock's Indians*, 222; Pickering Papers, reel 62: 52–3, 244–5.

[90] Mass. Archives, Unpassed Senate Legislation #2011. I am grateful to Daniel Mandell for bringing this incident to my attention and for supplying me with a copy of the document.

[91] *New American State Papers: Indian Affairs* (Wilmington, Delaware: Scholarly Resources, 1972), vol. 4: 149; Pickering Papers, reel 62: 231–231A.

[92] "Journal of John Sergeant," Dartmouth College, typescript copy, pp. 80–2; petition to Monroe quoted in Andrew McFarland Davis, "The Indians and the Border Warfare of the Revolution," in Justin Winsor, ed., *Narrative and Critical History of America*, 8 vols. (Boston: Houghton Mifflin, 1889), vol. 6: 613n.

group from New Stockbridge, led by John W. Quinney, moved to lands in Wisconsin that had been purchased by missionaries from the Menominees and Winnebagoes. Mtohksin's band and other Stockbridges soon joined them.[93] By the time Hendrick Aupaumut died in 1830, the Stockbridges and the Oneidas, faithful allies of the United States in the war for its birth, had moved to new reservation homes in Wisconsin, where they faced continued problems over land and, for a time, seemed to stare extinction in the face.[94]

In the aftermath of the Revolution, Americans took the position that Indian tribes who had fought alongside the British shared in the crown's defeat and forfeited their lands within the territorial boundaries of the new republic. The message for Indian country was clear: tribes who supported monarchy and tyranny deserved their fate; the friends of the republic would share its blessings. Yet the Stockbridges and their Oneida friends who had adopted the patriot cause found that republican blessings were reserved for white Americans. At the beginning of the Revolution, Stockbridge Indians and their American neighbors spoke a common rhetoric that depicted them as engaged in a shared struggle for rights and liberties. The Stockbridges made common cause with the patriots in the war that followed, and suffered uncommon casualties in the fighting. Nevertheless, the Revolution brought the final separation of the Indians from both their American neighbors and their Stockbridge lands. Indian patriotism did not earn Indian people a place in the nation they helped to create. For Native Americans, it seemed the American Revolution was truly a no-win situation.

---

[93] Brasser, *Riding on the Frontier's Crest*, 43. For nineteenth-century Stockbridge recollections of Mtohksin and Quinney, see Levi Konkapot, Jr., "The Last of the Mohicans," and "Death of John Quinney. By a Stockbridge Indian," *WHC* 4 (1859), 303–11.

[94] "Speech of John W. Quinney," and "Memorial of John W. Quinney," *WHC* 4 (1859), 314–20, 321–33.

# 4

## *Oquaga: dissension and destruction on the Susquehanna*

The American Revolution had perhaps no more direct and devastating impact than in Iroquois country. The conflict shattered the ancient unity of the Iroquois League and pitted brother against brother. Vicious border warfare disrupted normal patterns of Iroquois life, and American invasions crashed into Iroquoia, burning crops and villages, and sending refugees fleeing to the British for shelter. Ably recounted by Barbara Graymont in *The Iroquois in the American Revolution*,[1] the Six Nations' experience in the Revolution was one of almost total disaster.

Historians have usually approached the story by looking at tribes rather than towns: of the six nations composing the Iroquois League, the Mohawks, Cayugas, Senecas, and most of the Onondagas sided with the British, whereas the Oneidas and most of the Tuscaroras espoused the American cause, and therein lay the tragedy. However, by focusing attention on a particular community, we get a fuller sense of the divisions that the Revolution wrought in Iroquois society and a deeper appreciation of its impact on individual lives. The story of Oquaga or Onoquaga,[2] a melting pot for the Six Nations, mirrors the turmoil and suffering of Iroquoia in the Revolution, reminds us that in a civil war the lines of allegiance are not neatly drawn, and demonstrates that conflicts over church and state in the revolutionary era were not confined to white America. George III is reputed to have said that the Revolution was nothing more than "a Presbyterian rebellion."[3] If so, it was a rebellion with disastrous repercussions at Oquaga.

[1] Barbara Graymont, *The Iroquois in the American Revolution* (Syracuse, N.Y.: Syracuse University Press, 1972).
[2] A review of the records reveals the following spellings of the name: Oquaga/o, Onaquaga/o, Oghwaga/o/e, Oonoghquagey, Oghquaga/o, Onohoghgwage, Onohoguage, Onohokwage, Onohaghkwage, Onohghgwage, Oughquaga, Onoghquagey, Oughquagey, Ononhoghquage, Oughqugoe, Onoghquagy, Ochquaga, Onnaguaghe, Oghkwague, Onoghkwague, Aughquage, Aughquagey, Oghquaja, Oghquuge, Oughquaga, Ononquaga, Anaquaga, Onohquagwe, Ochgugu, Onenhoghkwage, Oequaga, Oughquagy, Onohoquagey, Onihohguago, Onohoghgwaga, Oghwaga, Aughquaga, Aaghquage, Aughquago, Achquage, Onohogwage, Occuagoe, Aquago, Ooghquaga, Anaquago, Auchquaga/o, Anaghakewage, Ouquagoe, Ochguaga, Aughguaga/o, Aughwaga/o, Oghgwaga, Oninghquagey, Ononkwakeh. Draper Mss. 17F142a provides some of the variant spellings.
[3] Edwin S. Gaustad, "Religion before the Revolution," in Jack P. Greene and J. R. Pole, eds., *The Blackwell Encyclopedia of the American Revolution* (Oxford: Blackwell Publisher, 1991), 68.

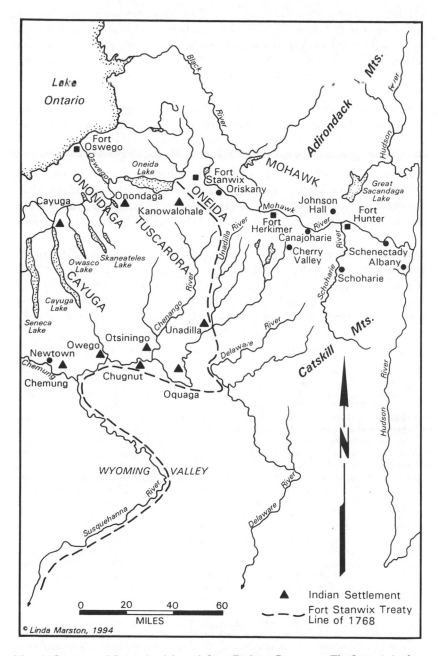

Map 6. Oquaga and Iroquoia. Adapted from Barbara Graymont, *The Iroquois in the American Revolution* (Syracuse, N.Y.: Syracuse University Press, 1972), p. xii.

Located on the banks of the upper Susquehanna near present-day Windsor
in Broome County, New York, in what was formerly Susquehannock hunting
territory, Oquaga was one of the most important Indian communities in the
area, and one of four main Oneida villages on the eve of the Revolution. It was
a frontier crossroads sitting astride major Indian trails, and a rendezvous for the
Susquehanna and Delaware rivers, where Indians from the south and west met
traders from Albany and Schenectady. Oquaga had been incorporating other
peoples from the beginning of the eighteenth century, as the upper Susquehanna
attracted immigrants from throughout the eastern woodlands. Tuscaroras,
displaced from their Carolina homes by the upheavals of the Tuscarora War in
1713, migrated north to accept shelter and subordinate status in the league
of their Iroquois relatives, and many took up residence around Oquaga.[4] Like
neighboring Otsiningo and other communities in the region, Oquaga seems to
have comprised several villages: a map made by Gideon Hawley in 1755 shows
Oquaga as four towns along a ten-mile stretch of the Susquehanna River, with
Tuscarora settlements to the north and south, and a Delaware settlement just
downstream.[5] Samuel Preston, who traveled through the area eleven years after
Oquaga's destruction, saw enough signs and ruins to convince him that Oquaga
in its heyday was "formidable and numerous," with towns on both banks of the
river and thousands of acres of land cleared, where the inhabitants cultivated
fruit trees, peas, pumpkins, and "an abundance of Indian corn."[6]

Massachusetts commissioners who met ten Oquaga delegates at Albany in

[4] Francis Whiting Halsey, *The Old New York Frontier: Its Wars with Indians and Tories, Its
Missionary Schools, Pioneers and Land Titles, 1614–1800* (New York: Scribner, 1901), 27–9; idem,
ed., *A Tour of Four Great Rivers: The Hudson, Mohawk, Susquehanna and Delaware in 1769, Being
the Journal of Richard Smith* (New York: Scribner, 1906), liii; Marjory Barnum Hinman, *Onaquaga:
Hub of the Border Wars of the American Revolution in New York State* (Privately printed, 1975), 1–
4, 16; Douglas W. Boyce, "'As the Wind Scatters the Smoke': The Tuscaroras in the Eighteenth
Century," in Daniel K. Richter and James H. Merrell, eds., *Beyond the Covenant Chain: The
Iroquois and Their Neighbors in Indian North America, 1600–1800* (Syracuse, N.Y.: Syracuse
University Press, 1987), 156–7; Barbara Graymont, "The Oneidas and the American Revolu-
tion," in Jack Campisi and Laurence M. Hauptman, eds., *The Oneida Indian Experience: Two
Perspectives* (Syracuse, N.Y.: Syracuse University Press, 1988), 31; Laurence M. Hauptman,
"Refugee Havens: The Iroquois Villages of the Eighteenth Century," in Christopher Vecsey and
Robert W. Venables, eds., *American Indian Environments: Ecological Issues in Native American
History* (Syracuse, N.Y.: Syracuse University Press, 1980), 128–39; Peter C. Mancall, *Valley of
Opportunity: Economic Culture along the Upper Susquehanna, 1700–1800* (Ithaca, N.Y.: Cornell
University Press, 1991), 29–39. Dolores Elliott examines a neighboring mixed village in "Otsiningo,
an Example of an Eighteenth Century Settlement Pattern," in Robert E. Funk and Charles
F. Hayes, III, eds., *Current Perspectives in Northeastern Archaeology: Essays in Honor of William
A. Ritchie. Researches and Transactions of the New York Archaeological Association* 17 (1977),
93–105.
[5] Hinman, *Onaquaga: Hub of the Border Wars*, 2, 4–5; Elliott, "Otsiningo," 94, 97–100.
[6] Samuel Preston, "Journey to Harmony on the Great Bend of the Susquehanna River . . . 1789,"
in Patricia H. Christian, ed., *Samuel Preston, 1789–1989: From Buckingham to Buckingham*
(Equinunk, Pa.: Equinunk Historical Society, 1989), 99–100. I am grateful to Alan Taylor for
bringing this source to my attention and for providing me with a copy of the journal.

1751 said they were "not a distinct Tribe but part of Several of the Tribes of the Six Nations." By the mid-1750s, Tuscaroras, Mahicans, and Shawnees, as well as Oneidas, lived at the village, and Oquaga continued to attract refugees displaced by war and people escaping the pressure of European settlement. British Indian superintendent Sir William Johnson got his start in the Iroquois trade by making a trading expedition in 1739 to "the cosmopolitan Indian town" of Oquaga, where he said the Indians mostly wanted alcohol. In 1756 Oquagas asked Johnson for a trading post "which would not only add greatly to our happiness, but would also increase our numbers, as it would draw Indians from all parts within 100 miles of us, to settle among us." Johnson reported in 1758 that there were people from almost every one of the Six Nations settled at Oquaga: "They are a flourishing and increasing People; as many of the upper Nations well affected to the English Interest & who are disgusted with the ruling Politics of their People leave their Castles & go & settle at Aughguaga." More Tuscaroras arrived in 1766. A delegation from Oquaga in the spring of 1768 included Oneidas, Tuscaroras, Cayugas, and Nanticokes. Increasing numbers of Mohawks settled at Oquaga after the Treaty of Fort Stanwix that same year. Oquaga sent 124 delegates to the council at German Flats in July 1770. By the eve of the Revolution, Oquaga, like other towns in the upper Susquehanna Valley, was a very mixed settlement and accustomed to functioning as such. In this refugee haven at "corn soup place," the shelter of the Great Tree of Peace helped to offset the trauma and societal disintegration that accompanied displacement of people from their original homelands, besides placing barriers to white settlement on the southern edges of Iroquoia.[7]

While the influx of displaced Indian peoples altered the tribal composition of the area, European colonists began to alter its economic orientation and, ultimately, its physical appearance. Together, though not always in cooperation, Indian and non-Indian newcomers reshaped the upper Susquehanna environment. The fur trade depleted the region's beaver population, and early colonists produced partial deforestation. After the Treaty of Fort Stanwix in 1768 opened more land to settlement, the number of settlers – or, more precisely, of landlords and their German and Scotch-Irish tenants – increased. The Stanwix boundary line lay to the east of Oquaga, but the newcomers nonetheless affected the region. They cleared fields, ran fences, built farms, erected mills, cut roads, and operated ferries, intent on creating a commercial agrarian society and linking themselves to a wider economic world. In doing so, they

[7] Mass. Archives, vol. 38: 166; *NYCD*, vol. 7: 582; vol. 8: 229; Thomas Elliot Norton, *The Fur Trade in Colonial New York, 1686–1776* (Madison: University of Wisconsin Press, 1974), 97; *Johnson Papers*, vol. 1: 6–7; vol. 9: 391, 903–4; vol. 12: 270, 273–5, 458; Elliott, "Otsiningo," 101. According to William N. Fenton (personal communication, July 11, 1991), the name Ononkwakeh means "corn soup place"; other names suggested include "the place of hulled corn soup" and "the place of the wild grapes."

continued the integration of native peoples into the Atlantic economy, and the disruption of native subsistence patterns, that the fur trade had begun. By the time of the Revolution, people from Oquaga were trading pelts for food.[8] Jack Campisi has also suggested that involvement in the fur trade generated political factionalism among the Oneidas and elevated warriors at the expense of sachems.[9]

Fundamental changes in the Indians' world left them susceptible to other European imports, especially alcohol and Christianity. As in seventeenth-century New England, missionaries did not always create factionalism. Entering native villages at a time of political upheaval, social disruption, and economic distress, they often aggravated and exploited existing divisions; sometimes Indians cultivated missionaries as a means of escaping traditional alliances or challenging in traditional relationships. At Oquaga, the religious and political factionalism that developed by the eve of the Revolution was not a simple division of "Christian" versus "pagan," if such divisions were ever simple. Rather, controversy between the established religion of the Church of England and the "new light" religion of New England Presbyterians and Congregationalists complicated existing divisions between traditionalists and Christians, and polarized the community. Moreover, if Campisi's model for the Oneidas holds true, the missionaries fueled existing divisions, giving warriors a religious validation for the challenges they were mounting to the hereditary chiefs, who derived power from the clan mothers on the basis of a traditional complex of beliefs.[10]

A mission station existed at Oquaga from 1748 to 1777, during which nearly two dozen missionaries, teachers, and interpreters came to the community, staying for periods ranging from a few weeks to eight years.[11] Several boys from Oquaga attended John Sergeant's school at Stockbridge, and Sergeant probably visited Oquaga in 1744, followed soon after by missionary David Brainerd. In 1748 Elihu Spencer came to the village, and during his short stay secured the conversion of Isaac Dekayenensere and Peter Agwrondougwas (Fig. 3), an Oneida chief of the Eel clan, henceforth known as Good Peter. That same year,

---

[8] Mancall, *Valley of Opportunity*, ch. 5; Jack Campisi, "Ethnic Identity and Boundary Maintenance in Three Oneida Communities," Ph.D. diss., SUNY Albany, 1974, 62.

[9] Jack Campisi, "Fur Trade and Factionalism of the Eighteenth Century Oneidas," *Occasional Publications in Northeastern Archaeology* 6 (1980), 37–46.

[10] Harold W. Van Lonkhuyzen, "A Reappraisal of the Praying Indians: Acculturation, Conversion, and Identity at Natick, Massachusetts, 1646–1730," *New England Quarterly* 63 (1990), 402–3; Campisi, "Fur Trade and Factionalism"; idem, "Ethnic Identity and Boundary Maintenance," 63, 65–8; James P. Ronda, "Rev. Samuel Kirkland and the Oneida Indians," in Campisi and Hauptman, eds., *Oneida Indian Experience*, 26; John C. Guzzardo, "The Superintendent and the Ministers: The Battle for Oneida Allegiances, 1761–75," *New York History* 57 (1976), 269–70; David Levinson, "An Explanation of the Oneida–Colonist Alliance in the American Revolution," *Ethnohistory* 23 (1976), 265–89.

[11] Hinman, *Onaquaga: Hub of the Border Wars*, 7; idem, *Onaquaga: Early Missionary Outpost, 1748–1777* (Old Onaquaga Historical Society, 1968), lists the various missionaries who served at Oquaga.

Figure 3. *Good Peter* (Peter Agwrondougwas) at age seventy-five. Oil on wood, by John Trumbull. The portrait was painted in Philadelphia in 1792, the year before Good Peter's death. Yale University Art Gallery, Trumbull Collection.

several Oquaga Indians attended Timothy Woodbridge's school at Stockbridge.[12] Rev. Jonathan Edwards noted the links between Stockbridge and Oquaga in 1751, and declared that the people at Oquaga had recently "made religion their

<hr>

[12] Halsey, *Old New York Frontier*, 52–7; idem, ed., *Tour of Four Great Rivers*, lvi. Good Peter was born on the Susquehanna River early in the century. His name was also given as Agwelentongwas and other variations. Walter Pilkington, ed., *The Journals of Samuel Kirkland* (Clinton, N.Y.: Hamilton College, 1980), 43, n. 9.

main concern, rather than war, or any worldly affairs."[13] He saw Oquaga as a potential center for missionary endeavors. The town lay within convenient access of other Six Nations settlements, in "a pleasant, fruitful country, surrounded by many settlements of Indians on every side" and was "on the road by which several of the nations pass as they go to war with Southern nations." With other Oneida villages close by, Edwards thought there was enough work for several missionaries in the area."[14] Missionaries from New England began arriving in the area and made Oquaga and the main Oneida castle of Kanowalohale the center of their operations.

Gideon Hawley, who had taught at the Stockbridge mission school, set off as missionary to Oquaga in 1753, in company with Timothy Woodbridge, but found that other aspects of European culture had preceded the Bible to the upper Susquehanna. The inhabitants of Oquaga had "more or less white blood in their veins," and Oquaga chiefs had to appeal to Sir William Johnson to help stop the flow of liquor into the village.[15] Following Hawley's departure in 1757, Good Peter carried on the missionary work alone, preaching at Oquaga and traveling to neighboring villages.[16]

Sir William Johnson ordered a fort or blockhouse built at Oquaga in 1756, and Oquaga supported the English during the Seven Years' War. In 1761 Good Peter requested that the fort "be pull'd down & kick'd out of the way," because "these Forts which are built among us disturb our Peace, & are a great hurt to Religion, because some of our Warriors are foolish & some of our Brothers soldiers don't fear God."[17] In 1762 Rev. Eli Forbes arrived at the village. He was impressed with Good Peter and the evidence of Christianity he saw in the town, and returned to New England the following year with four Indian boys for Eleazar Wheelock's Indian school.[18] Joseph Brant, who himself had spent two years in Wheelock's school, accompanied the Rev. Charles Jeffrey Smith to Oquaga as an interpreter, but Pontiac's War interrupted their work at the village.[19] Brant met his first wife in the village and his future father-in-law,

[13] *Collections of the Massachusetts Historical Society*, 1st series, 10 (1809), 146; Mass. Archives, vol. 38: 166.
[14] Quoted in Halsey, *Old New York Frontier*, 57–8.
[15] "A Letter from Rev. Gideon Hawley of Marshpee, containing an account of his services among the Indians of Massachusetts and New-York, and a Narrative of his Journey to Onohoghwage," *Collections of the Massachusetts Historical Society*, 1st series, 4 (1795), 50–67, esp. 65; Isabel Thompson Kelsay, *Joseph Brant, 1743–1807: Man of Two Worlds* (Syracuse, N.Y.: Syracuse University Press, 1984), 24; Halsey, *Old New York Frontier*, 62.
[16] Halsey, *Old New York Frontier* 68.
[17] Halsey, ed., *Tour of Four Great Rivers*, lxx, 65; *NYCD*, vol. 6: 361, 441, 447; *Johnson Papers*, vol. 9: 904; "Documentary Evidence of Onaquaga Fort," unpublished typescript supplied to the author by Marjory Hinman. Good Peter's request is quoted in Hinman, *Onaquaga: Early Missionary Outpost*, 19.
[18] Halsey, *Old New York Frontier*, 69–72. Only one of the boys graduated.
[19] *NYCD*, vol. 4: 322–3, 329–32.

Isaac Dekayenensere, told Sir William Johnson that he was "determined to follow the Words of Jesus Christ as near I can."[20] Although Brant's home was at Canajoharie, he reminisced after the Revolution that he owned a farm at Oquaga, with a comfortable log house, fifty acres of cleared land, an orchard, and a small herd of livestock.[21]

In 1764, the Presbyterian minister Samuel Kirkland, en route to take up missionary duties among the Senecas, accompanied Joseph Woolley to Oquaga. Woolley, a Delaware Indian and graduate of Wheelock's school, established a school in the village. Kirkland's "austere yet emotional brand of Calvinism" may have been "suited to a society suffering the worst effects of white contact,"[22] but it was not so well suited to Woolley, who found life at Oquaga hard. Kirkland had little patience with his complaints and pointedly told him he was living with "the most civilized Indians in all these parts" and had better get on with his work. Woolley died of consumption in late November 1765 or 1766, leaving the Oquagas to lament his passing and wonder if "perhaps God did this to try us, he Sent one among us, who had but a Short Time to live, to See how we Should be afflicted with it."[23]

They apparently bore their loss well. The Rev. Eleazar Moseley, a Presbyterian missionary from Boston, came to Oquaga to carry on the mission work, relying for interpretation on James Dean, then a boy of fifteen who had grown up among the Oquagas, and who became more proficient than any other white man in the Oneida language. Richard Smith, who visited Oquaga in June 1769, left a picture of an orderly and harmonious Christian Indian community of fifteen or sixteen large houses on the east side of the river, with a "suburb" on the west bank. The 140 or so inhabitants impressed him as "civil and sober" and hospitable. Each house had a small garden, in which the Indians grew corn, beans, watermelons, potatoes, cucumbers, cabbages, and turnips, and there were apple orchards. The town possessed two plows as well as cows, pigs, chickens, and horses. Oquaga shared a shad fishery with the Tuscarora town three miles downriver. On Sunday morning, the Indians attended divine service "which was conducted with regularity and solemnity." They sang psalms and read a portion of scripture, and Moseley preached a sermon.

> The congregation consisted of near 100 Indians, Men Women and Children, including the chief of the Tuscarora Town 3 miles below with some

[20] Kelsay, *Joseph Brant*, 99–100; *Johnson Papers*, vol. 11: 42.
[21] Hinman, *Onaquaga: Hub of the Border Wars*, 13.
[22] Campisi, "Fur Trade and Factionalism," 42.
[23] Woolley had entered Wheelock's school in 1757; by 1761 he was said to be reading Tully, Virgil, and the Greek Testament "very handsomely." Pilkington, ed., *Journals of Samuel Kirkland*, 3, 19; James Dow McCallum, ed., *Letters of Eleazar Wheelock's Indians* (Hanover, N.H.: Dartmouth College Publications, 1932), 263, 271–3; *NYCD*, vol. 4: 342. On Kirkland, see Ronda, "Reverend Samuel Kirkland and the Oneida Indians," 23–30.

of his People & they all behaved with exemplary devotion. The Indian Priest named Isaac sat in the Pulpit and the Indian clerk, Peter, below him, this Clerk repeated the Psalm in the Oneida Language and the people joined in the Melody with Exactness and Skill, the Tunes very lively & agreeable. The Sermon delivered in English was repeated by Dean, sentence by sentence. The Men sat on Benches on one Side of the House and the Women on the other. Before Meeting a Horn is sounded 3 several Times to give Notice."[24]

All seemed well at Oquaga. The Indians planned to build a church there, and Samuel Kirkland gloried in seeing crowded congregations and "a savage wolf of the Desert transformed into the Lamb of Christ."[25] However, Old Isaac had already complained to Sir William Johnson that many of Oquaga's Tuscarora residents refused to use the Book of Common prayer and were averse to the word of God, and Johnson had sent belts urging the Indians at Oquaga "to live united" and admonishing the Tuscaroras to follow Isaac's advice.[26]

Moseley found life at Oquaga lonely, having "no suitable companion for society – nor even a housekeeper to wash my dishes." He relinquished his office in 1771 to Rev. Aaron Crosby, a Harvard graduate and protégé of Eleazar Wheelock.[27] Crosby arrived at Oquaga unable to speak any Indian language, but he worked on his Oneida and, though not yet ready to preach in public, two years later Good Peter said he "begins to whisper to us the things of God in our own language."[28]

Whereas Oneidas expressed concern that denominational rivalries had transformed the "one true religion" into two rather uncertain religions, Kirkland was becoming depressed about the state of religion in Oneida country, fearing that the "Prince of Darkness" reigned there.[29] In March 1773, he made a grueling trip by snowshoe to Oquaga to assist Crosby. Crosby the Congregationalist declined to use the Church of England service, which the Mohawks, who had learned to use it at their Fort Hunter home, preferred. In addition, he refused to baptize children whose parents led what he thought were immoral lives. Kirkland found the community in some turmoil. With the exception of Good Peter, "who hath long been distinguished for his Piety & good sense," most of

[24] "Notes of a tour to the head of the Susquehanna in 1769 by Smith and Wells," in Halsey, ed., *A Tour of Four Great Rivers*, 64–8, 87; also quoted in modified form in idem, *Old New York Frontier*, 80–1.
[25] Ebenezer Moseley to Samuel Kirkland, Sept. 3, 1770; Kirkland to Rev. Levi Hart, Jan. 17, 1771, Kirkland Papers, Hamilton College Library, Clinton, N.Y., 10a, 14a.
[26] *Johnson Papers*, vol. 12: 270–1.
[27] Moseley to Kirkland, Sept. 3, 1770, Kirkland Papers, 10a. Wheelock apparently had expelled Crosby for breaking three of the commandments, Pilkington, ed., *Kirkland's Journals*, 90, n. 36.
[28] Samuel Kirkland to Andrew Elliott, Nov. 19, 1771; Kirkland to Moseley, Dec. 16, 1771; Kirkland to Crosby, Jan. 19, 1773; Kirkland to Elliott, March 28, 1773, Kirkland Papers, 23f, 24a, 37a, 39f; Pilkington, ed., *Kirkland's Journals*, 81.
[29] Guzzardo, "Superintendent and the Ministers," 280; Kirkland to Rev. Rodgers, June 30, 1772, Kirkland Papers, 30e.

the Indians seemed to believe that leading exemplary lives and learning the Ten Commandments by heart was all they needed to secure eternal life. He was shocked to find that the Indians "had no other idea of repentance than mere oral confession," expected that baptism "or mere external sprinkling" guaranteed eternal life, especially if the baptized person died in infancy, and celebrated baptisms with feasting and dancing. "I confess," Kirkland wrote to his wife, "I was astonished & grieved to the very heart to find such inexcusable ignorance & abominable infidelity prevail to such a degree among a people for whom so many hundreds hath been expended for their instruction, for nigh twenty years."[30] There may have been more to Oquaga resistance than Kirkland realized. Years later, Samuel Preston heard that in addition to their resident minister, the Oquagas "had a school of their own, taught by an old sagacious chief, where he educated their boys and young men in Indian learning, which I was told they kept secret from their minister, or at least he did not understand it."[31]

Kirkland spent hours talking with the leaders of the religious community at Oquaga, trying to reconcile differences between Good Peter and Isaac. He left Oquaga having effected a surface reconciliation, but in October 1774 the community was still divided, "chiefly by means of old Isaac (the Pharisee) and his party." Kirkland felt Isaac and his followers were determined to drive out the Presbyterians and introduce "the K–'s relign (so-called)." "By whom they are set on and employed," he wrote, "you may easily guess."[32]

The powers behind the turmoil, in Kirkland's mind, were the Johnson family and Joseph Brant. The Johnsons were Anglicans, and Sir William Johnson had encouraged the establishment of Rev. John Stuart's Church of England among the Mohawks. Sir William had been concerned for years about the weak state of the Church of England in his area of the country and feared that "the Number of Dissenters and the measures they pursue threaten more than our Religious libertys if not timely prevented."[33] Kirkland and the dissenting New Englanders complicated relations between the crown and the Indians in a time of escalating colonial tension, and Johnson's support of the Presbyterian minister declined sharply in the last years of his life. Johnson predicted that, unless he could remove Kirkland, the entire Iroquois Confederacy would be "set to quarrelling."[34] Religion was now entangled with local power struggles, and Oquaga was pulled between Kirkland's Presbyterian mission at Kanawalohale

[30] Pilkington, ed., *Kirkland's Journals*, 80–1; Kirkland to Jerusha Kirkland, March 24, 1773, Kirkland Papers, 39e.
[31] Preston, "Journey to Harmony," 100.
[32] Crosby to Kirkland, Jan. 25, 1774; Kirkland to Elliott, Oct. 24, 1774, Kirkland Papers, 47c, 51a; Pilkington, ed., *Kirkland's Journal*, 96–7, 116, n. 11.
[33] *Johnson Papers*, vol. 5: 388–9.
[34] For one interpretation of the struggle see Guzzardo, "Superintendent and the Ministers," 255–83. Levinson, "Oneida–Colonist Alliance," points out that the Oneida alliance was not just the result of Kirkland's influence but also a product of increasing Europeanization, growing ties with colonial neighbors, and weakening links with Iroquois neighbors.

and the Anglicanism of Johnson and Brant. Not only did the missionaries have two different words for their Indian congregations, but "the Word and the War" were also becoming "intimately entwined."[35]

In 1774, Johnson wrote to his "Brethren of Onoqhquagy," expressing concern over recent developments in the community. The Oquaga chiefs, "having been formerly instructed by some worthy divines of the church of England," had taken great pains to promote Christianity among their people; but, said Johnson, addressing his comments to the Tuscarora and other dissidents:

> I am sorry to find that for some time past, there is not that cordial affection between you and the rest of your village that ought to subsist between brothers and fellow Christians, but that you appear to be separating yourselves from the Oneida chiefs who are the proper heads of your settlement, and whom I know to be good men.

He reminded the Tuscaroras that the Oneidas had taken them in out of kindness, and that they should continue to heed their "civil and religious instructions."[36]

Johnson died suddenly in July 1774. His nephew and son-in-law, Guy Johnson, succeeded him as head of the Indian Department. Loyalist and Episcopalian, Guy Johnson opposed Kirkland on both religious and political grounds. He accused Kirkland of meddling in politics and said the chiefs had complained that children had died unbaptized because Kirkland and Crosby had refused the sacrament on account of the misconduct of the parents.[37]

In the winter of 1774–5, with Joseph Brant interpreting, Johnson held two councils at his home at Guy Park. In January, a delegation of Oneidas and Onondagas arrived, and Conoghquieson, a sachem from Old Oneida Castle who opposed Kirkland's Presbyterianism and his politics, apparently asked Johnson to remove Kirkland from Kanowalohale.[38] In February, twenty-one Oneidas and Oquagas came to the superintendent's home. The Oquagas offered condolences for Sir William's death and expressed concern that settlers were crossing the treaty line established at Fort Stanwix.[39] They were particularly distressed because the map used at the Treaty of Fort Stanwix was inaccurate and had deprived them of more land than they had realized. "Adam of Onoghquagey," who was Adam Addyngkahnorum, chief sachem of Oquaga and

---

[35] Kelsay, *Joseph Brant*, 189.
[36] *Johnson Papers*, vol. 8: 1174–5; vol. 12: 1110.
[37] Johnson to Kirkland, Feb. 14, 1775, Kirkland Papers, 53b; Pilkington, ed., *Kirkland's Journals*, 42.
[38] *NYCD*, vol. 8: 534–42.
[39] Causing their concern were the "Fair Play" settlers on the west branch of the Susquehanna, who angered not only the local Indians but also Pennsylvania provincial officials, who feared they would create further conflict with the Indians. Peter C. Mancall, personal communication, August 2, 1993. Mancall cites the main sources on the Fair Play settlers in *Valley of Opportunity*, 123n.

brother of Isaac Dekayenensere,[40] then asked Johnson to help them settle the dispute surrounding the Rev. Crosby. It had caused divisions in their village, "some taking part with him and others threatening to drive him away as he was not a member of the Church of England, and as he refused to Baptize the children of those who had led immoral lives, or did not approve of his worship." Adam delivered a letter from Crosby to Johnson in which the missionary defended his conduct on the issue of baptisms and reminded Johnson that he could not be bound by the superintendent in these matters but had to follow his own conscience. He admitted that Isaac and Captain Jacob had ordered him out of Oquaga, but claimed that "the rest of the Headmen, and all the Tuscaroras with united voice, desire me to continue with them, which request I am in duty bound to comply with; for there are 290 souls of those who desire my assistance."[41]

In reply, Johnson reminded them that shortly before he died his father-in-law had written to the Indians recommending that they continue to live under the direction of Old Isaac. He said he could not interfere in matters of religion and suggested that each faction at Oquaga try to decide matters for themselves, but he added that they should not permit the missionary "to force the consciences of those educated in a different persuasion." Since the Oneidas at the meeting were from Kirkland's congregation and defended their minister, Johnson told them he could not help noting "that the complaints against some of their Missionaries were too many and various to be destitute of some foundation."[42]

The Oquagas resolved to return home and, in an effort to restore peace in their town, "enter into a general resolution to abide by the Liturgy printed in the Indian Language." If the missionary would conform to it, they would let him stay on; if not, they would use the Liturgy themselves until a proper person could be appointed.[43] Kirkland, meanwhile, denied Johnson's accusations that he was meddling in politics, and claimed that the Indian speakers at Guy Park had been coached or had their words distorted. At the end of the month, four Oneida chiefs – including "Adam of Onighquagey" – sent Johnson a speech, interpreted and perhaps dictated by Kirkland, in which they refuted the charges against him, saying the minister was concerned only with religious matters. Kirkland complained that "certain great Men desire the six Nations have no instructions but such as have royal commissions, or bear the title of K-ng's Ministers."[44]

When the Oquaga delegates returned home from the conference, they related

---

[40] *Johnson Papers*, vol. 11: 38. I am grateful to Barbara Sivertsen for helping me to identify Adam of Onoghquagey.
[41] *NYCD*, vol. 8: 549–52. Johnson's meeting with the Oquagas and Oneidas is also in NAC, C-1223, vol. 11: 57–71.
[42] *NYCD*, vol. 8: 554.
[43] Ibid., 555.
[44] Kirkland to Johnson, Feb. 21, 1775; Speech of Oneida chiefs to Johnson, Feb. 23, 1775, Kirkland Papers, 53c, 53d; Pilkington, ed., *Kirkland's Journals*, 104–11.

only the part of the superintendent's speech that they thought likely to unite them; but when Brant returned, the delegates related the whole proceedings. Brant's hard-line interpretation of Johnson's words prevented the accommodation they had hoped for. Writing to Johnson in March, the Oquaga chiefs, Adam, Good Peter, Petrus (possibly "Little Peter"[45]), and Hendrick explained, "We think you meant that we should use that part of ye Book which we told you we had not used: But Joseph thinks the Minister must leave his manner of worship entirely & follow all ye forms of the Book; therefore the Difficulty Still Subsist." Isaac, bolstered by Johnson's endorsement, dug in his heels and refused to "do anything to ease the minds of those who are grieved." The chiefs felt the situation was beyond resolution, and Kirkland's devotees felt they had no choice but to move:

> We have no hope left of making peace among ourselves while we live together, for we have tried three years to unite. We have kept these troubles as secrets, hoping we should be able to settle them among ourselves without making them public, therefore have told you nothing till the other day; yet all our attempts have been fruitless. You may be sure Bro. we shall never willingly offend you yet we determine next summer, those of us who are united, together with our Brethren the Tuscaroras to remove towards Oneida, the place from whence we sprang, & join our Bros. there who have embraced Christianity & the Kings peace also – & carry our Minister with us, if he will go.[46]

In April 1775, responding to Johnson's reports about the troublesome missionaries, General Thomas Gage ordered, "You must by all means get the Indians to Rout them, as that is the only Method that can be fallen upon to keep them from Mischief."[47] But the mischief was already done. The long tug-of-war between Kirkland and the Johnsons, between new and old forms of Christianity, had polarized and split the Oquaga community even before the Iroquois civil war began.

Hector St. Jean De Crèvecoeur visited Oquaga in 1776 and, like Smith seventeen years before, he saw an orderly religious community. He described it as consisting of

> 50 odd houses, some built after the ancient Indian manner, and the rest of good hew'd logs properly dove-tailed at each end; they afford neat and warm habitations. The low lands on which it is built, like all the others, are excellent, and I saw with pleasure [a] great deal of industry in the cultiva-

[45] Thanks to Barbara Sivertsen for this.
[46] Speech of the Onoghkwage chiefs to Guy Johnson, March 7, 1775, Kirkland Papers, 54a. Cf. Guzzardo, "Superintendent and the Ministers," 282.
[47] Johnson to Gage, Feb. 13, 1775; Gage to Johnson, Apr. 13, 1775, Clements Library, Gage Papers, vols. 126, 127.

tion of their little fields. Corn, beans, potatoes, pumpkins, squashes appeared extremely flourishing. Many Indians had cows and horses tho' they seldom plough'd with them; they were greatly civilized and received me with their usual hospitality.

The women in particular seemed diligent in attending church. Crèvecoeur noted with surprise the presence of several white people in the town, who had come from different parts of Pennsylvania to put themselves under the care of Indians who were famous for their medical knowledge. Some of the patients were cured while Crèvecoeur was there, and he was intrigued to learn the Indians' methods of healing. The healers took great pains to conceal them from Europeans, so, like his contemporary Henry Tufts, who encountered similar medical secrecy among the Abenakis, Crèvecoeur resorted to getting one of the women drunk to learn her secrets.[48]

There was much that Crèvecoeur did not see, or foresee. He misidentified the residents of Oquaga as Senecas, he did not mention the religious dissension in the community, and he gave no indication of the storm that was soon to sweep Oquaga away.

Twelve Oneida sachems issued a declaration of neutrality in June 1775.[49] The next month, the Continental Congress recommended the commissioners of the Northern Indian Department to employ Kirkland to preserve the friendship of the Six Nations.[50] As the western tribes began to swing toward Britain by the spring of 1776, Kirkland reported to Schuyler that the Oneidas alone held an unshaken friendship for the colonists and a firm attachment to their council fire at Albany.[51] In March, the Cayuga chief, Fish Carrier, reproached the Oneidas for paying more regard to the new council fire at Albany than to the ancient one at Onondaga. By June, though they still hoped "to be still and bear no part in your dispute," the Oneida and Tuscarora chiefs feared it was no longer possible for them to remain neutral. Oquaga chiefs requested powder, lead, and flints from the colonists.[52]

Joseph Brant, in England in the spring of 1776, lobbied Colonial Secretary George Germain to look into the grievances of the Mohawks and Oquagas over

---

[48] H. L. Bourdin and S. T. Williams, eds., "Crèvecoeur on the Susquehanna, 1774–1776," *Yale Review* 14 (1925), 581–2; cf. *A Narrative of the Life, Adventures and Sufferings of Henry Tufts* (Dover, N.H.: Bragg, 1807), 73.

[49] Oneida Declaration of Neutrality, June 1775, Kirkland Papers, 57b; also in *Revolution and Confederation*, 4.

[50] "Proceedings of the 2nd Continental Congress, July 18, 1775" (copy), Kirkland Papers, 58b.

[51] Kirkland to Schuyler, March 11, 1776, Kirkland Papers, 64b.

[52] James Dean to Schuyler, March 10, 1776; Kirkland to Schuyler, June 8, 1776, Kirkland Papers, 67a; *American Archives*, 4th series, vol. 6: 710–11, 763–4; also Graymont, *Iroquois in the American Revolution*, 101, citing same Kirkland–Schuyler correspondence, *PCC*, item 153, vol. 2: 202–4, 192–6.

encroachment on their lands.[53] Adam of Oquaga voiced the same concern to the American commissioners when Schuyler met the Six Nations at German Flats in August, complaining that, in contravention of the Treaty of Fort Stanwix, "some of your people have of late made encroachments upon our lands, by surveying our hunting-grounds close up to our habitations."[54]

Meanwhile, many more Mohawks migrated to Oquaga to escape the political turmoil and disease raging in their valley. Mohawks had been moving into Oquaga since 1768, producing a shift in the population there,[55] but their presence at Oquaga now alarmed settlers, and New York raised three companies of rangers to patrol the woods along the frontier. Hearing that the rangers intended to shoot any Indians they found wearing paint and feathers, Isaac and other warriors from Oquaga sent a message in October, interpreted by Aaron Crosby, asking for assurances of safe conduct when they were out hunting. They informed the rangers they had always worn paint and feathers and were not about to stop now.[56]

In December 1776, en route to Niagara after his return from England, Brant stopped at Oquaga and called the warriors to arms. According to Daniel Claus, he told them "to defend their Lands & Liberty against the Rebels, who in a great measure began this Rebellion to be sole Masters of this Continent." Claus claimed that Oquaga "unanimously agreed with him in Sentiment" and "unanimously engaged to put themselves under his Command" against the rebels. John Norton, Brant's Cherokee-Scot protégé and an abopted Mohawk, later wrote that Brant's influence and family connections at Oquaga "entirely influenced" the people there to support the crown, and that the Oquagas were "his steady adherents in the cause of Loyalism throughout the War." Claus and Norton both probably exaggerated the degree of unanimity at Oquaga. The Anglican faction, the Mohawks, and many others alarmed over American encroachments on their land were certainly ready to follow Brant and accept his assurances that Germain would redress their grievances once the rebellion was quashed. But even with Good Peter and others of the Presbyterian faction removed to Oneida, it is unlikely that the community was yet unanimous in its support of the Mohawk and the king.[57] When John Harper, an old schoolmate of Brant's and an individual well known to the Indians of the region, visited Oquaga in late January 1777, he was convinced that the Indians would remain neutral, even though some of them had just returned from Niagara, where they

[53] NYCD, vol. 8: 670–1, 678.
[54] American Archives, 5th series, vol. 1: 1049; Schuyler Papers, NYPL, box 13, reel 7.
[55] Hinman, Onaquaga, Hub of the Border Wars, 16.
[56] American Archives, 5th series, vol. 2: 1193.
[57] American Archives, 5th series, vol. 3: 1500; NAC, Claus Papers, MG 19 F1, reel C-1478: "Observations of J. Brant," vol. 2: 209; "Anecdotes of Brant," vol. 2: 48; Carl F. Klinck and James J. Talman, eds., The Journal of Major John Norton, 1816 (Toronto: Champlain Society, 1970), 270, 279.

said they had gone to trade for "the necessities of life." They voiced their concern over encroachments on their lands and asked that the trespassers be removed, and at this point they may still have hoped for redress of their grievances. Redress was not forthcoming, and tensions remained high between Oquaga and neighboring colonists when Brant returned in the spring.[58]

Old Isaac of Oquaga warned Oneida messengers that winter that his son-in-law would soon return from Niagara "& take Oneida in his way."[59] When Brant did return, he raised the British flag at Oquaga, transforming the village into a recruiting station for Indians and Loyalists. In time about a hundred Loyalists from the area between the Hudson and the east branch of the Susquehanna joined the Mohawk, calling themselves Brant's Volunteers. From Oquaga, Brant's warriors ranged the surrounding countryside, initiating border warfare in the Susquehanna Valley. In the eyes of the colonists, the village finally had shown its true colors. Oquaga was now a military headquarters. "Here," observes Barbara Graymont, "was a classic example of a warrior chief seizing the leadership from the sachem chiefs."[60]

In August, the impending Iroquois civil war exploded at the bloody Battle of Oriskany. After more than a quarter of a century, the mission station at Oquaga closed, the Rev. Crosby remaining to the end.[61] The same month, Johannes Oosterhout Jr. and "Nicholas the Indian" returned from Indian country with news that the Indians had pulled back to Oquaga and sent out scouting parties, ostensibly because they had heard that two thousand American soldiers were coming to destroy them. Most of the young warriors had gone to join John Butler at Fort Stanwix, but the chiefs sent a message via Oosterhout and Nicholas "to see how times are" and requested that the road be kept open. The New York Council of Safety treated the message as an insult, and responded that unless the chiefs called in their young men immediately, they would be treated as enemies. "Tell the Indian," retorted Governor Clinton, "that if their young Men are fond of Fighting and choose to be in War that they can come & join us who are their Brethren born, in the same Country against our common Enemies and we will pay them as we do our own young Men who go out & fight for us." The Committee of Safety declared on September 3 that the Oquaga Indians, most of whom by now probably were Mohawks, "be considered and treated as open Enemies."[62]

[58] Halsey, *Old New York Frontier*, 169–71; Hinman, *Onaquaga*, 24–6; Paul L. Stevens, "His Majesty's 'Savage' Allies," Ph.d. dissertation, SUNY Buffalo, 1984, 954–5; *Penn. Archives*, 1st series, vol. 4: 450.

[59] Kirkland to Schuyler, Jan. 25, 1777, Kirkland Papers, 72c.

[60] Halsey, *Old New York Frontier*, 172, 176; Kelsay, *Joseph Brant*, 189–91; Graymont, *Iroquois in the American Revolution*, 110, 115–16; Haldimand Papers, 21774: 51; 21765: 376, 409.

[61] Hinman, *Onaquaga, Hub of the Border Wars*, 36.

[62] Hugh Hastings, ed., *Public Papers of Governor George Clinton*, 10 vols. (Albany, N.Y.: State Printers, 1899–1914), vol. 2: 271–4; Hinman, *Onaquaga: Hub of the Border Wars*, 36.

Most of the Loyalists and Indians returned to Niagara in the winter of 1777–8, but enough Indians and "disaffected Scotch Inhabitants" remained at Oquaga and Unadilla to alarm the settlers of Cherry Valley. Some evacuated their farms and retreated down country; the others petitioned Governor Clinton for rangers to guard the frontiers.[63] In the spring and summer, Clinton sent out scouting parties as news of Indian and Loyalist activities around Oquaga increased dramatically. By September, reports estimated there were between four and six hundred Indians in the area, with the majority centered at Oquaga under Brant's command, although other ranger captains and Indian Department officers operated out of Oquaga. The village was serving as a staging area for summer raids against the frontier. Oquaga was now a military target.[64]

In the first week of September, Clinton wrote to Colonel John Cantine that he could see no prospect of peace on the frontier "untill the Straggling Indians & Tories who infest it are exterminated and drove back & their Settlements destroyed. If, therefore, you can destroy the Settlement of Achquago it will in my Opinion be a good Piece of Service."[65] Plans for an expedition against the town gathered momentum during the fall. In October Clinton drew Washington's attention to the necessity of destroying Oquaga as "the Principal Place of Rendezvous for the Enemy." The frontiers could never be safe so long as Oquaga existed. Washington agreed and ordered Colonel Philip Van Cortlandt and Lieutenant Colonel William Butler of the Fourth Pennsylvania Regiment to march against the town.[66]

That same month, Butler led his expedition against Oquaga and Unadilla. His troops met no resistance as they crossed the Susquehanna and entered Oquaga at night, "the Enemy having that day left the Town, in the greatest Confusion." "It was the finest Indian town I ever saw," said Butler; "on both sides the River, there was about 40 good houses, Square logs, Shingles & stone Chimneys, good Floors, glass windows &c. &c." The Americans burned the town the next morning and destroyed some two thousand bushels of corn. The troops left only one house standing, which belonged to a friendly Oneida, probably Good Peter. Years later, a veteran of the expedition told Samuel Preston that "when they were mowing the corn they found several small children hid there, and he boasted very much, what cruel deaths they put them to, by

[63] Hastings, ed., *Governor Clinton Papers*, vol. 2: 821–3; Stanley J. Idzerda et al., eds., *Lafayette in the Age of the American Revolution: Selected Letters and Papers, 1776–1790*, 5 vols. (Ithaca, N.Y.: Cornell University Press, 1977–83), vol. 1: 324.

[64] Hastings, ed., *Governor Clinton Papers*, vol. 3: 250, 368, 402, 458, 505, 540, 597, 711–12; vol. 4: 16; Ernest Cruikshank, *The Story of Butler's Rangers and the Settlement of Niagara* (Niagara Falls, Ont: Renown, 1988; original ed. Lundy's Lane Historical Society, 1893), 51–2; *PCC*, reel 179, item 162: 213.

[65] Hastings, ed., *Governor Clinton Papers*, vol. 3: 742.

[66] Ibid., vol. 4: 66, 113–14, 163–4, 167, 169; *MPHC*, vol. 19 (1891): 354; *Writings of Washington*, vol. 13: 94, 97–8, 111, 131.

running them through with bayonets and holding them up to see how they would twist and turn." Unadilla shared the same fate. Clinton, Washington, and frontier inhabitants in New York, New Jersey, and Pennsylvania breathed a sigh of relief.[67]

From Indian country, however, came suggestions that Oquaga had not been unanimous in its support of Brant, and that the innocent had suffered along with the guilty. At a council in Albany soon after the attack, Good Peter told American Indian commissioner Volkert P. Douw that many of the Indians from Oquaga had fled, some into the woods, others taking refuge at Oneida:

> Many of the Indians who lived at *Ochguaga* are as true Friends to the thirteen united States as any of us. They were in the same Situation as many of your Friends are who are now in New York and elsewhere, who could not remove where the Enemy took possession. Their Houses and other property are now destroyed and many of those Friends are our Blood Relations. They will now come to us for Relief and protection.

Peter admitted that many Oquagas might have been "misled by Want" and "false Insinuations" to act against the Americans, but the Oneidas hoped to make them see their error and "make them hearty Friends to the united States." Peter requested a guarantee of protection for them. Douw gave him a certificate of protection for those Oquagas who had remained friendly to the United States, but said he must defer to Congress on the fate of those who had joined Brant.[68] Seventeen Indians from Oquaga took refuge with the Oneidas; the rest dispersed "for other parts of the Indian country."[69]

The destruction of Oquaga deprived Brant of his forward base, although he was back there periodically during subsequent border conflicts, and some of the inhabitants may have returned to the Oquaga area until American expeditions passed through in the summer of 1779.[70] But Oquaga's demise did not bring frontier settlers the security they had hoped for. The Indians retaliated with a series of attacks, notably the infamous assault on Cherry Valley. In December, four Indian chiefs wrote Colonel Cantine a "Threatening Letter," saying "your Rables came to Oughquago when we Indians were gone from our place, and

---

[67] Butler's report of his expedition is in Hastings, ed., *Governor Clinton Papers*, vol. 4: 222–8. An account of the expedition and a map showing Butler's line of march, both by Captain William Gray, appear in Frederick Cook, ed., *Journals of the Military Expedition of Major General John Sullivan* (Auburn, N.Y.: Knapp, Peck & Thomson, 1887), 288–90. Graymont, *Iroquois in the American Revolution*, 181–2; *Writings of Washington*, vol. 13: 135; PCC, reel 179, item 162: 213; Preston, "Journey to Harmony," 100–1. Butler's British namesake's account is in Haldimand Papers, 21761: 124–5.

[68] At a meeting with six Indians of Three Nations, Oct. 21, 1778, in Penrose, ed., *Indian Affairs Papers*, 161–5; also PCC, reel 173, item 153, vol. 3: 372–82; and *Revolution and Confederation*, 73–4, 76.

[69] Hastings, ed., *Governor Clinton Papers*, vol. 4: 437; Kelsay, *Joseph Brant*, 228.

[70] Barbara Sivertsen, personal communication, n.d.

you Burned our Houses, which makes us and our Brothers the Seneca Indians angrey, so that we Destroyed men, women, and Children at Chervalle."[71]

British, Indian, and American armies continued to devastate the upper Susquehanna Valley, destroying their enemies' crops and supplies even while short of food themselves. Oquaga became just one name on a long list of upper valley settlements laid waste during the war.[72] American troops marched through the ruins of Oquaga in their campaigns through Iroquoia in the summer of 1779, and Brant and Butler's war parties continued to pass through the area until the end of the war, making it unsafe for habitation by Indian or white.[73] More than 150 Oquagas joined fellow Iroquois refugees at Niagara and served on campaign with the British and Loyalists stationed there. They received promises, first from Governor Carleton and then from Governor Haldimand, that their services and sufferings would be rewarded at the end of the war with a restoration of their homelands.[74] A few people returned to the Oquaga region after the war,[75] but many Oquagas retreated even farther from home after the war, joining new communities on the Grand River in Ontario.[76]

Meanwhile, the Oquagas' Oneida relatives suffered equally heavy losses. Although some Oneida sachems remained pro-British, the warriors led by Kirkland's friend and confidant, Shenandoah, supported the Americans. Driven from their homes into squalid refugee camps around Schenectady, the pro-American Oneidas petitioned the United States Congress to compensate them for losses that included frame houses, wagons, livestock, farm equipment, kitchen utensils, clothing, teacups and saucers, punch bowls, rugs, looking glasses, jewelry, and other items large and small that constituted the material culture of their once-flourishing communities.[77] Congress eventually provided financial compensation, but by that time most of the Oneidas' lands, together with those of their Oquaga relatives, friends, and enemies, had been swallowed up by private land speculators, the State of New York, and the United States. At the Treaty of Fort Herkimer in June 1785, despite objections from Good Peter,

---

[71] Hastings, ed., *Governor Clinton Papers*, vol. 4: 364.

[72] Mancall, *Valley of Opportunity*, ch. 6, 149, 152.

[73] Hastings, ed., *Governor Clinton Papers*, vol. 5: 181–3, 192, 245–7, 941; vol. 6: 169–79; Anthony F. C. Wallace, *The Death and Rebirth of the Seneca* (New York: Knopf, 1969), 142; Halsey, *Old New York Frontier*, 265–9; Haldimand Papers, 21760: 173–4; Graymont, *Iroquois in the American Revolution*, 231; James J. Talman, ed., *Loyalist Narratives from Upper Canada* (Toronto: Champlain Society, 1946), 58–9.

[74] Haldimand Papers, 21765: 82; Talman, ed., *Loyalist Narratives*, 59; NAC, Claus Papers, vol. 2: 74, 89–90; *MPHC*, vol. 19 (1891): 422. Guy Johnson "confirmed" several Oquaga chiefs at Niagara by presenting them with gorgets; NAC, C-1223, vol. 12: 111–12, 122–3. The Oquagas' losses in the Revolution were estimated at £718, New York currency, in 1784: Haldimand Papers, 21775: 242.

[75] Old Seth, a Tuscarora, returned with his wife Elizabeth. Draper Mss. 17F142a; I am grateful to Barbara Sivertsen for drawing my attention to this source.

[76] See this volume, ch. 5.

[77] Massachusetts Historical Society, Pickering Papers, reel 62: 157–74.

Governor George Clinton secured the Indians' acquiescence in the transfer to New York of lands east of the Chenango River, which included Oquaga and Unadilla.[78] By 1790 the white population of the Susquehanna Valley was around thirty-five thousand; by the end of the century it had passed seventy-five thousand.[79] Indians who tried to return to the upper Susquehanna found new settlers living on their lands.

Moreover, the war in the upper valley left a searing impression on the minds of Indians and non-Indians alike. Cooperative relations such as the fur trade required, or such as Crèvecoeur had noted in 1776, were impossible a decade later. Settlers now associated Indians with the brutality and destruction of the war, and race relations never recovered; "Refugee Indians could no longer find sanctuary in the upper Susquehanna Valley."[80]

Most of the Oquagas, who had backed the losers in the Revolution, found themselves driven from their lands to new homes in Canada; most of their Oneida neighbors, who had backed the winners, also found themselves pushed from their lands to new homes in Wisconsin and Ontario, despite repeated treaty guarantees that they would not be deprived of their lands. After the war, the Oneidas split into two communities: the warriors or Christian party of Shenandoah at Kanowalohale, and the chiefs or pagan party at Oriske. In time they separated further, the warriors moving to Wisconsin and the sachems to Ontario, "where each asserted beliefs consonant with their political objectives."[81] Some other Oneidas continued to live in their New York homelands.

In the course of a generation, Oquaga had gone through many changes. From a refugee haven, it became a mission village. Split by internal factionalism, religious dissension, and external pressures, it then became a military headquarters. From military headquarters, it was reduced to burning ruins and its residents scattered. With the war over and New York opened to settlement, it underwent a final change. Settlers from Vermont and Connecticut invaded the Susquehanna Valley. The Oneidas sold the State of New York the present counties of Broome and Chenango in 1785 for $11,500. By 1791, there were three hundred New Englanders living near the site of Oquaga, in a town they

[78] Franklin B. Hough, ed., *Proceedings of the Commissioners of Indian Affairs . . . for the Extinguishment of Indian Titles in the State of New York* (Albany: Munsell, 1861), 84–108; Good Peter's Narrative of Transactions respecting Indian Lands, April, 1792, Pickering Papers, reel 60: 121; Grant of land from Oneidas to John Harper, Nov. 20, 1784, in Francis Jennings et al., eds., *Iroquois Indians: A Documentary History of the Diplomacy of the Six Nations and Their League*, 50 reels (Woodbridge, Conn.: Research Publications, 1985), reel 38; *Revolution and Confederation*, 332–8; J. David Lehman, "The End of the Iroquois Mystique: The Oneida Land Cession Treaties of the 1780's," *William and Mary Quarterly*, 3d series, 48 (1990), 524–47; Hinman, *Onaquaga: Hub of the Border Wars*, 94–8.
[79] Mancall, *Valley of Opportunity*, 180.
[80] Ibid., 147–8, 158–9.
[81] Campisi, "Fur Trade and Factionalism," 43, 45; idem, "Ethnic Identity and Boundary Maintenance," 88, ch. 3, and ch. 5.

called Windsor.[82] A town that had been a crossroads and a melting pot of Indian cultures had been replaced by one whose name obscured its Indian past.

Ronald Hoffman, surveying the southern backcountry in the American Revolution, concludes that "in times of severe social stress, societies lay bare their essential structural elements. A basically cohesive community will remain reasonably united in a period of adversity while one containing divisive elements will fragment."[83] The pattern held true at Oquaga. A community that had flourished as a refugee haven in times of relative tranquillity was pulled apart amid the pressures of a revolutionary age even before the fighting of the Revolutionary War began. Some Indian communities were able to exploit their internal divisions as a way of keeping both enemies and allies at arm's length. Other towns, in which there was not the same prewar religious ferment, suffered a similar fate to that of Oquaga – Sullivan's assault on Iroquoia in 1779 was relentless. But Oquaga's demographic makeup rendered it incapable of reconciling the deep divisions created by religious dissension before the war; its key location in a hotly contested area rendered it particularly vulnerable to early destruction once the fighting started. The community mirrored the Iroquois League as a haven for many peoples. Like the league, it could not survive the nationalistic and tribal rivalries the Revolution imposed upon it.

[82] Halsey, *Old New York Frontier*, 341–3; Hinman, *Onaquaga*, 98; Campisi, "Ethnic Identity and Boundary Maintenance," 93.
[83] Ronald Hoffman, Thad W. Tate and Peter J. Albert, eds., *An Uncivil War: The Southern Backcountry during the American Revolution* (Charlottesville: University Press of Virginia, 1985), xii.

# 5

## Fort Niagara: the politics of hunger in a refugee community

The role of Fort Niagara as a frontier outpost and headquarters for British and Indian operations against the American frontier is well known.[1] Preoccupation with the military activities at the fort, however, obscures the complex nature of the society that developed there during the Revolution. One of the "upper posts," along with Detroit and Michilimackinac, Fort Niagara in the Revolution was a military headquarters, a trading post, a supply depot, a diplomatic hub, and a multiethnic, multiclass society. Indian people who had lost everything in the war became increasingly dependent on the patronage of their allies at the fort. It emerged as a new community of peoples displaced from America by the chaos of war, and served as a conduit for the formation of other new communities in Canada. It was also a community whose communication with Quebec took six weeks when navigation was open, and that was sometimes totally isolated in winter.[2] The composition and isolation of the community created a situation in which competition for wealth and power flourished in the midst of misery and hunger.

As Laurence Hauptman and Richard White have shown, the refugee experience was nothing new for native peoples in northeastern North America. Iroquois villages took in people seeking shelter under the Great Tree of Peace, and in the eighteenth century, Conoys, Housatonics, Mahicans, Miamis, Mohegans, Montauks, Nanticokes, Narragansetts, Saponys, Shawnees, Susquehannocks, Tuscaroras, Wappingers, Esopus, and various remnants of New England tribes found refuge in Iroquois villages along the upper Susquehanna Valley and in

---

[1] Howard Swiggett, *War out of Niagara: Walter Butler and the Tory Rangers* (New York: Columbia University Press, 1933); Robert West Howard, *Thundergate: The Forts at Niagara* (Englewood Cliffs, N.J.: Prentice-Hall, 1968) More recent considerations of the fort include Paul L. Stevens, *A King's Colonel at Niagara, 1774–1776: Lt. Col. John Caldwell and the Beginnings of the American Revolution on the New York Frontier* (Youngstown, N.Y.: Old Fort Niagara Association, 1987).

[2] Ernest A. Cruikshank, ed., "Records of Niagara: A Collection of Documents Relating to the First Settlement, 1778–83," *Publications of the Niagara Historical Society* 38 (1927), 8. On Michilimackinac see David A. Armour and Keith R. Widder, *At the Crossroads: Michilimackinac During the American Revolution* (Mackinac Island, Mich.: Mackinac Island State Park Commission, revised ed., 1986).

the area south and west of the Mohawk Valley. In many ways the Iroquois were the true assimilationists of early America. Many of the people who fled to Fort Niagara in the Revolution were themselves refugees, or the children of refugees, who had fled to Iroquoia and been incorporated into the Iroquois world. The difficulties of adjusting to new homes, living alongside other refugees, and of coping with social disruption and elements of dysfunctional behavior were not new to these people.[3]

At Niagara, however, the Indian refugees settled in and around an existing and evolving community that included British soldiers; Indian Department personnel of English, Scottish, Irish, French, Canadian, and Indian descent; Loyalists who were themselves refugees from the American colonies; frontier traders; and even captives taken from the American frontier.[4] In fact, Fort Niagara in the Revolution comprised five or six separate communities, with varying degrees of physical separation and interaction between different groups. Within the fort walls, garrison contacts with the Indians were strictly curtailed.[5] The members of the Indian Department and the trading community were much closer both physically and socially to the Indians, as were the rangers. Across the river at Navy Hall was the marine corps. According to Seneca chief Blacksnake, the Indian camps that grew up around the fort stretched for eight miles, "presenting the appearance of one continued village from Fort Niagara to Lewiston." In fact, the Indian camps probably formed a large teardrop, with the heaviest concentration of population on the flat grounds close to the fort. Keeping the fort militarily defensible required keeping the Indian camps at a distance so that they did not obstruct the lines of fire, but some Indians enjoyed easier access to the fort than others. Influential individuals such as John and Walter Butler, Guy and John Johnson, Joseph Brant, and his sister Molly Brant (who had a house just outside the fort walls), and Sayengeraghta of the Senecas – all refugees from New York – congregated at Fort Niagara in the course of the Revolution.[6]

Competition for power and patronage predominated in the wartime community at Fort Niagara. Indian refugees contributed to these competitions. Indian

[3] Laurence M. Hauptman, "Refugee Havens: The Iroquois Villages of the Eighteenth Century," in Christopher Vecsey and Robert Venables, eds., *American Indian Environments: Ecological Issues in Native American History* (Syracuse, N.Y.: Syracuse University Press, 1980), 128–39. "Only in a refugee context," argues Hauptman, "can the Indian side of the New World drama of colonization and expansion be fully understood." Richard White, *The Middle Ground: Indians, Empires, and Republics in the Great Lakes Region, 1650–1815* (Cambridge University Press, 1991), 1–49.

[4] Niagara was home, at least temporarily, to white captives of several Indian nations, and there were various proposals for exchanges of prisoners. See, for example, Haldimand Papers, 21765: 83.

[5] At Michilimackinac, Major De Peyster forbade Indian women from spending the night in the fort; Armour and Widder, *At the Crossroads*, 103.

[6] Thomas S. Abler, ed., *Chainbreaker: The Revolutionary War Memoirs of Governor Blacksnake* (Lincoln: University of Nebraska Press, 1989), 114; Dennis P. Farmer, personal conversations, Old Fort Niagara, 5/8/92.

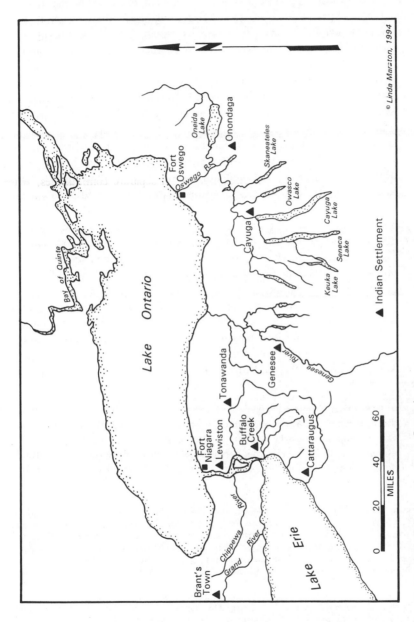

© Linda Marston, 1994

Map 7. Fort Niagara and western Iroquoia.

chiefs sought a place in a new social and political environment; army officers, traders, and Indian Department officials competed for rewards made more lucrative by the presence of refugees. Each group used others to validate its position, legitimize its actions, and bolster its support. Rival chiefs had plenty of opportunity to attach themselves to one or another rival factions or families within the British Indian Department; rival personnel within the department could likewise cultivate chiefs from different tribes, bands, clans, and families. The Indian people who came to Niagara tried to rebuild their refugee societies around a community that was itself experiencing significant change as new classes disturbed the status quo.[7]

Niagara was a traditional place for holding councils. An Iroquois speaker at the end of the Revolution referred to Niagara as "the great Council Fire where all our Business has been transacted during the War," and western Indians refused to accompany Six Nations delegates to Fort Stanwix in 1784, saying that they recognized "no fire place but that of Niagara where whatever relates to public business should be transacted."[8] Fort Niagara also sat on Seneca land. The Senecas regarded the British "as mere leasees of the Niagara riverbank" and visited the fort regularly to trade and keep an eye on their tenants.[9]

Captured by the British from the French in 1759, the fort was of crucial strategic and symbolic significance in the Revolution. Despite persistent shortages and logistical difficulties, the Saint Lawrence–Great Lakes transportation route gave better access to the interior than any controlled by the Americans.[10] Fort Niagara depended for its defense on a network of Indian alliances, and the Indians had good reason to protect the fort, as the Seneca chief Sayengeraghta, often known as Old Smoke, explained to the Hurons in a council at Niagara in 1779:

> It is also your Business Brothers to exert yourselves in the Defense of this Road by which the King, our Father, so fully supplied our Wants. If this is once stopt we must be a miserable People, and be left exposed to the Resentment of the Rebels, who, notwithstanding their fair Speeches, wish for nothing more, than to extirpate us from the Earth, that they may

[7] Bruce Wilson, "The Struggle for Wealth and Power at Fort Niagara, 1775–1783," *Ontario History* 68 (1970), 137–54. Cf. Richard White's discussion of the situation at Detroit in the French period. The congregation of many peoples at Detroit made it a "nexus of village and tribal rivalries, intrigues, and violence." When the French failed to mediate these disputes, various chiefs sought to use the French against their rivals. White, *Middle Ground*, 152.

[8] "Inventory of Indian councils held at Niagara June 30 1783," Haldimand Papers, 21765: 384; C.O. 42/15: 370. E. A. Cruikshank, ed., "Records of Niagara, 1784–89," *Publications of the Niagara Historical Society* 40 (1929), 6. Also see Haldimand Papers, 21779.

[9] *MPHC*, vol. 19 (1891): 10; Paul L. Stevens, "His Majesty's 'Savage' Allies," Ph.d. dissertation, SUNY Buffalo, 1984, 115–16; Cruikshank, ed., "Records of Niagara, 1778–83," 9–10.

[10] R. Arthur Bowler, *Logistics and the Failure of the British Army in America, 1775–1783* (Princeton, N.J.: Princeton University Press, 1975), 238.

possess our Lands, the Desire of attaining which we are convinced is the Cause of the present War between the King and his disobedient Children.[11]

An Oneida told American interpreter James Dean at the beginning of the war that "the Capture of that Fort is the only Thing that will unite the Minds of the Indians in their Friendship to the Colonies."[12] Despite the recurrent threat of American assault, however, and despite occasional attacks of the jitters, the small British garrison – fewer than four hundred men, with sometimes a mere handful on active duty as a result of sickness – saw no direct action in the war. Their main duty, in addition to restoring the fort's run-down defenses, was to protect supply lines where the Niagara River flowed into Lake Ontario.[13] Indian allies and Butler's green-jacketed Loyalist rangers carried the war to the Americans – and did so with grim effectiveness: "Scalps & Prisoners are coming in every day which is all the News this Place affords," Lieutenant Colonel Mason Bolton reported in June 1778.[14]

Nevertheless, the army was all-powerful in the social, political, and economic life of the community, and civilians looked to the military to protect and promote their interests. The military hierarchy made recommendations for major commissions in the Indian Department and the Loyalist corps. Supplying the army was the path to profit, and the merchant community assiduously cultivated their military connections. Since private shipping and storage facilities were expensive and prohibited, merchants competed to secure licenses from the military to ship their goods on military vessels. As the number of Indians at the fort increased dramatically during the war, provisioning the Indian Department became "the real El Dorado." The supplies necessary to retain the active support of the Indians cost about £500 per annum, New York currency, at the start of the war; by 1781 that amount had increased to £100,000. Goods for Indians were supposed to come from Britain, but in practice the Indian Department often turned to local merchants to supplement inadequate or delayed shipments. Merchants competed for contracts and stimulated Indian demand. They had private accounts with individual soldiers, made huge profits from the sale of rum, and, if disgruntled and disdainful officers are to be

---

[11] Haldimand Papers, 21779: 21.

[12] *PCC*, reel 172, item 153, vol. 2: 81, also quoted in Ralph T. Pastore, "Congress and the Six Nations, 1775–1778," *Niagara Frontier* 20 (Winter 1973), 89.

[13] Wilson, "Wealth and Power," 137; Haldimand Papers, 21756: 63. In August 1782, for example, there were a total of 476 troops stationed at Fort Niagara and its dependencies. For reductions by sickness see Ernest Cruikshank, *The Story of Butler's Rangers and the Settlement of Niagara* (Niagara Falls, Ont.: Renown, 1988; original ed., 1893), 38, 83. By the end of 1780 the fort had been transformed from a rundown structure into a strong fortification capable of repelling any American assault. For a plan of the fort around 1780 see Brian Leigh Dunnigan and Patricia Kay Scott, *Old Fort Niagara in Four Centuries: A History of Its Development* (Youngstown, N.Y.: Old Fort Niagara Association, 1991), 34–5.

[14] Haldimand Papers, 21762: 136.

believed, "cheated the army blind" every chance they got. At the same time, they relied on the army to curtail and control the random violence that erupted in the form of assaults, robberies, and brawls between soldiers and civilians, Indians and whites, and Indians and Indians.[15]

Two major firms were in operation at Fort Niagara at the beginning of the Revolution: that of Edward Pollard, who had been post sutler for fifteen years, and Taylor and Duffin. If the charges of Daniel Claus, no friend of John Butler, are to be believed, Butler, acting superintendent of Indian affairs in the northern department while Colonel Guy Johnson was away in England, entered into an alliance with Pollard, and together they effectively monopolized trade at Niagara. Butler was directly responsible for the distribution of provisions and presents to the Indians, and people who did business with anyone but Pollard risked being denied the king's bounty. Pollard retired to England a wealthy man in 1779.[16] The flood of Indian refugees that year increased the stakes and also brought a number of individual chiefs who proved to be capable players in the competition.

Fort Niagara was a hive of Indian activity even before Sullivan's expedition. In the spring and summer of 1776, John Butler and post commander Lieutenant Colonel John Caldwell held councils with Six Nations delegates in which they gradually overcame the resistance of Kayashuta and other chiefs to engaging warriors in the king's service. Butler's fluency in Seneca enabled him "to deal confidentially with the leaders of that nation."[17] In the fall of 1777, Butler persuaded Molly Brant, who had taken refuge at Cayuga after the Oneidas and Americans pillaged her Canajoharie home, to move to Niagara and exert her considerable influence among the tribes. Molly did so, but complained to Taylor and Duffin that "the Manner She lives here is pretty expensive to her: being obliged to keep, in a manner, open house for all those Indians that have weight in the 6 Nations Confederacy." The merchants assured her she would not be in want.[18] A "great number of Indians" were at the fort in December 1777, and most seemed loyal to the king, despite the news of Burgoyne's defeat.[19]

---

[15] This paragraph is based on Wilson, "Wealth and Power." For examples of the quantities of rum sold at Niagara, see Haldimand Papers, 21759: 5, 38; 21764: 16, 17. For Governor Haldimand's opinions on merchants at the upper posts, see Haldimand Papers, 21705: 48–9; 21717: 90–2, 137–8.

[16] Wilson, "Wealth and Power," 144; C.O. 5/78: 228; *DAR*, vol. 14: 249. Paul Stevens believes the evidence of "a clandestine mercantile partnership" between Butler and Pollard is "sketchy, unreliable, and not entirely convincing," and he suggests that Wilson accepted Claus' charges too readily. Stevens, "His Majesty's 'Savage' Allies," 521–4, 2040–3, n. 29.

[17] Barbara Graymont, *The Iroquois in the American Revolution* (Syracuse, N.Y.: Syracuse University Press, 1972), 97–100; Stevens, "His Majesty's 'Savage' Allies," 658–65; idem, *King's Colonel at Niagara*, 42, 56, 80, n. 57.

[18] H. Pearson Gundy, "Molly Brant, Loyalist," *Ontario Historical Society Papers and Records* 55 (1953), 100; Barbara Graymont, "Koñwatsi?tsiaiéñni," *Dictionary of Canadian Biography*, vol. 4: 417; NAC, Claus Papers, MG19 F1, vol. 2: 131–3; Haldimand Papers, 21774: 9–10, quoted in Maryly B. Penrose, comp., *Indian Affairs Papers: American Revolution* (Franklin Park, N.J.: Liberty Bell, 1981), 168.

[19] Haldimand Papers, 21765: 4.

↑ dependence
of British
of supplies

As their energies became diverted from the seasonal round of subsistence to the demands of war, the Indians grew increasingly dependent on British sources of supply. John Butler reported on a tour of Indian country in the fall of 1778 that as the young men were either out at war or on a war footing, "they had nothing to subsist upon but the remains of last Years Corn which was near expended, their hunting being neglected." Frequent war parties in the summer prevented Indian people from cultivating the usual quantities of corn, and much of what they did grow was destroyed before it was ripe. As a result many Iroquois families had not so much as an ear of corn that winter, and those who had cattle were compelled to eat them; many of those without cattle lived on roots.[20]

In the winter months between November 1778 and March 1779 a total of 7,365 Indians, of whom more than 4,700 were women and children, received provisions and clothing at Fort Niagara. In the first twenty-six days of the new year alone, more than 2,600 Indian people from twenty-two different tribes or bands came and went. Nations represented at the fort included Mohawks, Senecas, Onondagas, Oneidas, Cayugas, Nanticokes, Delawares, Conoys, Tuscaroras, Schoharies, Missisaugas, Shawnees, and others. The provisions given to Indian males usually included a blanket, a breechclout, a shirt, leggings, a musket, ammunition, a knife, vermilion, brass wire, a razor, awls, gun worms, fire steels, flints, combs, looking glasses, tobacco, and pipes. Indian women received a blanket, a shift, a petticoat, gartering, leggings, a small ax, beads, scissors, needles and thread, thimbles, rings, clasp knives, awls, and a kettle. Children were "cloath'd in proportion to their age." Chiefs and principal warriors were distinguished with gifts of a three-point or scarlet blanket, a coat and waistcoat, a hat and feathers, fine ruffled shirts, scarlet leggings and ribbons, black silk handkerchiefs, and silver jewelry. Each war chief also received ammunition, vermilion, and knives to distribute to his warriors. In this way the British enhanced the standing of their client chiefs and enabled them to carry out traditional chiefly responsibilities even as they fueled divisions within Indian society. Joseph Brant led war parties against the frontier, and most of the Indians returned to their villages once they had received their presents, but the Mohawks and Oquagas, together with some Onondagas, remained at Niagara, "having no Homes to go to," since the rebels had either burned or surrounded their villages.[21] The Indians made it clear that they expected the British to supply them and support their families while the warriors were fighting "in what they call a war amongst ourselves."[22] When Butler loaned his rangers' tents as temporary shelter for visiting Indians, the tents left when the Indians did.[23]

---

[20] Ibid., 34–5, 115–16.
[21] Returns of Indians at Fort Niagara from November 1778 to March 1779, and from December to January, are in Haldimand Papers, 21769: 16; 21760: 88; and 21765: 79. See also Haldimand Papers, 21765: 82, and *DAR*, vol. 17: 138.
[22] *MPHC*, vol. 19 (1891): 405.
[23] Haldimand Papers, 21765: 128.

Indians were not the only refugees at the fort; others included "distressed families" of Loyalists, mostly driven from the Mohawk Valley.[24] Walter Butler found himself "plagued" with the families of "Royalists," and prayed the government could do something for "those distress'd people."[25] The influx of refugees strained British supplies and taxed their transportation system, causing concern that shortages would prompt the Indians to believe American propaganda "that we meant only to deceive them and leave them in the lurch."[26] The numerous councils held with Indian delegations at Fort Niagara during the war aggravated the supply crunch.

The situation reached crisis proportions after the summer of 1779. Reeling from the invasion of their homeland by Sullivan and Brodhead, Iroquois people sought safety in what Washington called "precipitate flight to the British fortress at Niagara."[27] One of Sullivan's New Hampshire officers offered a more cautious assessment: "The nests are destroyed, but the birds are still on the wing."[28] In spite of their losses, the Indians remained firm in their allegiance to the crown and determined to exact revenge on the rebels once their women and children were safe.[29] More than five thousand Indians fled to Niagara and were drawing rations daily in October. Although the British sent out war parties almost immediately, more than three thousand Indians remained in the region of the fort throughout the fall. Governor Haldimand recognized that Indian allies were vital to the defense of the upper country and to the harassment of the Susquehanna and Mohawk valleys, but he shared the fears of post commander Bolton that the fort could not support so many people. Expecting an American attack in the spring, Haldimand ordered Bolton to encourage the Indians to send their women and children, along with the garrison's families, to Carleton Island and Montreal, where they could be protected without draining Niagara's supplies.[30] Molly Brant was one of those who departed, taking her family first to Montreal, then to Carleton Island. Bolton was glad to see her go: evidently she had been a thorn in his side during her stay at Niagara.[31]

Fifty-six Mahicans and some Cayugas left for Carleton Island, but most of the Indians remained at Niagara. The Iroquois refused to give their enemies the satisfaction of seeing them scatter and were determined to remain united in case

[24] Wilbur H. Siebert, "The Loyalists and the Six Nations in the Niagara Peninsula," *Transactions of the Royal Society of Canada*, 3d series, 9, section 11 (1915), 86.

[25] Haldimand Papers, 21765: 107; 21760: 149.5.

[26] *MPHC*, vol. 19 (1891): 461, 464; *DAR*, vol. 17: 203–4.

[27] *Writings of Washington*, vol. 16: 478, 492–3.

[28] Frederick Cook, ed. *Journals of the Military Expedition of Major John Sullivan against the Six Nations of Indians in 1779* (Auburn, N.Y.: Knapp, Peck, Thomson, 1887), 101.

[29] Haldimand Papers, 21760: 220; 21756: 45; 21765: 141.

[30] Ibid., 21760: 220; 21764: 62, 74; *MPHC*, vol. 10 (1886): 360; National Library of Scotland, Edinburgh, Stuart Stephenson Papers, Ms. 8250: 34–6; *DAR*, vol. 17: 231; C.O. 42/39: 378.

[31] Gundy, "Molly Brant, Loyalist," 102; Graymont, "Koñwatsi?tsiaiéñni," 418; Isabel Thompson Kelsay, *Joseph Brant, 1743–1807: Man of Two Worlds* (Syracuse N.Y.: Syracuse, University Press, 1984), 272.

of renewed rebel attacks. They had sent belts and messages to other nations and would not think of separating before they had received answers. Twethorechte, a Cayuga chief, admitted that his people were "much cast down" by their losses, but they had not given in. They would suffer if they must and try to support themselves through the winter by hunting, "and then we mean once more to meet our Enemies and see whether we are to live or die." The British promised to supply them with ammunition for hunting, and the Indians dug in for a long winter.[32]

The same season that brought hundreds of refugee Indians to Niagara also brought a return of superintendent of Indian affairs, Guy Johnson, nephew and son-in-law of Sir William (Fig. 4.). Driven from his Mohawk Valley home in 1775, along with his family and his Mohawk and loyalist followers, Johnson was known to the Iroquois as Uraghquadirha.[33] His arrival destroyed the lucrative monopoly of Butler and his business associates, and raised the politics of patronage to new levels. Taylor now became the garrison sutler and the supplier to the Indian Department. He entered into a partnership with George Forsyth, and the new firm of Taylor and Forsyth now controlled the private supply of the Indian Department, with the blessing of its head. Johnson apparently approved without checking the bills they submitted, often at greatly inflated prices and often for goods that were never delivered to the Indians.[34]

By now, the composition of the refugee community at Fort Niagara reflected the pattern of American assaults on Indian villages. On November 4, 1779, 3,329 Indians drew rations at Niagara. The majority – 959 Senecas, 582 Cayugas, 435 Delawares, and 182 Chugnuts – were refugees from the Sullivan – Brodhead invasions. American attacks on Onondaga villages in April 1779 accounted for the presence of most of the 179 Onondagas. There were also 154 Oquagas, homeless since 1778. One hundred seventy-four Mohawks had made Niagara their second home after their villages became untenable. Two hundred and forty Tuscaroras and eleven Oneidas preferred British alliance and asylum at Niagara to their relatives' American alliance and squalid refugee camps around Fort Stanwix and Schenectady. There were also several Oneida prisoners at Fort Niagara. Lesser numbers of Shawnees, Owegos, Nanticokes, Toderighoes, and Mahicans had also been caught up in the revolutionary diaspora and deposited at Fort Niagara.[35]

[32] Haldimand Papers, 21779: 60–2, 244–5; 21765: 148; NAC, C-1223, vol. 12: 55–9.
[33] Harley L. Gibb, "Colonel Guy Johnson, Superintendent General of Indian Affairs, 1774–82," *Papers of the Michigan Academy of Science, Arts and Letters* 27 (1941), 595–613. For Johnson's Iroquois name see for example *NYCD*, vol. 8: 519, 523, 534, 539.
[34] Wilson, "Wealth and Power," 145; Gibb, "Colonel Guy Johnson," 607–8. A record of Johnson's dealings with the Indians at Fort Niagara, and the patronage that undergirded them, is in NAC, C-1223, vol. 12.
[35] Haldimand Papers, 21769: 34; 21760: 262–3; 21764: 86–7. Captive Luke Swettland witnessed the Onondaga movements after the Americans burned their towns in April, in Swettland, *A Narrative of the Captivity of Luke Swettland, in 1778 and 1779, among the Seneca Indians* (Waterville, N.Y.: Guernsey, 1875), 19–29.

Figure 4. *Guy Johnson and Karonghyontye* (Captain David Hill), 1776. Oil on canvas
by Benjamin West. National Gallery of Art, Washington, D.C., Andrew W. Mellon
Collection. The close association between Johnson and certain Iroquois leaders
suggested in West's portrait continued during the war years at Fort Niagara and
ultimately resulted in charges of corruption being brought against the superintendent.

With such a concentration of Indian peoples around Niagara, local politics required delicate handling. In September, Governor Haldimand received a king's commission intended for Joseph Brant but decided to suppress it for the time being. He appreciated Brant's loyal service, but since the Mohawk was "but recently known upon the warpath," it would not do to bypass more experienced warriors. Moreover, Brant's connections with the Johnson family and his adoption of English ways had earned him enemies among his own people as well as friends among the British. Those enemies included Sayengeraghta, the principal Seneca war chief, who had fought alongside Sir William Johnson at the capture of Fort Niagara in 1759. Haldimand described him as "king of the Senecas and by many degrees the most leading and the man of greatest influence in the whole Six Nations, by whose intrigues Major Butler has been able to carry through many essential points." To have passed Sayengeragtha over for Brant would have had serious repercussions.[36]

The winter of 1779–80 was one of the worst on record. Mary Jemison in old age remembered it as the hardest winter she had known. The snow lay five feet deep for months, and the spring thaw revealed vast numbers of deer carcasses frozen on the ground. Some of Jemison's Senecas died of cold and hunger.[37] The Niagara River was frozen from January to March, and in the miserable refugee camps that lined the road to the fort, Indian families huddled in "poorly constructed wigwams" and dugouts. Colonel Bolton established a weekly relief line, and the fort's physician had nightmares about outbreaks of smallpox and yellow fever. The death toll from starvation and exposure is unknown, although survivors and historians estimated it at several hundred. Blacksnake said many people died from "salt food and exposure"; another Indian said three hundred died of dysentery. In the spring, work details from the garrison threw in quicklime and filled in dugouts where, in some cases, whole families had frozen to death.[38]

The Indians were not alone in their suffering at Niagara that winter. Dr. James McCauseland, the surgeon general to the king's Eighth Regiment, confronted a severe medical crisis. His patients included refugee Indians, refugee Loyalists, British soldiers, rangers, and prisoners. Many of these people arrived at the fort suffering from exhaustion, malnutrition, wounds, and a variety of chronic complaints. Transportation from Montreal to Fort Niagara was laborious at the best of times and perilous in the winter months; frequent gales battered

---

[36] Thomas S. Abler, "Kaieñ?kwaahtoñ" [Sayengeraghta], *Dictionary of Canadian Biography* 4 (1979) 404; Haldimand Papers, 21717: 39–40; *DAR*, vol. 17: 211–12; C.O. 42/39: 259.

[37] *MPHC*, vol. 19 (1891): 519; June Namias, ed., *Narrative of the Life of Mary Jemison by James Seaver* (Norman: University of Oklahoma Press, 1992), 105.

[38] Howard, *Thundergate: The Forts at Niagara*, 140–1; William T. Hagan, *Longhouse Diplomacy and Frontier Warfare* (Albany, N.Y.; Bicentennial Commission, 1976), 47. Anthony F. C. Wallace, *The Death and Rebirth of the Seneca* (New York: Knopf, 1969), 195.

the lakes in the fall and winter of 1779–80. Fresh meat and vegetables were soon in short supply. Although the fort seems to have escaped smallpox that winter, McCauseland treated scurvy, malnutrition, nausea, diarrhea, constipation, dysentery, stomach complaints, bowel pains, bladder infections, dropsy (from eating spoiled meat), gout, croup, headaches, tetanus, hernias, chilblaines, colds, fevers, ague, rheumatism, skin diseases, and various wounds, bruises, and burns.[39]

McCauseland had inadequate medical supplies and no trained medical assistance to meet this crisis. The soldiers assigned to hospital duties also cut wood, fed horses, swept chimneys, made coffins, and buried the dead.[40] Requests for medical supplies produced few results, and the doctor turned to a variety of home remedies. On one occasion, he recommended that an allowance of spruce beer be made to the garrison to help combat scurvy, only to learn two months later that the expensive provisions of it had never been intended for regular soldiers and would be struck from future supply lists.[41] The Senecas at the fort evidently could have offered advice on the external application of petroleum, which occurred in pools in their western New York homelands, as a treatment for toothaches, headaches, and rheumatism, as well as muscular aches and pains; but it is not known whether McCauseland benefited from their knowledge.[42]

Persistent delays of vital medical supplies from Quebec finally prompted the good doctor to order them direct from Europe, paying for them out of his own pocket, and sending the list to Haldimand. The situation improved little in subsequent years: "The great Sickness that often takes place among the Troops at Niagara," said McCauseland in the fall of 1782, was well known "to every Officer who has been Quartered here." Robert Hunter, a young English merchant who visited Niagara after the war, thought it an unhealthy place.[43]

Despite their sufferings, the Iroquois remained firm. When four Indians arrived at Niagara in February 1780, carrying messages from the Americans and talking of peace, Sayengeraghta returned their belts to them. During the course of the discussions, he drank to the health of the other Indians, "omitting the four Rebels as a mark of Contempt." The British threw the emissaries in jail,

[39] H. A. Verne, "Medical Crisis at Fort Niagara, 1779–80," *Niagara Frontier* 24 (Winter 1977), 89–94; Haldimand Papers, 21760: 376. For a broader view of the dietary and health conditions common for British soldiers during the Revolution, see Sylvia R. Frey, *The British Soldier in America* (Austin: University of Texas Press, 1981), ch. 2.

[40] Vane, "Medical Crisis," 92.

[41] Haldimand Papers, 21760: 279; Vane, "Medical Crisis," 90–1.

[42] Vane, "Medical Crisis," 93; Virgil J. Vogel, *American Indian Medicine* (New York: Ballantine, 1973), 389; Adolph B. Benson, ed., *Peter Kalm's Travels in North America*, 2 vols. (New York: Wilson-Erickson, 1937), vol. 2: 608.

[43] Vane, "Medical Crisis," 92–3; Haldimand Papers, 21760: 377, 416; 21765: 302–3; Louis B. Wright and Marion Tinling, eds., *Quebec to Carolina in 1785–1786: Being the Travel Diary and Observations of Robert Hunter, Jr., a Young Merchant of London* (San Marino, Calif.: Huntington Library, 1943), 110.

one of whom, the Mohawk Little Abraham, died in confinement.[44] Even before
Johnson assembled the chiefs of the various tribes and symbolically sharpened
their war ax in March, war parties were going out against the American frontier.
At least sixty Indian war parties left Niagara each year in 1780–1.[45] Such parties
reflected the composition of the refugee community and illustrated the mix of
allies produced by a war that was at once an imperial, a civil, and a racial
conflict. A war party of more than three hundred warriors led by Joseph Brant
in July 1780 showed a preponderance of Onondagas, Senecas, and Cayugas; a
substantial number of Mohawks, Oquagas, Tuscaroras, and Canaghsargys; and
a smattering of Delaware, Chugnut, Mahican, and Esopus Indians. The last
great raid of the war out of Niagara – the expedition led by Major Ross in the
fall of 1781, on which Walter Butler met his death at the hands of Oneida
Indians – comprised 33 regulars from the Eighth Regiment, 150 Loyalist rangers,
and 200 Indians.[46]

The raids struck the pro-American Oneidas and Tuscaroras as well as American settlers, and many of these Indians succumbed to the pressure and switched
their allegiance to the British at Niagara. In July 1780, some three hundred
Onondagas, Tuscaroras, and Oneidas "who were deemed in the rebel interest"
arrived at Niagara and more followed, a movement for which Johnson claimed
credit but which Haldimand feared was part of a rebel plot to add to the
growing consumption of supplies at the fort.[47]

In the spring of 1780, more than a thousand Indians, including Sayengeraghta
and his family, crossed over the portage from Niagara and took up abandoned
farmlands on Buffalo Creek. By May, Johnson reported a total of 1,142 men,
women, and children planting at Kadaragas (Cattaraugus), Chenusio, and along
Buffalo Creek, with more expected to follow suit. The British encouraged the
resettlement as a way of reducing the strain on the fort's food supplies, but they
could not keep up with the Indians' demands for hoes and corn.[48]

[44] Haldimand Papers, 21779: 73–8; Charles M. Johnston, ed., *The Valley of the Six Nations: A
Collection of Documents on the Indian Lands of the Grand River* (Toronto: Champlain Society,
1964), xxxiii; NAC, C-1223, vol. 12: 151–74, quote at 169; Thomas S. Abler, ed., *Chainbreaker:
The Revolutionary War Memoirs of Governor Blacksnake* (Lincoln: University of Nebraska Press,
1989), 144–5.
[45] Haldimand Papers, 21779: 83–8; *Frontier Retreat*, 141; Hagan, *Longhouse Diplomacy and Frontier
Warfare*, 43; Haldimand Papers, 21769: 122, 124, 165.
[46] Haldimand Papers, 21760: 333; 21761: 179. See also: NAC, C-1223, vol. 12: 138, 147, 149, 170,
193, for other mixed war parties.
[47] *NYCD*, vol. 8: 796; Haldimand Papers, 21760: 334; 21767: 139; 21769: 68; Hagan, *Longhouse
Diplomacy and Frontier Warfare*, 47; Hugh Hastings, ed., *Public Papers of Governor George
Clinton*, 10 vols. (Albany, N.Y.: State Printers, 1899–1914), vol. 5: 883–4.
[48] Haldimand Papers, 21767: 63–4, 73, 81–2; 21769: 62; Abler, "Kaieñ?kwaahtoñ," 406. According
to Blacksnake, the Senecas divided after spending the winter of 1779–80 at Fort Niagara. Some
went to Tonawanda for a couple of years and then to Allegheny; others went to Cattaraugus;
others moved to the Old Allegheny settlement, which became known as the Cornplanter Grant.
Abler, ed., *Chainbreaker*, 118–19.

In a similar effort to relieve the pressure on supplies, Haldimand implemented plans to establish a temporary agricultural settlement of reduced rangers and refugee Loyalists on the west bank of the Niagara River. He ordered Johnson to purchase a tract of land from the local Missisauga Indians, and then distribute plots of land to Loyalists judged capable of improving them and supporting their families. Butler's appointment as superintendent of the settlement, with responsibility for selecting suitable settlers, provided him with a new source of patronage. Trade monopolies and Indian presents were not the only paths to profit at Fort Niagara. Several Loyalists cleared fields and erected houses and barns in readiness for spring planting.[49]

Haldimand continued his efforts to meet Indian needs with goods supplied from England. He requested annual estimates and urged Bolton to do everything he could to save money.[50] British concerns about the cost of maintaining Indian allegiance were not new. The giving and receiving of gifts that was an essential lubricant of Indian diplomacy struck parsimonious British officials as unnecessary extravagance. British efforts at retrenchment after the Seven Years' War had sent a clear message of hostility to Indian people who saw them cutting the ties that bound friends together. But the governor was becoming alarmed at the costs of supporting the Indians at the upper posts, and particularly concerned about his superintendent's management of those costs at Niagara. Moreover, Indian chiefs competing for influence in trying times had no other access to the goods they needed than from their British allies.

It was soon apparent that, as between officers and men, there were degrees of suffering between Indians and chiefs at Niagara. Joseph Brant's salary from the Indian Department enabled him to provide quite well for his family (although his father-in-law, Isaac of Oquaga, died soon after moving to Niagara), but evidently cost him influence among his people, which suggests he may not have been redistributing his wealth in the expected manner. While other Indian parents struggled to feed their hungry children, Brant explored with Johnson the possibility of starting a school and getting a teacher for his offspring. Sayengeraghta likewise drew a salary and, along with the Mohawk chief Johannes Tekarihoga, was one of ten or twelve sachems and principal warriors of whom Johnson "took especial care." While other Indian people survived on soup made of fish heads, writes Isabel Kelsay, "Tekarihoga and his kind supped on fresh beef and butter, and tea and wine and sugar and sago, and delicacies such as raisins, almonds, and prunes, and essence of peppermint."[51] On December 16,

[49] Wilson, "Wealth and Power," 143–4; *MPHC*, vol. 19 (1891): 543–4; Cruikshank, ed., "Records of Niagara, 1778–83," 17; Haldimand Papers, 21764: 120; 21762: 19–20; Siebert, "Loyalists and the Six Nation Indians," 87–8; R. Arthur Bowles and Bruce G. Wilson, "John Butler," *Dictionary of Canadian Biography*, vol. 4: 118–19.

[50] Haldimand Papers, 21766: 34; 21767: 67; 21764: 114.

[51] Ibid., 21766: 72; NAC, C-1223, vol. 12: 97; Kelsay, *Joseph Brant*, 272–4. Sayengeraghta's annual pension in 1781 was £40; Haldimand Papers, 21770: 51.

1779, Johnson met with the Mohawks and told them he would supply them with the necessary articles for making snowshoes and help take care of their families while they prepared to go on campaign; he "then privately acquainted Kayangaraghta [Sayengeraghta] and some other Chiefs that he was preparing some handsome Cloaths as a particular Compliment for their good services." Four days later he gave Sayengeraghta "a fine blue Coat, trimmed with Gold-Lace, and a gold-embroidered Waist Coat." On New Year's Day, when Sayengeraghta and several other chiefs called on him with the compliments of the season, Johnson presented them with "some Silver Works & other things of high Estimation among them." Later that month he gave "a few Silver Works and Cloathing" to a daughter of Cornplanter, pointing out that she was a relative of Sayengeraghta "and a Woman of some Consequence among the Senecas." In March, Johnson gave Sayengeraghta's son Nagwarikwha (known to the British as the Infant) a scarlet coat with gold epaulets and a gorget with his name engraved on it.[52]

Guy Johnson justified such extravagance as the product of shifting Iroquois consumer tastes and past indulgence. "Many of the Indians will no longer wear Tinsel Lace and are becoming Good Judges of Gold & Silver," he explained. They frequently demanded wine, tea, coffee, and candles, and were particularly fussy in selecting the finest "Cloth for Blankets and the best Linnen & Cambric." Items that satisfied Indians in the western department would not do for the Six Nations, who were "not so fond of gaudy Colours, as of good & substantial things," and were "passionately fond of Silver Ornaments & neat Arms."[53]

By a curious logic, Johnson justified his "favored chief" policy as necessary response to the consequences of such a policy. Sayengeraghta, he said,

> is a good and prudent Man, and Still retains a Considerable Influence over his people, although I shou'd observe that the True Chiefs have lost much of their . . . ascendancy since the Commencement of the Rebellion, by a neglect of their old Customs, in introducing Young Men of little Experience and Interest to be heads of Partys who can't make any sufficient body without loading them with favors, and I know some Young Men who have Strong attachments to Government, and have done very good Service, that must depend on the Superintendents interest and Indulgence to make up any party of Consequence, as they have not acquired Sufficient reputation according to the Indian Mode, Whereas the real Chiefs have an Influence derived from long Service in the Indian way.[54]

---

[52] NAC, C-1223, vol. 12: 96–7, 99, 102–3, 117, 239. John Trumbull painted a portrait of the Seneca known as the Infant in 1792; Theodore Sizer, *The Works of Colonel John Trumbull, Artist of the American Revolution*, revised ed. (New Haven, Conn.: Yale University Press, 1967), fig. 107.
[53] Haldimand Papers, 21767: 89.
[54] Ibid., 21767: 151.

Johnson had evidently not changed the opinion he expressed six years earlier that the chiefs' influence depended mainly on "the Strength and Reputation of their Connections."[55]

By Johnson's estimate, "above one third of the Indian Confederacy" had "lost their all," and were camped around the fort, living on rations.[56] Haldimand feared that the Indians, who "absolutely depend upon us, for every Blanket they are covered with," wanted to prolong the war at British expense. He warned Johnson to guard against what he called their "little Arts and Deceipts" in drawing provisions, and stressed the "indispensable necessity" of keeping Indian families in their villages during the winter months.[57] Johnson tried to cut costs late in the fall, by encouraging the Indians to go off hunting for the winter and reducing the rations of those that remained. Chiefs who met him in council, however, "Spoke on a large Belt" and pointed out in no uncertain terms that only their loyalty to Britain had brought destruction of their towns and reduced them to dependence on the garrison in the first place."[58]

The new year brought more of the old problems. Johnson had to purchase more than he anticipated because another severe winter had destroyed much of the game or driven it south. Heavy snow cut off communication between posts, and severe spring gales battered the fort's stockades. Losses at sea pushed up the prices of goods at the fort. Fitting Indians out for campaigns added extra expenses: in the first ten months of 1781, seventy-five war parties, totaling almost three thousand warriors, went out from Fort Niagara.[59] In April, John Butler was confronted with a "naked store" and had to put the Indians off with promises that their needs would be met when the first vessels made it through to Niagara in the spring. Lest he be proved a liar, he then turned around and urged Haldimand to send "a Supply of Indian Presents by the very first Boats."[60]

Empty storehouses heightened tensions and highlighted existing discontents. In April, Joseph Brant got involved in some kind of drunken brawl with someone in the Indian Department. Apparently blowing the affair out of proportion, Molly Brant said that her brother was "almost murdered" by some of Colonel Johnson's men. She asked Daniel Claus to forward her complaints to Haldimand. Joseph led war parties on dangerous missions only to be mistreated "by those of the King's people who stay quietly at home & in the Fort," she said. "The whole Matter is, that the Officers at Niagara are so haughty & proud, not

---

[55] Milton W. Hamilton ed., "Guy Johnson's Opinions on the American Indian," *Pennsylvania Magazine of History and Biography*, 77 (1953), 321.
[56] Haldimand Papers, 21767: 147.
[57] *MPHC*, vol. 10 (1886): 416; Haldimand Papers, 21764: 154; 21767: 139.
[58] Haldimand Papers, 21767: 153.
[59] Ibid., 21767: 165; Cruikshank, ed., "Records of Niagara, 1778–83," 32. Returns of war parties are in Haldimand Papers, 21769: 122, 124, 165.
[60] Haldimand Papers, 21765: 213.

knowing or considering that the Kings Interest is so nearly connected with that of the Indians."[61]

By May, 1,540 Indians in Guy Johnson's department had gone to plant crops on Buffalo Creek, and the superintendent supplied them with hoes and what corn he could get from Detroit. Only a few barrels of the corn coming from farther afield reached the Indian settlements in time for spring planting, which caused hunger and discontent among the Indians and compelled Johnson "to be more Liberal to them in other things." The Senecas produced larger crops than most of the other tribes, and Johnson gave presents of clothing to Indians who supplied corn to families in distress.[62]

Johnson and the new commander at the fort, Brigadier General H. Watson Powell (Bolton had handed over command and sailed for home only to go down with his ship in a storm on Lake Ontario in November 1780[63]) endeavored to enforce Haldimand's orders restricting the consumption of rum at the post. Always a problem at frontier posts, rum became more expensive in time of war. By 1781, rum purchased in Montreal for eight shillings a gallon was selling at Niagara for twenty to twenty-four shillings. Such exorbitant prices made Haldimand determined to have it supplied exclusively from the king's stores, and he ordered the commanding officers of the upper posts "upon no account whatever" to purchase rum or anything else on behalf of the crown from local traders. Annual rum consumption at Niagara regularly exceeded seven thousand gallons. This was less than the ten thousand gallons consumed at Detroit, and not all of it was drunk by Indians; but rum caused concern "for the Pernicious effects it has upon their Warriors and Young Men, and the poverty and decease [sic] it brings upon their families."[64]

Post commanders, acutely aware of the importance of gifts in Indian diplomacy, found it difficult not to resort to local traders at times when crown supplies were too little and too late, as Guy Johnson frequently pointed out in his own defense. Johnson reduced the number of people immediately dependent upon the fort, but some Indians had the opportunity to indulge more extravagant tastes during the war. Johnson purchased wine, especially port, as well as sugar, tea, soap, and other items that, he claimed, were not only absolutely necessary for sick chiefs, "but from long custom expected for various uses by the Head men and some of their Families." He gave tea, coffee, sugar, wine, candles, soap, and "all kinds of Groceries" to "the principal people of the *Mohawks*,

---

[61] Kelsay, *Joseph Brant*, 307–8; Penrose, comp., *Indian Affairs Papers: American Revolution*, 271.

[62] Haldimand Papers, 21761: 110; 21767: 181, 199, 205, 226–7; 21769: 120.

[63] Ibid., 21760: 380, 387–8.

[64] Ibid., 21761: 144; 21767: 195–6, 215–16; 21764: 16–17; *MPHC*, vol. 10: 491; vol. 19: 640–1; Wilson, "Wealth and Power," 140; Armour and Widder, *At the Crossroads*, 170–1. Figures used for rum consumption at the upper posts are in *Haldimand Papers*, 21759: 5–38, *MPHC*, vol. 19: 644–5.

*Onoghquagys*, and many others, with Shoes, Saddlery &c besides real Gold and Silver Lace, as well as fine Cloth, fine Linen & Cambric." Even then some Indians were dissatisfied with the best he had to offer. Johnson's accounts for September 1781 included £10 for "a Scarlet Coat & Waistcoat to a Cahuga Chief;" £17 for "a Rich Brocade Waistcoat to Seyanderacta," and "a Ruffled Shirt & Feathers to Christian, an Oneida." The "list of goods wanting for the service" at Niagara in October included a category of stores for "sick chiefs" that included orders for tea, brown sugar, eight barrels of port wine, four barrels of Madeira, and a hundred pounds of chocolates.[65]

Haldimand authorized the purchases for sick chiefs and women, but did not accept Johnson's rationale for other expenses. Determined to restrict purchases from traders and eliminate gifts that were not included in the estimates sent to England, he warned against gratifying the "whims" of Indians who wanted things they saw in the traders' stores. Royal supplies fulfilled the Indians' needs; anything else served only "to Effeminate them, & to Create Wants, unknown to their Forefathers."[66] Johnson admitted that the Indians ought to be weaned from luxury items but did not think it prudent to do so in wartime. After all, when the British courted their services at the start of the war, the Indians had been promised that all their needs would be taken care of. Now, driven from their homes by Britain's enemies, the Indians "availed themselves of all Old Promises." The warriors of the Six Nations cost no more to support than a similar number of white men, Johnson argued; besides, "the name of their Attachment is of Value."[67]

With the opening of shipping in the summer months of 1781, the British were able to promise good-quality supplies from England, and the Indians at Niagara received supplies of rum, vinegar, pork, fresh beef, and butter, or so the account books said.[68]

Stimulated by the lavish expenditure and eager to compete for the opportunity to supply soldiers, Loyalists, and Indians, several small trading firms challenged the monopoly of Taylor and Forsyth. That monopoly collapsed suddenly in 1781 when one of its clerks, a former employee of the Butler-sponsored firm, "blew the whistle" on the firm, and informed the military authorities that Taylor and Forsyth had been padding their accounts and overcharging the government. An investigation followed; Taylor and Forysth were arrested and sent to Quebec to stand trial, dismissed from their position as sutlers, and denied permission to trade at the upper posts. Implicated, Guy Johnson was called to Montreal in the fall of 1781 with his account books to explain himself.

---

[65] Armour and Widder, *At the Crossroads*, 170–1, 190; Haldimand Papers, 21767: 205, 215–16; 21769: 138, 156.
[66] *MPHC*, vol. 19: 661; Haldimand Papers, 21767: 218–19.
[67] Haldimand Papers, 21767: 238–41.
[68] Ibid., 21761: 161–7, 21767: 195–6.

Although he expended much energy in his own defense, his reputation was permanently damaged. Aspiring entrepreneurs such as Richard Cartwright and Robert Hamilton quickly stepped into the void left by Taylor and Forsyth. Hamilton and Cartwright built up strong connections with the military as well as with Isaac Todd of the Montreal fur-trading firm, Todd and McGill. John Butler took over as acting superintendent in Johnson's absence, but his hopes to benefit from Sir Guy's disgrace were disappointed. The provisioning scandal confirmed the British military in its prejudices against local merchants and Indian Department personnel, and Haldimand looked to someone of status and respectability to head the Indian Department. Butler was bypassed in favor of Sir John Johnson, son of Sir William.[69]

Meanwhile, Indian demands increased anew with the imminent return of winter. The small amount of corn supplied to Indian families for spring planting meant inadequate crops in the fall, and many families returned from their planting grounds to the fort. "The Chief part of the Onondagas are already come in, and I fear many of [the] different Nations will follow their example," Butler reported in early December. Two weeks later, Butler had clothed 2,441 people and had "not a yard of Linen left for the rest." When Sayengeraghta asked for a gold-laced hat and a good coat, which he said Johnson had promised him, Butler was unable to provide them. He offered Sayengeraghta anything else in the store, but the Seneca replied "that if the King was grown too poor, and not able to purchase a Hat for him he wou'd do it himself," which he promptly did and boasted of it. "I imagine I shall have many such haughty Speeches this Winter," sighed Butler.[70] The same day that Butler recorded his encounter with Sayengeraghta, Guy Johnson, now in Montreal, was describing the chief to Haldimand as "a Thoughtfull Man, who looks forward to the future State of the Indians, and one that must be fed with Success, as well as with favors to keep his Zeal alive."[71]

Keeping alive the zeal of the Indians became a central theme of Guy Johnson's defense during his trial. Johnson showed, to his own satisfaction at least, that he had "preserved the Spirit of the Indians" in spite of their chagrin at the lack of military assistance. Before he arrived at Niagara in 1779, the nearest Iroquois village had been a hundred miles away, and the British had called upon Six Nations' warriors as they needed them. But once the Iroquois had had to abandon everything and retreat to Niagara, they expected to be supported at

---

[69] Wilson, "Wealth and Power," 146, 149, 151; Cruikshank, ed., "Records of Niagara, 1778–83," 36. Proceedings of the board of enquiry into Johnson's management, and Taylor and Forsyth's accounts, together with Johnson's defenses, are in Haldimand Papers, 21770. Guy Johnson's case was not unique. Patrick Sinclair, the commander of Michilimackinac, was summoned to Quebec to answer similar charges about the same time; Gibb, "Colonel Guy Johnson," 610. On John Johnson, see Earle Thomas, *Sir John Johnson, Loyalist Baronet* (Toronto: Dundurn, 1986).
[70] Haldimand Papers, 21765: 263–4; 21767: 273.
[71] Ibid., 21767: 271.

government expense, as they had been promised. Johnson claimed he had done his best to induce the Indians to settle away from the fort and cultivate their crops, and that he "liberally rewarded the families of Influence at additional Expence to set the Example to the rest." His house, he said, "was perpetually thronged by Indians," and the number of chiefs and their families caused "vast trouble and an Expence which it was impossible to ascertain with exactness."[72]

While Johnson struggled to justify his extravagant administration of the Indian Department, Butler struggled to satisfy Indian expectations from empty stores. Logistics and transportation were not the only problems. The Indian presents shipped to Niagara often did little to alleviate shortages of essential supplies. The first vessels that made it through to Niagara in the spring of 1782 failed to bring the clothing Butler had been promising all winter.[73] With the news of Cornwallis's surrender spreading through the tribes, post commander Powell had no choice but to make purchases from local traders to appease the Indians. Powell's fears of Indian disloyalty proved unfounded, however, as he himself acknowledged when the Indians asked him to visit and christen their new village at Lewiston, which they called "The Loyal Confederate Valley." In this predominantly Mohawk settlement about eight miles downriver from Niagara, Powell found them "very comfortably settled, and their fields well planted with Indian Corn."[74] The little Loyalist colony on the west bank of the Niagara River, which now held eighteen men, seventeen women, and forty-nine children, was making similar progress.[75]

Intertribal politics and personal rivalries also demanded Powell's attention that spring. When Joseph Brant returned to Niagara after a year's absence, he encountered a cold reception from Sayengeraghta, who apparently had grown accustomed to his pivotal role in Anglo-Indian relations at the fort. Powell did his best to smooth over difficulties between the rival chiefs, and finally sent Sayengeraghta on a mission toward Fort Pitt, which served the dual purpose of assuaging the Seneca's feelings and getting him out of the way.[76]

Whatever else they hid, the Indian Department's account books did reflect the continuing pattern of life at Niagara in the fall of 1782. War parties continued to come and go, as indicated by the purchase of a cow for a war dance; Indians continued to be hungry, as indicated by the $15 per head paid for horses for them to eat.[77] The inequitable distribution of supplies gave some

---

[72] "A Review of Colonel Johnson's Proceedings from the end of 1775," Haldimand Papers, 21766: n. p.; and 21768: 13–15.
[73] Haldimand Papers, 21762: 40.
[74] Ibid., 21762: 45–6, 93–5. For the location of the Loyal Confederate Valley see Helen H. Tanner, ed., *Atlas of Great Lakes Indian History* (Norman: University of Oklahoma Press, 1987), map 15.
[75] Siebert, "Loyalists and the Six Nations," 90; Cruikshank, ed., "Records of Niagara, 1778–83," 42.
[76] Kelsay, *Joseph Brant*, 324.
[77] Haldimand Papers, 21769: 155; 21770: 112.

people an impression of plenty in the Indian Department in the midst of scarcity in the garrison. Brigadier General Allen MacLean, who took over as commander in 1782, found the garrison short of every kind of stores: "There is not a Single Blanket, nor is there a pot to Cook for the Men; We shall be under the Necessity, if some Blankets do not come soon to Borrow from the Indian Department."[78] Disgruntled army officers with cold and hungry men looked with resentment on an Indian Department whose list of presents that fall included not only blankets, guns, flints, powder, lead and shot, fishhooks, hoes, and awls, but also gorgets, arm bands, earrings, hair plates, brooches, scarlet cloth, shoe buckles, steel spurs, ribbon, lace, vermilion, thread, rings, bells, looking glasses, razors, scissors, Jew's harps, combs, thimbles, paint, laced hats, Indian flags, plumes, coats, bridles, kettles, mugs, brass tomahawks, beads, pipes, and tobacco. Compelled to make up the gaps by borrowing from local merchants, MacLean complained loudly of "the slovenly, irregular manner" in which Indian presents were sent from Montreal. The Indians were desperately short of clothing, but instead the shipments included kettles and gartering, of which they already had more than enough, and "two large Trunks of Sponges, what use they are intended for, no Man here can tell."[79]

As rumors of the preliminary peace terms agreed upon in Paris filtered into Niagara, the British and the Indians entered a difficult period of transition, readjusting a wartime relationship to the new realities of peace. Nevertheless, the old wartime problems of dependency and the management of supplies continued to govern and plague the relationship. Joseph Brant complained that his warriors were kept idle while the peace terms were finalized and the Americans continued to attack Indian villages: "We think the Rebels will ruin us at last if we go on as we do one year after another, doing nothing only Destroying the Government goods & they Crying all the while for the great Expences so we are as it were between two Hells."[80]

Meanwhile, Haldimand redoubled his efforts to economize now that the fighting was ending. Young men no longer serving on war parties were to be sent out hunting instead of hanging around the British posts, "depending upon the King's Provisions, and Contracting Habits of Indolence which must ever keep them poor and dependent."[81] The dependency relationship that had sustained Indian allegiance for years was to be dismantled now that allegiance seemed less crucial.

The end of the war did not bring an end to violence within the refugee community at Niagara, where private animosities occasionally flared up in the midst of social dislocation. On the night of April 15, 1783, "a Cruel horrid

[78] Ibid., 21762: 215.
[79] Ibid., 21762: 234–5, 238; *MPHC*, vol. 20 (1892), 85.
[80] Haldimand Papers, 21775: 49.
[81] Ibid., 21775: 65–8.

murder" was committed. A "poor Delaware Indian," lying drunk, was struck in the head with an ax by one Jonathan Pray, and died two days later. According to Brant, the Delaware "was a very good man and a very inoffensive man." Pray "was a long time prisoner with the Indians," but evidently he "never had been ill used by them," and they had delivered him up the previous November. MacLean threw Pray into the fort's "blackhole" and intended to send him to Montreal for trial, but a court of enquiry found him guilty and Brant urged that the sentence be carried out at Niagara "as nothing else will Convince the Indians that they will have redress." MacLean noted in his report to Haldimand that the murdered Indian was the brother of Aaron, the Delaware interpreter, and "a real good man." He also observed, "Many Indians have been lying Drunk about this place without ever coming to harm, nor is there the Shadow of Suspicion upon any other person but Jonathan Pray." The murder worried Haldimand, and he agreed that Pray's sentence should be carried out "upon the Spot where the Offence was committed, as requested by the Indians." In the tense atmosphere generated at Niagara by rumors of British betrayal of their Indian allies and impending withdrawal of British garrisons, this was not the time to disregard Indian demands.[82]

MacLean reported that the Indians were quiet and seemed glad the fighting was over, but they did not yet know the exact boundaries and did not believe what they had heard. "The Indians from the Surmises they have heard of the Boundaries, look upon our Conduct to them as treacherous and Cruel," he wrote to Haldimand in May, expressing the sentiments of dismayed officers as much as betrayed Indians. The Indians told MacLean they could not believe the British had given up their country without their consent; "it was an Act of Cruelty and injustice that Christians only were capable of doing." Brant was in Canada, and MacLean recommended keeping him there until things calmed down at Niagara "for Joseph knows too much and too little, tho a good fellow in the main, he is a perfect Indian." With all the news he had picked up in Canada "he would be so much more sensible of the miserable Situation in which we have left this unfortunate People." "I do from my Soul Pity these People," concluded MacLean, "and should they Commit Outrages at giving up these Posts, it would by no means Surprise me."[83]

While the British and Indian inhabitants of Niagara wondered what was to become of them, the post commander examined the expenses that the Indian Department had run up at the fort. Haldimand had ordered a minute investigation "into the Merits of this Wonderful Charge." The governor could not imagine "that Such Amazing Issues could have been made without the knowledge of Col. Butler and the principal Officers of the Department, & Joseph, and

---

[82] Ibid., 21763: 48–9, 54, 56–9; 21764: 366–7.
[83] Ibid., 21756: 138; 21763: 104, 108; Johnston, ed., *Valley of the Six Nations*, 35–7.

the principal Chiefs." He also suggested that it might not be a bad idea to let Brant inspect some of the accounts so that he could see that the government did "not cry out at the Expense of the Indian Department without some cause."[84]

MacLean's investigations revealed abuses throughout the Indian Department. As Guy Johnson's own attempts to vindicate his conduct revealed, much of his crime consisted of perpetuating a system of patronage and profit that had been entrenched as a way of life and a modus operandi in the department since the days of Sir William Johnson: "I was compelled to keep an Issue constantly occupied in supplying their wants from my Quarters, which was their common Rendezvous, as it was for many of the Chiefs, and their families, both by Night and day."[85] Butler remained tight-lipped, denying any knowledge of "how & from whom such amazing assortments of *Private* Stores could have been formed," but admitted that Johnson "kept a very expensive house, that Chiefs frequently dined at his table, and Drank Wine," and that the Mohawk women and the wives of principal chiefs often got tea and sugar. Other witnesses said that Johnson and his wife, as well as Captain John Dease, kept their tables well supplied with raisins, almonds, and prunes for visiting Indians. Other irregularities included an auction of private property in which a box of chocolates was sold. When Johnson left Niagara, there were eight and a half barrels of brown sugar and two barrels of white wine in his house. Despite the enormous quantities of provisions supposedly issued to Indians, it appeared that they never received regular issues of tea, sugar, chocolate, raisins, prunes, butter, vinegar, or fresh beef, though Johnson "used a good deal for himself, and when he killed a Bullock he generally gave some Pieces to some of the favorite Chiefs." Every item Johnson purchased from the local merchants had come from Taylor and Forsyth. "In short," said MacLean in concluding his investigation into Johnson's accounting,

> I have reason to think it Extravagant, Wounderfull & fictitious, and the quality of Articles so Extraordinary, New, & Uncommon, that one may Exclaim with Hamlet when he sees his fathers gost [*sic*], "he comes in so questionable a shape, that I must speak to it." – I should think the first Lord of the Treasury would be the best person to settle it.[86]

---

[84] Haldimand Papers, 21764: 360; 21756: 134–5.

[85] Robert S. Allen, *His Majesty's Indian Allies: British Indian Policy in the Defence of Canada, 1774–1815* (Toronto: Dundurn, 1992), 37; Haldimand Papers, 21766: n. p.; 21768: 127–32; also 21770: 242–6.

[86] Haldimand Papers, 21763: 114–15. Further enquiries into Johnson's accounts, as well as Johnson's explanations, are in Haldimand Papers, 21770: 134, 142–3, 150, 163–79, 214, 232, 253–63. Johnson's trial dragged on for two years and was reopened on appeal in England. The evidence suggested that he inherited and perpetuated a system that was already corrupt. Johnson brought charges against Haldimand for defamation of character, which the court found justified, but not before Johnson died in 1788. Gibb, "Colonel Guy Johnson," 608, 612–13.

MacLean butted heads with the Indian Department but, with three thousand Indians still receiving daily provisions at the fort, was unable to effect the clean sweep he wanted. He and Butler disagreed over the amount of rum issued, and MacLean was unable to cap the flow, not less than 422 gallons being issued in one sixteen-day period. He lamented that "the People at the head of Indian department Seem to Vie with Each other who Shall Expend most Rum, and the great Chiefs are Striving who Shall Drink most Rum."[87]

MacLean thought Indian councils served no purpose but to create expense and should be avoided whenever possible. However, when John Johnson finally met with 1,685 Iroquois in July, their council provided more evidence that the real causes of expense often lay elsewhere. Johnson came to Niagara to reassure the Indians that their father had not abandoned them and had sent presents for them. Sayengeraghta said the Indians were happy to hear it, but hoped that this time "we may receive the Presents intended for us, & that they may not be applied to the use of the white people, & at the same time charg'd to us, which has often been the case, & has frequently, & undeservedly given us the Character of been [sic] Extravagently expensive to the King our Father." The Seneca paused and pointed at some of the officers present.[88]

The Indians remained fearful that they would be left alone to deal with the Americans, who seemed determined to overrun their country. Sayengeraghta requested the king "not to permit his Loyal subjects to wander, & scatter themselves, but encourage them to settle on Lands on the opposite side of the Waters, and Erect Posts for our mutual Protection in Trade, & by this means cement us as one people which we are assured will be a general advantage to all concerned."[89]

The peace terms that ended the war, and the American attitudes that outlived it, were scarcely more favorable to the refugee Loyalists than to their Indian neighbors, and most of Butler's Rangers reconciled themselves to finding new homes and obtaining land grants. By mid-1783, 837 people (469 men, 111 women, and 257 children) were listed as Loyalists incorporated in Butler's Rangers, and many of the officers were selecting lands. Butler, without permission, had already begun to lay out permanent lots for his favorites. The Eighth and thirty-fourth regiments were reduced to a peace footing in March 1784, and the soldiers allowed to claim lands; Butler's Rangers were disbanded three months later, and many signed up for lands on the Niagara Peninsula. The Loyalist colony counted forty-six families in April 1784; a little over a year later it had grown to 770 people. Robert Hunter thought that "the settlements on the British side are very capital. New settlers are coming every week." Crop failure

[87] Haldimand Papers, 21763: 192, 199, 225–6; Maclean to Ephraim Douglas, 16 July 1783, Schuyler Papers, NYPL, box 14.
[88] Haldimand Papers, 21779: 125.
[89] C.O. 42/15: 37071; Haldimand Papers, 21779: 126, 143–5.

and famine, familiar visitors to the Niagara Peninsula when it was inundated by population influxes, returned in 1789, but the region continued to attract settlers, many from the new republic to the south.[90]

The problem of new homes for Indian Loyalists proved more difficult. Brant sought land for his refugees and expected the British government to honor its promises. The Senecas offered the Mohawks land in the Genesee Valley, but the Mohawks were no keener than Butler's Loyalists to return to the United States. The British proposed a grant of lands on the Bay of Quinté, across Lake Ontario, but the Senecas felt increasingly isolated and vulnerable as they clung to their lands in the Genesee Valley and objected to the Mohawks seeking "an Asylum at so great a Distance from our Abodes." Brant then asked for six miles of land on either side of the length of the Grand River in Ontario. Haldimand, acknowledging that the war and peace had cost the Iroquois their homelands, agreed to Brant's request. John Butler met with the Six Nations and the Miss.saugas in May 1784, and for £1,180 the "Sachems, War Chiefs & Principal Women" of the Missisaugas agreed to sell 2,842,480 acres of land "to the King our Father, for the use of His people, and our Brethren the Six Nations.[91] John Deserontyon and his people accepted a 92,700 acre tract of lands at the Bay of Quinté, and became known as the Tyendinaga Mohawks. Brant later accused Deserontyon of fomenting divisions within the nation.[92]

When John Dease took over as acting deputy superintendent during Butler's absence in the summer of 1784, he found the Indian Department short of everything, and key chiefs disappointed that Butler had left without even saying goodbye. Dease complained that there was no alcohol; the Indians complained that there was not enough ammunition during the passenger-pigeon hunting season. Worse, the Indians at the various neighboring villages were "Extremely Sickly; A Yellow fever has Already Carried Off Numbers & some principal Chiefs." The Indians asked daily for food and medicines, and Dease planned to visit their villages when he had the time.[93]

In the winter and spring of 1784–5, the Mohawks and their neighbors moved once again, this time to permanent homes on the Grand River. The Mohawks congregated around Brant's Ford; the other refugee communities settled to the

[90] Siebert, "Loyalists and the Six Nations," 90–2, 120; Cruikshank, ed., "Records of Niagara, 1778–83," 68–72; Wilson, "Wealth and Power," 144; Haldimand Papers, 21765: 375–7, 388; Wright and Tinling, eds., *Quebec to Carolina in 1785–1786*, 94.

[91] Siebert, "Loyalists and the Six Nations," 93–4; Johnston, ed., *Valley of the Six Nations*, 44–50, 52–3; Carl F. Klinck and James J. Talman, eds., *The Journal of Major John Norton, 1816* (Toronto: Champlain Society, 1970), 280; Haldimand Papers, 21723: 75–6; 21724: 13, 112; 21725: 17–19; C.O. 42/46: 224–5; Cruikshank, ed., "Records of Niagara, 1778–83," 18–22, 29, 30–2; idem, "Records of Niagara, 1784–87," *Publications of the Niagara Historical Society* 39 (1928), 12–15, 17–18, 28–32, 55.

[92] E. A. Cruikshank, "The Coming of the Loyalist Mohawks to the Bay of Quinté," *Papers and Records of the Ontario Historical Society* 26 (1930), 390–430; Haldimand Papers, 21737: 182–4.

[93] Cruikshank, ed., "Records of Niagara, 1784–89," 4–7.

Figure 5. *A View of Niagara from the Heights near Navy Hall*, c. 1783. Watercolor by James Peachey. Courtesy National Archives of Canada, c-2035.

southeast. The Onondagas took up residence immediately adjacent to the Mohawk tract on the east bank of the river, the Tuscaroras did likewise on the west. The Senecas and Oneidas lived closest to the Tuscaroras, and the Cayugas took lands near the mouth of the Grand. The Delawares, Tutelos, Nanticokes, and others took lands close by. A census of the Indians living on the Grand River in 1785 counted 1,843 people from a variety of tribes, illustrating the dislocation and continuing displacement of Indian peoples during the Revolution. There were 448 Mohawks, 174 "Council Fire" Onondagas, 51 Onondagas of Bear Foot's party, 20 Onondagas "from the West," 47 Senecas, 31 Senecas "from the West," 198 Upper Cayugas, 183 Lower Cayugas, 55 Upper Tutelos, 19 Lower Tutelos, 113 Oquagas, 49 Oquagas of "Joseph's party," 129 Tuscaroras, 16 Mohawks from Saint Regis, 183 Delawares, 48 Delawares of "Aaron's party," 15 "Montours," 11 Nanticokes, and 53 Creeks and Cherokees. Though as many as seventeen hundred Senecas and six hundred Oneidas chose not to accompany their relatives to Canada and remained in the United States, other Indians found life in the United States untenable. Way-Way, a Nanticoke woman born at Chugnut, recalled that she was "a little gal when the white man destroyed our crops and run us off in the war." Her family fled to Niagara, then moved to Genesee; they returned with other Nanticokes after the war only to find their lands in the upper Susquehanna Valley occupied by white settlers. After a couple of years, Way-Way and other Nanticokes migrated to the new communities on the Grand River. Niagara was both a magnet for Indian people who had lost their homes in the Revolution and a path to new homes in the conflict's aftermath.[94] In time, the separation of the Iroquois became permanent between those in Ontario and those who remained in New York, with one council fire in central New York at Onondaga (after it was moved from Buffalo Creek) and another at Ohsweken on the Grand River in Ontario.[95]

In such mixed communities, some disagreements were inevitable. John Johnson blamed Joseph Brant, accusing the leader of the Upper Mohawks from Canajoharie of wanting to be head of the whole settlement and thereby alienating the Lower Mohawk chiefs.[96] But Patrick Campbell saw few signs of discord in 1792. Whereas the Seneca towns on the Allegheny were becoming "slums in the wilderness,"[97] the communities Campbell visited on the Grand River appeared to be flourishing. "The habitations of the Indians are pretty close on each side of the river as far as I could see," Campbell wrote, "with a very few white people interspersed among them, married to squaws and others of half-blood,

[94] Johnston, ed., *Valley of the Six Nations*, xl, xli.n, 52. Way-Way's story is given in Peter C. Mancall, *Valley of Opportunity: Economic Culture along the Upper Susquehanna, 1700–1800* (Ithaca, N.Y.: Cornell University Press, 1991), 147.
[95] Wallace, *Death and Rebirth of the Seneca*, 168.
[96] Johnston, ed., *Valley of the Six Nations*, xli, 54.
[97] Wallace, *Death and Rebirth of the Seneca*, ch. 7.

their offspring." Some disbanded soldiers had taken up residence among the Indians, and Brant actually encouraged the presence of white settlers, although his attempts to sell lands to them caused a crisis in his relations with the British government later in the decade. Campbell noted that there was a church and schoolhouse, both built by the British government, and Brant entertained his visitor with an elegant dinner, served on handsome china by two black servants in livery and buckled shoes.[98] Such a mix of Indians, soldiers, and occasionally blacks did not seem strange to people who had lived for years in the polyglot frontier community at Fort Niagara.

The fragmented societies that congregated at Niagara displayed many of the classic characteristics of refugee communities. The trauma of land loss was compounded by the hardships of life at the post. Heavy use of alcohol, outbreaks of violence, "and perhaps even apathy leading to starvation" were all symptoms of societal disintegration. Lieutenant Colonel John Enys of the Twenty-ninth Regiment saw Sayengeraghta, now an old man, at a council at Niagara in the summer of 1787. "He is a sensible old man and has been a very good Warrior in his day," noted Enys, "but like all the rest is very much addicted to Liquor, for no sooner was the council over than his Majesty was dead drunk rolling in an Outhouse amongst Indians, Squaws, Pigs, Dogs, &c.&c." Enys's comment reveals most about his own attitudes, but it also says something about the breakdown and upheaval experienced by Native American refugee societies. John Norton, the Scot-Cherokee, adopted Mohawk, and member of the British Indian Department, later wrote that although the influx of refugees to Niagara caused the government great expense, it did more serious damage to the Indians, as it reduced them to "abject dependence" on the British, "and exposed them and their families to be contaminated by all the vices attendant on a Dependant Situation."[99]

At Niagara, ingrained corruption and competition made a bad situation worse, aggravating factionalism and creating glaring inequities. The army fought the Indian Department; rival factions within the department fought each other; merchants competed for army contracts and Indian Department monopolies; a new group of entrepreneurs began to edge out an older gentleman class; Indian agents cultivated client chiefs with lavish presents while Indian families went

---

[98] Johnston, ed., *Valley of the Six Nations*, 59–65, 70–119; idem, "Joseph Brant, the Grand River Lands, and the Northwest Crisis," *Ontario History* 55 (1963), 267–82; Cruikshank, ed., "Records of Niagara, 1784–89," 14–15; Haldimand Papers, 21737: 40.

[99] Hauptman, "Refugee Havens," 138; Elizabeth Cometti, ed., *The American Journals of Lt. John Enys* (Syracuse, N.Y.: Syracuse University Press, 1976), 144. Klinck and Talman, eds., *Journal of Major John Norton*, 278. See also Wallace, *Death and Rebirth of the Seneca*, 199–202 for the social pathology of increasing alcoholism. Lest one conclude that alcoholism was a uniquely Indian response to times of painful change after the Revolution, see W. J. Rorabaugh, *The Alcoholic Republic: An American Tradition* (New York: Oxford University Press, 1979), esp. ch. 5.

hungry and naked; Indian chiefs competed for government largess; personalities clashed in the competition for high stakes in the midst of poverty.

Despite the cold and hunger, the corruption and factionalism, the greed and brutality, Niagara served as more than just a shelter in time of war for its Indian inhabitants. As manifested in earlier Iroquois refugee communities, the stress experienced in the refugee camps around Niagara required adaptation and resilience from the inhabitants.[100] More than a place, Fort Niagara was also an experience through which Indians of different tribes lived shared lives, and out of which they created new communities at what is now the Six Nations Reserve in Ontario. Whether they rebuilt their lives on the Grand River or on the Seneca reservations established in postwar New York at Tonawanda, Buffalo Creek, and Cattaraugus, Indian people on both sides of the Niagara River faced a future of dependency for which their hard winters at the fort during the Revolution had prepared them all too well.

[100] Hauptman, "Refugee Havens," 138.

# 6

## *Maquachake: the perils of neutrality in the Ohio country*

The image of the Shawnees in the historiography of the old Northwest has been not unlike that of the Apaches in the desert Southwest. Settlers on the frontiers of Pennsylvania, Ohio, Virginia, and Kentucky feared and hated the Shawnees even as they battled to take their lands, and the image of Shawnee warriors stalking frontier cabins proved too tempting for most later historians to abandon. The Shawnees' capture of Daniel Boone, their siege of Boonesborough, and their resolute resistance to American expansion would seem to suggest that their role in the American Revolution was clear, and certainly few tribes made such common cause with the redcoats.

The Shawnees, however, exemplify the inadequacy of standard portrayals of Indian experiences during the Revolution. Like other Indian peoples, they struggled to survive in a tumultuous situation not of their making. The revolutionary era brought a renewal and intensification of familiar pressures on Shawnee lands and culture; the Revolutionary War was one phase in a long and brutal contest for the Ohio River, in which the Shawnees occupied the front lines. As village chiefs from Chillicothe told the British in 1779, "We have always been the Frontier."[1] The Shawnees occupied a precarious position between the frontiers of Virginia and Kentucky and militant Mingo bands closer to Detroit. Tribes already allied to the British threatened to attack them if they contemplated peace with the Virginians. They became embroiled in the escalating conflict, but participation was never total, at least before the last year of the war. Different groups and individuals had different ideas about the best course to pursue.[2] The American Revolution in Shawnee country translated into a story of political fragmentation and burning villages. Shawnee people struggled to hold their communities together in the midst of conflict and migration. In the case of the Maquachake division of the tribe, it was also a story of persistent

---

[1] Haldimand Papers, 21782: 302. John Sugden, *Blue Jacket and the Shawnee Defence of the Ohio* (unpublished manuscript), presents a thorough account of the Shawnee war of resistance.
[2] P. Henry to George Morgan, March 12, 1777; Answers to Queries, Jan. 1778, George Morgan Papers, Library of Congress; George Morgan Letterbook, vol. 1: 13, 32; *Pennsylvania Archives*, 1st series, 5 (1853): 258–9, 443–4.

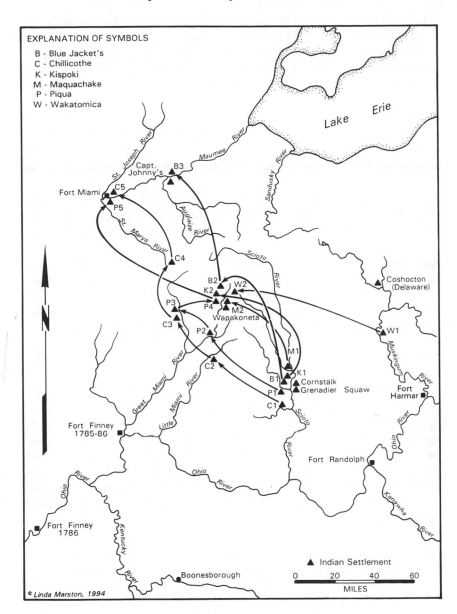

EXPLANATION OF SYMBOLS

B - Blue Jacket's
C - Chillicothe
K - Kispoki
M - Maquachake
P - Piqua
W - Wakatomica

Map 8. The location and relocation of Shawnee towns during the revolutionary era. Composite map showing general patterns of movement, 1774–94. Based on Helen H. Tanner, ed., *Atlas of Great Lakes Indian History* (Norman: University of Oklahoma Press, 1987), maps 16, 17, and 18.

*vain attempt MG ~to maintain*

*5 divisions*

efforts to live in peace, and of vain endeavors to maintain some kind of middle ground as militants on both sides created a new world of war.

The Shawnees traditionally comprised five divisions, each with specific responsibilities. According to Thomas Wildcat Alford, a nineteenth-century Shawnee, and other sources, the Chillicothe and Thawekila divisions took care of political concerns that affected the whole tribe and generally supplied tribal political leaders; the Maquachakes were concerned with health and medicine and provided healers and counselors; the Piquas were responsible for matters of religion and ritual, and the Kispokis generally took the lead in preparing and training for war and supplying war chiefs. Before the Revolution these divisions seem to have functioned as semiautonomous political units, occupied particular towns, and possessed their own sacred bundles.[3] As the traditional divisions fragmented, the allocation of specific responsibilities became at least partly redundant. In addition, the Maquachakes may have had greater influence than this division suggests. There is evidence that they acted as "counsellors for the whole nation," with primary responsibility for treating with outsiders and providing the head civil chief. They may even have acted as keepers of the tribe's sacred bundle, a duty usually attributed to the Chillicothe division. Much of what we know about traditional Shawnee life comes from the writings of C. C. Trowbridge, who relied heavily on information from Tenskwatawa, the Shawnee Prophet; and Tenskwatawa may have deliberately downplayed the importance of the Maquachakes as the division to which his chief rival, Black Hoof, belonged.[4]

In 1673 Marquette described the Ohio Valley as the place "where dwell the people called Chaouanons in so great numbers that in one district there are as many as 23 villages, and fifteen in another quite near one another." But the Iroquois drove them out early in the 1680s. Several hundred Shawnees migrated west to Starved Rock on the Illinois River, taking refuge around French Fort Saint Louis. They returned east in 1692, accepting an invitation from the Delawares and establishing a new town on the lower Susquehanna River in Pennsylvania. Most Shawnees migrated to the southeast, establishing villages along the Savannah River in Georgia and South Carolina, and some remained

---

[3] Spellings of the names of these divisions vary considerably. Vernon Kinietz and Erminie Voegelin, eds., "Shawnese Traditions: C. C. Trowbridge's Account," *Occasional Contributions from the Museum of Anthropology of the University of Michigan* 9 (June 1939), xiii–xiv, 8; Thomas Wildcat Alford, *Civilization and the Story of the Absentee Shawnees, as told to Florence Drake* (Norman: University of Oklahoma Press, 1936), 44; James H. Howard, *Shawnee!: The Ceremonialism of a Native American Tribe and Its Cultural Background* (Athens: Ohio University Press, 1981), 25–30, 213–22; Edmund De Schweintz, *The Life and Times of David Zeisberger* (Philadelphia: Lippincott, 1870), 374.

[4] John Sugden, personal communication, March 27, 1992; Sugden, *The Shawnee in Tecumseh's Time* (Nortorf, Germany: Abhandlugen der Völkerkundlichen Arbeitsgemeinschaft, Heft-66, 1990), 32–3, 74.

there, living in Creek country. Delawares, Shawnees, and Senecas, reacting to European-induced pressures farther east, resettled the upper Ohio Valley in the early eighteenth century, and most Shawnees had reassembled in southeastern Ohio by the middle of the century.[5] Others moved to the Wabash and Illinois country sometime before 1750 "for fear of finding themselves exposed to a cruel war on the part of the English," lived there for a couple of years, then moved south to Creek country.[6] War, migrations, political fragmentation, disease, economic disruption, and cultural changes had already taken their toll by the time the core of Shawnees returned to their historic homeland, and the new communities of the Ohio country were increasingly multiethnic in composition.

The Shawnees and their neighbors confronted the challenges of living between competing empires and colonies, but the pretensions of Britain, France, Virginia, Pennsylvania, and the Six Nations rarely translated into real influence in the upper Ohio Valley, where local concerns and regional loyalties held sway.[7] The Shawnees exercised increasing independence of action in the face of Iroquois claims over the region, fought in Pontiac's War contrary to advice from the league (as did some Senecas), and denounced Iroquois actions in selling their lands from under them at the Treaty of Fort Stanwix in 1768.[8] Continuing European pressures accelerated trends toward intertribal responses, however, and two years later Shawnees on the Scioto plains were working to form a confederacy of tribes in opposition to the Stanwix cession.[9]

Increasing tensions between Shawnees and Virginian frontiersmen produced a series of petty frontier skirmishes and exploded in Dunmore's War in 1774. In 1773 the Seneca chief Kayashuta told Sir William Johnson that 170 Shawnee families had "packed up everything," harvested their corn, and moved from the Scioto rather than "be Hemmed in on all Sides by the White People, and then be at their mercy." This was but the first of many movements of Shawnee people during the revolutionary era; Johnson interpreted it as evidence of the

[5] Howard, *Shawnee*, 4–5, 31, 127–8; Reuben G. Thwaites, ed., *The Jesuit Relations and Allied Documents*, 73 vols. (Cleveland: Burrows, 1896–1901), 59: 144–5; Helen Hornbeck Tanner, "The Greenville Treaty, 1795," in Erminie Wheeler-Voegelin and Tanner, *Indians of Ohio and Indiana Prior to 1795*, 2 vols. (New York: Garland, 1974), vol. 1: 66–7; Kinietz and Voegelin, eds., "Shawnese Traditions," 9; Michael N. McConnell, *A Country Between: The Upper Ohio Valley and Its Peoples, 1724–1774* (Lincoln: University of Nebraska Press, 1992).

[6] *MPA, FD*, vol. 5: 48.

[7] McConnell, *A Country Between*.

[8] Michael N. McConnell, "Peoples 'In Between': The Iroquois and the Ohio Indians, 1720–1768," in Daniel K. Richter and James H. Merrell, eds., *Beyond the Covenant Chain: The Iroquois and Their Neighbors in Indian North America, 1600–1800* (Syracuse, N.Y.: Syracuse University Press, 1987), 93–112, examines the limited influence of the Six Nations among the Indians of the Ohio country. Francis Jennings, "The Indians' Revolution," in Alfred F. Young, ed., *The American Revolution: Explorations in the History of American Radicalism* (DeKalb: Northern Illinois University Press, 1976), 324.

[9] *DAR*, vol. 1: 159, 315; vol. 2: 22, 24, 28, 87, 105, 166, 169, 204, 253–4, 261–2; vol. 3: 43.

Shawnees' hostile intentions toward the English.[10] The British Indian Department effectively isolated the Shawnees, and when the Shawnees sent a war belt soliciting Iroquois assistance, the Onondagas threw it back at them.[11]

Cornstalk, principal chief of the Maquachakes, counseled against war, but the cautionary voices of the civil chiefs were drowned out by the increasing clamor for war: "Our People at the lower Towns have no Chiefs amongst them," the Shawnees told Alexander McKee, "but all are Warriors." In the end Cornstalk had no choice but to follow his warriors. During the daylong conflict at Point Pleasant in 1774, Virginian troops heard his voice ringing out over the din of battle, urging his warriors to stand firm. After Point Pleasant and the destruction of their towns on the Muskingum River, most Shawnees were ready to heed Cornstalk's advice. They followed him to the treaty grounds at Camp Charlotte to make peace with Lord Dunmore. Kishanosity or Hardman, leading civil chief of the Maquachakes, was discredited by the war "on which acct. the Shawanees have thrown him down and have taken all his Power out of his Hands," although this apparent fall from favor, as historian John Sugden points out, could refer to the customary transfer of power from civil to war chiefs in times of conflict. At any rate, Kishanosity henceforth pursued peaceful policies, along with Cornstalk, Nimwha, and Wryneck of the Piquas.[12] Peace proved expensive: Dunmore's terms required the Shawnees to yield their lands south of the Ohio and send four hostages to Williamsburg as a guarantee of future good behavior.

The four hostages were Wissecapoway, a son of Cornstalk whom Dunmore later set free, Chenusaw, who escaped, and Cutenwha (the Wolf) and Newa, who both remained.[13] Nicholas Cresswell saw the hostages as they made their

[10] *Johnson Papers*, vol. 12: 1052, 1056–7.

[11] Jack M. Sosin, "The British Indian Department and Dunmore's War," *Virginia Magazine of History and Biography* 74 (January, 1966), 34–50; Alexander McKee, "Journal of Negotiations with Indians at Pittsburgh, May–June 1774," LC, Peter Force Transcripts, Series 8D, reel 49, item 93; "Extract of a Journal of Indian Transactions, from Feb. 27, 1774," and [John Connolly], "Journal of my Proceedings . . . from April 6, 1774," and "Extract from my journal from 1 May, 1774," all in NYPL, Chalmers Collection, Papers relating to Indians; *DAR*, vol. 7: 143, 174, 223, 263; vol. 9: 24, 47; *NYCD*, vol. 8: 506–8.

[12] Alexander McKee: Journal of Negotiations with Indians at Pittsburgh, May–June 1774, 10–18; NYPL, Chalmers Collection, Papers relating to Indians, "Extract of my Journal," 50; PCC, reel 91, item 78, vol. 1: 420; Draper Mss. 1H17 (Wryneck for peace), 1H44 (Nimwha to discuss Delaware peace initiative at Shawnees' main town); Paul Lawrence Stevens, "His Majesty's 'Savage' Allies" British Policy and the Northern Indians During the Revolutionary War. The Carleton Years, 1774–1778," Ph.D. dissertation, SUNY Buffalo, 1984, 217–18, 1940; Sugden, *Blue Jacket.* Wryneck is identified as a Piqua war chief in NAC, C-1223, vol. 12: 257. On Dunmore's War see Reuben G. Thwaites and Louise P. Kellogg, eds., *Documentary History of Dunmore's War* (Madison: Wisconsin State Historical Society, 1905); and Draper Mss. 3D1–39.

[13] Robert L. Scribner, ed., *Revolutionary Virginia, The Road to Independence: A Documentary Record*, 7 vols. (University Press of Virginia, 1973–83), vol. 3: 316, 151, n. 3, 274, n. 11; vol. 4: 127, 128, n. 3; *Revolution on the Upper Ohio*, 41–3.

way to Williamsburg and left us a word portrait of Shawnee warriors as they appeared to an itinerant and impressionable young Englishman on the eve of the Revolution:

> They are tall, manly, well-shaped men, of a Copper colour with black hair, quick piercing eyes, and good features. They have rings of silver in their nose and bobs to them which hang over their upper lip. Their ears are cut from the tips two thirds of the way round and the piece extended with brass wire till it touches their shoulders, in this part they hang a thin silver plate, wrought in flourishes about three inches diameter, with plates of silver round their arms and in the hair, which is all cut off except a long lock on the top of the head. They are in white men's dress, except breeches which they refuse to wear, instead of which they have a girdle round them with a piece of cloth drawn through their legs and turned over the girdle, and appears like a short apron before and behind. All the hair is pulled from their eye-brows and eyelashes and their faces painted in different parts with vermilion. They walk remarkably straight and cut a grotesque appearance in this mixed dress.[14]

Cresswell's observation on surface acculturation belied the essential conservatism of Shawnee society. Though, like everybody else, they borrowed selectively from European and Indian neighbors, they were resolute in holding onto their culture. In part, at least, this prompted Shawnees to follow a history of migration rather than accept the consequences of living alongside Europeans.[15] The Rev. David Jones, a contemporary of Cresswell who visited the Shawnee villages looking for converts, encountered this conservatism, and it gave him no high opinion of the Shawnees. Kishanosity, "a man of good sense," ate breakfast with Jones and seemed willing "to be instructed in knowledge of God." But, lamented Jones, "he was only one, and there were many against me." Othaawaapeelethee, Yellow Hawk, gave the minister a long speech, telling him they did not want his religion: "They had lived a great while in the way they do now, and were *resolved* to *continue* so."[16] David McClure, another visitor at the time, confirmed that the Shawnees "have always shown great opposition to christianity and have great hatred of the *Long Knife*, which is the name given by them to the *Virginians*."[17]

For many Shawnees, the outbreak of the Revolution simply meant that one war merged into another and that the struggle against Virginian aggression would continue. Land speculators targeted Shawnee hunting territory, and

[14] *The Journal of Nicholas Cresswell, 1774–1777* (New York: Dial, 1924), 50.
[15] Jerry Eugene Clark, "Shawnee Indian Migration: A System Analysis," Ph.D. dissertation, University of Kentucky, 1974.
[16] Rev. David Jones, *A Journal of Two Visits made to some Nations of Indians on the west side of the River Ohio, in the years 1772 and 1773* (Burlington, n. p. 1774), 37–9, 46–8, 52.
[17] Franklin B. Dexter, ed., *Diary of David McClure* (New York: Knickerbocker, 1899), 93.

American encroachments destroyed and drove away the game. In June 1775, Shawnees complained that the Virginians were "killing our deer and destroying our trees." The next month, Cornstalk, Nimwha, Kishanosity, and other chiefs told the Virginians, "We are often inclined to believe there is no resting place for us and that your Intentions were [*sic*] to deprive us entirely of our whole Country."[18] Some Shawnees saw the Revolution, and the promise of British support, as an opportunity to renew their assault on American invaders of their Kentucky lands.

American commissioners traveling Indian country in the summer of 1775 to invite the tribes to meet at Fort Pitt in the fall found the Shawnees "Constantly Counseling." The commissioners acknowledged the Maquachakes as the treaty-making body of the Shawnees, and sought out Shawnee women since they had the reputation of knowing what was going on. Women sometimes spoke in council because, said the Shawnees, "some Women were wiser than some Men." The women "all seemed very uneasy in Expectation that there would be War." A Maquachake woman told Commissioner Richard Butler that the Shawnees were divided, with the Chillicothe and Piqua divisions of the tribe displaying growing militancy.[19]

The Maquachakes were most prominent among the Shawnees who showed up at the Fort Pitt treaty council that October. Cornstalk addressed his concern to the Virginia commissioners:

> Brothers
>     I imagined all Matters were settled last fall and that we were as one People. I now find that there is a bad Wind Blown up. I know not from whence it has Arisen but I desire the White People will search into it. I hope they will not let that Interrupt the Good work we are now about. If we are Strong and finish the good work we have begun our Children now Growing up will live in peace but if we regard what wicked or foolish People do it may be an Impediment to our living in Friendship.

Nimwha likewise expressed his hope "that we will be able to Conclude a Peace and that our Childrens Children may reap the Blessings and advantages of it." Caught between the encroaching American frontier to their south and east, and the Mingoes, Wyandots, and other pro-British militants to the north and west, as well as with other Shawnees opting for war, the Maquachakes' chances of

---

[18] Haldimand Papers, 21845: 483; Scribner et al., eds. *Revolutionary Virginia*, vol. 7: 770–1; *Revolution on the Upper Ohio*, 61. For discussion of "the contagion of the ethic of speculation" in Kentucky lands during the revolutionary era, see Stephen Aron, "Pioneers and Profiteers: Land Speculation and the Homestead Ethic in Frontier Kentucky," *Western Historical Quarterly* 27 (1992), 179–98.

[19] "Butler's Journal," *Western Pennsylvania Magazine of History* 47: 145, 148, 152, n. 66; *Revolution on the Upper Ohio*, 24–5, 39, 41–2, 58, 60–1, 75; Scribner et al., eds., *Revolutionary Virginia*, vol. 3: 208–66, 316–17, 377, 383–4, 388–90.

being able to bequeath that peace to their children were slim indeed. Conscious that young Shawnee warriors were already slipping away and committing hostilities, Cornstalk acknowledged that some of his "foolish Young Men" had burned several houses at the mouth of the Kanawha River, but blamed the Mingoes for putting "evil stories" into their heads. He promised to send runners "to direct my People to sit still and do no mischief while we are doing Business," and said he would take no notice if any of those rash young warriors were killed by the Americans. The Shawnee delegates promised to adhere to their agreements at Camp Charlotte, which included the return of all captives, black and white, although Cornstalk balked at the idea of returning the offspring of a black woman and a Shawnee father as "we thought it very hard they shou'd be made Slaves of." At the end of the council, with the Virginia commissioners' reminders ringing in their ears of the treatment they had received in Pontiac's War and Dunmore's War, the assembled Indians confirmed the Ohio River as the boundary between Indian and white territory.[20]

In the spring and summer of 1776, Cornstalk assured American Indian agent George Morgan of his people's determination to remain neutral in the growing conflict. He and his Maquachake kinsfolk continued to talk peace in the towns along the Miami and the Scioto rivers, but many Chillicothes, Piquas, and Kispokis were not listening. These Shawnee divisions remained unreconciled to the Maquachakes' acquiescence in the consequences of Dunmore's War, and saw only continued American encroachment on their lands.[21] When Indian agent Matthew Elliott – still in the service of the Americans at the time – visited the Kispoki Shawnee towns in the summer of 1776, he feared a general Indian war. In August, Shawnee emissaries carried a nine-foot war belt to the Cherokees, helping to precipitate bloody warfare on the borders of Virginia and the Carolinas.[22]

Nevertheless, that fall, Shawnee peace advocates attended another multitribal treaty council at Fort Pitt, which the American agent George Morgan misread as a broader commitment to neutrality by the tribes.[23] In private conference, Cornstalk, Nimwha, and other Maquachakes assured Morgan that the source of the troubles lay not with the British at Detroit but in the villages of the Mingo "Banditti" around Pluggy's Town. Cornstalk expected a reciprocal exchange of information between the Maquachakes and the Americans: "I depend upon you

[20] Scribner et al., eds., *Revolutionary Virginia*, vol. 4: 140–1, 184–90, 193–6, 208–9, 222–4; *Revolution on the Upper Ohio*, 92–3; *North Carolina Colonial Records*, vol. 10: 386; *Revolution and Confederation*, 104–6.

[21] *PCC*, reel 80, item 163: 245–7; Speech of Cornstalk, June 21, 1776, George Morgan Letterbook, 1776, Pennsylvania Historical Commission, Harrisburg; Stevens, "His Majesty's 'Savage' Allies," 732–6.

[22] *North Carolina Colonial Records*, vol. 10: 660–1; 763–85; *DAR*, vol. 12: 191–208.

[23] *Revolution on the Upper Ohio*, 216–17; *American Archives*, 5th series, vol. 3: 599–600; Morgan Letterbook, Carnegie Library, vol. 1: 13, vol. 2: 19–21.

that I may remove out of danger with my Children & you may rely you shall not be ignorant of what passes among the red people – I will give you constant notice & will never deceive you."[24]

Nonetheless, American invasion of Shawnee country rankled with the Maquachakes as much as with their more belligerent relatives. Settlers and land speculators pushed into Kentucky even as the Maquachakes were trying to stem the Shawnee drift to war. In early November, Cornstalk addressed his concerns to Congress via George Morgan:

> When God created this World he gave this Island to the red people & placed your younger Brethren the Shawnees here in the Center – Now we & they see your people seated on our Lands which all Nations esteem as their & our heart – all our Lands are covered by the white people, & we are jealous that you still intend to make larger strides – We never sold you our Lands which you now possess on the Ohio between the Great Kenhawa & the Cherokee, & which you are settling without ever asking our leave, or obtaining our consent – Foolish people have desired you to do so, & you have taken their advice – We live by Hunting & cannot subsist in any other way – That was our hunting Country & you have taken it from us. This is what sits heavy upon our Hearts & on the Hearts of all Nations, and it is impossible for us to think as we ought to do whilst we are thus oppress'd with your [blank]. Now I stretch my Arm to you my wise Brethren of the United States met in Council at Philadelphia – I open my hand & pour into your heart the cause of our discontent in hopes that you will take pity of us your younger Brethren, and send us a favorable Answer, that we may be convinced of the sincerity of your profession.[25]

Maquachake peace advocates continued to keep the Americans informed about developments in Indian country and among their own people. In late February 1777, Cornstalk, Kishanosity, the civil chief Moluntha, the war chief Oweeconne, and other Maquachake head men and women sent messengers to George Morgan, reassuring him of their desire for peace. Once again they blamed the Mingoes for corrupting their young warriors. The chiefs could do little to prevent warriors going out against the encroaching Americans: "They will not listen to me – when I speak to them they will attend for a Moment & sit still whilst they are within my Sight. – at night they steal their Blankets & run off to where the evil Spirit leads them." They assured Morgan that only a few warriors were causing trouble, but the Maquachake peace faction clearly was in the minority and losing ground. The chiefs said they intended to separate

[24] At a private conference, Oct. 26, 1776, Morgan Letterbook, 1776.
[25] Speech of Cornstalk, Nov. 7, 1776, Morgan Letterbook, 1776, reproduced in Francis Jennings et al., eds., *Iroquois Indians: A Documentary History of the Diplomacy of the Six Nations and Their League,* 50 reels. (Woodbridge, Conn.: Research Publications, 1985), reel 32; and in *Revolution and Confederation,* 147.

from those who wanted war and to build a new town. In March, the Delaware council reminded the Shawnees of what had befallen them three years previously and invited them to settle at the Delaware capital, Coshocton. Cornstalk planned to move his people closer to the Delawares where, he said, they would be safer from Mingo threats.[26]

As the war party continued to gain strength in their villages, many Shawnee warriors accepted the war belt from Governor Henry Hamilton at Detroit and joined the Mingoes in raiding the American frontier. George Morgan and General Edward Hand reported in July that two tribes of the Shawnees had "become unmanageable," although two others remained in the American interest. That summer, Cornstalk's sister, Nonhelema, known to the Americans as the Grenadier Squaw, carried a warning to the garrison at Fort Randolph that her nation had joined the British.[27] Such factionalism was not uncommon in wartime, often splitting towns as well as nations: old men early in the next century could not remember an occasion when "more than one-half of the nation have been at war at the same time."[28]

American militia helped to heal the split for many Shawnees. On October 6, 1777, Captain Matthew Arbuckle, commanding at Fort Randolph on the Kanawha, informed Edward Hand that he had detained two Shawnees who came into the fort professing friendship and asking for information. A few days later, Cornstalk's son, Elinipsico, came to the fort to see why they were being detained and said his father would be there shortly. Arbuckle resolved to detain "as many as fall into my hands" as hostages for the Shawnees' good behavior. A month later, Arbuckle reported that he had confined Cornstalk and two other Shawnees. He requested instructions as to what he should do with them, "as I am well satisfied the Shawanese are all our enemies." Cornstalk, his son, and two other Shawnees named Red Hawk and Petalla were now in confinement. On November 10th, in supposed retaliation for the killing of a white man near the fort, members of the militia broke into the cabin where the Indians were being held and killed them all. Cornstalk and his son met their deaths as the soldiers burst through the door; Red Hawk was killed as he tried to escape up the chimney; "the other Indian was shamefully mangled." According to one

---

[26] *American Archives*, 5th series, vol. 3: 600; *Revolution on the Upper Ohio*, 14–15; *Frontier Defense*, 164–7; Stevens, "His Majesty's 'Savage' Allies," 965–6, 1508–12; *PCC*, reel 180, item 163: 269–70; Edward Hand Papers, LC, Force Transcripts, series 7E, reel 13, item 55, Letterbook: 61; Morgan Letterbook, vol. 1: 47–8, 57–9.

[27] Draper Mss. 1U68; *PCC*, reel 180, item 163: 278; *Frontier Defense*, 20, 25; Hand Papers, reel 13, item 55, Letterbook: 40–2; Stevens, "His Majesty's 'Savage' Allies," 1299–1300.

[28] John Johnston, "Recollections of Sixty Years," in Leonard U. Hill, *John Johnston and the Indians in the Land of the Three Miamis* (Piqua, Ohio, 1957), 189. It is not clear whether Johnston's informants were speaking about the Indians in Ohio generally or about the Shawnees in particular. Johnston certainly knew the Shawnees best, and the recollections of division fit them better than any other tribe.

account, which may have been a posthumous invention, Cornstalk had a pre-monition of death and just an hour before his murder had sat in council with the Americans:

> His countenance was dejected; and he made a speech, all of which seemed to indicate an honest and manly disposition. He acknowledged that he and his party would have to run with the stream, for all the Indians on the lakes and northwardly, were joining the British.[29]

The Governors of Pennsylvania and Virginia sent urgent messages of regret to the Shawnees; George Morgan conveyed Congress's sorrow, and Patrick Henry publicly denounced the murders. But the damage was done. As General Hand recognized, "If we had anything to expect from that Nation it is now Vanished."[30] The Chillicothe war chief, Black Fish, raided into Kentucky in the winter of 1777–8, capturing Daniel Boone and twenty-six companions in a snowstorm. In May 1778 Shawnee warriors struck the Kanawha Valley around Fort Randolph.

But revenge was not the only engine driving the Shawnees. The Maquachakes remained predominantly neutral. In accordance with Cornstalk's final wishes, his followers moved to the Delaware capital of Coshocton. White Eyes, the pro-American leader of the Delaware Turtle clan, traveled to Cornstalk's town on the upper Scioto in midwinter and accompanied some Maquachakes back to Coshocton. The Delawares and the Moravians provided the newcomers with corn to see them through the winter. According to White Eyes, the Maquachakes did "not take it so much to Heart that their Chief at the Canhewa is killed, but take hold to the Chain of Friendship & mind nothing else." More Maquachakes migrated in the spring, and by April seventeen families under Kishanosity, Oweeconne, and Nimwha had settled at Coshocton. In White Eyes's words, they "became the same people" with the Delawares.[31]

The Maquachake division remained the most inclined to peace throughout the war, and Maquachake delegates continued to affirm that "all the Mischief that has been done is by the Mingoes, who live among us and will not listen to us." They themselves were "determined to sit still and preserve their women

[29] *Frontier Defense*, 125–8, 149–50, 157–62, 175–7; Hand Papers, reel 13, item 55, Letterbook: 35–9, 44–8; Draper Mss. 2YY91–4; 3NN69–71; 3D164–73; Charles A. Stuart, ed. *Memoirs of Indian Wars, and Other Occurrences; By the late Colonel Stuart, of Greenbrier* (New York: Arno, 1971), 58–62. Another version of the "drift with the stream" speech is in Draper Mss. 2YY92; Stevens, "His Majesty's 'Savage' Allies," 1510, is justifiably suspicious of it as a later invention.

[30] *Frontier Defense*, 188–92, 205–9, 234–7, 258–61; Morgan Letterbook, vol. 3: 18–20.

[31] Haldimand Papers, 21782: 297: Hand Papers, reel 13, item 55, Letterbook: 16: 55; *PCC*, reel 91, item 78, vol. 1: 420; *Frontier Defense*, 166, 242; *Frontier Advance*, 91, 110, 143, 193, 234, 245; Morgan Letterbook, vol, 3: 27, 54, 56, 96; *Revolution and Confederation*, 164; John Heckewelder, *Narrative of the Mission of the United Brethren among the Delaware and Mohegan Indians* (Philadelphia: McCary & Davis, 1820), 149; Erminie Wheeler Voegelin, "Ethnohistory of Indian Use and Occupancy in Ohio and Indiana Prior to 1795," in Tanner and Voegelin, *Indians of Ohio and Indiana*, vol. 2: 497; Stevens, "His Majesty's 'Savage' Allies," 1593–4, 2372, n. 40.

and Children, and think of nothing but peace."[32] Cornstalk's sister, Nonhelema, consistently supported the American cause. She left her people and moved to Fort Randolph, bringing cattle to the garrison and frequently acting as an interpreter and messenger for the Americans. Her people disowned her and in old age and poverty she was compelled to petition the United States for support. She requested a grant of 2,000 acres on the west bank of the Scioto River where she once lived and where her mother was buried; Congress granted her a suit of clothes and a blanket each year, and daily rations for life, "which she may receive at any post in the western territory she shall chuse."[33]

Meanwhile, by late 1777 and early 1778, a general exodus of Shawnees from the Scioto Valley was taking place. Several towns moved to the Miami River and its tributaries, where they would be less vulnerable to assault. Cornstalk's faction of Maquachakes had moved east to Coshocton, leaving Cornstalk's town all but deserted. The Grenadier Squaw's Town was also probably abandoned by this time, as were the towns at Maquachake on the Scioto River, Piqua on Deer Creek, Blue Jacket's Town and McKee's Town on Paint Creek, and others. Most of the Maquachakes, presumably under Moluntha, joined other Shawnees in withdrawing to the north and west. From 1778, Maquachake became located on the Mad River near present-day West Liberty, Ohio.[34]

As concern over American encroachments grew, more Shawnees accepted Hamilton's war belt in the spring of 1778.[35] At some point, the nation split over the question of continued, and perhaps endless, resistance to the Americans. Though many Maquachakes and Kispokis wanted peace, most Chillicothes and Piquas remained cool to the Americans and favored joining the Mingoes.[36] Kikusgawlowa (Kishkalwa) led part of the Thawekilas south into Creek country in 1774, brought them back to the Ohio years later, and then moved west of the Mississippi.[37] Beginning around 1779 or 1780, Yellow Hawk and Black Stump led some twelve hundred Shawnees, primarily from the Thawekila, Piqua, and Kispoki divisions, down the Ohio Valley. Eventually, many of these people migrated west to Missouri, where they took up lands after the Revolution near Cape Girardeau under the auspices of the Spanish government. Long-distance

---

[32] J. Almon, *The Remembrancer* (London, 1775–1784), 1780, part 1: 152–8; Hand Papers, reel 13, item 55, 262: 234.

[33] *Frontier Advance*, 67–70; Louise P. Kellogg, "Non-hel-e-ma, Shawnee Princess," in William A. Galloway, *Old Chillicothe* (Xenia, Ohio: Buckeye, 1934), 283–95; *PCC*, reel 37, item 30: 371–3; reel 69, item 56: 165, 169–70; Draper Mss. 3D39, 14S158–60: Hand Papers, Letterbook: 40.

[34] Voegelin in Tanner and Voegelin, *Indians of Ohio and Indiana*, vol. 2: 532–3, 647–8; Helen Hornbeck Tanner, ed., *Atlas of Great Lakes Indian History* (Norman: University of Oklahoma Press, 1987), map 16.

[35] "McKee's report," June 28, 1778, NYPL, Chalmers Collection, Papers relating to Indians; Haldimand Papers, 21781: 28; *MPHC*, vol. 9: 434, 442–58; *Frontier Defense*, 282.

[36] Hand Papers, reel 13, item 55: 262, 234; *Penn. Archives*, 1st series, vol. 12: 179–80.

[37] Alford, *Civilization*, 200–1; Thomas L. McKenney and James Hall, *History of the Indian Tribes of North America, with Biographical Sketches and Anecdotes of the Principal Chiefs*, 3 vols. (Philadelphia: Biddle, 1836–44), vol. 1: 15–18; Galloway, *Old Chillicothe*, 40.

migration to the west was nothing new: some Shawnees moved to the Illinois River in the 1680s; Shawnee traditions say they began to cross the Mississippi as early as 1763, and Missouri Indians killed a Shawnee chief in the west in 1773. But no early migrations split the nation like this one. Shawnee movements in the west continued, and Shawnee history after the Revolution has to be traced in Missouri, Kansas, Texas, and Oklahoma, as well as in Ohio, Alabama, and Indiana.[38]

The Shawnees who remained in Ohio were mainly Chillicothes and Maquachakes, with an amalgam of members from other divisions who refused to leave their homelands. The Maquachakes may have continued to hope they could reach an accommodation with the Americans, but conflicting reports left the American frontier unsure of Shawnee intentions.[39] In February 1779, Shawnees attending a multitribal council at Detroit took up the hatchet against the Big Knives.[40] In March the Delaware council at Coshocton urged the Shawnees, Mingoes, and Wyandots to consider their women and children and refrain from the warpath. The Shawnees responded by choosing Nimwha, their "oldest brother," to go with them to the main town, "The place w[h]ere all the Heads of the Nations gather," and consider it.[41] In April, Daniel Brodhead, the commander at Fort Pitt, stepped up the pressure and sent the Shawnees a speech advising them that this was their last chance to listen to the Delawares. On the same day the Delawares sent another plea to the Maquachakes. But when Shawnee warriors burned Brodhead's speech in defiance, the general was in no doubt how to treat them.[42] Meanwhile, Shawnee emissaries met with western tribes and carried war belts south to Creek and Chickasaw country.[43]

With Shawnee hostility apparently well established, American invasions of Shawnee country became an almost annual event. American troops burned crops and villages, while American forts on the perimeters of their country kept Shawnee communities on a war footing. While the rest of the nation gravitated

[38] Clark, "Shawnee Indian Migration: A System Analysis," 52–3, 64; Kinietz and Voegelin, eds., "Shawnese Traditions," xiv; Howard, *Shawnee*, 15–16; Alford, *Civilization*, 10n–11n, 201; Galloway, *Old Chillicothe*, 41–2, 56, 181–2. Voegelin thought 1774 marked the beginning of the Shawnee westward movement; Voegelin in Tanner and Voegelin, *Indians of Ohio and Indiana*, vol. 2: 382. References to a Shawnee who had been to New Orleans, and to the chief killed by Missouris, are in *DAR*, vol. 4: 374–5; vol. 5: 279. For mention of Shawnees visiting Saint Louis in 1769, and around Cape Girardeau after the Revolution, see Louis Houck, ed., *The Spanish Regime in Missouri*, 2 vols. (New York: Arno Press and New York Times reprint of 1909 ed.), vol. 1: 45, 210; vol. 2: 50–94. For observations on the Shawnees living around Cape Girardeau in the 1790s, see Clements Library, Louis Vincent, "Journal de Mes Voyages," 133–41.
[39] *Frontier Advance*, 242–7.
[40] Ibid., 220.
[41] Draper Mss. 1H44.
[42] Ibid. 1H51–4; 1H66–7; 2H10; *Penn. Archives*, 1st series, vol. 12: 120; *Frontier Advance*, 279–81, 349, 358.
[43] Haldimand Papers, 21782: 181–2, 247; John D. Barnhart, ed., *Henry Hamilton and George Rogers Clark in the American Revolution, with the Unpublished Journal of Lieutenant Governor Hamilton* (Crawfordsville, Ind.: Banta, 1951), 168–9.

toward the British, the Maquachake civil chiefs once again endeavored to seek peace. They sent peace feelers to Brodhead via their Delaware allies and went to Fort Pitt in September 1779 to meet the commander on his return from his expedition against the Allegheny Seneca and Munsee towns, even though the rest of the tribe remained obdurate. The Delaware, Killbuck, advised them: "It is true, you have done no harm, but I see some stains of blood upon you, which the mischief and folly of your young men have occasioned." The only way to wash away the blood was for the Maquachakes to return to Brodhead all the horses and captives their people had taken. Moreover, peace with the Americans could be bought only at the cost of going to war against the English and the Mingoes. "The thirteen United States and I are one," said Killbuck, who had already fought for the Americans; "now I offer you the flesh of the English and Mingoes to eat, and that is the only method I know of, by which your lives may be preserved, and you allowed to live in peace." The Maquachakes took the string of wampum and two scalps that Killbuck handed them and sang the war song, probably with little enthusiasm. "I think the Maquichees are honest," Killbuck reported to Brodhead. "In former times they were the best of the Shawanese nations. I think we may take them by the hand."[44]

Faced with the prospect of war despite their best efforts for peace, the Maquachakes realized that Coshocton offered them no sanctuary in a world at war. The Delaware capital itself was in an increasingly perilous position as warriors from the Great Lakes tribes congregated in the area, and the Americans failed to live up to their promise of building a blockhouse to protect the town. Deep snow prevented Brodhead from bringing in any supplies, even though the Delawares and Maquachakes had previously asked him to send them traders "as our women & Children are poor & naked & in danger of perishing by the severity of the winter." Finally, Nimwha, who had been a constant advocate of peace and accommodation since Dunmore's War, died. The Maquachakes around Coshocton decided to return to the Scioto and rejoin the Maquachakes under Moluntha. They explained their decision to their Delaware hosts in February 1780: "*Grandfathers* listen: My chief Nimwha is dead whom I used to listen to & whom Kishanosity set before you the king of the Maquichees has sent for me & I am going to him as soon as I see him I will know better where I shall live."[45] The Maquachakes read the signs accurately: Brodhead burned Coshocton the next year.[46] A few Delawares clung to their American allegiance and took refuge at Fort Pitt, but most joined the flow to the British. In November, responding

---

[44] *Penn. Archives*, 1st series, vol. 12: 131–2, 157–8; *Frontier Advance*, 33, 142–3, 368–9; *Frontier Retreat*, 73–5; *Revolution and Confederation*, 194–5; *Remembrancer*, 1780, pt. 1: 153–8.

[45] Voegelin, in Tanner and Voegelin, *Indians of Ohio and Indiana*, vol. 2: 505; Heckewelder, *Narrative*, 208; Draper Mss. 1H126; *Frontier Retreat*, 139. Heckewelder said the Maquachakes returned to the Scioto, but it is more likely that they passed through the area on their way to join Moluntha's people.

[46] *Frontier Retreat*, 391.

to British interrogation about the whereabouts of the Coshocton Indians, the Moravians replied that they were "dispersed everywhere, as they have deserted their villages."[47]

Shawnee war parties were active on the frontiers in the spring of 1780: the British at Detroit reported the Shawnees and their allies were bringing in scalps every day, "having at present a great field to act upon."[48] Thomas Jefferson wanted to see the Ohio Shawnees exterminated or driven from their lands, and he advocated turning other tribes against them. Brodhead too now regarded them as the primary target, "because I am persuaded they are the most hostile of any Savage Tribe, and could they receive a severe Chastisement it would probably put an end to the Indian war."[49] In August 1780, the Delawares at Coshocton sent a message to the Shawnees and Delawares at Wakatomica; though the latter obstinately refused to heed their advice and make peace with the Americans, the Coshocton Delawares felt compelled to warn them of the danger they were in as an American army assembled at Fort Pitt, ready to march against them.[50]

After George Rogers Clark invaded Shawnee country that summer, the Delawares interceded on behalf of their Shawnee "grandchildren." But Brodhead replied that the Shawnees had done much mischief and would have to pay for it before long. "It may be," he said in reference to Matthew Elliott, Alexander McKee, and the Girty brothers, who had gone over to the British early in 1778, "that the Shawanese would not have been so foolish if it was not put into their heads by some bad people who live with them & are paid by the English to tell them lyes."[51]

Most Shawnees required little incitement by foreign agents by this time. In the spring of 1781, Wryneck led a multitribal delegation to Detroit and, speaking for the confederacy of Ohio tribes, urged the British to gather their soldiers and muster the lake tribes to support the Shawnee war effort. "We see ourselves weak and our arms feeble to the force of the Enemy," declared Wryneck. "'Tis now upwards of Twenty years since we have been alone engaged against the Virginians."[52]

The conflict had become a total war for the Shawnees. Traditionally, Shawnees had often adopted captives to help maintain population levels. Now, with the war taking a heavy toll, captives were painted black and marked for death with

[47] MPHC, vol. 10: 539–40.
[48] Haldimand Papers, 21781: 74.
[49] Julian P. Boyd, ed., The Papers of Thomas Jefferson (Princeton, N. J.: Princeton University Press, 1950–), vol. 3: 259, 276; Draper Mss. 50J7, 50J39; James Alton James, ed., George Rogers Clark Papers, 1771–1781 (Springfield: Illinois State Historical Library, 1912), 390, 419; Penn. Archives, 1st series, vol. 12: 238.
[50] Haldimand Papers, 21782: 384.
[51] Frontier Retreat, 299.
[52] MPHC, vol. 10 (1886): 462–5.

increasing frequency. Even so, the Shawnee still held in "mild captivity" the prisoners they had formerly taken; only those recently captured who had threatened their extermination were put to death.[53] Shawnee warriors continued to carry the war to the Americans, participated in the rout of the Kentuckians at Blue Licks in the summer of 1782, and assisted in the defeat of William Crawford's expedition that same year.[54] Clark invaded Shawnee country again in the fall.[55] That winter, Shawnees congregated around Maquachake, Girty's Town, Blue Jacket's Town, and Wakatomica, the only towns Clark had not attacked.

Despite the destruction of their crops and villages, and the disruption of their cycles of subsistence and ceremony, Shawnees survived the recurrent invasions. Physical movement was a relatively simple operation for people whose lodges "could be built easily in a few days, and were abandoned with little concern."[56] They pulled back when American armies invaded their country, watched as the troops torched villages and cornfields, then returned or rebuilt new homes in safer locations after the enemy departed. Cornfields and hunting territories beyond the reach of American strikes, as well as British supplies from Detroit, sustained their war effort.[57] Colonel William Christian, writing to Governor Benjamin Harrison of Virginia in September 1782, lamented that "Kentucky employs the attention of the Bulk of the Shawnee Nation" and predicted that if the war continued for another year all the inhabitants of Kentucky would be killed, carried off as captives to Detroit, or driven away.[58] The Shawnees were holding their own.

Suddenly, British officers and agents were urging chiefs to restrain their warriors and tried to sell them the Peace of Paris as offering a new era of peace with the Americans. When hunters from Chillicothe lost stock to American horse thieves in the summer of 1783, Major De Peyster at Detroit regretted their loss but pointed out "the times are very Critical[;] the World wants to be at Peace & its time they should be so." If the Shawnees took action, "it must be an affair of your own, as your Father can take no part in it."[59] British actions

[53] NAC, Claus Papers, vol. 3: 147–8, 156; Haldimand Papers, 21762: 116; C. C. Trowbridge, "Shawnee Traditions," cited in Howard, Shawnee, 125.

[54] Haldimand Papers, 21762: 149–50; 21781: 85–6.

[55] Draper Mss. 8J320–2, 11J24, 11S160–2, 1AA275–7; Claus Papers, vol. 3: 189–90; C.O. 5/109: 49; C.O. 42/15: 381; Haldimand Papers, 21717: 158; 21775: 49; 21756: 88, 91, 93–5, 125–8, 132, 135; 21762: 238; 21763: 1; 21775: 49; 21779: 109–10; 21781: 88; "Journal of Daniel Boone," Ohio Archaeological and Historical Publications 13 (1904), 276; Virginia State Papers 3 (1883), 381–2.

[56] Thomas Wildcat Alford, in Galloway, Old Chillicothe, 175.

[57] James, ed., George Rogers Clark Papers, 381–3, 605; Draper Mss. 26J127–8; MPHC, vol. 19 (1891): 598.

[58] Virginia State Papers, vol. 3 (1883): 331.

[59] Colin G. Calloway, Crown and Calumet: British–Indian Relations, 1783–1815 (Norman: University of Oklahoma Press, 1987), 3–23; Claus Papers, vol. 3: 219; MPHC, vol. 20 (1892): 122–3, 153–4; J. Watts De Peyster, Miscellanies by an Officer. By Colonel Arent Schuyler De Peyster, 1774–1813 (New York: Chalmers, 1888), xxxix–xl; NAC, C-1223, vol. 13: 231.

lent force to the gloating words of American major Wall to the Shawnees during an exchange of prisoners at the Ohio falls in July: "Your Fathers the English have made Peace with us for themselves, but forgot you their Children, who Fought with them, and neglected you like Bastards."[60]

This was the real disaster of the Revolution for the Shawnees. Between 1775 and 1790 some eighty thousand people poured into Shawnee hunting territories, an invasion of settlers and land speculators that gathered pace dramatically after Independence.[61] Any hopes the Shawnees had of recovering their Kentucky lands disappeared with the end of the Revolution. Having carried the fight south of the Ohio and lost, Shawnees henceforth fought to preserve their lands north of the river. They were left to face American aggression on their own, but remained committed to the defense of their lands. With Simon Girty interpreting, Captain Johnny, or Kekewepelethe, who was Maquachake war leader along with Oweecone,[62] told the Americans in 1785, "You are drawing so close to us that we can almost hear the noise of your axes felling our Trees and settling our Country." He warned that if settlers crossed the Ohio, "we shall take up a Rod and whip them back to your side."[63]

The Maquachakes returned their war belts to the British in 1784, signifying their intention to remain at peace, and acted as intermediaries conveying Virginian peace talks to their nation's great council fire. "Wee are Hear in the Center and It is not in our power at Present, to send you an answer," Moluntha, Peniwesica, and White Wolf informed the Virginians. They promised to meet with them as soon as they heard from the great council fire and hoped to make a peace that would "Last Whilst Gras Groes and Waters Runes."[64] But peace remained elusive. Many Shawnees carried on the fight for another dozen years and took a leading role in an emerging multitribal confederacy.

The Shawnees refused to participate in the multitribal land cession at Fort McIntosh in 1785. The Americans regarded an accommodation with the Shawnees as crucial to establishing peace with the western tribes, and Congressional emissaries traveled from Pittsburgh to meet with the Shawnees in council at Maquachake in the summer of 1785. The Shawnees and Indians

---

[60] Haldimand Papers, 21779: 117.
[61] Peter H. Wood, "The Changing Population of the Colonial South: An Overview by Race and Region, 1685–1790," in Peter H. Wood, Gregory A. Waselkov and M. Thomas Hatley, eds., *Powhatan's Mantle* (Lincoln: University of Nebraska Press, 1989), 86; *MPHC*, vol. 19 (1891): 519; G. Imlay, *A Topographical Description of the Western Territory of North America* (London: Debrett, 1792), 24, 67.
[62] I am grateful to John Sugden for identifying Captain Johnny as Kekewepelethe, despite some confusion in the documents.
[63] "At a Council held at Wakitunikee, May 18, 1785," British Museum, Miscellaneous American Papers, Additional Mss., 24322; also in C.O. 42/47: 370–1, and *MPHC*, vol. 25 (1896): 691–3; cf. *PCC*, reel 69, item 56: 113–15; and *North Carolina State Records*, vol. 17: 159–60.
[64] *MPHC*, vol. 25 (1896): 690; *Virginia State Papers*, vol. 3: 565. Kekewepelethe and other warriors also sent speeches to Virginia "as our Great Chief Rynack, was taken from us by Death, before he could finish the Business." *Virginia State Papers*, vol. 3: 566.

from other nations held several councils there, some in secret, "all of which," said Major Samuel Montgomery in his journal of the trip, "denoted a disinclination of accepting the protection and friendship offered to them." The Americans attributed Shawnee intransigence to the influence of British agents like Girty.[65]

Three hundred disgruntled Shawnees finally met the American commissioners Richard Butler and George Rogers Clark at Fort Finney in January 1786. The majority of the Shawnees were Maquachakes, fulfilling their traditional role as negotiators, but the discussions were heated. Kekewepelethe took a defiant stand, and the Shawnees complained "that we were putting them to live on ponds, and leaving them no land to live or raise corn on." Clark and Butler responded by rejecting the Shawnees' wampum belt and threatened that refusing the American terms would bring about the destruction of their women and children. Moluntha stepped in to counsel moderation and accommodation, and the Shawnees ceded tribal lands east of the Great Miami. But they warned the Americans, "This is not the way to make a good or lasting Peace to take our Chiefs Prisoners and come with Soldiers at your Backs."[66] Moluntha, Oweeconne, and Musquaconah or Red Pole all signed the treaty.[67]

The commissioners realized that the elder chiefs from whom they obtained the cession were losing authority to a new generation of warriors who came of age during long years of recurrent warfare. Richard Butler noted "that many of the young fellows which have grown up through the course of the war, and *trained like young hounds to blood*, have a great attachment to the British; . . . the chiefs of any repute are and have been averse to the war, but their influence is not of sufficient weight to prevent them from committing mischief, which they regret very much." Six years later, in meetings held at the Glaize, Shawnee war leaders sat *in front* of civil leaders during councils. Traditional seating arrangements reflected the primary influence of the village chiefs and the primacy of their peaceful role except when the nation was on a war footing.[68]

---

[65] *PCC*, reel 69, item 56: 248–9, 377–82; David Bushnell, Jr., "The Journal of Samuel Montgomery: A Journey Through the Indian Country beyond the Ohio, 1785," *Mississippi Valley Historical Review* 2 (1915–16), 272–3.

[66] *The Military Journal of Major Ebenezer Denny* (Philadelphia: Lippincot, 1859), 63–75; "Journal of General Butler," in Neville B. Craig, ed., *The Olden Time*, 2 vols. (Cincinnati, Ohio: Clarke, 1876), vol. 2: 512–31; *Revolution and Confederation*, 340–7.

[67] Charles J. Kappler, ed., *Indian Affairs: Laws and Treaties*, 2 vols. (Washington, D.C.: Government Printing Office, 1904), vol. 2: 16; *Revolution and Confederation*, 349–51; Voegelin in Tanner and Voegelin, *Indians of Ohio and Indiana*, vol. 2: 568–9. Thanks to John Sugden for identifying Musquaconah as Red Pole, or possibly Reed Pool.

[68] Craig, ed., *Olden Time*, vol. 2: 515; B. H. Coates, ed., "A Narrative of an Embassy to the Western Indians from the Original Manuscript of Hendrick Aupaumut," *Memoirs of the Historical Society of Pennsylvania* 2 (1827), pt. 1, 118. Howard, *Shawnee*, 96, 108. C. C. Trowbridge said that the position of war chief, which could be achieved only by merit, was more prestigious than that of the village chiefs, but by the time he gathered his information from the Shawnee Prophet, generations of warfare may have altered old patterns. Kinietz and Voegelin, "Shawanese Traditions," 11–13, 17.

Many Shawnees were outraged by the land cessions made by Moluntha and other chiefs, and Matthew Elliott convinced them to disavow what had happened at Fort Finney.[69] In April, Moluntha and the Shade appealed to the British for help, claiming the American commissioners had deceived them as to the real purpose of the treaty.[70] At the same time, Moluntha endeavored to maintain peace with the Americans and to carry out the commitments he had made. He asked the United States to be patient and consider the workings of Shawnee consensus politics:

> It is not with us as it is with you, for if you say to a man do so why it must be done, but consider we are a lawless people and can do nothing with our people only but by fair words and likewise our people is very much scattered and our business cannot be done as soon as what you would expect likewise we have a great deal of business upon hand at this time and has had for some time past which entirely lays on us at Mackochek town so I would have you not to think hard of us for we are determined to hold fast our friendship.

The Maquachakes faced the same old problems in trying to steer a middle course. Moluntha could accept no responsibility for the actions of the Mingoes and Cherokees who continued to commit hostilities, though he did provide the Americans with information as to their whereabouts. The nation remained divided. The Chillicothe Shawnees took a more intransigent stance and refused to give up their captives, which often entailed binding and handing over adopted children who in any case would run back to them at the first opportunity. Younger warriors refused to listen to the older chiefs, whom they accused of having sold out. Moluntha ended his speech by asking for a little tobacco to smoke in council and a little ink and paper, as it was impossible to get any at Maquachake.[71]

Even as the Maquachakes were endeavoring to keep the peace, border skirmishes continued and pressure mounted in Kentucky for another "campaign into the towns."[72] In October 1786, as Richard Butler received word from Indian country that "there is one town of the Shawnee, called Mackachack, that

---

[69] Richard White, *The Middle Ground: Indians, Empires, and Republics in the Great Lakes Region, 1650–1815* (Cambridge University Press, 1991), 438–9; Reginald Horsman, *Matthew Elliott, British Indian Agent* (Detroit: Wayne State University Press, 1964), 54–55; *MPHC*, vol. 24 (1895): 34.

[70] C.O. 42/49: 349.

[71] *PCC*, reel 64, item 150, vol. 1: 265, 431–3, 435–57; *Military Journal of Ebenezer Denny*, 87. Two Shawnees brought in a white boy at Fort Finney in January 1786, "and being asked if they did not think the boy would run back again, they candidly told us, that he certainly would, if not bound or confined some way." The boy was put on a boat and taken away weeping. *Military Journal of Ebenezer Denny*, 83.

[72] *Military Journal of Ebenezer Denny*, 64, 85, 93.

has done all in their power to keep the Shawnees from going to war," Kentucky had already launched an attack on the Maquachakes.[73] Benjamin Logan, with a force of 790 Kentucky militiamen, conducted "a wild scampering foray" into Shawnee country. Maquachake at this time consisted of two settlements: one on the west side of Mackachack Creek, a tributary of the Mad River, comprising twenty or thirty wigwams; and Moluntha's town on the other bank, which was smaller. Meeting little resistance – most Shawnee warriors seem to have been away on the Wabash, where Clark threatened an invasion – Logan's men killed the few Indians they found at Maquachake and burned the town. When they reached Moluntha's town, which was about a mile away, the old chief met them clutching a copy of the Fort Finney peace treaty while his people hoisted an American flag. Simon Girty said the Maquachakes could not believe the Americans would attack them and "rose their Yankee colours to receive them." To no avail. The Kentuckians destroyed the town and rounded up the Maquachakes. Colonel Hugh McGary, who in large measure had been responsible for the precipitate Kentuckian assault and subsequent rout at Blue Licks, asked Moluntha if he had been at the battle. Moluntha, who may not have understood the question, apparently nodded in the affirmative, smiling. McGary promptly killed him with an ax. Logan's report stated that the expedition destroyed seven Shawnee towns, killed ten chiefs, took thirty-two prisoners, burned some two hundred houses and an estimated fifteen thousand bushels of corn, carried off horses and cattle, and "took near one thousand pounds value of Indian furniture besides an unknown quantity burnt." Josiah Harmar considered the attack "a breach of faith on our part." Ebenezer Denny said "Logan found none but old men, women and children in the towns; they made no resistance; the men were literally murdered." A court martial that investigated McGary's murder of Moluntha suspended the colonel for one year.[74]

A month after Logan's attack, the Shawnees took a leading role in a multitribal council at the mouth of the Huron River. The united Indian nations resolved to present a united front to American aggression against their lands, "the Result

---

[73] Draper Mss. 1W249, quoted in Wiley Sword, *President Washington's Indian War* (Norman: University of Oklahoma Press, 1986), 37.

[74] *PCC*, reel 85, item 7, vol. 2: 471; William Henry Smith, ed., *St. Clair Papers: The Life and Public Services of Arthur St. Clair, ... With His Correspondence and Other Papers*, 2 vols. (Cincinnati, Ohio: Clarke, 1882) 2: 19; Draper Mss. 8J242, 11YY13; Haldimand Papers, 21736: 262–3; *MPHC*, vol. 24 (1895), 34–7; "Logan's Campaign – 1786," *Ohio Archaeological and Historical Publications* 22 (1913), 520–1; Charles G. Talbert, "Kentucky Invades Ohio – 1786," *Register of the Kentucky Historical Society* 54 (1956), 203–13; Voegelin in Tanner and Voegelin, *Indians of Ohio and Indiana*, vol. 2: 567, 569–70, 652; Clements Library, Josiah Harmar Papers, Letter Book B: 17–18, 23, 27–9; *Military Journal of Major Ebenezer Denny*, 94. McGary's court martial is in Draper Mss. 12S133–9; *Virginia State Papers*, vol. 4: 202, 212. Charles Gano Talbot, *Benjamin Logan, Kentucky Frontiersman* (Lexington: University of Kentucky Press, 1962), 209–12, describes the expedition. Musquaconah and the Shade were also reported killed, but Musquaconah died in Pittsburgh in 1797; thanks to John Sugden for this.

of which," noted British observers, "may deluge the Frontiers in Blood." The Shawnees continued to stress their desire for peace, but made it clear that no lands west of the Ohio would be given up without a fight.[75]

Each American invasion caused a renewed shift to the northwest until Shawnee population became congregated in new towns on the Auglaize and Maumee rivers; following the attack on the Shawnee towns in 1786, there was a general exodus toward the Miami towns at the head of the Maumee. Matthew Elliott moved his base of operations to the Maumee region also.[76] Others may have moved south to join relatives who had already taken up residence in Cherokee and Creek country, and there were four Shawnee towns on the Tallapoosea River by 1791.[77] More Shawnees migrated across the Mississippi – some two hundred Shawnees and Delawares left their villages on the Miami in the summer of 1787 and settled in the West – but British predictions that the Shawnees' fight for their lands would continue proved accurate.[78]

In 1787 Robert Todd burned the old Chillicothe town on Paint Creek and killed a handful of Indians, but just which Indians were the enemies remained subject to doubt. Benjamin Logan noted in May that some Chickamauga Cherokees were living on the Scioto and that "part of the Shawnies may be doing damage while the others are amongst us in a friendly manner. The matter is disputed among the People."[79] The new towns on the Maumee River became the targets of renewed American expeditions intending to cow the northwest confederacy. In 1790 General Josiah Harmar's army spent much of its time "burning and destroying everything that could be of use: corn, beans, pumpkins, stacks of hay, fencing and cabins, &c." but achieved little else (Fig. 6).[80] The Shawnees now moved their towns downstream to the Glaize region.

The war altered the composition as well as the location of Shawnee towns.

*[handwritten marginal note: War altered composition & location of Shawnee towns]*

[75] Haldimand Papers, 21763: 262–3. The proceedings of the Indian council are in C.O. 42/50: 66–73; the united nations's message to Congress is in *ASPIA*, vol. 1: 8–9; and in *Revolution and Confederation*, 356–8. PCC, reel 69, item 56: 113.

[76] On the movement of the various Shawnee towns, see Voegelin in Tanner and Voegelin, *Indians of Ohio and Indiana*, vol. 2: passim, esp. 532–6, 553; and Tanner, *Atlas of Great Lakes Indian History*, 79–91; Hill, *John Johnston and the Indians in the Land of the Three Miamis*, 6. John Bennett, *Blue Jacket, War Chief of the Shawnees and his Part in Ohio's History* (Chillicothe, Ohio, np. 1943), 16; Horsman, *Matthew Elliott, British Indian Agent*, 56.

[77] *DAR*, vol. 17: 121; Caleb Swan, "Position and State of Manners and Arts in the Creek or Muscoggee Nation in 1791," in Henry Rowe Schoolcraft, ed., *Historical and Statistical Information Respecting the History, Condition, and Prospects of the Indian Tribes of the United States*, 6 vols. (Philadelphia: Lippincott, Grumbo, 1851–7), vol. 5: 263; Henry Harvey, *History of the Shawnee Indians, from the Year 1681 to 1854* (Cincinnati: Morgan, 1855), 98–9.

[78] Haldimand Papers, 21775: 178; 21781: 86; *MPHC*, vol. 10: 650; *Military Journal of Ebenezer Denny*, 105.

[79] Voegelin, in Tanner and Voegelin, *Indians of Ohio and Indiana*, vol. 2: 535–6, citing Draper Mss. 9BB57, 60, 20S59–60, 23CC42–3, 4BB112; *Virginia State Papers* 4 (1884), 286.

[80] "General Harmar's Expedition," *Ohio Archaeological and Historical Publications* 20 (1911), 74–108; *Military Journal of Ebenezer Denny*, 146–7.

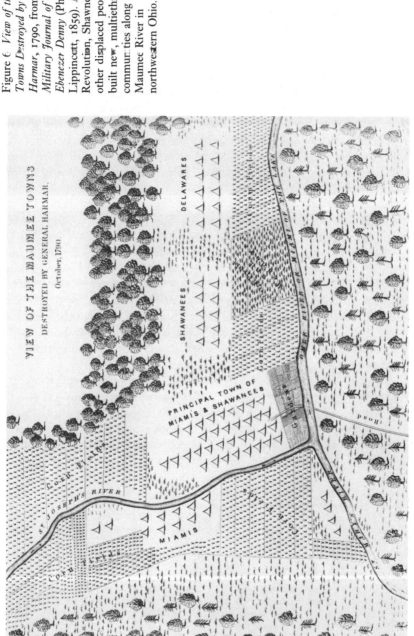

Figure 6 *View of the Maumee Towns Destroyed by General Harmar*, 1790, from *The Military Journal of Major Ebenezer Denny* (Philadelphia: Lippincott, 1859). After the Revolution, Shawnees joined other displaced peoples and built new, multiethnic communities along the Maumee River in northwestern Ohio.

Shawnee communities splintered and restructured. Mingoes, Senecas, and Cherokees joined Shawnee communities to continue the war effort. Moravian missionary John Heckewelder reported that "the Shawnees lost many of their men during these contests; but they were in a manner replaced by individuals of other nations joining them." He said that about one hundred "turbulent Cherokees" came over to the Shawnees. Samuel Montgomery noted the presence of Cherokee warriors at Maquachake in 1785. Shawnee towns took on the appearance of renegade strongholds in American eyes.[81] The distinctions and particular responsibilities of the five ancient divisions also seem to have become blurred as some groups moved west of the Mississippi and families from the several divisions crowded into the towns not destroyed by Clark. Kekewepelethe seems to have established a town on the Auglaize River around 1789. The residents of "Captain Johnny's Town" probably were predominantly Maquachakes, but the divisional composition of Shawnee towns becomes increasingly difficult to discern in the chaos of movement at the end of the Revolution. By 1791, the Shawnee communities themselves became part of a multitribal settlement that developed on the Glaize.[82]

Maquachake was not the only community in the Ohio country to attempt neutrality and pay heavily for the effort. Pacifist Moravian Delawares suffered removal by the British and Wyandots, and then massacre at the hands of American militia. The Delaware capital at Coshocton struggled to accommodate conflicting tensions and keep out of the war, but found itself pushed ever closer to the British, and was burned by American troops in 1781. Like the Maquachakes, these Delaware towns found the Ohio country no place to espouse neutrality in the American Revolution.[83]

Shawnees fought at Fallen Timbers in 1794, and many boycotted the Treaty of Greenville in 1795. A new generation of warriors carried the fight into the next century, and new leaders like Tecumseh attracted followings that cut across traditional patterns.[84] Most of Tecumseh's followers came from other tribes. A Maquachake chief, Black Hoof, pursued accommodation after the Treaty of Greenville and better reflected the peaceful desires of the majority of

*[margin annotation: miserable attempts at neutrality]*

---

[81] John Heckewelder, *History, Manners, and Customs of the Indian Nations Who Once Inhabited Pennsylvania and the Neighboring States* (New York: Arno, 1971), 89; Bushnell, ed., "Journal of Samuel Montgomery," 272; Haldimand Papers, 21763: 25; *PCC*, reel 69, item 56: 249; *Frontier Retreat*, vol. 1, 173; *MPHC*, vol. 20 (1892), 96; *Pennsylvania Archives*, 1st series, vol. 12: 223.

[82] Alford in Galloway, *Old Chillicothe*, 21; Howard, *Shawnee*, 86; R. David Edmunds, *Tecumseh and the Quest for Indian Leadership* (Boston: Little, Brown, 1984), 46–7; Sugden, *Blue Jacket*; Helen Hornbeck Tanner, "The Glaize in 1792: A Composite Indian Community," *Ethnohistory* 25 (Winter 1978), 15–39.

[83] Gregory Evans Dowd, *A Spirited Resistance: The North American Indian Struggle for Unity, 1745–1815* (Baltimore: Johns Hopkins University Press, 1992) describes the experiences of Coshocton and nearby Indians who sought to stand apart from the hostilities in ch. 4: "Neutrality, A World Too Narrow, 1775–1781."

[84] Johnston, "Recollections of Sixty Years," in Hill, *John Johnston and the Indians*, 154.

Shawnee people.[85] Nevertheless, the long struggle of the Maquachakes to preserve peace proved to no avail. Indian peoples who found themselves perpetually on the edge of the frontier had little chance of maintaining a middle ground in either the border warfare of the Revolution or in the national expansion to which independence gave birth.

[85] R. David Edmunds, "'Our Friendship is Strong and Pure': Black Hoof and the Loyal Shawnees," paper presented at the United States Capitol Historical Society, March 4–5, 1992.

# 7

# Chota: Cherokee beloved town in a world at war

By the eve of the American Revolution the Cherokee Indians in Georgia, the Carolinas, and Tennessee had undergone generations of wrenching changes that had produced alterations in the number and nature of their townships and in the structure of their society. Disrupted subsistence patterns, devastating smallpox epidemics in 1738 and 1759–60, involvement in the colonial wars of European powers, and the scorched-earth campaigns of British armies in 1760 and 1761 intensified a prolonged population decline that reduced the Cherokees from an estimated 22,000 people early in the century to perhaps 3,000 warriors (about 12,000 people) in 1775. Cherokee towns declined in number, from more than sixty to forty-three reported in 1775, although that decline may reflect population concentration more than population loss.[1] New technology and new values, overhunting of wildlife and adoption of domestic animals, combined with demographic decline, prompted major changes in Cherokee ecological relationships and set in motion modifications in settlement patterns as tribal towns began to give place to more individual farms and isolated settlements.[2] Political relationships within and between Cherokee towns altered: colonial

---

[1] Gary C. Goodwin, *Cherokees in Transition: A Study of Changing Culture and Environment Prior to 1775* (University of Chicago, Department of Geography, research paper 181, 1977), 111; Russell Thornton, *The Cherokees: A Population History* (Lincoln: University of Nebraska Press, 1990), esp. 21–32, compiles and discusses the data for Cherokee population decline; Betty Anderson Smith, "Distribution of Eighteenth-Century Cherokee Settlements," in Duane H. King, ed., *The Cherokee Indian Nation: A Troubled History* (Knoxville: University of Tennessee Press, 1979), 46–60, examines cartographic evidence for Cherokee towns and settlements; Raymond D. Fogelson and Paul Kutsche, "Cherokee Economic Cooperatives: The Gadugi," in William N. Fenton and John Gulick, eds., *Symposium on Cherokee and Iroquois Culture* (Bureau of American Ethnology, Bulletin 180, Washington, D.C., 1961), 88–98, also discuss eighteenth-century Cherokee towns and populations. See also Tom Hatley, *The Dividing Paths: Cherokees and South Carolinians through the Era of the Revolution* (New York: Oxford University Press, 1993).

[2] Goodwin, *Cherokees in Transition*, 2, 65, 81–2, 93, 103–4, 107, 113–14, 122–3, 145, 150–1; M. Thomas Hatley, "The Three Lives of Keowee: Loss and Recovery in Eighteenth-Century Cherokee Villages," in Peter H. Wood, Gregory A. Waselkov, and M. Thomas Hatley, eds., *Powhatan's Mantle: Indians in the Colonial Southeast* (Lincoln: University of Nebraska Press, 1989), 223–48; Samuel Cole Williams, ed., *Adair's History of the American Indians* (New York: Promontory, 1966), 238–45.

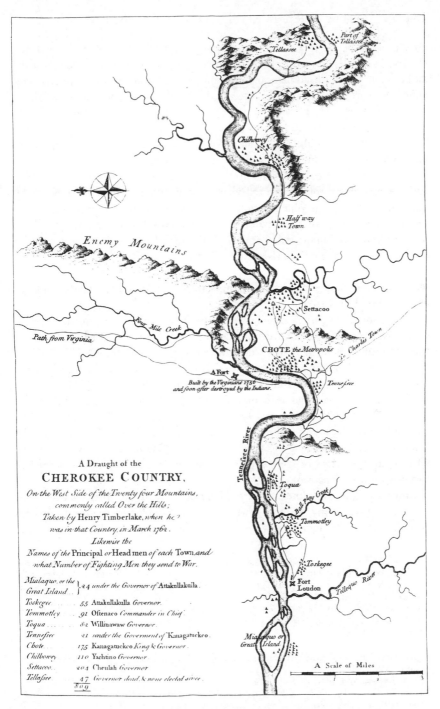

Within the map:

Part of Tellassee

Tellassee

Chilhowey

Half way Town

Enemy Mountains

Settacoo

CHOTE the Metropolis

To Charles Town

Five Mile Creek

Path from Virginia

A Fort
Built by the Virginians 1756
and soon after destroyed by the Indians.

Tennessee

Tennessee River

Toqua

Bell Play Creek

Tommotley

Toskegee

Fort Loudon

Tellequo River

Mialaquo or Great Island

A Scale of Miles

A Draught of the
**CHEROKEE COUNTRY,**

On the West Side of the Twenty four Mountains,
commonly called Over the Hills;
Taken by Henry Timberlake, when he
was in that Country, in March 1762.

Likewise the
Names of the Principal or Head men of each Town and
what Number of Fighting Men they send to War.

Mialaquo, or the } 24 under the Governor of Attakullakulla.
Great Island

Toskegee ....... 55 Attakullakulla Governor.
Tommotley ..... 91 Ostenaco Commander in Chief.
Toqua ........... 82 Willinawaw Governor.
Tennessee ...... 21 under the Goverment of Kanagatuckeo.
Chote ........... 175 Kanagatuckeo King & Governor.
Chilhowey ...... 110 Yachtino Governor.
Settacoo ........ 204 Cheulah Governor.
Tellassee ....... 47 Governor dead, & none elected since.
                  ———
                  809

Map 9. *A Draught of the Cherokee Country* by Lieutenant Henry Timberlake, 1762, showing the location of Chota – "the Metropolis" – and the warrior strength of the Overhill towns. From *The Memoirs of Lieut. Henry Timberlake* (London: Author, 1762).

governments began to hold all Cherokees responsible for the actions of any Cherokees, traders and their alcohol fueled the young men's challenge to the authority of village headmen, and the influence of women seems to have declined as Europeans, primarily interested in military alliances and deerskins, dealt almost exclusively with warriors and hunters.[3] New markets and new people induced Cherokees to shift from taking Indian war captives to trafficking in, and eventually holding, African slaves.[4] Cherokee religion also appears to have undergone drastic changes in the eighteenth century.[5]

While the Cherokees wrestled with far-reaching changes within their culture and society, other forces ensured that they would not be left in peace by outsiders. Their geographic location made them strategically important to the English colonies "as they form a barrier against powerful incursions of Indians on the Ohio and Illinois tribes and as a counterbalance against the Creeks in case of war with them."[6] It also rendered them susceptible to assault by other tribes. Their fertile valleys, which colonial surveyor William De Brahm reported were "of the richest Soil equal to Manure itself,"[7] ensured their lands would be coveted by white settlers.

Chota, the diplomatic, ceremonial, and political capital town of the Overhill Cherokees, rose to prominence amid the upheavals of the mid-eighteenth century, at a time when Cherokees were under pressure to centralize their dealings with European colonists. The American Revolution reversed the trend. Chota was not only a Cherokee community caught up in the Revolutionary War; it was also the stage on which were played out major developments and key events in a revolution in Cherokee society. The town itself would survive and then succumb to the forces unleashed by the American Revolution. Its decline as the Cherokee capital reflected the fragmentation of Cherokee society as regions, villages, and warriors reasserted their autonomy and new groups emerged to battle American expansion.

Chota's origins are rather obscure. Hanging Maw, a headman in 1791, said simply, "Chota is my beloved town – very old." Historian David Corkran described it as "the mother town of all the Cherokees," which contained "the

---

[3] Goodwin, *Cherokees in Transition*, 120; Fred O. Gearing, "The Rise of the Cherokee State as an Instance in a Class: The 'Mesopotamian' Career to Statehood," in Fenton and Gulick, eds., *Symposium on Cherokee and Iroquois Culture*, 127–34; Hatley, *Dividing Paths*, 50–1; Theda Perdue, "Cherokee Women and the Trail of Tears," *Journal of Women's History* 1 (1989), 14–17.

[4] Theda Perdue, *Slavery and the Evolution of Cherokee Society, 1540–1866* (Knoxville: University of Tennessee Press, 1979), chs. 2–3.

[5] Raymond D. Fogelson, "Change, Persistence, and Accommodation in Cherokee Medico-Magical Beliefs," in Fenton and Gulick, eds., *Symposium on Cherokee and Iroquois Culture*, 213–25; idem, "Who Were the Ani-Kutani? An Excursion into Cherokee Historical Thought," *Ethnohistory* 31 (1984), 260.

[6] *DAR*, vol. 2: 279; Hatley, *Dividing Paths*, ch. 6.

[7] Louis De Vorsey, Jr., ed., *De Brahm's Report of the General Survey in the Southern District of North America* (Columbia: University of South Carolina Press, 1971), 105.

eldest of Cherokee councils."[8] Archaeological investigations at Chota, prior to the flooding of the area when the Tellico Dam was built in 1979, indicate intermittent occupation of the area on the outside bend on the east bank of the Little Tennessee River dating back into the Archaic period (c. 8,000 B.C. to 1,000 B.C.). But the vast majority of recovered materials derive from the historic period, suggesting that the town itself may have existed for less than a hundred years. Cartographic evidence points to Chota's emergence as a distinct political entity sometime between 1730 and 1756, and supports speculation that Chota may have developed as a hamlet of the town of Tanasi across the creek and later eclipsed its mother town in importance.[9]

Chota lay at the terminus of one of the many trade routes radiating out of Charleston and Savannah, and received a steady stream of European trade goods. Deerskin hunting to fuel this trade became a major Cherokee industry – and a major cause of Cherokee dependency.[10] Archaeological excavations over seven field seasons recovered almost eighty thousand European artifacts from Chota-Tanasee. Most of these items were glass beads, but by the eve of the Revolution, Cherokees at Chota were using a large inventory of trade goods that also included guns, hoes, axes, chisels, hinges, pins and needles, nails, keys, bells, fishhooks, combs, glass bottles (and their alcoholic contents), mirrors, scissors, rings, and pewter spoons. At least one resident wore eyeglasses and others drank from a teapot.[11]

The British divided the Cherokees into four divisions: the Overhill towns in the north, mainly on the Little Tennessee and Tellico rivers; the Valley and Middle settlements in the Blue Ridge region, and the Lower towns in South Carolina.[12] By 1750 Chota had replaced Great Tellico as the most powerful of

[8] Draper Mss. 15U21; David H. Corkran, *The Cherokee Frontier: Conflict and Survival, 1740–1762* (Norman: University of Oklahoma Press, 1962), 16–17.

[9] Gerald F. Schroedl, ed., *Overhill Cherokee Archaeology at Chota-Tanasee* (Knoxville: University of Tennessee, Department of Anthropology, Report of Investigations No. 38, 1986); Paul Gleeson, ed., *Archaeological Investigations in the Tellico Reservoir, Interim Report 1969* (Knoxville: University of Tennessee, Department of Anthropology, Report of Investigations No. 8, 1970), 49, 81, 131; idem, ed., *Archaeological Investigations in the Tellico Reservoir, Interim Report 1970* (Knoxville: University of Tennessee, Report of Investigations No. 9, 1971), 19, 31, 59–76, 97, 99. Smith, "Distribution of Eighteenth-Century Cherokee Settlements," 56, indicates that Chota may have appeared as Charna on a 1725 map, but Gerald F. Schroedl and Kurt C. Russ, "An Introduction to the Ethnohistory and Archaeology of Chota and Tanasee," in Schroedl, ed., *Overhill Cherokee Archaeology at Chota-Tanasee*, 9–10, believe this is incorrect.

[10] Perdue, *Slavery and the Evolution of Cherokee Society*, 27. John Phillip Reid, *A Better Kind of Hatchet* (University Park: Pennsylvania State University Press, 1976), examines the impact of the deerskin trade on the Cherokees.

[11] Gleeson, ed., *Archaeological Investigations . . . Interim Report 1969*, 81–99; idem, *Archaeological Investigations . . . Interim Report 1970*, 59–76, 97–8; Robert D. Newman, "Euro-American Artifacts," in Schroedl, ed., *Overhill Cherokee Archaeology*, 415–68; Gerald F. Schroedl and Emanuel Breitburg, "Burials," in ibid., 125–215, esp. 194–5.

[12] Goodwin, *Cherokees in Transition*, 115; C.O. 323/17: 242.

all the Cherokee towns.[13] John Phillip Reid explains Chota's rise as an ascendancy by default, arguing that political activity centered around Chota because the headmen there were politically active and successful at a time when those in other towns were not. The Lower towns were preoccupied with war against the Creeks in the 1740s, and the more strategically located Overhill towns assumed added importance to the British as key allies guarding transmontane Carolina.[14]

The "ascendancy by default" view gives insufficient credit to the statecraft of a remarkable triumvirate of leaders: Old Hop, the *uku* or "fire king" of Chota; Attakullakulla or Little Carpenter, the slender politician and "second man" who had visited George II in 1730; and the athletic and pockmarked Oconostota, the "great warrior" or military leader. These three matched wits with rival leaders in other towns; dealt with Virginia, South Carolina, Britain, and France, as well as other Indian nations; and pursued a series of diplomatic maneuvers intent on securing Overhill trade and security while keeping free of entangling alliances.[15] Duane Champagne, modifying Reid's arguments, suggests that Chota was the symbolic center of Cherokee society and became redefined as the political center in this period of crisis. In 1752, the *uku* of Chota and other headmen announced to Carolina that Chota was the mother town of the Cherokee nation and the legitimate political center.[16] Chota never gained undisputed authority – villages, regions, and clans retained considerable autonomy – but it consolidated its leadership in the 1760s and became recognized as the Cherokee capital as the Cherokees entered one of the most turbulent periods in their history.

Chota also had less tangible but equally significant influence as a town of peace, "a beloved Town, a City of Refuge," where no blood was to be shed. Trader James Adair called it "their only town of refuge."[17] The Prince of Chota

---

[13] Gleeson, ed., *Archaeological Investigations . . . Interim Report 1969*, 49; Schroedl and Russ, "Introduction to the Ethnohistory and Archaeology of Chota and Tanasee," 9.

[14] John Phillip Reid, *A Law of Blood: The Primitive Law of the Cherokee Nation* (New York University Press, 1970), 17–27; Corkran, *Cherokee Frontier*, details Chota's relationship with other powers and parties in the middle years of the century. See also Goodwin, *Cherokees in Transition*, 115–16; and Duane Champagne, *Social Order and Political Change: Constitutional Governments among the Cherokee, the Choctaw, the Chickasaw, and the Creek* (Stanford, Calif.: Stanford University Press, 1992), 55–9, 70.

[15] On Attakullakulla see Corkran, *Cherokee Frontier*, 43–44; Draper Mss. 30S73–4; and James C. Kelley, "Notable Persons in Cherokee History: Attakullakulla," *Journal of Cherokee Studies* 3 (1978), 2–34. On Oconostota see Draper Mss. 30S73; James C. Kelley, "Oconostota," *Journal of Cherokee Studies* 3 (1978), 221–38; William L. Anderson, "Oconostota," in Richard L. Blanco, ed., *The American Revolution, 1775–1783: An Encyclopedia*, 2 vols. (New York: Garland, 1993), vol. 2: 1261–3; and Duane King and Danny E. Olinger, "Oconastota," *American Antiquity* 37 (1972), 322–8. See also *Virginia Magazine of History and Biography* 7 (1900): 5.

[16] Duane Champagne, "Symbolic Structure and Political Change in Cherokee Society," *Journal of Cherokee Studies* 8 (1983), 88–90.

[17] Reid, *Law of Blood*, 110–11; Williams, ed., *Adair's History of the American Indians*, 85.

in 1767 said he sat "on a white Seat under a White Canopy," to hear good talks.[18] Cherokee warriors and headmen in the years immediately after the Revolution recalled that "in former days the Town of Chote was the place where all good Talks was held," and Abraham of Chilowee said "our young warriers of All our nation looks upon Chota as their Beloved Town, where the fire of Piece is Always kept Burning."[19]

The town also functioned as a diplomatic meeting ground. John Stuart said that in every Cherokee town were "Beloved men appointed by the Creeks, Chickasaws, Catawbas, & other Nations with whom they are at Peace,"[20] but Chota was preeminent in Cherokee diplomacy, and management of foreign affairs became centralized in the Chota town government. Emissaries came and went in freedom, even if the chiefs frowned upon the messages they brought. Cherokee town councils – the assemblies of all men and women in the town house whose purpose was to avoid rather than resolve difficulties, to conciliate rather than command – had no control over the activities of emissaries. The councils might refuse to listen, but they could not silence the talks, a fact of Cherokee life that was to prove of utmost importance in 1776.[21]

The efforts of its headmen notwithstanding, Chota was unable to avoid participation in the colonial wars of the midcentury. A listing of the towns in the Cherokee Nation compiled in 1757 shows Chota as one of the largest, with 140 men at a time when the whole nation totaled 2,000 men; Henry Timberlake's map of the Overhill Cherokee country in 1762 credited Chota with 175 warriors.[22] At the request of Governor Glen of South Carolina, it sent four hundred warriors under Oconostota to attack Choctaw towns along the Tombigbee River. Oconostota led a war party against the French and Indians in the Illinois and Wabash region in 1755, and waylaid French river traffic on the Ohio and Mississippi in 1757. The Overhills suffered most from French and Indian incursions. In response to Cherokee requests for protection and their dissatisfaction with the location of Fort Prince George, built in 1753, the British built Fort Loudoun, just a few miles downstream from Chota. But relations became strained and broke down in open war in 1759–61. Chota's influence may have faltered after British armies invaded Cherokee country and burned Cherokee

---

[18] "John Stuart's Journal of His Proceedings with the Indians and Traders at Augusta in Georgia about the Price of Goods," Clements Library, Gage Papers, vol. 137, item 6.

[19] *Virginia State Papers*, vol. 4: 342, 504.

[20] C.O. 323/17: 259.

[21] *DAR*, vol. 6: 157–9; C.O. 5/75: 220–2; C.O. 5/662: 49; Reid, *Law of Blood*, 30–1, 65–6; Champagne, "Symbolic Structure," 90. On the Chota town house see Gerald F. Schroedl, "Structures," in Schroedl, ed., *Overhill Cherokee Archaeology*, 219–24.

[22] William L. McDowell, Jr., ed., *Documents relating to Indian Affairs, 1754–1756* (Columbia: University of South Carolina Press, 1970), 412–13; *The Memoirs of Lieutenant Henry Timberlake* (London: Author, 1765), frontispiece. Thornton, *Cherokees: A Population History*, 31, gives figures of five thousand in 1757, but two thousand men in 1756 and 1760.

towns.[23] In 1764 John Stuart reported that Chota had a hundred warriors, fewer than some other Overhill towns.[24]

Nevertheless, Chota remained on the forefront of Cherokee public life as the Cherokees rebuilt their war-torn landscape amid the gathering storms of the Revolution. Indeed, in an effort to avoid the kind of unauthorized actions that had precipitated the war, the Chota leadership moved to integrate the warriors into the political decision-making process and to restrain them "from acting under the autonomous imperatives of the clan revenge."[25] Though Old Hop was long dead, Attakullakulla and Oconostota remained formidable leaders. Attakullakulla, frail and old (though not in his nineties as some writers have suggested), went off to war against the tribes of the Wabash in 1773.[26] Oconostota appears to have claimed the title of tribal chief in 1768.[27] Alexander Cameron reckoned Oconostota held "not only a vast sway with his own people but with other tribes," although John Stuart rather exaggerated when he told his home government that "the Great Warrior of Chote . . . is the Supreme Governor of His Nation where his Word is a Law, which ascendancy is entirely owing to his personal bravery and other Superior Talents." That Oconostota was inducted into the Saint Andrew's Club of Charleston in 1773 suggests he was not out of place in colonial society and among expatriate Scots. That Cameron accused him of double-dealing suggests Oconostota the warrior was not out of his depth in stratagems of statecraft.[28] The Cherokees needed to have their wits about them: Cameron himself – who lived among the Cherokees, and whom Stuart regarded as uniquely qualified to manage them – wrote to his superior in February 1774 asking whether he was to set the Cherokees "at variance" with the Creeks.[29]

Confronted with increasing tensions, Cherokee elders assembled in the town house at Chota, and Oconostota sent talks to British and Virginian authorities in an effort to prevent individual murders from escalating into full-blown war.[30]

[23] Corkran, Cherokee Frontier, 41, 61, 114, chs. 14–17; P. M. Hamer, "Anglo-French Rivalry in the Cherokee Country, 1754–1757," North Carolina Historical Review 2 (1925), 303–22; Schroedl and Russ, "Ethnohistory and Archaeology of Chota and Tanasee," 13. On the Cherokee War of 1759–61, see Hatley, Dividing Paths, chs. 9–11.

[24] C.O. 323/17: 233.

[25] Champagne, "Symbolic Structure and Political Change in Cherokee Society," 90.

[26] DAR, vol. 6: 233.

[27] Schroedl and Russ, "Ethnohistory and Archaeology of Chota and Tanasee," 13; Fred O. Gearing, "Priests and Warriors: Social Structures for Cherokee Politics in the 18th Century," American Anthropological Association 64, No. 5, pt. 2, Memoir 93 (1962), 100.

[28] DAR, vol. 6: 232; vol. 7: 148; LC, C.O. 5/75: 9. Oconostota's certificate of induction to the Saint Andrew's Club is in PCC, reel 85, item 71, vol. 2: 205.

[29] North Carolina Colonial Records, vol. 10: 767; Stuart to Gage, Jan. 18 1775, Clements Library, Gage Papers, vol. 125; DAR, vol. 7: 69.

[30] Taitt to Stuart, July 18 1774 in Stuart to Haldimand, Aug. 8 1774, and "Talk of the Great Warrior and the other Heads of the Overhills to Alexander Cameron" in Stuart to Gage, Aug. 8 1774, Clements Library, Gage Papers, vol. 122; Virginia Magazine of History and Biography 13 (1906), 418.

Nevertheless, the pressure on Cherokee lands continued to mount, and with it the challenge to the aging Attakullakulla and Oconostota, who had dominated the council house at Chota for half a century.[31] By the eve of the Revolution, Cherokees had seen their lands handed away at the Treaty of Fort Stanwix by Iroquois delegates who wanted to ensure that white expansion went south, not north; whittled away as colonial traders encouraged the people to run up large debts that could be paid off only with land; and snatched away in formal treaties, and in illegal transactions with private companies.[32] At the Treaty of Hard Labor in 1768, South Carolina fixed the Kanawha and New rivers as the boundary of Cherokee country. Two years later, at Lochaber, a new line was run from the mouth of the Kanawha to Long Island on the Holston River. At the Lochaber congress, Attakullakulla complained about the encroachments of settlers who drove away the game and built cabins in Cherokee country. Five months later, Alexander Cameron was summoned to the council house at Chota, where Oconostota and the young warriors expressed their anger at settlers who occupied their lands without their consent: "They say that they see the smoke of the Virginians from their doors," reported Cameron. In 1771 Attakullakulla agreed to Virginia moving the boundary line westward to the Kentucky River. In July 1774, Oconostota was still entreating Virginia to stop its people crossing the boundary.[33]

The process of land transfer and dispossession evidently was not as simple and complete as it often appears, however. Tom Hatley has suggested that the land-sales policy of older village headmen like Attakullakulla represented an attempt to resolve the dilemma of keeping open trade contacts while preserving some kind of boundary line against backcountry settlers. Incurring debts and ceding land to métis traders might have created a cultural buffer that could provide trade and help fend off colonial expansion.[34] In November 1775, Cameron noted that Attakullakulla was just back from the settlements at Watauga and Nolachuky, "where he had been Collecting his rent."[35]

The situation reached a crisis with the infamous Sycamore Shoals Treaty in March 1775. A group of North Carolina land speculators led by Richard

---

[31] Jerry Clyde Cashion, "North Carolina and the Cherokee: The Quest for Land on the Eve of the American Revolution," Ph.D. diss., University of North Carolina at Chapel Hill, 1979, esp. 124.

[32] *DAR*, vol. 3: 72–3, 85–6, 126–7, 174, 272–5; vol. 5: 113, 116.

[33] *DAR*, vol. 2: 213; vol. 3: 70–3; Draper Mss. 3QQ142; Hatley, *Dividing Paths*, 213. See also C.O. 5/72: 210–11; C.O. 5/74: 22–5; C.O. 5/75: 194, 200. The treaties at Hard Labor and Lochaber and relevant documents are reprinted in W. Stitt Robinson, ed., *Virginia Treaties, 1723–1775*, vol. 5 of Alden T. Vaughan, gen. ed., *Early American Indian Documents: Laws and Treaties* (Frederick, Md.: University Publications of America, 1979). On the Virginia–Cherokee frontier in the decade before the Revolution see John Alden, *John Stuart and the Southern Colonial Frontier* (Ann Arbor: University of Michigan Press, 1944), chs. 15–16 and Appendix B on the new boundary run by Virginian surveyor John Donelson.

[34] Hatley, *Dividing Paths*, 205–8.

[35] Clements Library, Clinton Mss., vol. 12: 5.

Henderson and Nathaniel Hart met with Attakullakulla, Oconostota, and Savanukah, the Raven of Chota,[36] and in defiance of royal proclamation and tribal law, pulled off one of the biggest land deals in frontier history. In return for a cabin full of trade goods, Henderson secured "an immense Territory" – 27,000 square miles – between the Kentucky and Tennessee rivers, "to which they allure Settlers very fast." The cession cut the Cherokees off from the Ohio River and their Kentucky hunting grounds. Governor Josiah Martin of North Carolina feared it would have dire consequences; John Stuart commented that obtaining fraudulent titles to large tracts of land had become common practice, but realized that "in our present state of anarchy and confusion there can be no remedy for this Evil." The Cherokees declared that they were deceived as to what they were signing, and Old Tassel later denounced Henderson as a liar and a rogue who had forged Oconostota's signature. Attakullakulla's son, Tsi'yugûnsi'ny or Dragging Canoe, the chief of Big Island town, stormed from the conference on the second day and, according to legend at least, promised to make the ceded lands "dark and bloody."[37]

The outbreak of the Revolution offered Dragging Canoe and younger Cherokees an opportunity to win back some of the lands that had been lost in previous years. That required challenging the actions and authority of the village headmen and gaining the upper hand in the council house at Chota (Figs. 7 and 8). The elder chiefs did not want the Cherokees to get involved in the quarrel and neither, apparently, did most Cherokee women, who feared the impact of war on their already decimated villages and families.[38] Contrary to rumor and propaganda in the colonies, John Stuart and Alexander Cameron

---

[36] The title of "the Raven" belonged to the "Red War Chief," who headed the war organization responsible for conducting affairs during military emergencies and acting as a liaison with other towns and foreign powers. Raven was a war title given to a leader who scouted ahead of a war party in search of enemies. Every Cherokee town had "Ravens," but the Raven of Chota was the most prominent. Savanukah was Oconostota's nephew. Fogelson and Kutsche, "Cherokee Economic Cooperatives: The Gadugi," 92; William L. Anderson, "Raven of Echota," in Blanco, ed., *American Revolution: An Encyclopedia*, vol. 2: 1374–5.

[37] Cashion, "North Carolina and the Cherokees," 115–26; *Colonial Records of North Carolina*, vol. 10: 246; Stuart to Gage, May 26, 1775, Clements Library, Gage Papers, vol. 129; *Virginia State Papers*, vol. 1: 282–92, 296–7, 303–11, 315. The Sycamore Shoals Treaty is reprinted in *Revolution and Confederation*, 203–5. Draper Mss. 1CC 160–94 contains depositions regarding Henderson's purchase; papers relating to the purchase are also in Draper Mss. 4QQ. A printed proclamation by Governor Josiah Martin, dated Feb. 10, 1775, against Henderson's proposed schemes is in C.O. 5/318. Old Tassel's accusations at the Treaty of Hopewell in 1785 are in *The New American State Papers: Indian Affairs* (Wilmington, Del.: Scholarly Resources, 1972), vol. 6: 51. On Dragging Canoe, see John P. Brown, *Old Frontiers: The Story of the Cherokee Indians from Earliest Times to the Date of Their Removal to the West, 1838* (Kingsport, Tenn: Southern, 1938), book 2; and Raymond E. Evans, "Notable Persons in Cherokee History: Dragging Canoe," *Journal of Cherokee Studies* 2 (1977), 176–89. On Dragging Canoe's name see James Mooney, "Myths of the Cherokee," *19th Ann. Report of the Bureau of American Ethnology*, part 1 (Washington, D.C.: Government Printing Office, 1900), 538.

[38] Hatley, *Dividing Paths*, 220.

were equally reluctant to see the Cherokees go to war, at least for the time being. Once it became clear that Britain would call on her Indian allies, Stuart hoped to restrain the Cherokees until he could coordinate their attacks with the operations of British troops in the southern colonies.[39] However, Cherokee involvement in the war came on Cherokee time and for Cherokee reasons.

The outbreak of the Revolution severed Cherokee trade routes to South Carolina. In 1776 John Stuart despatched his brother Henry with goods to fill the gap, and with orders to try and keep the Cherokees at peace but prepare them to fight the Americans when the British gave the word. The Cherokees were not particularly interested in fighting Britain's war, but younger warriors who felt hemmed in by encroachments and saw the country "in rebellion & chaos" *were* interested in driving out the settlers at Watauga and Nolachuky, on the western side of the mountains and on the Indian side of the 1763 boundary line.[40]

Henry Stuart met Dragging Canoe at Mobile. The Cherokee expressed his concern "that they were almost surrounded by the White People, that they had but a small spot of ground left for them to stand upon and that it seemed to be the Intention of the White People to destroy them from being a people." Stuart replied that the encroachments were contrary to the king's orders and that the Cherokees had no one to blame but themselves for making private land sales. Dragging Canoe, voicing the anger of young men for whom hunting and the preservation of hunting territory was central to their identity as both Cherokees and males, answered "that he had no hand in making these Bargains but blamed some of their Old Men who he said were too old to hunt and who by their Poverty had been induced to sell their Land but that for his part he had a great many young fellows that would support him and that were determined to have their Land." Stuart feared Dragging Canoe was "firmly bent on doing mischief." The talk of war caused considerable uneasiness among "the most thinking and sensible part of the Nation."[41] As Stuart headed for the Overhill towns,

---

[39] Philip M. Hamer, "John Stuart's Indian Policy During the Early Months of the Revolution," *Mississippi Valley Historical Review* 17 (1930), 351–66; idem, "The Wataugans and the Cherokee Indians in 1776," *East Tennessee Historical Society Publications* 3 (1931), 108–26; Robert Wilson Gibbes, ed., *Documentary History of the American Revolution*, 3 vols. (New York: Appleton, 1853–7), vol. 1: 159–60; *DAR* vol. 10: 83, 182, 361; vol. 11: 130–1; vol. 12: 189–90; C.O. 5/76: 177–9; 77: 28; *North Carolina Colonial Records*, vol 10: 38, 117–19, 392; *Collections of the New-York Historical Society* (1872), 223; Stuart to Gage, July 20, 1775, plus enclosure of Stuart to Drayton, July 18, 1775, Clements Library, Gage Papers, vol. 132.

[40] *DAR*, vol. 12: 16, 130–3, 189. The British policy of restraining Indians from going to war while preparing them for the eventuality of war continued into the next century; Colin G. Calloway, *Crown and Calumet: British–Indian Relations, 1783–1815* (Norman: University of Oklahoma Press, 1987), 228–30.

[41] *North Carolina Colonial Records*, vol. 10: 764–6; *DAR*, vol. 12: 192–3, For discussion of the importance of territorial preservation to the hunting culture of young Cherokee men see Hatley, *Dividing Paths*, 211–15, 217–18.

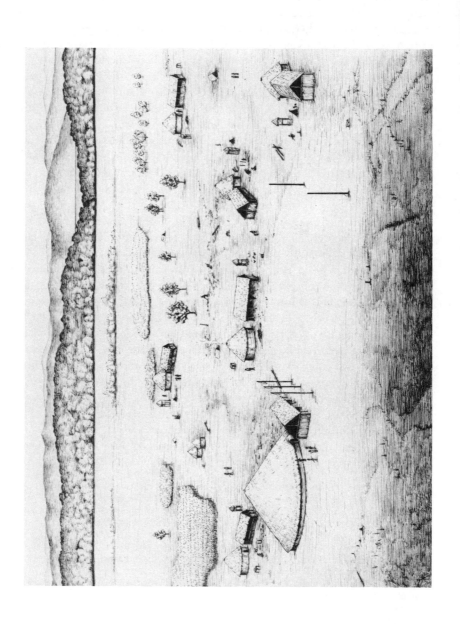

Figures 7 (opposite page) and 8. Exterior and interior views of the town house at Chota. Artistic rendering based on archeological and ethnohistorical evidence by Thomas Whyte. From Gerald F. Schroedl et al., eds., *Overhill Cherokee Archaeology at Chota-Tanasee* (University of Tennessee, Department of Anthropology, and Tennessee Valley Authority, 1986). Reproduced courtesy of the Frank H. McClung Museum and Department of Anthropology, University of Tennessee.

delegates from the Lower, Middle, and Valley settlements voiced their concerns about trespass on their lands when American commissioners solicited their neutrality at Fort Charlotte.[42]

Stuart arrived in Cherokee country in late April 1776, after a fifty-five-day journey from the Chickasaw villages. The Cherokees received him at Chota "with the greatest marks of Respect," displayed British colors in the town house, and performed the Eagle Tail Dance in the square. They assured him of their attachment to the king, but Stuart's was a difficult mission.[43] He assembled the headmen from the different parts of the Cherokee nation, distributed his supplies, and urged the chiefs to listen to Cameron and refrain from going to war. Stuart and Cameron, with the consent of the older chiefs, even sent letters to the Watauga settlers urging them to remove. But once the young warriors had received arms and ammunition, they "were with difficulty restrained by Mr Cameron and the Old Sensible People."[44]

While the Cherokees grew impatient and apprehensive, "a Deputation of fourteen Indians with a Cherokee fellow as interpreter arrived from the Northern Nations."[45] The delegates, members of the Shawnees, Delawares, Mohawks, Nanticokes, and Ottawas, made a dramatic entry into Chota painted black. They said they had traveled seventy days to get there, through country which used to be rich Shawnee and Delaware hunting territory but which was now "thickly inhabited and the people all in arms." The Mohawks brought disturbing news of events in the north and said the northern tribes had agreed to join the king's troops. If the Cherokees joined and attacked the Americans from this side, nothing could stop them. "After this day," wrote Stuart, "every young Fellow's face in the Overhill Towns appeared Blackened, and nothing was now talked of but War." Stuart and Cameron continued to argue against war and the principal chiefs agreed, but the warriors were impatient and suspicious of their intentions.[46]

[42] Journal of Negotiations with the Cherokees at Fort Charlotte, South Carolina in April 1776 and with the Creeks at Augusta in May 1776, Raleigh, North Carolina, Department of Cultural Resources, Division of Archives and Records, Secretary of State Records – Continental Congress – 1774–1779 (SS. 317). Excerpts from both meetings are in Revolution and Confederation, 208–11.

[43] LC, C.O. 5/77: 183–7; DAR vol. 12: 130–3. John Norton described the Eagle Tail Dance as one in which the warriors described their exploits; Carl F. Klinck and James J. Talman, eds., The Journal of John Norton 1816 (Toronto: Champlain Society, 1970), 47, 157.

[44] DAR, vol. 12: 194; Clements Library, Clinton Mss., vol. 18: 11; Philip M. Hamer, ed., "Correspondence of Henry Stuart and Alexander Cameron with the Wataugans," Mississippi Valley Historical Review 17 (1930–1), 451–9.

[45] The following paragraphs are based on Henry Stuart's long account of his mission to Chota, and the council with the northern delegates. Stuart's account is in C.O. 5/77: 169, printed in North Carolina Colonial Records, vol. 10: 763–85, and in DAR, vol. 12: 191–208. An account is also in Clements Library, Clinton Mss., vol. 18: 11. Gregory Evans Dowd, A Spirited Resistance: The North American Indian Struggle for Unity, 1745–1815 (Baltimore: Johns Hopkins University Press, 1992), 46–9, gives a good analysis of the Chota meeting; Brown, Old Frontiers, 141–6, also contains an account.

[46] North Carolina Colonial Records, vol. 10: 773–4; DAR, vol. 12: 198–200.

On the day appointed for the emissaries to deliver their grand talk, the war standard was erected and the posts of the Chota town house were painted black and red.[47] Stuart and Cameron could judge the inclinations of the assembled Cherokees from their appearances: "Those from the Great Island, except Outacite [Judd's Friend] and two or three more, were all black, also all the Chilhowie and Settico people, and some from every town were blackened."[48]

The principal deputy of the Mohawks spoke first, urging united Indian resistance, and presented a purple and white wampum belt to Dragging Canoe. The Ottawa deputy seconded with a talk urging the Indian nations to stop fighting among themselves and unite against their common enemies. Finally, the Shawnee deputy produced "a War Belt about 9 feet long and six inches wide of purple Whampum strewed over with vermilion." He recounted the grievances of the Shawnees and other Indian nations and reminded his listeners of the encroachments of the Virginians and how, in a very few years, the Indians had declined from a great people to a mere handful. The Americans clearly intended to destroy them, he said; "Better to die like men than to diminish away by inches." Dragging Canoe accepted the Shawnee war belt, and the warriors joined in singing the war song.[49]

Attakullakulla, Oconostota, and other chiefs, who "remembered the calamities brought on their nation by the last war," refused the northerners' wampum belts but voiced no opposition. "Instead of opposing the rashness of the young people with spirit," said Stuart, they "sat down dejected and silent."[50] Dragging Canoe, Doublehead, Young Tassel, Bloody Fellow, and others struck the war post against the Wataugans.

Dragging Canoe visited Stuart and Cameron two days later painted black, and the warriors proposed that the British agents should take up the belt. Traders made preparations to leave the towns, although Dragging Canoe assured them they would be safe if they stayed, and would not be required to join in the fighting. Stuart blamed Dragging Canoe for the trouble and said in his report that he "made him acknowledge himself before all the Chiefs the sole cause of the war." Stuart and Cameron also suggested to the Cherokees that the Shawnees might have deceived them. Some Cherokees agreed to wait until "the Great Warrior of the Nation," Oconostota, had given his opinion on war or peace,[51] but the die was cast. "It was in vain to talk any more of peace," said Stuart. All he could do was urge the warriors not to pass the boundary line, not to kill women, children, or Loyalists, and to cease hostilities whenever John

[47] The town house was built on a natural rise in one of the terraces on which Chota stood. For descriptions see Gleeson, ed., *Archaeological Investigations . . . Interim report 1969*, 124–9.
[48] *North Carolina Colonial Records*, vol. 10: 777; *DAR*, vol. 12: 201.
[49] *North Carolina Colonial Records*, vol. 10: 777–8; *DAR*, vol. 12: 202–3.
[50] *North Carolina Colonial Records*, vol. 10: 779; *DAR*, vol. 12: 203.
[51] *North Carolina Colonial Records*, vol. 10: 780–3; *DAR*, vol. 12: 204–6.

Stuart requested. Attakullakulla and the older chiefs assured him the warriors would restrict their attacks to the settlements on the Cherokee side of the boundary line. They sent Henry Stuart a string of white beads, symbolizing peace and sincerity, and apologized for "the precipitate behavior" of their young men. Stuart made dire predictions of the consequences of acting without British support. As he left, the Overhill warriors were making preparations for war, but many Cherokees were depressed and fearful of what was to come.[52]

John Stuart turned in a lengthy account of the events at Chota so that he would not be blamed for the sudden outbreak of the war.[53] Though he held Dragging Canoe responsible for the outbreak of the war at that time, Stuart knew the underlying causes that made war inevitable:

> In this district amazing great settlements have been made upon tracts held under titles obtained from individuals by taking advantage of their wants and poverty, or by forgeries and frauds of different sorts in which the nation never acquiesced; for they are tenants in common and allow no person, however so great, to cede their lands without the consent of the nation obtained in general council.[54]

Stuart and his brother were not the only ones to interpret the war as a generational clash. Moravian missionaries in the area held the same view, as did John McDonald, Stuart's deputy, who lived among the militant Chickamaugas. Attakullakulla's son, Turtle at Home, who also joined the Chickamaugas, told John Norton years later that the older chiefs opposed the war, "but the younger War Chiefs being eager to combine with their Northern Brethren in assisting the Great King, took up the War Hatchet, without being unanimous."[55]

The arrival of the northern delegation at Chota sparked a Cherokee revolution in the midst of the American Revolution.[56] It provided Dragging Canoe with the opportunity to commit the Cherokees to resistance against white intruders, and at the same time to mount a dramatic challenge to the leadership of his father's generation. Traditionally, young men were expected to be aggressive in certain circumstances and old men to be rational; Cherokee society

---

[52] *North Carolina Colonial Records*, vol. 10: 660–1, 665, 784; *DAR*, vol. 12: 190, 207, 214; Clinton Mss., vol. 18: 11.

[53] Clinton Mss., vol. 18: 11.

[54] *DAR*, vol. 12: 189.

[55] Adelaide L. Fries, et al., eds., *Records of the Moravians in North Carolina*, 11 vols. (Raleigh, N.C.: State Printers, 1922–54), vol. 3: 1065, 1077; Klinck and Talman, eds., *Journal of John Norton*, 42, 59.

[56] Cf. Raymond D. Fogelson, *The Cherokees: A Critical Bibliography* (Bloomington: Indiana University Press, 1978), 15: "The American Revolution was not a revolution for the Cherokees, but rather a series of diplomatic and military defeats in which they were once more losing pawns on an international gaming board." Although this is an apt summary of the consequences of the Revolution for the Cherokees, it nonetheless gives insufficient credit to what was going on within Cherokee society.

accommodated and harmonized the resulting tensions. However, in the Revolution the tensions became incompatible. The older chiefs who had sold lands to Henderson and built networks of accommodation with colonial traders and officials were hesitant to act now that their white counterparts were divided among themselves. Younger militants, no longer prepared to tolerate the illegal occupation of their lands, seized the initiative. The warriors' chanting of the northerners' war song at Chota constituted, in Gregory Dowd's words, "a vote of no confidence" in Attakullakulla and past policies. The war council at Chota also forged "a critical link in the militants' chain across the Eastern Woodlands," as Shawnees and Cherokees committed themselves to a united front against American expansion.[57]

The first blow to the Cherokee war effort came when the Creeks refused to join them.[58] Cherokee warriors swept down on the settlements of the trespassers on Cherokee land, but this was just the prelude to the main action of the war.

Many southern colonists seem to have been waiting for just such an opportunity. Charles Lee, the Continental commander in the south, welcomed the Cherokee war: North Carolina could "now with the greatest justice" make an example of the Cherokees "and as these Cherokees are not esteem'd the most formidable Warriors, we can probably do it without much risk or loss."[59] North Carolina's delegates to the Continental Congress urged swift retaliation "to carry fire and Sword into the very bowels of their country."[60] William Henry Drayton, a prominent Charleston Whig who had led a delegation from South Carolina to the Cherokees in 1775, recommended "that the nation be extirpated, and the lands become the property of the public. For my part, I shall never give my voice for a peace with the Cherokee Nation upon any other terms than their removal beyond the mountains." Thomas Jefferson declared, "I hope the Cherokees will now be driven beyond the Missisipi. [sic]"[61] The Cherokees had forfeited their rights to their land: private seizures of Indian lands, illegal before the war, now became a patriotic act.[62]

Retaliatory expeditions from Virginia, Georgia, and North and South Carolina

[57] Dowd, *Spirited Resistance*, 48–9, 52.

[58] *DAR*, vol. 10: 361, 394–5; vol. 12: 190, 200, 205, 207–8, 229–30, 239–40, 247; C.O. 5/94: 39; LC, C.O. 5/78: 52–3; *North Carolina Colonial Records*, vol. 10: 785; J. Almon *Remembrancer* 1776, pt. 3: 275; Gibbes, ed., *Documentary History of the American Revolution*, vol. 2: 32; David H. Corkran, *The Creek Frontier, 1540–1783* (Norman: University of Oklahoma Press, 1967), 298.

[59] *North Carolina Colonial Records*, vol. 10: 657, 659; *PCC*, reel 85, item 71, vol. 1: 45.

[60] *North Carolina Colonial Records*, vol. 10: 730–2.

[61] Gibbes, ed., *Documentary History of the American Revolution*, vol. 2: 29; Julian P. Boyd, ed., *The Papers of Thomas Jefferson* (Princeton N.J.: Princeton University Press, 1950–), vol. 1: 494; Hatley, *Dividing Paths*, 192–3.

[62] Edward J. Cashin, "But Brothers, It is Our Land We Are Talking About: Winners and Losers in the Georgia Backcountry," in Ronald Hoffman and Peter J. Albert, eds., *An Uncivil War: The Southern Backcountry During the American Revolution* (Charlottesville: University Press of Virginia, 1985), 269.

stormed through Cherokee country in the summer and fall of 1776. "Their numbers were much superior to any body of Warriors we could raise, even if we had been unanimous," recalled Turtle at Home.[63] In the course of a few months, the Cherokees were defeated, and their towns and cornfields destroyed. In Parliament, Edmund Burke denounced the government's Indian policy, saying the Cherokees had been "bribed and betrayed into war," and then abandoned to the Americans. Americans said the same thing.[64] Cherokees from the Lower, Middle, and Valley towns fled to the Overhills.[65] But they found no refuge there, as Virginian troops attacked the Overhill towns, driving the inhabitants into the woods.[66]

Chota, where the decision for war had been taken, survived the scourge that war unleashed. Colonel William Christian burned Big Island Town (Dragging Canoe's town), Tellico, Chilhowee, and Settico but spared Chota. According to one tradition, Christian's clemency was "out of respect to Nancy Ward," the *ghighau* or War Woman of the Cherokees.[67] That interpretation does little credit to the efforts of Cherokees to save their beloved town or to the unusual restraint exercised by Christian, who tried to negotiate a peace. Christian believed the old men and women were averse to the war and blamed Cameron and Dragging Canoe for leading the others into it. He sent word to the Raven of Chota that "I did not come to War with women and children but to Fight with men."[68] As the Virginian army approached Chota, the Raven sent a flag of truce. Attakullakulla, Oconostota, and "the greater part of the Nation, who," said Turtle at Home, "had been inclined to remain neuter," sued for peace. Christian demanded they hand over Dragging Canoe and Cameron, but the peace faction could not compel their surrender. The massive retribution visited on the Cherokees allowed the accommodationist chiefs to reassert a measure of authority among the majority of the Overhill people, while Dragging Canoe and younger warriors moved farther south and west to continue the war.[69]

Cut off from British support and supplies, and reeling from the American counterstrikes, the older chiefs had no choice but to make peace overtures to the Americans. As John Stuart watched Cherokee refugees from the Lower, Middle, and Valley towns trickle into Pensacola and dampen the spirits of the

[63] Klinck and Talman, eds., *Journal of John Norton*, 43.
[64] David H. Murdoch, ed., *Rebellion in America: A Contemporary British Viewpoint, 1765–1783* (Santa Barbara, Calif., and Oxford: Clio, 1779), 433, 565; Lilla M. Hawes, ed., "The Papers of Lachlan McIntosh, 1774–1779," *Collections of the Georgia Historical Society* 12 (1957), 56–60.
[65] *North Carolina State Records*, vol. 11: 346, 351–2.
[66] *DAR*, vol. 12: 253–4.
[67] Brown, *Old Frontiers* 159; Norma Tucker, "Nancy Ward, Ghigau of the Cherokees," *Georgia Historical Quarterly* 53 (1969), 196.
[68] *Virginia Magazine of History and Biography* 17: (1910) 57, 62–3.
[69] Ibid., 57; Brown, *Old Frontiers*, 156–61; Klinck and Talman, eds., *Journal of John Norton*, 43; Draper Mss. 1XX23.

Creeks, he received reports from Cameron and Dragging Canoe that Oconostota had endeavored to hand over Cameron to the Virginians.[70] He sent Oconostota a message of castigation, throwing the blame for the war away from the British and on to the shoulders of the older chiefs who had consistently wanted peace. According to Stuart, Oconostota should have prevented the young men from rashly taking up the hatchet. Having failed to do that, he should not then have made peace without consulting Stuart or Cameron:

> You say you are grown old and that you was obliged to act the part you did, in order to save your Corn – but I think you are very old indeed in your mind as well as your Body, or else the brave Oucconnastota would never have been induced through fear, to have laid a Trap for getting Mr. Cameron delivered to the Rebels – he was in a particular manner put under your protection, and I thought that the great Warrior of Chote would have died rather than have consented that their Beloved man should fall into the hands of the Rebells, or Suffer his Towns to be burnt without firing one gun. What then must I think of your becoming the Instrument for attempting to betray him – My Friend – it was not with the Virginians only that you attempted to play a double game – but this is a disagreeable Subject and I shall say no more upon it.[71]

The Cherokee chiefs conducted peace talks with the Americans throughout the spring. Meanwhile, the Americans and the British each sent messages into their towns advising for and against coming to terms and promising protection and the supplies which they knew the Cherokees desperately needed.[72] Oconostota was careful to point out that the chiefs were back in control: "The beloved men are now talking, & the boys on both sides sitting listening." Old Tassel or Corn Tassel of Toqua admitted he had taken up the hatchet "although it appeared dreadful," and fought against the Virginians, but now promised to go to Dragging Canoe with words of peace and assured the Americans that the young people would heed his words.[73]

In March, Colonel Nathaniel Gist, who had a Cherokee wife, traveled to Chota to invite the Overhill people to meet Virginia's peace commissioners in April at Long Island on the Holston, an ancient treaty ground considered sacred in Cherokee tradition.[74] The Overhills went to Long Island where, said the British, "they received some Powder, and as much Wheat Flour as they could carry with them to their Nation." Oconostota, Attakullakulla, and a

---

[70] *DAR*, vol. 13: 26, 73–4; vol. 14: 34–5.

[71] *PCC*, reel 85, item 71, vol. 2: 202–3.

[72] Draper Mss. 4QQ 76–148, 151–4; *North Carolina State Records*, vol. 11: 459; *DAR*, vol. 13: 121; vol. 14: 49, 94–5, 114–15.

[73] Draper Mss. 4QQ 96–7, 143.

[74] Duane H. King, "Long Island of the Holston: Sacred Cherokee Ground," *Journal of Cherokee Studies* 1 (1976), 113–27.

delegation of thirty Cherokees traveled to Williamsburg to talk peace, one of Attakullakulla's last acts.[75] In May 1777, the Lower Cherokees came to terms with Georgia and South Carolina at DeWitt's Corner, surrendering all remaining land in South Carolina except a narrow strip on the western border.[76] Two months later, the Overhill Cherokees met to make peace with Virginia and North Carolina at Long Island. Chains of friendship were established between Chota and Williamsburg, as well as Chota and New Bern; Virginia and North Carolina each appointed agents to live at Chota. Old Tassel delivered a spirited speech questioning the Americans' assumptions of conquest, but the Overhills ceded all lands east of Blue Ridge as well as a corridor through the Cumberland Gap. The Raven hoped the new boundary would act as "a wall that reached up to the skies." Together, the two treaties stripped the Cherokees of more than five million acres.[77]

The British and Americans both recognized that shortage of provisions drove the Cherokees to make peace. John Stuart said they "patched up a peace with the rebels," so as to be allowed to return to their homes. Hanging Maw, who stayed away from the peace talks, said they were "only a make-hast[e] to save corn."[78] Old Tassel hoped for a new era of peace: 'Let us all study raising up our Children, and let us consider the quarrel as short, like that of a day.'"[79] In the wake of the disastrous war, the Lower, Middle, and Overhill towns had reasserted their right to make peace independently. Chota never regained its ascendancy in foreign affairs, even though it continued to be recognized as head town until 1788.[80]

Many other Cherokees stayed away from the peace talks, perhaps hoping Britain would yet put down the rebellion. That spring, the homeless inhabitants of Big Island, Tellico, Toqua, and Chilhowee followed Dragging Canoe south and west and built new towns, with the same names, along the Chickamauga. Stuart's deputy and commissary, John McDonald, already lived on Chickamauga Creek. British supplies now went to Chickamauga, not to Chota. Seeing their northern

---

[75] James H. O'Donnell, III, *The Southern Indians in the American Revolution* (Knoxville: University of Tennessee Press, 1973), 55–7; LC, C.O. 5/558: 448–9; *DAR*, vol. 13: 121; Draper Mss. 1XX27; *Remembrancer*, 1777: 226; Brown, *Old Frontiers*, 164.

[76] The articles of the Treaty of DeWitt's Corner are in Archibald Henderson, "The Treaty of Long Island of Holston, 1777," *North Carolina Historical Review* 8 (1931) 76–8; *Remembrancer*, 1777: 343–4; and *Revolution and Confederation*, 218–20.

[77] Henderson, "Treaty of Long Island of Holston," 58–117 (Raven's quote at 96); *PCC*, reel 85, item 71, vol 2: 221–2. A copy of the treaty is in North Carolina State Archives, Raleigh, Treasurer's and Comptroller's Papers: Indian Affairs and Lands, box 1, Cherokee Nation, 1739–91. The proceedings and treaty are also reprinted in *Revolution and Confederation*, 226–55.

[78] C.O. 5/558: 449; Draper Mss. 1XX23; *DAR*, vol. 15: 285; Randolph C. Downes, "Cherokee–American Relations in the Upper Tennessee Valley, 1776–1791," *East Tennessee Historical Society Publications* 8 (1936), 36.

[79] Draper Mss. 4QQ142.

[80] Champagne, *Social Order and Political Change*, 77–8; idem, "Symbolic Structure and Political Exchange in Cherokee Society," 90–1.

neighbors dispossessed of their lands, many of the Lower and Middle Cherokees moved their towns to new locations on the headwaters of the Coosa, affiliating with Dragging Canoe and joining the Anglo-Chickamauga war effort. Outacite, Bloody Fellow, Hanging Maw, Young Tassel (John Watts), Oconostota's brother Kitegiska, and Dragging Canoe's brother Little Owl, moved.[81] Dragging Canoe's four or five hundred warriors remained steadfast in their hostility to the United States.[82]

The Chickamauga "secession," as it is often called, was not an unmitigated disaster. It relieved Chota of the need to hand over Dragging Canoe to the Americans as the price of peace, and it allowed the peace party to disavow the actions of dissidents over whom they had no control.[83] However, it split the Cherokee nation. Dragging Canoe and his followers called themselves *Ani-Yunwiya*, "the Real People," and referred to those who did not join them as "Virginians," a term of ultimate contempt.[84] The schism broke the old union of young warriors and ex-warriors as the nation separated along lines of age and status. The traditional "old equals good equals honor" ethos no longer applied in the minds of young warriors, who felt the old men had sold them out. In the view of anthropologist Fred Gearing, the divided Cherokees "slipped into virtual anarchy," with "amiable old men" in the older towns and "violent young men" in the Chickamauga towns. "The old men saw their priestly government crumble; the young men had thrown the political structure away. Neither one found an adequate substitute." Now that Dragging Canoe had led so many of the young families away from the Overhill towns, the "balanced determinations made by men in council were no longer available." The new Chickamauga communities were new in more ways than one, as young warriors acted free from the usual restraint of the old beloved men. Traditional ceremonies virtually ceased as the communities existed in a state of perpetual war alert. A social structure that had functioned for generations crumbled.[85]

Moreover, Chickamauga resistance jeopardized Chota's efforts to preserve neutrality, especially as the Chickamauga towns attracted younger militants from other tribes. Americans rarely distinguished between Chickamauga enemies

[81] *DAR*, vol. 15: 284–5; Draper Mss. 11S99–100; *Virginia State Papers*, vol. 3: 271; Brown, *Old Frontiers*, 163–4; R. S. Cotterill, *The Southern Indians: The Story of the Civilized Tribes Before Removal* (Norman: University of Oklahoma Press, 1954), 44–6; Hatley, *Dividing Paths*, 222–6. Gregory Dowd, echoing Brown, comments that Old Tassel "had not joined the secession, but he did remain popular with the secessionists." Dowd, *Spirited Resistance*, 63; Brown, *Old Frontiers*, 164. This aptly assesses Old Tassel's influence, but Old Tassel himself said that he had lived among the Chickamaugas. *Virginia State Papers*, vol. 4: 306–7.

[82] *North Carolina State Records*, vol. 11: 428; Draper Mss. 4QQ142.

[83] Cotterill, *Southern Indians*, 44–5.

[84] Brown, *Old Frontiers*, 161; James Paul Pate, "The Chickamauga: A Forgotten Segment of Indian Resistance on the Southern Frontier," Ph.D. diss., Mississippi State University, 1969, 81.

[85] Gearing, "Priests and Warriors: Social Structures for Cherokee Politics in the 18th Century," 60–1, 103–4.

and Overhill neutralists, and the headmen feared that the actions of the Chickamaugas threatened to involve the whole nation in another war. The British funneled supplies to the Chickamauga towns and provisioned about five hundred Cherokees who arrived "naked and forlorn" at Pensacola, but they cut off supplies to the peace party; the Americans were unable to pick up the supply, and Cherokees who tried to remain neutral suffered terrible deprivation.[86] Savanukah, the Raven of Chota, assured the Americans that he was working hard to convince the "Roagues at Chuckemogo" of their error, but he could do so with little conviction because the Treaty of Long Island did little to stop trespasses on Cherokee lands. The Raven complained to Governor Caswell of North Carolina that the people from Watauga were "marking trees all over my country and near to the place where I live." Caswell issued a proclamation forbidding such trespass, but it was to little avail.[87] Crop failures prompted more Cherokees to look to the British for help in 1778, and though Stuart knew they wanted neutrality, he also felt he could depend on the majority of Cherokees.[88]

The British capture of Savannah and Augusta in 1778–9 opened Cherokee country to British goods via the Savannah River, and many Cherokees rejoined the king's cause.[89] In January 1779, Governor Patrick Henry of Virginia initiated plans for an invasion of the Chickamauga towns, both to punish them for their hostilities and to stem the flow of new recruits. Joseph Martin, Virginia's agent to the Overhills, had reported that "the leading Men are much exasperated at the Conduct of the Seceders at & about Chickamogga who perpetually embroil their public Council, and, by repeated violence, instigated by British Emissaries, attempt to involve the nation at large in the suspicions of Hostility & consequent war." People continued to join the Chickamaugas, "notwithstanding the Remonstrance made against those Imigrations by the old Warriors, most of whom have expressed great wrath and Bitterness against the Headstrong & Lawless part of their nation." An expedition that drove home the prodigals, thought Henry, would be well received by the older chiefs.[90] North Carolina's agent, James Robertson, believed that the Lower towns and Chickamaugas were hostile and stirred up by Tories, but agreed that the Indians who remained in the Upper towns were firmly for peace, and that sending an expedition against Chickamauga was the only way to prevent a bloody war.[91]

---

[86] Cotterill, *Southern Indians*, 48; Samuel Cole Williams, Tennessee During the Revolutionary War (Nashville, 1944, reprinted Knoxville: Univerity of Tennessee Press, 1974), 61, 89; Clements Library, Clinton Mss., vol. 31: 4; *North Carolina State Records*, vol. 11: 654–5.

[87] *North Carolina State Records*, vol. 13: 90–1, 117–18, 135–6, 500–1.

[88] Pate, "Chickamauga," 85; *DAR*, vol. 13: 296.

[89] Downes, "Cherokee–American Relations," 37; C.O. 5/80: 177, 187.

[90] *North Carolina State Records*, vol. 14: 243–5.

[91] Ibid., 246–7.

After Evan Shelby destroyed eleven towns in April, Dragging Canoe led the bulk of his followers to the base of Chatauga (later Lookout) Mountain and established the "Five Lower Towns" in Creek territory.[92] John Stuart's death that same spring caused temporary confusion in the British Indian Department as the southern district was split in two. Alexander Cameron, the influential Cherokee agent, was appointed to the Choctaws and Chickasaws, whereas Thomas Brown received charge of the Creeks and Cherokees.[93] It seemed a good time to send out peace feelers, and Chota continued to function as the conduit for such efforts. The Chickamaugas sent a talk to Shelby, via Oconostota as intermediary, professing to have seen the folly of their ways and asking him to take them by the hand.[94] In July 1779, the Raven of Chota, heading a Cherokee peace delegation to the Delawares at Coshocton and Daniel Brodhead at Fort Pitt, declared that he had disowned his English brother over the water and signed a treaty with the Americans.[95] However, Americans remained incapable of alleviating Cherokee hunger or protecting Cherokee lands.[96] The same month that the Raven was talking peace to Brodhead and the Delawares, Dragging Canoe assured Shawnee delegates that although the Chickamaugas had had their towns burned and "now live in the grass as you see us," they were far from conquered.[97]

Cameron "found matters in great confusion" among the Cherokees. At Chota, Virginia's resident agent, Joseph Martin, was working "through the mediation of the Great Warrior" to treat with those Cherokees who remained at peace, and offered to supply them with all they needed if they would return to their old towns. Cameron's arrival frustrated Martin's plans and sent him scuttling back to Virginia, but General Williamson's invasion of Cherokee country caused renewed distress. Meanwhile, Cameron received news of his transfer to the western district, which further dejected him and his Cherokee friends.[98] Smallpox added to the Cherokees' woes in 1779–80.[99]

Despite such setbacks, many Cherokees remained firm in their attachment to

[92] Williams, *Tennessee During the Revolutionary War*, 91–9; Brown, *Old Frontiers*, 173–5; *PCC*, reel 85, item 71, vol. 1: 241–2; Draper Mss. 31S23–4. The Five Towns were: Lookout Mountain Town, Crow Town, Long Island Town, Nickajack, and Running Water.

[93] Clinton Mss., vol. 61: 40, 42.

[94] *PCC*, reel 85, item 71, vol. 1: 225–6, 259–61, 263.

[95] *Frontier Advance*, 392–400; Draper Mss. 1H111–14; *Revolution and Confederation*, 183–9.

[96] Downes, "Cherokee–American Relations," 37; *North Carolina State Records*, vol. 14: 220–2; *PCC*, reel 85, item 71: 265–7.

[97] Brown, *Old Frontiers*, 176.

[98] *DAR*, vol. 17: 232–3, 267–71; C.O. 5/81: 38. Martin enjoyed considerable influence at Chota. He was married to the daughter of beloved woman Nancy Ward, and Old Tassel referred to him during the peace talks in 1777 as "the beloved man who is pitched upon to hold the good talks fast with me." Richard A. Shrader, "Joseph Martin, Indian Agent, 1777–1789," M.A. thesis, University of North Carolina at Chapel Hill, 1973, 2, n. 2.

[99] *DAR*, vol. 17: 233; Brown, *Old Frontiers*, 182.

Britain.[100] As Cornwallis swept north in 1780, British agents intensified their efforts to get Cherokee warriors to act in concert with British troops, and increased their promises of food, ammunition, and clothing.[101] A former trader at Settico reported that the Raven of Chota went to treat with the British agent in Georgia that fall, received a war talk from Thomas Brown, and announced "that he was done with the Big Knife." The British apparently gave the Raven a medal as principal chief and he "was received as such by the warriors in the Room of Occouostota." Traders fled the Upper towns in anticipation of being killed.[102] By December, Virginia was convinced that the British had been successful and that another Cherokee war was inevitable. Thomas Jefferson recognized the root cause – "Their distress had too much ripened their alienation from us, and gathered to a head," – but resolved to strike first.[103]

Jefferson dispatched Arthur Campbell and John Sevier, fresh from his bloody victory at King's Mountain, into Overhill country in December 1780. Only Chilhowee offered any resistance. "We were soon in possession of their beloved Town, in which we found a welcome supply of provisions," said Campbell. From Chota he sent out parties of men to destroy neighboring towns. After the Virginians destroyed Toqua, Chilhowee, and several smaller towns, the Cherokees sent Nancy Ward with overtures for peace. Campbell gave an evasive answer, "as I wished first to visit the vindictive part of the nation . . . and to distress the whole as much as possible by destroying their habitations and provisions." He proceeded to burn Settico, Tuskegee, and Chota. The Virginians destroyed about a thousand houses, fifty thousand bushels of corn, and all but a few small towns. In the baggage abandoned by Oconostota in his flight, they found "various manuscripts, Copies of Treaties, Commissions, Letters, and other Archives of the nation, some of which shews the double game that people has been carrying on during the present war." Blaming British intrigue, Campbell concluded, "Never did a people so happily situated, act more foolishly in loosing their livings, and their Country." The Raven of Chota told the British the following year that the Virginians attacked "in such numbers last fall there was no withstanding them, they dyed their hands in the Blood of many of our Woman [sic] and Children, burnt 17 towns, destroyed all our provisions by which we & our families were almost destroyed by famine this Spring."[104]

[100] DAR, vol. 18: 56.
[101] Downes, "Cherokee–American Relations," 37; Williams, Tennessee During the Revolutionary War, 182; H.M.C., Report on American Mss., vol. 2: 221.
[102] "Deposition of William Springstone, Dec. 11, 1780," Virginia Magazine of History and Biography 27 (1919), 313–14, and Virginia State Papers, vol. 1: 446.
[103] Draper Mss. 14U237; 1XX41; Downes, "Cherokee–American Relations," 37; O'Donnell, Southern Indians in the American Revolution, 106; Virginia Magazine of History and Biography 27 (1919), 315.
[104] Pate, "Chickamauga," 109–110; Brown, Old Frontiers, 194–5; Draper Mss. 9DD24, 30S140–80; Virginia State Papers, vol. 1: 434–7. The Cherokee archives captured by Campbell are in PCC, reel 85, item 71, vol. 2, and discussed in John R. Alden, "The Eighteenth-Century Cherokee Archives," American Archivist 5 (1942), 240–4. The Raven's speech is in C.O. 5/82: 287, and quoted in O'Donnell, Southern Indians in the American Revolution, 118–19.

Confronted with starvation, Hanging Maw declared for peace with the Americans in open council early in 1781.[105] In March, Sevier followed up on his fall campaign by burning fifteen Middle towns.[106] In April, Oconostota, Hanging Maw, and Old Tassel sent messengers to Colonel Martin, bearing blue and white beads – blue signifying that times had been dark, white that the time was now good. They said they were "in a bad situation Out in the Woods perishing," and blamed the British for their distress.[107] The Spanish capture of Pensacola in May ended any hope of Creek aid, and the Cherokees were left to face the victorious Americans alone.[108] Arthur Campbell proposed launching another expedition against the Chickamaugas and raising tribes in the Illinois country to attack the Cherokees.[109] Sevier and Christian met 500 Overhill Cherokees at Long Island. While Old Tassel and Oconostota spoke to make the way clear for peace and cited land seizures as the cause of the troubles, the Americans looked for more land as reparation. Christian told the Cherokees that if they wanted peace they should hand over their prisoners, drive British agents from the Chickamauga towns, and send delegates to Congress.[110]

That summer, however, while Oconostota and two other chiefs went to Williamsburg, the Raven traveled to Savannah. On September 1, he assured Thomas Brown of the Cherokees' loyalty and said that Oconostota's peace mission was "only to save the Corn upon the Ground & prevent our Towns being burnt." Once the corn was in, said the Raven, they would attack the rebels with as much spirit as ever.[111] By year's end, however, Oconostota and other Overhill chiefs were urging the Virginians to attack Chickamauga, fearing themselves "in imminent danger unless we do something shortly."[112]

The collapse of the Anglo-Indian war effort in 1781 unleashed a settlers' invasion of the upper Tennessee country. The Cherokees appealed to Governor Alexander Martin of North Carolina, who in turn ordered Sevier to warn off the intruders, but the squatter invasion continued unabated throughout 1782.[113] The British credited the Cherokees with "manly spirited perseverance" in the

[105] *Virginia State Papers*, vol. 1: 495; Draper Mss. 11S24–5.
[106] Brown, *Old Frontiers*, 196; *Virginia State Papers*, vol. 2: 24.
[107] Draper Mss. 1XX43.
[108] Downes, "Cherokee–American Relations," 38.
[109] Campbell to Robert Lanier, May 27, 1781, Nathanael Greene Papers, Duke University, Perkins Library, Durham, N.C.
[110] Downes, "Cherokee–American Relations," 38. The Treaty of Long Island is in Draper Mss. 1XX45–9, reprinted in *Revolution and Confederation*, 265–70. A damaged report of the treaty proceedings, July 26–Aug. 2, 1781, is in the Nathanael Greene Papers, reel 2, Davis Library, University of North Carolina at Chapel Hill, microfilm #1–842. Arthur Campbell hoped the Cherokees would cede so much land as to not only defray the cost of the war against them, "but also raise a fund for a Peace establishment which might prevent future outbreakings." Campbell to George Washington, July 10, 1781, Southern Historical Collection, University of North Carolina, Revolutionary War Papers, Addition 2194.
[111] C.O. 5/82: 287–8 (same speech in LC, C.O. 5/82: 509–11).
[112] Draper Mss. 11S71–3; *Virginia State Papers*, vol. 2: 679.
[113] Downes, Cherokee–American Relations," 39–40.

face of great adversity, recurrent assault, and rebel atrocities.[114] But the Cherokees were on their last legs. The "friendly" chiefs sent messages to the Americans, blaming their woes on the "roguery of the Tories that come among us, and the Thieves of our people that join them that we cannot restrain." Many of their people were "lying out," not knowing what to do and afraid of both the British and the Americans. They were short of provisions, had no ammunition, and dared not risk hunting lest Americans kill them, as they had a group from the Valley towns, "we hope thro' mistake, thinking they were from Chickamogga." It seemed that those who had been the first to make peace were suffering the most. Joseph Martin and Shelby both urged Virginia to do something to help the Cherokees: "I cannot help pitying the wretches," wrote Shelby.[115] In July, Oconostota, now almost blind and perhaps suffering from tuberculosis, formally resigned his authority "with the consent of the whole nation" to his son Tuckasee, the Terrapin.[116]

That summer, the Chickamaugas were reported to want peace. The chiefs of Chota worked to facilitate the treaty and the Chickamaugas gathered their prisoners for delivery to the Americans.[117] But Virginia planned to destroy the Chickamauga towns and then dictate a treaty that would require the Chickamaugas to return to the old towns they had left, deliver up all Tories and runaway slaves, and strip the Cherokees of their lands to the Ohio and Mississippi.[118] Governor Martin of North Carolina recognized that the Overhills had been generally neutral but told Old Tassel and the other "friendly" chiefs that he expected them to apprehend the people from Chickamauga "who are enemies to us both."[119] That fall Sevier and McDowell launched another attack on the Chickamauga towns.[120] At "the Old Chota Town which professed to be at peace," Sevier met with Oconostota, Old Tassel, and Hanging Maw, and made peace.[121] Meanwhile, backcountry settlers continued to encroach on Overhill lands.[122] Crop failures added to the miseries of the Cherokees. William Christian

---

[114] C.O. 5/82: 277, 343; *DAR*, vol. 21: 122; H.M.C., *Report on American Mss.*, vol. 3: 157.

[115] Draper Mss. 11S77–83; *Virginia State Papers*, vol. 3: 171–2, 243.

[116] Draper Mss. 11S90–1; 9DD35; King and Ollinger, "Oconastota," 227; Colyer Meriwether, ed., "Gen. Joseph Martin and the Cherokees," *Publications of the Southern History Association* 8 (1904), 449.

[117] Draper Mss. 11S94–8, 107; Meriwether, ed., "Gen. Joseph Martin and the Cherokees," *Publications of the Southern History Association* 8: 449; vol. 9: (1905) 27.

[118] *North Carolina State Records*, vol. 16: 710–11.

[119] Ibid., vol. 16: 461; vol. 19: 939.

[120] Cotterill, *Southern Indians*, 55; Williams, *Revolutionary War in Tennessee*, 211; *North Carolina State Records*, vol. 16: 461; Haldimand Papers, 21762: 203; H.M.C. *Report on American Mss.*, vol. 3: 326.

[121] Major James Sevier to L. C. Draper, Aug. 19. 1839, Tennessee State Library and Archives, John Sevier Papers, box 1, folder 1, and Tennessee Historical Society, Misc. files, reel 7, box 14, S-39.

[122] Draper Mss. 60J156–9; *North Carolina State Records*, vol. 16: 461.

found their plight beyond description by the end of the year.[123] In January, Oconostota delivered a talk to Joseph Martin at Chota, signifying the demise of the town and the peace efforts it had cultivated: "All the old warriors are dead. There are now none left to take care of the Cherokees, but you & myself, & for my part I am become very old. And this beloved town of Chote belongs to you"[124] Oconostota died soon after, probably in the spring of 1783.[125]

Virginia continued to hope that Chota could exert its influence to bring the Chickamaugas back into the fold and make peace.[126] But the miseries of the Overhill people only served to swell the ranks of the Chickamauga dissidents, and the efforts of the older chiefs to maintain peace and keep the Americans apprised of Chickamauga intentions only widened the gulf between the groups.[127] Increasingly, when the British referred to Cherokees, they meant those who continued the war from Chickamauga. In January 1783, a deputation of twelve hundred Cherokees and northern Indians arrived in Saint Augustine intent on forming a confederacy against the Americans. Delegates passed between Cherokee country and Detroit for the same purpose. A hundred Cherokees fought out the last months of the war among the Shawnees.[128] At Chota, Kenoteta or the Rising Fawn publicly and symbolically "threw away" the British, scattering dust between them and his people and handing his royal medal and commission to Joseph Martin. News of the Peace of Paris confirmed the Overhill chiefs' belief that Britain had been the ruin of the Cherokees.[129] At Chickamauga, the fight went on.

Rebuilt after Campbell burned it in December 1780, Chota was still one of the largest of the Cherokee towns on the Tennessee River, numbering "something over thirty houses" when Moravian Brother Martin Schneider visited it at the end of the war.[130] Though the war was over, the usual pressures on Cherokee lands continued.[131] Although Bloody Fellow of the Chickamaugas threatened to kill illegal settlers if the authorities did not remove them, at Chota Old Tassel and the Raven continued to try and avoid hostilities by sending their

[123] Draper Mss. 11S122; *Virginia State Papers*, vol. 3: 398.
[124] Draper Mss. 12S11.
[125] King and Ollinger, "Oconastota," 222–3; Jefferson Chapman, *Tellico Archaeology: 12,000 Years of Native American History* (Knoxville: University of Tennessee, Department of Anthropology, Report of Investigations No. 43, 1985), 118; Draper Mss. 14DD16.
[126] Draper Mss. 1XX56; Meriwether, ed., "Gen. Joseph Martin and the Cherokees," vol. 9: 29.
[127] Fries, ed., *Records of the Moravians in North Carolina*, vol. 5: 1982.
[128] H.M.C., *Report on American Mss.*, vol. 3: 325–6; Carleton Papers, PRO 30/55/60, doc. 6742: 6–11; *Virginia State Papers*, vol. 3: 426–7; *DAR*, vol. 19: 429; C.O. 5/82: 347; C.O. 42/39: 113; 40: 258; Draper Mss. 12S19.
[129] Draper Mss. 12S13–14, 18–19; *Virginia State Papers*, vol. 3: 420–1; C.O. 5/82: 447.
[130] Samuel Cole Williams, ed., *Early Travels in the Tennessee Country* (Johnson City, Tenn.: Watauga, 1925), 256; Fries, ed., *Records of the Moravians in North Carolina*, vol. 5: 1981.
[131] Stephen B. Weeks, "General Joseph Martin and the War of the Revolution in the West," *Annual Report of the American Historical Association* (1893), 444.

complaints through channels to the governors of Virginia and North Carolina. People were ranging through Cherokee country, marking the land, complained Old Tassel to Governor Martin: "When one goes off two comes in his place."[132] Old Tassel struggled to restructure the old system, but it was a lost cause. He could speak only for the Overhills and could not get the Lower and Middle towns to follow Chota's example and make peace. Some of Tassel's own warriors slipped away to join Dragging Canoe as Chickamauga war parties passed by the Overhill towns, and his people sometimes fell victim to American militia marching to attack the Chickamauga villages.[133]

The Cherokees were in a hopeless situation, caught in jurisdictional disputes between the federal government, various state governments, and backcountry settlers attempting to create the new "state" of Franklin. The new national government had little authority and was concentrating its attention on Indian affairs north of the Ohio, where it could sell Indian lands to fill an empty treasury; North Carolina was impecunious and powerless, and wanted to use Indian lands to settle its debts; Franklin, frankly, was land hungry.[134] Spain, as Britain's successor in the South, cultivated relations with the Creeks, Seminoles, Choctaws, and Chickasaws as buffers against American expansion, but had no need for Cherokee allegiance. Indeed, until Baron de Carondelet took over as governor of Louisiana and West Florida in 1791, Spain regarded the Cherokees as beyond its sphere of influence. The Spanish crown gave permission for Cherokee refugees to settle near Pensacola, but otherwise the Cherokees were on their own.[135] The British predicted accurately that, in their exposed situation, the Cherokees would be compelled to give up part of their hunting grounds to the Americans as the price of keeping the rest.[136]

In June 1785, the Cherokees signed the Treaty of Dumplin Creek with Franklin, which they evidently regarded as only a tentative agreement. In August, Joseph Martin reported that the Cherokees were "in Great Confusion the people from Franklyn have actually Settled or at least built houses within Two miles of their Beloved Town Chota." Old Tassel continued to appeal to Virginia and to Congress for help in stopping the Franklinites' encroachments, "which make some of our young men in a bad way of thinking." But Oconostota's death had deprived Martin of much of his influence at Chota.[137]

[132] *North Carolina Colonial Records*, vol. 9: 825–6; *North Carolina State Records*, vol. 17: 11–12 175–6; Draper Mss. 12S18–19.

[133] Gearing, "Priests and Warriors," 103.

[134] Downes, "Cherokee–American Relations," 39.

[135] Ibid., 38; A. P. Whitaker, "Spain and the Cherokee Indians, 1783–1791," *North Carolina Historical Review* 4 (1927), 252–69.

[136] Carleton Papers P.R.O. 30/55: 93 doc. 10139; Joseph Galvez to Gov. of Florida, Dec. 31, 1783, Library of Congress, East Florida Papers, reel 16, bundle 39M3.

[137] *North Carolina State Records*, vol. 22: 649–50; *Revolution and Confederation*, 386–87, 389; Samuel Cole Williams, *History of the Lost State of Franklin*, revised ed. (New York: Press of the Pioneers, 1933), 77–8; Draper Mss. 2XX5; 12S18, 38–9; *Virginia State Papers*, vol. 4: 54.

In November 1785, the Cherokees signed their first treaty with the new United States. Old Tassel attended the Treaty at Hopewell on the Keowee River in South Carolina with thirty-six chiefs and more than nine hundred of his people. He reasserted the Cherokees' attachment to their lands and even drew the American commissioners a map depicting Cherokee boundaries. Nancy Ward hoped the treaty would mark a new beginning: "I have seen much trouble in the late war. I am now old, but hope yet to bear children who will grow up and people our Nation, as we are now under the protection of Congress and have no more disturbances." Signed over the protests of North Carolina's agent, William Blount, whom the Cherokees called "the Dirt King," the Treaty of Hopewell confirmed Cherokee boundaries, but it did little to stop the encroachments on their lands.[138] More Cherokees joined the Chickamaugas and resorted to violence to defend their lands.

In July 1786, Sevier ordered out the Franklin militia. When the troops reached Chota, Old Tassel and Hanging Maw tried to smooth things over and keep the peace. They said the recent killings had been committed by two or three warriors from Cawatie, not Chota: "My Town is not so," asserted Tassel. They offered to deliver up the murderers if given time, but the Franklinites marched to Cawatie and burned it. They then compelled the chiefs to accept the Treaty of Coyotee or Chota Ford, which basically reaffirmed the terms of Dumplin Creek, and stripped the Cherokees of their lands between the French Broad and Little Tennessee rivers.[139]

Speaking to Joseph Martin in council at Chota in September, Old Tassel reflected bitterly, "Your people settle much Faster on our Lands after a Treaty than Before."[140] By the beginning of the new year, a convention of Cherokee chiefs at Chota had resolved to migrate to new homes "as the white people tell them they will plant corn in their Towns this Spring."[141] By early spring, the Franklinites had opened a land office for all the lands between the French Broad and Tennessee rivers. "It Includes part of their Beloved Town, Chota, and several of their Corn Fields," Martin told Governor Randolph. Again, Old Tassel's complaints went unheeded. Chota's peaceful stance began to unravel. Martin found the inhabitants "in Greater Confusion Than I Ever saw them." Forty warriors had gone to war against the settlers of Cumberland and Kentucky to take revenge for the killing of some Cherokee hunters. Martin assembled the chiefs at Chota and secured their promise "that if the White People will let Them Remain in peace that nothing will Induce them To Take up the Hatchett

---

[138] The proceedings of the Treaty of Hopewell are in *New American State Papers: Indian Affairs*, vol. 6: 46–54; *ASPIA*, vol. 1: 40–3; and *Revolution and Confederation*, 393–402, 405–8.
[139] Pate, "The Chickamauga," 170; *North Carolina State Records*, vol. 18: 696–70; vol. 22: 655–9; *Virginia State Papers*, vol. 4: 164.
[140] *PCC*, reel 69, item 56: 417–18.
[141] *Virginia State Papers*, vol. 4: 235.

or Join the Spaniards," but the chiefs insisted that "if they are to be killed whenever they Go to Hunt, they must have Satisfaction."[142]

Alarmed by reports of hostilities, Virginia sent talks to Chota warning of the dire consequences such actions would precipitate. Old Tassel did not like the tenor of the talk, and told Governor Randolph so, in a speech delivered from Chota in June. "It seems as if you was fond of Believing Lies and Looking over Truth," he said, blaming Creek and Shawnee militants for the hostilities. "If you are a Just Man you will Enquire into matters Before you write so Rash, and stand to the Truth." Old Tassel had done everything in his power to preserve peace, hold fast to the treaties, and prevent his young men from doing mischief, but every treaty made seemed only to increase the trespasses on Cherokee land. "It is well known that you have Taken almost all our Country from us without our consent. That Don't seem to satisfy my Elder Brother, but he still Talks of fire and sword." "Truth is," reflected Old Tassel, "if we had no Land, we should have Fewer Enemies." "I make no Doubt but you are a great man," he continued, "and suppose we are a foolish people; but we have seen Enough to know we are Used Ill." He went on:

> You Suffer your People to settle to our Towns and say nothing about it, but if the Creeks or Shonies does you any mischief you Threaten us with fire and sword. For my part I love peace. I formerly Loved War, and Lived at Chicamogga, but Colo. Martin sent for me to come away. Being his Relation, I came, and six winters is past that I have taken his talk and assisted him in keeping peace. I now live in Chuister, the Middle Ground between Chota and Chickamogga. I stand up like a wall between Bad people and my Brothers, the Virginians. Both Creeks and Chickamoggians has been turned back from doing mischief by me.

If Virginia forced him to it, Tassel would have to look for "new friends."[143]

In May 1788, a Cherokee named Slim Tom murdered the family of John Kirk; they were squatting about nine miles from Chota on land reserved to the Cherokees. The Cherokees blamed the Creeks and Chickamaugas, but Sevier marched 150 men into Cherokee country in retaliation, while Colonel James Hubbard led a supporting move to Chota. At Chilhowee, John Kirk murdered Old Tassel, Old Abraham, and several other Cherokees under a flag of truce. The inhabitants of Chota fled before Hubbard arrived, but not before "the white flag which had for three years been flying at Chota had been taken down." Old Tassel's murder sent many more warriors to join Dragging Canoe's resistance movement. Tired of being caught between the Americans and the Chickamaugas and Creeks, the rest of the people of Chota fled across the mountains to their relatives in South Carolina, "where we hope to live in

---

[142] Ibid., 261; *North Carolina State Records*, vol. 22: 493–4.
[143] *Virginia State Papers*, vol. 4: 306–7.

Peace," said Black Dog, one of the refugees. The "Prince of Notoly" sent a talk
to the Americans "concerning my elder Brothers of Chota," who "have come
over here for peace where it is light & clear." Their greatest desire was peace,
he said. "They left their Towns that the Creeks & the white men may fight it
out themselves, as I suppose they both love fighting."[144]

The Cherokees now moved their capital from Chota to Ustanali on the
Coosawati River in northern Georgia. Cherokees no longer expected the national
council to meet at Chota; the council elected Little Turkey, not a member of
the Chota leadership, as principal chief. Even before the assassination of Old
Tassel, Chota had ceased to function as the coordinating center of the annual
festivals. "What was left," according to Duane Champagne, "was a coalition of
villages."[145]

In 1799, two Moravian missionaries, Abraham Steiner and Fredrick De
Schweintz, visited Chota. The town comprised "only five houses which were
well scattered over the plain." Besides some women and children they met only
one old man, called Arcowee, in front of his house. Arcowee was the current
"beloved man of Chota," and, consistent with the concerns of his predecessors
for peace, he produced a copy of a speech made by President Washington three
years before, urging the Cherokees to live in peace. "The old man was told that
all of this was intended for their good," wrote the Moravians, "but it did not
happen to be the matter concerning which *we* had come hither." Informing him
of their mission, the brothers invited Arcowee to follow them to Tellico for
further discussion, which he did. Considering their talks, the old man reviewed
the history of his people's relations with the whites and the decline of his
beloved town. "I am delighted that there is thought for the old loved town of
Chota," he said.

> When you came there you could not see my house, so much has the place
> been overgrown with grass, yet you found it; that rejoices me exceedingly.
> I am now quite alone. The other loved ones are gone, though they ever
> desired to maintain peace (therewith he signified allegorically that they had
> been murdered by the whites.) Never, however, will I leave Chota but
> remain there till I die or perish.[146]

By the end of the fighting generated by the Revolution, "the Cherokees were
no longer sure of their place in the universe." Their population had dropped to
perhaps ten thousand; they had lost three-quarters of their homelands and
hunting grounds; more than half of their towns had been destroyed. The major

[144] Downes, "Cherokee–American Relations," 46–7; Brown, *Old Frontiers*, 277–8; *Virginia State
Papers*, vol. 4: 452; Draper Mss. 12S193–4; *PCC*, reel 69, item 56: 425, 432–3.
[145] Chapman, *Tellico Archaeology*, 106; Champagne, *Social Order and Political Change*, 76–7.
[146] Williams, ed., *Early Travels in the Tennessee Country*, 472–3, 497. The Steiner-Schweintz
journal is also printed in *North Carolina Historical Review* 21 (1944), 330–75 (Arcowee passages
346–7, 359–60).

cleavages that the Revolution had produced between the Lower towns around Chickamauga and those that had favored neutrality continued to divide the Cherokees into the nineteenth century. Their cultural framework suffered severe shocks, disrupting the harmony that was vital to Cherokee well-being and relations with the spirit world. "Disorder was everywhere," wrote William McLoughlin, "between old chiefs and young chiefs, between one town and another, between parents and children, between man and the retreating animals. Somehow they had lost control of their destiny as a people." Thousands of Cherokees moved farther inland into what was left of their nation and began to rebuild. Their experiences in the Revolution convinced the Cherokees that, in Russell Thornton's words, "they could not preserve themselves by war." Despite internal cultural conflicts over whether to make the transition to farming, many tried the path of acculturation. They did so on "the promise of equal citizenship in the new nation," and won admiration from many Americans as a "civilized tribe." The Cherokee people, wrote William McLoughlin, "were reborn like the phoenix from the ashes of defeat and confusion." The new Cherokee nation that arose from the ruins of the Revolution was very different from that of the eighteenth century.[147]

But it was too late. The Revolution marked an emphatic divergence between the Cherokees and their colonial neighbors as the warriors of both societies "took control of the path."[148] Cherokee participation in the Revolution proved a powerful, durable, and usable image. As the clamor grew in the nineteenth century to remove Cherokees from their remaining lands, the peace efforts of village headman before the war, the role of Chota during the war, and the new societies built from the ruins of war, were ignored in favor of the memory of Cherokee hostility in the Revolution. The Cherokees would have to begin again the process of rebuilding, in new homes beyond the Mississippi.

---

[147] William G. McLoughlin, *Cherokee Renascence in the New Republic* (Princeton, N.J.: Princeton University Press, 1986), xv, 3–4, 25; Russell Thornton, "Boundary Dissolution and Revitalization Movements: The Case of the Nineteenth-Century Cherokees," *Ethnohistory* 40 (1993), 363; Hatley, *Dividing Paths*, 232–3; Champagne, *Social Order and Political Change*, 93–4; James H. O'Donnell, III, *The Cherokees of North Carolina in the American Revolution* (Raleigh, N.C.: Department of Cultural Resources, Division of Archives and History, 1976), 23.
[148] Hatley, *Dividing Paths*, 228, 231.

# 8

## *Tchoukafala: the continuing Chickasaw struggle for independence*

By the time of the American Revolution, the Chickasaw Indians were already veterans in their own struggles to preserve their independence. Located in northern Mississippi and western Tennessee in a strategic area between the Yazoo and Tombigbee rivers,[1] with powerful Indian nations as neighbors and ambitious European nations as suitors and enemies, the Chickasaws offset their numerical weakness with skilled diplomacy and military prowess. They fought against De Soto's Spaniards in 1540–1, resisted French and Choctaw assaults in the eighteenth century, and maintained their place in the swirling world of Spanish, French, English, and tribal war, trade, and diplomacy.[2] The Revolution in Chickasaw country was a small affair in terms of fighting, but it significantly changed the Chickasaws' diplomatic landscape. They responded to the new competition between Spain and the United States in much the same way as they had dealt with the old competition between France and England. Factions formed, but the Chickasaws' common and consistent goal, in the words of Piomingo, chief of Tchoukafala for more than a decade after the Revolution, was to preserve their independence as a "people to our Selves."[3] In time, however, American independence and expansion delivered a body blow to Chickasaw independence.

Chickasaw traditions, as handed down at the time of the Revolution, remembered that they were "only a family from a great rich nation towards the sun

---

[1] For a description of traditional Chickasaw territorial boundaries, see Piomingo's account in James H. Malone, *The Chickasaw Nation* (Louisville, KY: Morton, 1922), 57, and *ASPIA*, vol. 1: 286.

[2] Arrell M. Gibson, *The Chickasaws* (Norman: University of Oklahoma Press, 1971), provides a convenient survey of this history.

[3] D. C. Corbitt and Roberta Corbitt, eds. "Papers from the Spanish Archives relating to Tennessee and the Old Southwest," *East Tennessee Historical Society Publications* 40 (1968), 101. The Chickasaw word for long is *falaha*; the Choctaw is *falaya*. Tchoukafala or Chuckafalaha is therefore sometimes written as Chuckafalaya. John R. Swanton, *Social and Religious Beliefs and Usages of the Chickasaw Indians*, Bureau of American Ethnology, Forty-fourth Annual Report (1926–7), 213. Choctaw and Chickasaw are mutually intelligible languages except for differences in vocabulary; Betty Jacob, "Choctaw and Chickasaw," *International Journal of American Linguistics* 46 (1980), 43. Americans often referred to Tchoukafala as Old Pontotoc.

setting," who had migrated east after their fathers dreamed "that away towards the sun rising was land of life."[4] Compared to their Choctaw neighbors, the Chickasaws were a small nation. They said they had ten thousand warriors when they first came from the west, but chronic warfare steadily reduced the population. The Chickasaws bolstered their population by adopting captives, absorbing small neighboring tribes, and accommodating Natchez refugees after the French destroyed that nation in 1730. A French report in 1731 estimated the Chickasaws at six hundred men, roughly three thousand people, plus "250 or 300 Natchez who have joined them."[5] The Chickasaw population nucleus seems to have fallen steadily to about 1,600 by the end of the French wars, perhaps rebounding to about 2,300 people and 450 warriors before the Revolution.[6] English trading alliances and French conflicts tugged at the unity of Chickasaw society. Warriors ranged farther afield; some people relocated in search of deerskins and slaves, and others migrated rather than commit to an English alliance. One band migrated to the protection of the Creek confederacy and became known as Breed Camp; another settled for a time among the Choctaws.[7]

Chickasaw traditions recalled living in a world at war from time immemorial. "They say that as far back as they can learn by their ancestors, verbally handed

[4] Dawson A. Phelps, ed., "Extracts from the Journal of the Reverend Joseph Bullen, 1799 and 1800," *Journal of Mississippi History* 17 (1955), 264. See also Henry Warren, "Chickasaw Traditions, Customs, Etc.," *Publications of the Mississippi Historical Society* 8 (1904), 543–53.

[5] John R. Swanton, *The Indian Tribes of North America*, Bureau of American Ethnology, Bulletin 145 (Washington, D.C. 1952): 179; *MPA, FD*, vol. 4: 81.

[6] Samuel Cole Williams, ed., *Adair's History of the American Indians* (New York: Promontory Press reprint of 1930 ed.), 377–8; Wilbur R. Jacobs, ed., *Indians of the Southern Colonial Frontier: The Edmund Atkin Report and Plan of 1755* (Columbia: University of South Carolina Press, 1954), 42–3; "An Estimate of the Indian Nations, Employed by the British in the Revolutionary War," *Massachusetts Historical Collections*, 1st series, 10 (1809), 123; Peter H. Wood, "The Changing Population of the Colonial South," in Wood, Gregory A. Waselkov, et al., eds., *Powhatan's Mantle: Indians in the Colonial Southeast* (Lincoln: University of Nebraska Press, 1989), 68. Cf. John Ferdinand Dalziel Smyth, *A Tour in the United States of America*, 2 vols. (New York: New York Times and Arno, 1968), vol. 1: 347, estimated their number at 750 warriors. One French estimate from 1726 said the Chickasaws had 800 men, but more commonly the French spoke of 450 warriors, and in 1740, after years of conflict, they estimated the Chickasaws to be reduced to scarcely 300 men; *MPA, FD*, vol. 1: 315, 450, 461; vol. 3: 538. An undated British list of warrior counts, Clements Library, Germain Papers, vol. 17: 11, gives the Chickasaws as 500; John Stuart in 1764 estimated they had 450 warriors, C.O. 323/17: 254. Various other estimates of Chickasaw warrior strength are given in Helen Louise Shaw, *British Administration of the Southern Indians, 1756–1783* (Lancaster, Pa: Lancaster Press, 1931), 194–5.

[7] *MPA, FD*, vol. 4: 65. On "Breed Town," the Chickasaw group among the Creeks, see Duane Champagne, *Social Order and Political Change: Constitutional Governments among the Cherokee, the Choctaw, the Chickasaw, and the Creek* (Stanford, Calif.: Stanford University Press, 1992), 63. According to John Stuart in 1764, Breed Camp contained thirty-three Chickasaw warriors and twenty Natchez. He said the Chickasaws of Breed Camp were "despised by their brave Countrymen who remain at home, as Dastards, who basely deserted their Country." C.O. 323/17: 238, 244. Patricia Galloway, "The Necessity of the Other: Choctaw Indian Identity in the Eighteenth Century," paper presented at the 1992 meeting of the American Historical Association.

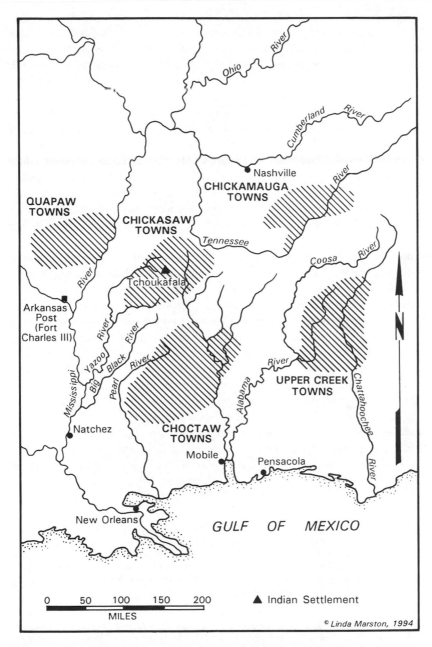

Map 10. Tchoukafala, the Chickasaws, and their neighbors during the revolutionary
era. Based on Lester J. Cappon, ed., *Atlas of Early American History: The
Revolutionary Era, 1760–1790* (Princeton, N.J.: Princeton University Press, 1976),
map 19.

down & extended from family to family," reported one postrevolutionary traveler, "that there was nothing but war[;] all nations were at war. The Chickasaws were at war with all nations."[8] French movement down the Mississippi and the penetration of English traders from Charleston by the end of the seventeenth century brought guns and slave-raiding warfare to Indian villages on both sides of the river.[9] When the Chickasaws and Choctaws met the French in conference at Mobile in 1702, the Chickasaws had already lost more than eight hundred men. Nevertheless, Pierre Le Moyne d' Iberville estimated they could still muster two thousand warriors, of whom seven or eight hundred had guns, and the Indians reported that the Chickasaws still lived in eighteen villages, totaling 588 huts. Tchoukafala contained thirty huts. Six years later, South Carolina Indian agent Thomas Nairne estimated Chickasaw warrior strength at seven hundred, but by his method of counting there were only eight villages.[10]

Toting English guns, raiding for slaves, and existing on what amounted to a permanent war footing, the Chickasaws won a reputation as the most warlike people on the Mississippi – courageous if somewhat vainglorious warriors. Nairne described them as "arrogant and conseited [sic], high minded[,] touchy as tinder." He also noted that escalating warfare had increased the prestige of Chickasaw war chiefs, as "the head Military Officers carry all the sway." Sieur De Bienville, governor of Louisiana, wrote in 1726: "These people breathe nothing but war and are unquestionably the bravest of the continent." An Indian identified as an Abenaki who had lived among several southern tribes described the Chickasaws as "real warriors, even braver than the Catawbas." The French said the more numerous Choctaws were afraid of the Chickasaws, "who are almost all warriors," and Chickasaws boasted that they had "only to beat drums in our cabins" to make the Choctaws run away. Jean-Bernard Bossu said their bravery was unsurpassed. Bernard Romans thought them "the most fierce, cruel, insolent, and haughty people" of the southern nations. A less hostile observer, English trader James Adair, called them "our friendly gallant

---

[8] Jesse D. Jennings, ed., "Nutt's Trip to the Chickasaw Country," *Journal of Mississippi History* 9 (1947), 52.

[9] Gibson, *Chickasaws*, 39–41; Dawson A. Phelps, "The Chickasaws, the English, and the French, 1699–1744," *Tennessee Historical Quarterly* 16 (1957), 117–33. For a brief but informative source on the Chickasaws and Choctaws "as they emerged into the destructive currents of European global politics," see Patricia Galloway, "Henri de Tonti du Village des Chacta, 1702," in Galloway, ed., *La Salle and His Legacy: Frenchmen and Indians in the Lower Mississippi Valley* (Jackson: University Press of Mississippi, 1982), 146–75.

[10] Daniel H. Usner, Jr., *Indians, Settlers, and Slaves in a Frontier Exchange Economy: The Lower Mississippi Valley Before 1783* (Chapel Hill: University of North Carolina Press, 1992), 16, 18, 21 (table). Richebourg Gaillaird McWilliams, ed., *Iberville's Gulf Journals* (University: University of Alabama Press, 1981), 171–4. George C. H. Kiernon, trans., "Documents Concerning the History of the Indians of the Eastern Region of Louisiana," *Louisiana Historical Quarterly* 8 (1925), 39; Alexander Moore, ed., *Nairne's Muskhogean Journals: The 1708 Expedition to the Mississippi River* (Jackson: University Press of Mississippi, 1988), 36–8.

Chikkasah." John Stuart said they were "esteemed the bravest Indians on the Continent." Peter Chester, British governor of West Florida at the time of the Revolution and a man not given to praising Indians, referred to them as "this brave tho' small Nation," whom surrounding tribes regarded with awe. British traveler John F. D. Smyth referred to their heroic reputation and "unconquerable spirit."[11]

Nairne identified the town of Hallachechoe as the mother town in 1708, but James Adair stated that "Chooka Phraa" (Tchoukafala) was the mother town in 1720, and historian Arrell Gibson described it as the tribal capital by midcentury, with more than two hundred households.[12] Tchoukafala ("longhouse" or "long town") seems to have had warlike associations even among a people with a warlike reputation, and may have functioned as a "red" or war town. Anthropologist John R. Swanton "was told that the Tcuka falaha were warlike and lived on a flat or prairie country, while the Tcukillissa were peaceful people living in the timber."[13]

The core of the Chickasaw settlements appears to have been a large prairie area north and west of Tupelo, Mississippi, known as the Chickasaw Old Fields, although the exact locations, divisions, and relationships of the Chickasaw towns are difficult to ascertain.[14] French reports in the 1730s described "six or seven villages" built on commanding eminences in a large prairie; all the villages appeared to merge into one. Some of the villages were fortified with earthen embankments and palisades; all were protected by, or built around, fortified

---

[11] Moore, ed., *Nairne's Muskhogean Journals*, 36–8; *MPA, FD*, vol. 1: 211, 228–9; vol. 3: 538, 695; vol. 4: 126, 147; Seymour Feiler, trans. and ed., *Jean-Bernard Bossu's Travels in the Interior of North America, 1751–1762* (Norman: University of Oklahoma Press, 1962), 172; Williams, ed., *Adair's History of the American Indians*, 271, 341n; C.O. 323/17: 244; Bernard Romans, *A Concise Natural History of East and West Florida* (New Orleans: Pelican, 1961), 40; *Publications of the Mississippi Historical Society* 5 (1925), 46–8; Smyth, *A Tour in the United States of America*, vol. 1: 360–3.

[12] Moore, ed., *Nairne's Muskhogean Journals*, 37, 69n; Williams, ed., *Adair's History of the American Indians*, 378; Gibson, *Chickasaws*, 6.

[13] Swanton, "Social and Religious Beliefs and Usages of the Chickasaw Indians," 193–5.

[14] For discussion of Chickasaw town sites see, for example, Jesse D. Jennings, "Chickasaw and Earlier Indian Cultures of Northeast Mississippi," *Journal of Mississippi History* 3 (1941), 155–226; James R. Atkinson, "The Ackia and Ogoula Tchetoka Chickasaw Village Locations in 1736 during the French–Chickasaw War," *Mississippi Archaeology* 20, No. 1 (June 1985), 53–72; and Jay K. Johnson, Patricia K. Galloway, and Walter Belokon, "Historic Chickasaw Settlement Patterns in Lee County, Mississippi," *Mississippi Archaeology* 24, No. 2 (Dec. 1989), 45–52. Sometime during the fifteenth century and before European contact, the Chickasaws had shifted their settlements from large village locations in the river bottomlands to small hamlets in the uplands, a move that suggests a corresponding decentralization in patterns of authority; Jay K. Johnson, "Prehistoric Mississippi," in Barbara Carpenter, ed., *Ethnic Heritage in Mississippi* (Jackson: University Press of Mississippi, 1992), 18–20. A French copy of an Indian map dated September 1737 shows the position of Tchoukafala in relation to the other Chickasaw towns; Gregory A. Waselkov, "Indian Maps of the Colonial Southeast," in Wood et al., eds., *Powhatan's Mantle*, 299. "Notes sur les deux cartes desseinés par les Chikachas," *Journal de la Sociéte des Americanistes* 13 (1921), 7–9; *MPA, FD*, vol. 1: 357; NAC, reel F-513, f. 66–8.

cabins.[15] Writing in 1775, James Adair said the Chickasaws in 1720 had four large settlements, divided into seven towns. Tchoukafala was about four miles long and a mile wide, and more populous then than the whole nation was by 1775. Bernard Romans said they lived in one long town, which they divided into seven others. Chickasaws shifted their towns in response to enemy threats, and appear to have extended their settlements in peacetime and contracted them when at war. They inhabited seven autonomous towns at the time of the Revolution, but by 1800, most had deserted the prairie towns and were living in scattered single-family settlements throughout northeastern Mississippi. Visitors still identified four major districts, but the transition to white settlement patterns and land-use practices further obscured traditional arrangements.[16]

Threatened by the Anglo-Chickasaw trading alliance, and thwarted in their drive to link their Illinois and Louisiana settlements, the French tried "to persuade all the nations to dip their hands in our blood." "We can't tell You the Names of all our Enemies, there are so many of them," Chickasaws told the English in 1756. But the Chickasaws more than held their own in open war with the French and their Choctaw allies in 1720–5 and 1733–43.[17] Chickasaws from other villages pinned the blame for long-standing conflicts with the Choctaws on the villages of Phalachelo and Tchoukafala: "It is they who have always worked to perpetuate the war that is destroying us," they told Red Shoes, war captain of the Choctaw town of Couechitto, in an attempt to divert a Choctaw assault. In 1736, Governor De Bienville agreed to an attack on Tchoukafala in large part because of the insistence of his Choctaw allies, who told him Tchoukafala was the Chickasaw town nearest to them and "gave them more trouble than all the othrs." But a pro-Tchoukafala faction among the Choctaws precipitated an attack on the town of Ackia instead. Choctaws attacking undefended Tchoukafala in 1737 apparently dug open Chickasaw graves to scalp the corpses. Another assault in 1740 failed, but Chickasaw towns and cornfields suffered more devastating attacks in 1741 and 1742.[18]

---

[15] Another report said there were twelve villages, seven of which were fortified. *MPA, FD*, vol. 1: 163, 307–8n, 357, 393–4; vol. 3: 538; vol. 4: 150.

[16] Williams, ed., *Adair's History of the American Indians*, 378; Warren, "Chickasaw Traditions," 550; Romans, *Concise Natural History of East and West Florida*, 42; Swanton, "Social and Religious Beliefs and Usages of the Chickasaw Indians," 212; Gibson, *Chickasaws*, 6, 21; Jennings, ed., "Nutt's Trip to the Chickasaw Country," 34–5; Phelps, ed., "Excerpts from Bullen's Journal," 262n–3n.

[17] Gibson, *Chickasaws*, 41–56; Usner, *Indians, Settlers, and Slaves*, 81 7; Michael J. Foret, "War or Peace? Louisiana, the Choctaws and the Chickasaws, 1733–1735," *Louisiana History* 31 (1990), 273–92; Norman W. Caldwell, "The Chickasaw Threat to French Control of the Mississippi in the 1740s," *Chronicles of Oklahoma* 16 (1938), 465–92. *MPA, FD*, vol. 1, passim; vol. 4: 41, 147; vol. 5: 112, 217, 257; John T. Juricek, ed., *Georgia Treaties, 1733–1763*, vol. 11 in Alden T. Vaughan, gen. ed., *Early American Indian Documents: Treaties and Laws, 1607–1789* (Frederick, Md.: University Publications of America, 1989), 76.

[18] *MPA, FD*, vol. 1: 304; vol. 3: 733–4; vol. 4: 150, 154, n. 25; Patricia Galloway, personal communication, February 24, 1993.

Under siege by the French and Choctaws, who infested their trading routes and rendered hunting perilous, the Chickasaws depended for their survival on English guns and ammunition. The British were more than happy to help frustrate French designs in the Mississippi Valley. In 1737, Tchoukafala had not only a store of English arms and ammunition but also a small pile of grenades, which the English had taught the warriors how to use.[19] Recurrent war took a heavy toll. The Chickasaws told Governor Glen of South Carolina in 1754 that once they "did not mind how many our Enemies were," but that now the Chickasaws were reduced to "a Handful of Men."[20] Nevertheless, they withstood their many enemies: "All the northern and the southern tribes, as well as the French, have waged war against them without being able to drive them from their lands," reported Jean-Bernard Bossu in 1759.[21]

Britons referred repeatedly to the Chickasaws as their "antient Friends," dutiful children, and faithful allies, "the Nation the most attached to the English of any in the Southern District," with a friendship "as Strong as Iron." In conferences with the two tribes, British superintendent John Stuart held up the Chickasaws as a model of fidelity that the wayward Choctaws should emulate.[22] At the Mobile conference in 1765, Paya Mataha, the principal chief and war prophet of the Chickasaw nation, declared: "My Heart & the Superintendants are as one, it is well known I never deserted the British Interest and I never will. Tho' I am a Red Man my Heart is white from my Connections with & the Benefits I have received from the white People, I allmost [sic] look upon myself as one of them."[23]

But the Chickasaws were nobody's mercenaries. Their goal was to protect their own interests, not tamely to serve King George's. They tempered their resistance to French expansion by skillfully playing France and Britain against

[19] Juricek, ed., *Georgia Treaties, 1733–1763*, 75–6, 125–6; *MPA, FD*, vol. 4: 150.

[20] William L. McDowell, Jr., ed., *Colonial Records of South Carolina: Documents relating to Indian Affairs, 1750–1754* (Columbia: South Carolina Archives Dept., 1958), 458–9, 511–13; idem, ed., *Documents Relating to Indian Affairs, 1754–1765* (Columbia: South Carolina Archives Department, 1970), 17, 109–14, 292–3, 413–16, 458–61, 490–1.

[21] Feiler, trans. and ed., *Jean-Bernard Bossu's Travels*, 172.

[22] Edward Mease, "Narrative of a Journey through several parts of the province of West Florida in the Years 1770–1771," and "Papers Relating to Congress with Choctaw and Chickasaw Indians," in Eron O. Rowland, "Peter Chester," *Publications of the Mississippi Historical Society* 5 (1925), 80, 136–41; Dunbar Rowland, ed., *Mississippi Provincial Archives, 1763–1766: English Dominion* (Nashville: Brandon, 1911), vol. 1: 511, 227; Williams, ed., *Adair's History of the American Indians*, vol. 1: 384; Smyth, *Tour in the United States of America*, vol. 1: 361–2; "The Letters of Hon. James Habersham, 1756–1775," *Collections of the Georgia Historical Society* 6 (1904), 200; Clarence Edwin Carter, ed., *The Correspondence of General Thomas Gage*, 2 vols. (New Haven, Conn.: Yale University Press, 1931–3), vol. 1: 332; *DAR*, vol. 8: 127; "Proceedings of a Congress held by John Stuart with the Chickasaw and Chactaw Nation, Dec. 31, 1771," enclosed in Stuart to Gage, May 23, 1772, Clements Library, Gage Papers, vol. 137, item 14: 5; George Germain to Peter Chester, Feb. 7, 1777, Mississippi Department of Archives and History, RG 25: English Provincial Archives, vol. 14.

[23] Rowland, ed., *Mississippi Provincial Archives, 1763–1776: English Dominion*, vol. 1: 245.

each other in a country where Indians, not Europeans, called the shots. They cultivated alliances to maintain a flow of trade goods, but regarded themselves as independent of all foreign powers.[24] The competition for Chickasaw allegiance generated divisions, and there was a small Francophile party in the nation, but the Chickasaws remained essentially united during the intense warfare and turbulent diplomacy of the eighteenth century.[25]

The competing interests at work in Chickasaw country aligned along economic and class lines as well as national ones. The principal chief, Paya Mataha, and superintendent John Stuart each looked to the other to help fend off challengers. During the 1760s, a number of traders challenged Stuart's commissary John McIntosh by allying themselves to Chickasaw headmen led by war chief Mingo Houma, who were rivals of Paya Mataha; the rival headmen in turn employed their trade connections to bolster their challenge to Paya Mataha. "Payamataha our Firm Friend & their great Leader loses his influence," said Stuart in 1766. Both Paya Mataha and Mingo Houma remained pledged to their British allegiance, but the new situation complicated Anglo-Chickasaw diplomacy. At the Mobile conference in 1772, Stuart tried to reaffirm Paya Mataha as the conduit through whom all Chickasaw business with the British should pass. Mingo Houma, however, declared that he was king of his nation, "& Paya Mataha is my warrior."[26] Since Mingo Houma signified "war chief" and Paya Mataha (*hopaii imataha*) meant "war prophet," both chiefs may have been asserting their actual and distinct functions in Chickasaw politics.[27]

Chickasaw leaders were unanimous in denouncing the effects of European trade on their society and lamenting the influence of trader cliques. Paya Mataha and first war chief Piomingo (Mountain Leader) of Tchoukafala[28] attempted to stem the tide of change that threatened their authority. Increasing numbers of

---

[24] Gibson, *Chickasaws*, 58–9.
[25] *MPA, FD*, vol. 4: 65; Champagne, *Social Order and Political Change*, 50, 63. Cf. Richard White, *The Roots of Dependency: Subsistence, Environment, and Social Change among the Choctaws, Pawnees, and Navajos* (Lincoln: University of Nebraska Press, 1983), ch. 3; and Patricia K. Galloway, "Choctaw Factionalism and Civil War," *Journal of Mississippi History* 44 (1982), 289–327, for the effects of competition and "play-off strategies" in Choctaw politics.
[26] Williams, ed., *Adair's History of the American Indians*, vol. 1: 351; C.O. 5/75: 350; Romans, *Concise Natural History of East and West Florida*, 43; Stuart to Gage, Jan. 11, 1766, Clements Library, Gage Papers, vol. 47; "Proceedings of a Congress held by John Stuart with the Chickasaw and Chactaw Nation," 10; 'Papers Relating to Congress with Choctaw and Chickasaw Indians," 146; George C. Osborn, "Relations with the Indians in West Florida During the Administration of Governor Peter Chester, 1770–1781," *Florida Historical Quarterly* 31 (1953), 245–51.
[27] Patricia Galloway, Personal Communication, March 24, 1993.
[28] For rather stereotypical thumbnail sketches of Piomingo, Wolf's friend, and some other leaders, see Harry Warren, "Some Chickasaw Chiefs and Prominent Men," *Publications of the Mississippi Historical Society* 8 (1904), 555–70. Champagne, *Social Order and Political Change*, 79, identifies Piomingo as first war chief. Piomingo's historical importance for a long time was obscured by historian Samuel G. Drake's confusing him with James Colbert; Albert V. Goodpasture, "Indian Wars and Warriors of the Old Southwest," *Tennessee Historical Magazine* 4 (1918), 108.

colonists settled in Chickasaw country after the Seven Years' War, and traders established themselves in and around Chickasaw villages, peddling alcohol to stimulate deerskin production. British authorities tried to check the independent traders by employing a commissary and licensing system, but Chickasaw spokesmen at the Mobile conference complained "grievously" and said "their little nation is distracted and split in parties by the jarring interest of traders as well as the number of vagabonds that resort to it who are only suffered to live because they are white men and British subjects." Paya Mataha said his nation was "once great but now much diminished by death," and he placed much of the blame on traders who corrupted his people, and made them ungovernable and disrespectful of old ways.[29]

Chickasaw government and society experienced additional change as growing numbers of mixed-bloods exercised influential intermediary roles.[30] James Colbert, a Scot, lived with the Chickasaws from his childhood, spoke Chickasaw fluently, and had three Chickasaw wives. His half-dozen sons exerted tremendous influence in Chickasaw councils well into the nineteenth century. Colbert operated a lucrative trade, established a plantation, and owned cattle and slaves. Many mixed-bloods not only cultivated a new life-style but also distanced themselves from the full-bloods and congregated around the headquarters of commissary John McIntosh at Tokshish (later McIntoshville) on the Natchez Trace.[31] The British authorities looked on men like Colbert with suspicion and disdain, but Colbert was to prove a loyal ally of the crown in the Revolution.[32]

On the eve of the Revolution, the Chickasaws' diplomatic landscape became more complicated even as internal tensions escalated in Chickasaw country. Spain began to step up espionage activities in the region, members of the old French party within the nation began to look to Spain for allegiance, and the British geared more of their Chickasaw diplomacy to counteracting Spanish influence.[33] Northern Indians harassed the Chickasaws, who retaliated in kind. The British planned to use the Chickasaws in combination with the Cherokees to check Kickapoo hostilities in the Illinois country, and in combination with the Quapaws of Arkansas to form a buffer protecting the Floridas. But Chickasaw murders of French Canadian hunters in the Illinois country threatened their

---

[29] *DAR*, vol. 1: 279; vol. 2: 105, 179, 281–2, 303; vol. 3: 106, 180; vol. 5: 37–8; C.O. 5/73: 316–17; Rowland, ed., *Mississippi Provincial Archives: English Dominion*, vol. 1: 125; "Papers relating to a Congress with the Chickasaw and Choctaw Indians," 47, 142, 144; Gibson, *Chickasaws*, 65–9; Usner, *Indians, Settlers, and Slaves*, 126; Osborn, "Relations with the Indians in West Florida During the Administration of Governor Peter Chester, 1770–1781," 249.

[30] Gibson, *Chickasaws*, 64–5.

[31] Williams, ed., *Adair's History of the American Indians*, vol. 1: 398; Gibson, *Chickasaws*, 65; *DAR*, vol. 2: 303; Dawson A. Phelps, "Tockshish," *Journal of Mississippi History* 13 (1951), 138–45.

[32] *DAR*, vol. 2: 304.

[33] Light Townshend Cummins, "The Governors of Spanish Colonial Louisiana and Espionage in the Southeastern Borderlands, 1766–1795," *Locus: Regional and Local History of the Americas* 6 (1993), 23–38; Gibson, *Chickasaws*, 70.

favored status in British eyes.[34] As Choctaws and Creeks tired of their war, they asked the Chickasaws to mediate a peace, but the British stepped in to prevent it and to strengthen Chickasaw allegiance to the crown in apprehension of further Anglo-Creek hostilities.[35] The Chickasaws resisted getting involved with the Shawnees in Dunmore's War, reaffirming British confidence in their loyalty.[36]

In the early phases of the Revolution, the Choctaws and Chickasaws occupied a key place in British strategy, which concentrated on the Atlantic seaboard while establishing a network of Indian allies to prevent American thrusts toward the Mississippi. John Stuart was confident that the two tribes were "absolutely at our disposal." At Detroit, Henry Hamilton planned to unite the northwestern Indians in a coalition with the Chickasaws and Cherokees to raid the American frontier, and war belts circulated between Chickasaws, Cherokees, Delawares, and Shawnees.[37]

British confidence soon appeared to be misplaced. Chickasaws seemed reluctant to become involved in the war. They were supposed to patrol the Mississippi and Tennessee rivers, but "refused to go out" late in 1776 as that was their hunting season, and allowed Spanish boats to slip by.[38] The government in London continued to believe in the reputation they had given the Chickasaws of unswerving loyalty to the king,[39] but things were more complicated in Chickasaw country. Early in 1777, John Stuart sent his Choctaw deputy Charles Stuart on a tour of the Mississippi country, inviting delegates to meet him at Mobile in the spring, where he planned to enlist their assistance. But Charles Stuart sent only bad news. Drunkenness and chaos reigned in the Choctaw towns, and the Choctaws would promise nothing until they heard what the Chickasaws intended to do. The Chickasaws, said Stuart, were "a spoiled Nation, Proud and Insolent."[40] John Stuart feared the Chickasaws had been tampered with by the rebels and looked to the Mobile conference to defeat their machinations.[41]

Some twenty-eight hundred Creek, Choctaw, and Chickasaw Indians attended Stuart's monthlong conference in May and June. The superintendent warned

---

[34] *DAR*, vol. 1: 216; vol. 2: 105; vol. 7: 257; Arrell M. Gibson, *The Kickapoos: Lords of the Middle Border* (Norman: University of Oklahoma Press, 1963), 31; Stuart to Gage, Nov. 19, 1774, and Gage to Stuart, Dec. 28, 1774, Clements Library, Gage Papers, vols. 124–5; LC, C.O. 5/76: 13–15; "Letters of Hon. James Habersham," 200.

[35] *DAR*, vol. 5: 35, 38, 224, 265; vol. 8: 35, 49, 126.

[36] *DAR*, vol. 9: 24.

[37] Clements Library, Clinton Mss., vol. 14: 28; *Collections of the Illinois Historical Society*, vol. 1: 232–3.

[38] *DAR*, vol. 12: 277.

[39] George Germain to Peter Chester, Feb. 7, 1777, Mississippi Dept. of Archives and History, RG 25: English Provincial Archives, vol. 14.

[40] James H. O'Donnell, III, *The Southern Indians in the American Revolution* (Knoxville: University of Tennessee Press, 1973), 63; *DAR*, vol. 14: 50, 69.

[41] *DAR*, vol. 13: 80, 118.

them to avoid smooth-talking enemies and listen only to the king's agents. If the Americans ever got a foothold in Chickasaw country or forced their way down the Tombigbee River, he predicted, they would cut off British trade, and the Chickasaws would be "a lost people." Only forty Chickasaws attended the conference because they had heard rumors of an impending rebel invasion down the Tennessee River and "thought it prudent to remain at home to defend their country, which they were determined to do to the last extremity." Nevertheless, they made "a spirited speech" reciting the benefits of an English alliance and declared their willingness to "venture their lives in the cause." They also reminded Stuart that adequate and well-regulated trade was a pre-requisite to their effective military assistance.[42] In June, James Colbert confirmed Chickasaw loyalty, despite the work of Spanish and American emissaries. He raised parties to patrol the Mississippi, Tennessee, and Ohio rivers, although many Chickasaws had been drunk on British rum ever since the Mobile confer-ence.[43] By August, Stuart felt the Choctaws and Chickasaws were restored to "their usual good disposition." Scouting parties headed out to the Mississippi and Tennessee that fall.[44]

Chickasaw and Choctaw parties stopped and searched passing vessels on the Mississippi that winter. Governor Bernardo de Galvez at New Orleans com-plained that they fired on Spanish boats coming down from the Illinois coun-try.[45] But the Indians grew tired of the watching, and Captain James Willing demonstrated the vulnerability of the Chickasaw rear guard when he slipped down the Mississippi in February 1778, raiding Loyalist settlements in West Florida. "Had the Chickasaws done what was required of them we might have had earlier intelligence of this invasion," Stuart complained.[46] The Chickasaws had other things on their minds – in March they held a war council with the Quapaws and agreed to fight against the powerful Osages west of the Mississippi.[47] In April, Stuart dispatched John McGillivray, "a gentleman of fortune intimately acquainted with the Choctaw and Chickasaw Indians," with 100 men and ample

---

[42] The Mobile conference, and Stuart's reports of it, are in *DAR*, vol. 14: 79–82, 112–15, 147–8; C.O. 5/78: 143, 153, 205; LC, C.O. 5/78: 197–204.

[43] C.O. 5/558: 675–8, 683–6; LC, C.O. 5/558: 517–19; *DAR*, vol. 13: 173.

[44] *DAR*, vol. 14: 167–9, 195; C.O. 5/78: 186; 79: 29.

[45] C.O. 5/79: 67; John Walton Caughey, *Bernardo de Galvez in Louisiana, 1776–1783* (Gretna, La.: Pelican, 1972), 141.

[46] *DAR*, vol. 13: 246; LC, C.O. 5/79: 170; O'Donnell, *Southern Indians*, 72–3; John W. Caughey, "Willing's Expedition Down the Mississippi, 1778," *Louisiana Historical Quarterly* 15 (1932), 5–36; J. Barton Starr, *Tories, Dons, and Rebels: The American Revolution in West Florida* (Gainesville: University Presses of Florida, 1976), ch. 3. Willing's report of his expedition is in *PCC*, reel 104, item 78, vol. 23: 491–4. On the British response, see Kathryn T. Abbey, "Peter Chester's Defense of the Mississippi after the Willing Raid," *Mississippi Valley Historical Review* 22 (1935), 17–35.

[47] Gilbert C. Din and A. P. Nasatir, *The Imperial Osages: Spanish–Indian Diplomacy in the Missis-sippi Valley* (Norman: University of Oklahoma Press, 1983) 115, citing De Villiers to Galvez, Apr. 13, 1778, AGI, PC, leg. 1.

supplies of gifts and ammunition to rally the Choctaws and Chickasaws.[48] McGillivray raised only five warriors in the Choctaws' Six Towns district, where Spanish influence was at its strongest, and the continuing disruption of rum limited his success in securing Chickasaw recruits. Charles Stuart held another round of talks with Chickasaw and Choctaw "medal and gorget chiefs" in June to try and counteract Spanish intrigues.[49]

John Stuart had to explain Chickasaw foot-dragging to the home government, which assumed the Chickasaws were ready and willing to do Britain's bidding. He pointed out to Secretary of State George Germain that their towns lay exposed to rebel incursions down the Ohio and Tennessee rivers, but he thought a more likely disincentive came from traders, who dissuaded warriors from going on campaign as it was bad for business. Paya Mataha, who had visited Stuart in Pensacola that summer, gave the superintendent a different slant on Chickasaw hesitation in this civil war:

> In the course of my conversations with the chief I found that it was with the utmost difficulty he could place in the light of enemies those men whom from his earliest infancy he had been taught to consider as his dearest friends, whom he had assisted and defended upon many occasions at the risk of his life. I had also the greatest difficulty to make him comprehend that they had forfeited their right to the protection of the Great King and the British nation by their apostasy and rebellion; and he at last observed that although these might be considerations of sufficient weight to engage us to make war upon them, yet he could not bring himself to imbrue his hands in the blood of white people without the greatest reluctance, and that he shuddered at the apprehensions of committing some fatal blunder by killing the King's friends instead of his enemies.

"These sentiments," said Stuart, "could not fail of impressing me with a very high esteem and respect for his character." The superintendent assured Paya Mataha that the Chickasaw role would be purely defensive, and the chief returned to his people reassured and "fully determined to take an active part."[50] Governor Peter Chester of West Florida remained unconvinced: in his view, one British regiment on the Mississippi would be more use than the entire Choctaw and Chickasaw nations, "were they even all firmly united in our interest."[51]

As Spanish influence continued to make headway in both Choctaw and Chickasaw towns, Stuart took countermeasures. He dispatched Farquar Bethune to the Choctaws, instructed commissary John McIntosh to do everything he could to frustrate Spanish efforts among the Chickasaws, and submitted lists of

[48] *DAR*, vol. 15: 94–7; C.O. 5/79: 81; LC, C.O. 5/79: 133, 117–19.
[49] *DAR*, vol. 15: 112–14; 152–8; C.O. 5/79: 136, 196.
[50] *DAR*, vol. 15: 183–4; C.O. 5/79: 184, 189–90; LC, C.O. 5/79: 262–3.
[51] *DAR*, vol. 15: 188; C.O. 5/594: 653.

presents, including "a considerable quantity of scarlet coats," in anticipation of another round of meetings with the chiefs. No novice in Indian diplomacy, Stuart knew the Chickasaw alliance was a reciprocal relationship that had to be cemented and sustained by gifts and trade goods.[52] American initiatives made little headway: George Rogers Clark, who regarded the Chickasaws as the "most potent nation" south of the Ohio, sent peace proposals via Kaskaskia emissaries late in 1778, but "their conversation on the subject was cool and answered no great purpose."[53]

In November, General John Campbell issued a commission appointing James Colbert "Leader and Conductor of such Volunteer Inhabitants and Chickasaw, Choctaw, Creek or other Indians as shall join you for the purpose of annoying[,] distressing[,] attacking[,] or repelling the King's Enemies."[54] Chickasaw and Choctaw scouts continued their river patrols that winter, while John Stuart went about the old task of explaining to his cost-conscious government that Indian allies were worth the expense: "We have not been able to do without them."[55] Stuart's death in March 1779 brought a reshuffling in the southern Indian Department, with Cherokee agent Alexander Cameron reluctantly re-assigned to the Chickasaws and Choctaws.[56]

Despite threatened invasions by the Americans,[57] the Chickasaws showed little fear of their various enemies. In March, Mingo Houma, Paya Mataha, and other headmen sent the Spaniards a message, telling them they had only them-selves to blame for Chickasaw hostilities that past winter, as they had been "sending bad Talks to the Chactaws endeavoring to set them against us & our friends the English." The chiefs had heard that the French and Spanish were supplying ammunition to their enemies, "therefore shou'd We lose any of our People in their hunting grounds by your red people We shall not go to them for redress as We know what quarter to take Satisfaction in, for it is no New thing to us for We always knew that the french bought our Hair till lately."[58]

In May, while their war parties brought prisoners into Mobile and set off to join Henry Hamilton at Vincennes,[59] the Chickasaws received a white belt of peace from Virginia, with a message offering them the choice between friend-ship and destruction. Mingo Houma, Paya Mataha, and his brother, Tuskau

[52] *DAR*, vol. 13: 351, 395; vol. 15: 187–8, 212; LC, C.O. 5/80: 111.
[53] James Alton James, ed., *George Rogers Clark Papers, 1781–1784* (Springfield: Illinois Historical Society, 1926), 136; Draper Mss. 47J1.
[54] *PCC*, reel 104, item 78, vol. 24: 435.
[55] *DAR*, vol. 17: 29–30.
[56] C.O. 5/80: 123; HMC, *Report on American Mss.*, vol. 2: 59; *DAR*, vol. 17: 154–5.
[57] *PCC*, reel 85, item 71, vol. 1: 251.
[58] LC, C.O. 5/80: 243–5. The Chickasaw speech, dated March 8, is enclosed in Charles Stuart's letter of May 6 to Lord Germain; a copy is also in NYPL, Rare Books and Manuscripts Division, Bancroft Collection, vol. 242: 191–6.
[59] *DAR*, vol. 17: 121–2.

Pautaupau, responded that they did not see how the Virginians could call them brothers when the northern Indians were constantly warning that the Americans intended to destroy them and take their lands. With all of 450 warriors behind them, the chiefs declared:

> We desire no other friendship of you but only desire you will inform us when you are Comeing and we will save you the trouble of Coming quite here for we will meet you half Way, for we have heard so much of it that it makes our heads Ach, Take care that we dont serve you as we have served the French before with all their Indians, send you back without your heads. We are a Nation that fears or Values no Nation as long as our Great Father King George stands by us for you may depend as long as life lasts with us we will hold him fast by the Hand.

The Chickasaws could not understand why the Americans had allied with the French, their former enemies. If the Americans truly wanted peace, they said, they should bury the hatchet they had raised against King George, and turn it against the French, "for they are a people we will never make peace with as long as Oak grows and Water runs." The chiefs ended by asking the Virginians to print their speech in the newspapers, "that all your people may see it and know who it was from, We are men & Warriors and dont want our Talks hidden."[60]

Spain declared war on Britain in June 1779, and the American Revolution in West Florida became an Anglo-Spanish war. The Spanish ambassador in London cited as a major grievance British attempts to incite the Choctaws, Chickasaws, and Cherokees to wage war on Louisiana.[61] Now Bernardo de Galvez openly courted Indian allegiance, and Spanish agents stepped up their operations in Choctaw and Chickasaw towns.[62] Although the British complained that the Choctaws would sell to the highest bidder, they retained their esteem for the Chickasaws as "a proud & politick people known to be brave & of a more free & independent spirit." According to Charles Stuart, they prided themselves on being able to support themselves by hunting rather than depending on the king's largess. Stuart stressed the need to pay attention to Paya Mataha. Mingo Houma often placed his mark first on talks sent from the Chickasaw nation, but Stuart identified the mix of sacred and political power in the position of war prophet. Paya Mataha's influence was "not only great in his own Nation but extends over the whole Choctaw Nation who look upon him as an Oracle or as they term it a Witch."[63] Paya Mataha was getting on in years, however: in

---

[60] "Chickasaw Talk to the Rebels," May 22, 1779, LC, C.O. 5/81: 139–41; also in *PCC*, reel 65, item 51, vol. 2: 41–2, and *Revolution and Confederation*, 262–3.
[61] N. M. Miller Surrey, ed., *Calendar of Manuscripts in Paris Archives and Libraries Relating to the History of the Mississippi Valley to 1803*, 2 vols. (Washington D.C.: Carnegie Institution, Department of Historical Research, 1926–8), vol. 2: 1582.
[62] LC, C.O. 5/81: 111, 295; *DAR*, vol. 16: 238.
[63] C.O. 5/81: 97–8; LC, C.O. 5/81: 78–9.

the winter of 1771–2 he had described himself as "an old warrior with Grey Hairs."[64]

While the British cultivated the Chickasaws, the Americans alienated them further. In January 1780, Thomas Jefferson advocated turning their old enemies, the Kickapoos, against them, and ordered the construction of Fort Jefferson on Chickasaw land five miles below the confluence of the Ohio and Mississippi rivers. The fort was built that spring, but the Chickasaws so harassed it that they forced the Americans to abandon it in June 1781.[65]

Reports of Spanish-American inroads and recurrent factionalism caused Britain to despair of the Choctaws as allies. Even Lord Germain, four thousand miles away, realized that they were not anxious to "involve themselves in a war for the sake of either party." The Chickasaws were now more important than ever to British plans for a multitribal coalition in the South.[66] They continued their small-scale warfare on the Mississippi, Ohio, and Tennessee rivers, and resisted Spanish and American diplomatic efforts. Spain sent them flags by the Quapaw chief Anguska, who frequently served Spain as a scout and ambassador in Indian diplomacy. But, reported James Colbert, "the majority of the Nation would not allow them to be hoisted." Paya Mataha told Alexander Cameron that they had received talks from the Spaniards – "but they was not bad Talks," apparently urging neutrality – and from the Virginians, who warned the Chickasaws that the English would get them all killed. Paya Mataha was not impressed: "Ever Since I was a young man, I was Taken Notice off [sic] in Charleston & Elsewhere, but now I am Grown Old, what Should Enduce me to Leave or forsake the Inglish[?]" He said he would never take the French or Spaniards by the hand as long as he lived, and warned the Choctaws that if they did not "return immediately to the English," he would send for the Chickamaugas and Shawnees, march into their country, "and talk to them with powder and ball." Cameron believed this "had a very good effect upon them."[67]

Choctaws rallied to the defense of Pensacola that fall, and handed over their Spanish medals, flags, and commissions to Cameron. The Indians gave effective

[64] "Papers Relating to Congress with Choctaw and Chickasaw Indians," 145.
[65] Julian P. Boyd, ed., *The Papers of Thomas Jefferson* (Princeton N.J.: Princeton University Press, 1950– ), vol. 3: 276; Kathryn M. Fraser, "Fort Jefferson: George Rogers Clark's Fort at the Mouth of the Ohio, 1780–1781," *Register of the Kentucky Historical Society* 81 (1983), 1–24; Kenneth C. Carstens, "The 1780 William Clark Map of Fort Jefferson," *Filson Club History Quarterly* 67 (1993), 23–43; James, ed., *George Rogers Clark Papers, 1771–81*, 427; Samuel Cole Williams, *Tennessee During the Revolutionary War* (Knoxville: University of Tennessee Press, 1944, reprint ed., 1974), 171; *Virginia State Papers*, vol. 3: 346. Clark had believed the fort would overawe the Chickasaws; "Letters from the Canadian Archives," *Collections of the Illinois Historical Society*, vol. 1 (1903), 453.
[66] *DAR*, vol. 18: 73, 78–9, 175; C.O. 5/81: 105; 82: 92–6; 597: 148, 248; HMC, *Report on American Mss.*, vol. 2: 159.
[67] LC, C.O. 5/81: 280–1, 293–4, 515; 82: 187; *DAR*, vol. 16: 367; 18: 121. Paya Mataha's talk to Cameron is enclosed in Cameron's July 18 letter to Germain.

service, but General John Campbell alienated them by thinking he could call them out and dismiss them at will. Cameron said that Campbell did not understand anything about Indians and thought they could "be used like slaves or a people devoid of natural sense."[68] Campbell's stringent economy compelled the Indians to disperse for hunting; only half a dozen Chickasaws remained in a force of almost eight hundred Indians at Pensacola on February 1, 1781. The Indian allies became dispirited at the lack of supplies and furious at the lack of support they received in the fighting. Pensacola fell in May and the Choctaws and Chickasaws returned home.[69]

Spanish conquest of West Florida was now complete.[70] Spain claimed the territory between the mouth of the Yazoo River and the Ohio. The Chickasaws had no intention of tamely transferring allegiance to the new masters of West Florida, but it was the beginning of a new era. Chickasaw leaders took stock of the new situation and increasingly shaped their foreign policies in response to Spanish and American, rather than British, initiatives. In the emerging struggle between Spain and the United States for control of the lower Mississippi Valley, the Chickasaws sought to take advantage of both sides, but the diplomatic shuffling aggravated and crystallized factions within the nation. The old French party, which had survived as the anti-British faction during the war, embraced the Spaniards. Piomingo and his followers remained strongly anti-Spanish and, as British allies faded from the scene, transferred their allegiance to the Americans. Paya Mataha, the old friend of Britain, looked to mend diplomatic fences and sent mixed signals to both Spaniards and Americans.[71]

In the summer of 1781, Balthazar de Villiers, commandant at Post Charles III on the Arkansas,[72] planned to send Quapaw emissaries to the Chickasaws, but Anguska demurred, saying that to go with messages of peace so often would convey the mistaken impression that the Quapaws were afraid of the Chickasaws.[73] Nevertheless, the following March, Chickasaw delegates, presumably from the anti-British faction, accompanied Shawnee, Delaware, and Cherokee emissaries carrying four large blue-and-white belts, customary symbols of peace, to Saint

[68] DAR, vol. 18: 219–22; C.O. 5/82: 111–22, 128–33; Report on American Mss., vol. 2: 159–60; O'Donnell, Southern Indians in the American Revolution, 95–7, 99–105; George C. Osborne, "Major General John Campbell in British West Florida," Florida Historical Quarterly 27 (1949), 317–39.

[69] C.O. 5/82: 120, 130–3, 143, 204, 208; DAR, vol. 20: 58–60, 149–51; LC, C.O. 5/82: 243, 369–73.

[70] On the Anglo-Spanish war and conquest of West Florida see Starr, Tories, Dons, and Rebels; and Albert W. Haarman, "The Spanish Conquest of British West Florida, 1779–1781," Florida Historical Quarterly 39 (1960), 107–34.

[71] Gibson, Chickasaws, 74–5.

[72] For an account of the small Spanish post in the Revolution, see Gilbert C. Din, "Arkansas Post in the American Revolution," Arkansas Historical Quarterly 40 (1981), 3–30.

[73] Spain in the Mississippi Valley, vol. 2, pt. 1: 430. On Anguska's role in the Revolution, see W. David Baird, The Quapaw Indians: A History of the Downstream People (Norman: University of Oklahoma Press, 1980), 43–6.

Louis, and requested peace with Spain in the name of 130 tribes.[74] Spain increased the political and economic pressure on other Chickasaw groups to come to a new understanding.

Chickasaw country remained a thorn in Spain's side, however. By 1782, according to some reports, there were almost three hundred whites and perhaps a hundred blacks living in Chickasaw country, many of them Loyalist refugees from a failed rebellion at Natchez.[75] James Colbert fashioned these men into a band of resistance fighters near Chickasaw Bluffs; they stepped up assaults on Spanish vessels on the Mississippi, exacting reprisals for what Colbert considered the unduly harsh treatment of the captured leaders of the Natchez rebellion.[76] The raids climaxed in the capture of a boat carrying Señora Nicanora Ramos, wife of Governor Cruzat of Saint Louis. The lady was well-treated and eventually released.[77]

Governor Estevan Miró of Louisiana moved to Natchez and began operations to secure peace with the Chickasaws and to separate them from Colbert's influence. He despatched Anguska and Choctaw messengers to the Chickasaw villages.[78] In fact, most Chickasaws seem to have had little to do with Colbert's band, and in the new diplomatic situation that was emerging, the chiefs apparently tried to distance themselves from the partisan leader. Spanish reports said the rebels resided five leagues from the Chickasaws, who would not have them in their villages. Colbert himself told Miró that he had urged the Chickasaws to make peace "with you & the Americans & with all the world as it is proper that no Indians ought to interfere with what Concerns None but white [people]."[79]

Nevertheless, Miró resolved to bring the Chickasaws to book because,

---

[74] Louis Houck, ed., *The Spanish Regime in Missouri*, 2 vols. (Chicago: Donnelley, 1909), vol. 1: 209–10.

[75] Wilbur H. Siebert, "The Loyalists in West Florida and the Natchez District," *Proceedings of the Mississippi Valley Historical Association* 8 (1914), 120–1; *Spain in the Mississippi Valley*, vol. 2, pt. 1: 428–30; 3, pt. 2: xi, 32–3, 60; *PCC*, reel 50, item 41, vol. 4: 196; John W. Caughey, "The Natchez Rebellion of 1781 and Its Aftermath," *Louisiana Historical Quarterly* 16 (1933), 57–83; Robert V. Haynes, *The Natchez District and the American Revolution* (Jackson: University Press of Mississippi, 1976). Villiers to Piernas, Sep. 16, 1781, AGI, PC, leg. 194, describes the Natchez rebels in Chickasaw country.

[76] D. C. Corbitt, "James Colbert and the Spanish Claims to the East Bank of the Mississippi," *Mississippi Valley Historical Review* 24 (1938), 457–72; Gilbert C. Din, "Loyalist Resistance after Pensacola: The Case of James Colbert," in William S. Coker and Robert Rea, eds., *Anglo-Spanish Confrontation on the Gulf Coast During the American Revolution* (Pensacola: Gulf Coast History and Humanities Conference, 1982), 158–76; *Spain in the Mississippi Valley*, vol. 3, pt. 2: xi; C.O. 5/82: 292, 412.

[77] *Spain in the Mississippi Valley*, vol. 3, pt. 2: 15, 21–34; Houck, ed., *Spanish Regime in Missouri*, vol. 1: 211–34; Miró to Grimarest, June 3, 1782, Miró to Cruzat, July 20, 1782, Miró to Villars, Oct. 3, 1782, AGI, PC, leg. 3A.

[78] Miró to Villars, May 22, 1782 and Miró to Cruzat, July 20, 1782, AGI, PC, leg. 3A.

[79] Din, "Loyalist Resistance after Pensacola," 162, 166–7; idem, "Arkansas Post in the Revolution,", 15–16, 20–1; *Spain in the Mississippi Valley*, vol. 3, pt. 2: 32, 50, 60. Colbert is also quoted in Caughey, *Galvez in Louisiana*, 236. Information that the Chickasaws would not allow the rebels in their villages is in Villars to Miró, July 6, 1782, AGI, PC, leg. 2359, cited in Din, "Arkansas Post," 20.

"although this nation has not taken part in the hostilities, nor has it declared itself against us, still it is evident that the deeds are done under its protection." In light of the Chickasaws' military reputation and past French experiences, Miró knew better than to try a direct attack. He estimated it would take a thousand troops, supported by militia and Indian auxiliaries, to defeat Colbert's force if the Chickasaws joined them. Instead, Miró sought a peaceful resolution by offering a general pardon to refugees from Natchez who returned home and launched a diplomatic offensive to isolate and win over the Chickasaws. While Choctaw intermediaries carried messages of peace to Tchoukafala and other towns, Governor Cruzat dispatched Captain Jacobo Dubreuil on a secret mission to induce the Kickapoos and Mascoutens to attack the Chickasaws, telling the northern tribes that the Chickasaws had captured the goods intended for them. The plan worked. As Kickapoo and Mascouten raids took their toll and curtailed Chickasaw hunting, Chickasaw chiefs hurried to Saint Louis that summer. They asked Governor Cruzat to intervene to halt hostilities and promised to deny refuge to Colbert's partisans. By October, they were reported to be preventing Colbert's men from committing further attacks on Spanish river traffic. The chiefs were caught between Spanish subterfuge and economic necessity: "The Chickasaws are poor and there are no other white people except the Spaniards who can supply their necessities."[80]

In fact, there were other options. Paya Mataha was not quite ready to take the Spaniards by the hand, and practiced some diplomatic foot-dragging. In the late summer of 1782 he welcomed a Choctaw peace emissary sent by Spain but said he could not go to Natchez yet as he had been ill. He promised to send his brother Tuskau Pautaupau with some warriors and hoped the Spaniards would give his people ammunition "in view of the fact that for some time past he has embraced friendship with the Spaniards." A second Choctaw delegation in October found Paya Mataha absent, apparently off making peace with the Cherokees and Tallapoosa Creeks. Tuskau Pautaupau promised that the Chickasaws would come to confirm peace with their Spanish father once Paya Mataha returned, but "could not say whether it would be carried out in a month or two, or in the middle of winter. Only the return of Paymataa could decide the time." Miró decided it was futile to send missions to the Chickasaws.[81]

The Chickasaws were also talking to the Americans. The Kaskaskia chief, Jean Baptiste de Coigne, who had traveled to Chickasaw country in vain for the

---

[80] *Spain in the Mississippi Valley*, vol. 3, pt. 2: xii, 20, 50–4, 57–8, 61–3; Corbitt, "James Colbert," 465–6; Houck, ed., *Spanish Regime in Missouri*, vol. 1: 214–15, 232; Miró to Villars, Oct. 18, 1782, AGI, PC, leg. 3A. The French in the 1730s had displayed similar trepidation about invading Chickasaw country without ample numbers of suitably trained troops and Indian allies; *MPA, FD*, vol. 1: 163.

[81] *Spain in the Mississippi Valley*, vol. 3, pt. 2: 57–8, 61–2; Miró to Villars, Aug. 15, 1782, AGI, PC, leg. 3A.

Americans in 1778, now led a second, successful, mission.[82] In July 1782, after sending out some tentative peace feelers via Indian intermediaries, Paya Mataha, Mingo Houma, Tuskau Pautaupau, and Piomingo sent Simon Burney, an Englishman living in Chickasaw country, and four warriors with a message to "the Commanders Of Every different Station Between This Nation and the Falls of the Ohio River." The Chickasaws offered to make peace "for the Bennifitt of our Child[ren]." What little fighting had occurred between them, they said, had resulted from the Americans building Fort Jefferson on their land. Now they wanted to sit down and smoke with the Virginians as friends and brothers. But they also wanted to keep their options open:

> Youl Observe at the Same time Our making A Peace with you doth Not Intitle Us to Fall out With Our Fathers the Inglish for we Love them as They were the First People that Ever Supported Us to Defend Our Selves Against Our former Enimys The French & Spaniards & All their Indians. & We are a People that Never Forgets Any Kindness done Us by Any Nation.[83]

George Rogers Clark took the initiative and dispatched Captain Robert George and John Donne with peace talks. He assured the Chickasaws of the Virginians' desire for peace, but denied that Fort Jefferson was the cause of the war and advised the Chickasaws to sell George all their lands in Kentucky so Virginia could build a town there as a center for Chickasaw trade. Clark then wrote to Governor Benjamin Harrison of Virginia, asking his approval, and Harrison laid it before the Virginia House of Delegates. Harrison wanted a land cession if it could be obtained.[84]

When George reached the Chickasaws in the fall, he found them so opposed to the idea of a land cession that he did not raise it in council, opting instead to express Virginia's desire for peace, promise trade and supplies, and treat the Chickasaws to a Virginian interpretation of the Revolution. A land cession was unacceptable, but, carefully mending their diplomatic fences, Paya Mataha, Mingo Houma, Piomingo, and others offered acceptable words instead, blaming Britain for past misunderstandings:

---

[82] Stanley Faye, "Illinois Indians on the Lower Mississippi, 1771–1782," *Journal of the Illinois State Historical Society* 35 (1942), 71–2; Villars to Grand Pré, July 6, 1782, AGI, PC, leg. 2359; James, ed., *George Rogers Clark Papers, 1781–84*, 73–5.

[83] The Chickasaw message is in Draper Mss. 1XX50, reprinted in James, ed., *George Rogers Clark Papers, 1781–84*, 73–5, and *Revolution and Confederation*, 270–1. See also *Clark Papers*, 99–104, 123; *Virginia State Papers*, vol. 3: 277–9, 337–8. The tentative steps toward a peace are outlined in Robert S. Cotterill, "The Virginia–Chickasaw Treaty of 1783," *Journal of Southern History* 8 (1942), 483–96.

[84] Cotterill, "Virginia–Chickasaw Treaty," 487; James, ed., *George Rogers Clark Papers, 1781–84*, 136, 166, 171; *Virginia State Papers*, vol. 3: 346; *Official Letters of the Governors of the State of Virginia* 3 (1929), 393–4, 407–8.

> The English put the Bloody Tomahawk into our hands, telling us that we
> should have no Goods if we did not Exert ourselves to the greatest point
> of Resentment against you, but now we find our mistake and Distresses.
> The English have done their utmost and left us in our adversity. We find
> them full of Deceit and Dissimulation and our women & children are
> crying out for peace.[85]

Meanwhile, Harrison appointed Joseph Martin and John Donelson to meet
with the Chickasaws, conclude a firm peace and, if it could be done without
creating undue anxiety among them, obtain a land cession.[86]

The international settlement concluded in Paris by British and American
diplomats was incomplete. It left relations between Spain and the new United
States to be worked out and, in the lower Mississippi Valley, this often meant
that the new relations had to be worked out in concert with the Indian nations
and in the context of Indian diplomacy.[87] In such a situation, individuals like
James Colbert exerted a complicating influence. Colbert continued to harass the
Spaniards, and in April 1783 he crossed the Mississippi with a hundred Loyalists and some Indians in an abortive attack on the post of Charles III, the only
battle of the Revolution in Arkansas.[88] In late July, when John Donne was in the
Chickasaw nation, Colbert gave him a letter for Governor Harrison, pointing
out that the Chickasaws had to turn somewhere for trade now that Britain had
abandoned them. Many young men in the tribe were pro-Spanish, but the
chiefs wanted to make peace with the United States. Colbert reminded Harrison
that having the Chickasaws as allies on the Mississippi would be a useful buffer
against Spain's Indian allies.[89] Donne found the Chickasaws generally in favor
of peace and said they had expelled Colbert's refugee bands "lest their residence
should give umbrage to our Chiefs." Colbert himself was anxious to establish
that he had fought as a British officer, not just a guerrilla leader, and pressed a
copy of his commission on Donne. Donne thought the United States should
encourage Colbert's newfound friendship; otherwise, he might prove "a Stum-
bling block in the way against our conciliating the affections of the Chickasaws."[90]
Colbert's influence among the Chickasaws seems to have been limited to his
relatives, however, and whatever influence he had ended abruptly when he was
killed by a fall from his horse sometime before January 1784.[91]

[85] Cotterill, "Virginia–Chickasaw Treaty," 489–90; *Virginia State Papers*, vol. 3: 356–8.
[86] Cotterill, "Virginia–Chickasaw Treaty," 487; Draper Mss, 1XX56.
[87] Arthur Preston Whitaker, *The Spanish–American Frontier, 1783–1795* (Lincoln: University of
Nebraska Press, 1969 reprint of 1927 original), ch. 1 et passim.
[88] Jack D. L. Holmes, "Spanish–American Rivalry over the Chickasaw Bluffs, 1780–1795," *East
Tennessee Historical Society Publications* 34 (1962), 30; Din, "Loyalist Resistance after Pensacola,"
168–9; idem, "Arkansas Post in the Revolution," 23–30. A lengthy account of the attack by the
post commander, Jacobo Dubreuil, is in Dubreuil to Miró, May 5, 1783, AGI, PC, leg. 107.
[89] *Virginia State Papers*, vol. 3: 513–14.
[90] PCC, reel 104, item 78, vol. 24: 439–43.
[91] Din, "Loyalist Resistance after Pensacola," 172; John Walton Caughey, *McGillivray of the Creeks*
(Norman: University of Oklahoma Press, 1938), 68.

Three days after Colbert wrote his letter to Harrison, Mingo Houma, Paya Mataha, Piomingo, and other headmen met in council and sent a message to Congress, alluding to their difficulty of making peace with the United States. The king of England had advised them to take the Americans by the hand and, said the chiefs, "our hearts were always inclined to do so & *as far as our circumstances permitted us*, we evinced our good intentions" [emphasis added]. But, it was now almost a year since their initial overtures and, with so many pressures and offers, they were confused and uncertain.

> The Spaniards are sending talks amongst us, and inviting our young Men to trade with them. We also receive talks from Georgia to the same effect – We have had speeches from the Illinois inviting us to a Trade and Intercourse with them – Our Brothers, the Virginians Call upon us to a Treaty, and want part of our land, and we expect our Neighbors who live on Cumberland River, will in a Little time Demand, if not forcibly take part of it from us, also we are informed they have been marking Lines through our hunting grounds: we are daily receiving Talks from one Place or other, and from People we Know nothing about. We know not who to mind or who to neglect.

If Congress was head of the thirteen states, why had the Chickasaws not heard from that body? They hoped Congress would stop encroachments on their lands and supply them with the trade they desperately needed: "We can supply ourselves from the Spaniards but we are averse to hold any intercourse with them, as our hearts are always with our Brothers the Americans."[92]

Economic realities dictated political and diplomatic choices. The cutoff of British trade had to be made up somewhere, especially as the Chickasaws became embroiled again in hostilities with the Kickapoos.[93] More than three hundred Chickasaws set out for Saint Augustine in the spring of 1783 in search for presents; their arrival with as many Choctaws in the summer took the British by surprise as they struggled to cope with the influx of refugees from Savannah and Charleston, and though they welcomed and provisioned the visitors, they were eager to have them leave as soon as possible.[94] The Chickasaws would have to look elsewhere.

Different groups had different opinions about where to turn, and the result was a series of conflicting commitments to Spain and the United States that pulled Chickasaw diplomacy in different directions. The surface appearance of a unified and somewhat duplicitous Chickasaw foreign policy obscures more complex realities of division and disunity that both limited and expanded diplomatic choices. As British, American, and Spanish officials tried to cut through

---

[92] *Virginia State Papers*, vol. 3: 515–17; also in *PCC*, reel 104, item 78, vol. 24: 445–9, and *Revolution and Confederation*, 370–1.
[93] *PCC*, reel 69, item 56: 113; *Spain in the Mississippi Valley*, 3, pt. 2: 133–5.
[94] *Spain in the Mississippi Valley*, 3, pt. 2: 72; Carleton Papers, PRO 30/55/60: 6782.

multiple and shifting Chickasaw foreign policies, they saw only the tips of intratribal politics as one party or another extended feelers and solicited their trade. The Americans represented one source of trade and protection, but only one, and the advantages offered by American allegiance were always tempered by American land hunger.[95]

After a series of delays, Virginia and a number of Chickasaw chiefs held a treaty at French Lick near Nashville in November 1783. Martin and Donelson demanded that the Chickasaws return their prisoners and expel Delaware Indians and hostile whites who had taken up residence in their country. After discussion, the Chickasaws agreed to remove the Delawares. Mingo Houma and Tuskau Pautaupau (called the Red King in the treaty[96]) in turn demanded a halt to white intrusions on to their land, described their boundaries, and made it clear they had no intention of ceding territory. The "king of the Chickasaws" said he had "no power vested in himself from his nation to sell Lands," only to make peace. Martin and Donelson did not push it. Piomingo, who was emerging as head of the American faction, concluded, "Peace is Now Settled, I was the first that proposed it, . . . & Am in hope No more Blood [may be] Shed by Either party."[97]

Although Piomingo and the Colberts leaned to the Americans, a growing majority led by the flamboyant second war chief Wolf's Friend or Ugulayacabe looked to Spain.[98] Chickasaw and Spanish Indian policies intersected in their goal of checking American expansion. Spain stepped up its efforts to include the Chickasaws in a multitribal alliance and moved toward an "uneasy modus vivendi" with the British merchants Panton, Leslie, Mather, and Strother as the key to keeping the tribes out of the American economic orbit.[99]

Spanish and American parties in the Chickasaw nation negotiated with Spain and the United States for favorable trade rates, while Spain and the United States competed for Chickasaw allegiance and the right to establish a post at

[95] *PCC*, reel 62, item 48: 277; *Spain in the Mississippi Valley*, vol. 3, pt. 2: xvii.
[96] For the identification of the Red King as Tuskau Pautaupau, see *Spain in the Mississippi Valley*, vol. 3, pt. 2: 62.
[97] Cotterill, "Virginia–Chickasaw Treaty," 495; Draper Mss. 1XX 55, 65; *Virginia State Papers*, vol. 3: 548, 581; *Revolution and Confederation*, 374–6.
[98] At the Nashville conference in 1792, Wolf's Friend's name was also given as Mooleshawskek. He impressed the American commissioners on that occasion as "a great man; in council ranks among the first of his nation; has a considerable property, is a large man, of dignified appearance." He appeared at the council wearing a coat of scarlet and lace and in the heat of the day had "a large crimson silk umbrella over him." *ASPIA*, vol. 1: 284–5.
[99] Miró to Grimarest, Dec. 23 and Jan. 20, 1783, AGI, PC, leg. 3A; Roper, "The Revolutionary War on the Fourth Chickasaw Bluff," 8; *Spain in the Mississippi Valley*, vol. 3, pt. 2: xv; Thomas D. Watson, "The Troubled Advance of Panton, Leslie and Company into Spanish West Florida," in Samuel Proctor, ed., *Eighteenth-Century Florida and the Revolutionary South* (Gainesville: University Presses of Florida, 1978), 68–86; D. C. Corbitt and Roberta Corbitt, eds., "Papers from the Spanish Archives Relating to Tennessee and the Old Southwest, 1783–1800," *East Tennessee Historical Society Publications* 9 (1937), 113.

Chickasaw Bluffs.[100] In the fall of 1783, the aging Paya Mataha earnestly requested a Spanish trader. The following spring, he traveled to Chickasaw Bluffs, where he fell mortally ill with fever. As he lay dying he told the Spaniards he had advised his young men to live in friendship with Spain. He said he was dying a Spaniard and asked that on his death his body be draped in a Spanish flag and cremated, which was done.[101] In June 1784, delegates from six Chickasaw villages, together with Choctaws and Upper Creeks, attended a conference with Spain at Mobile, secured assurances of continued trade, and negotiated new trade tariffs. Although Tchoukafala was the headquarters of Piomingo's pro-American party, the town sent enough delegates to the conference to consume almost a thousand pounds of bread and meat, and fifteen hundred pounds of rice.[102] When Mingo Houma died in 1784, his nephew and successor Taski Etoka (Hare Lip King), and Ugulayacabe, continued the Spanish alliance.[103] The Chickasaws resolved to expel refugee "vagabonds" who gave Spain cause for concern, declaring that they did not want their nation "to become a nest of thieves."[104]

Meanwhile, the pro-American chiefs sent black beads signifying Mingo Houma's death to the governor of North Carolina and assured him that Mingo Houma's passing changed nothing: they would still refuse to listen to Spain and would live in peace with the Americans.[105] At the Treaty of Hopewell in January 1786, the pro-American party granted the United States the same trade monopoly that the pro-Spanish party had granted Spain at Mobile.[106] Piomingo also made a bold announcement for the benefit of his American hosts:

[100] William S. Coker and Thomas D. Watson, *Indian Traders of the Southeastern Spanish Border-lands: Panton, Leslie & Company and John Forbes & Company, 1783–1847* (Pensacola: University of West Florida Press, 1986), 99–102, ch. 8; Jack D. L. Holmes traces this history in "Spanish–American Rivalry over the Chickasaw Bluffs, 1780–1795," *East Tennessee Historical Society Publications* 34 (1962), 26–57.

[101] *Spain in the Mississippi Valley*, vol. 3, pt. 2: 89–91; Din, "Loyalist Resistance after Pensacola," 171; Dubreuil to Miró, Aug. 26, 1783 and Apr. 20, 1784, AGI, PC, leg. 107.

[102] O'Neill to Galvez, Sept. 4, 1785, AGI, PC, leg. 37–36; Jack D. L. Holmes, "Spanish Treaties with West Florida Indians, 1784–1802," *Florida Historical Quarterly* 48 (1969), 143–4; Coker and Watson, *Indian Traders*, 59; *Spain in the Mississippi Valley*, vol. 3, pt. 2: 102. The Spanish text of the Mobile treaty is in Manuel Serrano y Sanz, *España y los Indios Cherokis y Chactas en la segunda mitad del Siglio XVIII* (Seville: Tip. de la Guía Oficial, 1916), 82–5. The new tariff, in the Panton, Leslie Papers, is cited in Usner, *Indians, Settlers, and Slaves*, 273–4.

[103] Champagne, *Social Order and Political Change*, 79. Taski Etoka, also called the Chickasaw King, also appears as Mingotuska, Tascaotuca, and other variations; Cotterill, *Southern Indians*, 69; *Spain in the Mississippi Valley*, 4, pt. 3: xv, 76, 80; Caughey, *McGillivray of the Creeks*, 351; Serraño y Sanz, *España y los Indios Cherokis y Chactas*, 49–57, passim.

[104] *Spain in the Mississippi Valley*, vol. 3, pt. 2: 137, 144, 146–7, 158. Spain was not alone in its concern about the vagrants in Chickasaw country: Alexander McGillivray blamed them for getting the chiefs to talk with the Americans and consider granting permission for a settlement on the Tombigbee. McGillivray to Fabrot, Nov. 7, 1785, AGI, PC, leg. 198 (North Carolina State Archives, box 26).

[105] *North Carolina State Records*, vol. 17: 85–6.

[106] Draper Mss. 14U103–6; *Revolution and Confederation*, 418–25; *North Carolina State Records*, vol. 18: 493–5.

> You see this now (pointing to the medal) it was worn by our great Man, he
> is dead and his daughter sent it for you to see it. I take place as head
> leading Warrior to treat with all Nations.[107]

Nevertheless, Piomingo and his followers worried about American encroachments on their lands. Piomingo demanded that the entire treaty be read aloud and asked for assurances that the American request for a trading-post site near Muscle Shoals required a tract of land only five miles in diameter. Only then did he agree, and personally marked the area on a map provided him.[108] Later that spring, however, the "great chief of the Chickasaws" (presumably Taski Etoka) visited Mobile in an effort to secure Spanish trade goods at a cheaper rate by pointing out that Americans offered them all they wanted if they would sell land.[109]

Piomingo enjoyed especially close relations with General James Robertson at Nashville, and pro-American Chickasaws provided Robertson with warnings of Creek hostile intentions.[110] But, in binding himself to the Americans, Piomingo was alienating himself from the pan-Indian alliance with Spain that Creek chief Alexander McGillivray was building, and that many Chickasaws supported. Tchoukafala was in a dangerous position.[111] McGillivray denounced Piomingo as "one or two Chiefs of the Chickesaw Nation" whom the Americans had deluded into granting land at Muscle Shoals. The Creeks claimed this land and promptly drove off the American settlers. "Such Conduct of the Chickasaw Chiefs has enraged Most of the rest of the Confederate Nations to attack & chastize that people," McGillivray told Governor O'Neill.[112]

Piomingo's faction sent messages to Congress, professing friendship, requesting trade, and agreeing to the construction of a post at Chickasaw Bluffs. Congress responded by sending medals for the chiefs and flags for their towns.[113] Piomingo told the Americans that he suspected they intended only to "jockey"

---

[107] Draper Mss. 14U100; *Revolution and Confederation*, 420.

[108] *Spain in the Mississippi Valley*, vol. 3, pt. 2: 151, 158; Corbitt and Corbitt, eds., "Papers from the Spanish Archives," *East Tennessee Historical Society Publications* 9 (1937), 139; Holmes, "Spanish–American Rivalry," 32; *ASPIA* vol. 1: 49–52; *Revolution and Confederation*, 420.

[109] *Spain in the Mississippi Valley*, vol. 3, pt. 2: 173; Corbitt and Corbitt, eds., "Papers from the Spanish Archives," *East Tennessee Historical Society Publications* 10 (1938), 141.

[110] James Robertson to John Sevier, Aug. 1, 1787, Nashville: Tennessee State Library and Archives, V-K-1, Box 1; *ASPIA*, vol. 1: 466.

[111] Caughey, *McGillivray of the Creeks*, 90–3; *Spain in the Mississippi Valley*, vol. 3, pt. 2: 170; Arthur Preston Whitaker, trans. and ed., *Documents Relating to the Commercial Policy of Spain in the Floridas* (Deland: Florida State Historical Society, 1931), 63; David H. White, "The Indian Policy of Juan Vicente Folch, Governor of Spanish Mobile, 1787–1792," *Alabama Review* 28 (1975), 260–75.

[112] Corbitt and Corbitt, eds., "Papers from the Spanish Archives," *East Tennessee Historical Society Publications* 10 (1938), 135, 137–9.

[113] Caughey, ed., *McGillivray of the Creeks*, 238–40; "A Message from the Secretary of War of the United States to Chamby, one of the principal Chiefs of the Chickasaws in answer to his Message to Congress, . . . June 27, 1787," Clements Library, Harmar Papers, vol. 6.

the Chickasaws out of their land.[114] Nevertheless, he cultivated notorious land grabbers John Sevier and the breakaway "state" of Franklin in search of the trade neither Spain nor the United States seemed capable of supplying. The United States was willing to send him munitions to help fight the Creeks.[115]

Piomingo's party may have numbered no more than a hundred, but McGillivray feared that any American foothold in Chickasaw country threatened Creek security. In the spring of 1787, McGillivray despatched a party of Creeks who, after a sharp skirmish, drove off the Americans and took possession of the fort they were building: "A few Chickesaws and Chactas Stood by Spectators of the engagement & upon the defeat went of with their friends," McGillivray reported to his Spanish backers. Chickasaws again took no action when a Creek war party carrying a Spanish flag returned from attacking American settlements at Cumberland. The Spaniards believed their policy of soliciting Chickasaw friendship was paying off.[116] Tensions between McGillivray's Creeks and Piomingo's Chickasaws escalated into open conflict in the summer of 1789 when a Creek war party killed Piomingo's brother and nephew as they returned home from a mission to the United States capital.[117]

A Chickasaw messenger presented himself to Carlos De Grand-Pré at Fort Panmure in Natchez in the spring of 1787, announcing that he had great news. He spread out a bundle of cloth on the ground and took out a wampum belt, three parts of which were made of white beads, the rest mixed white and black. He said he had been sent with "this collar which never lies" to warn the Spaniards that Americans were active in the Chickasaw villages: "Half the Chickasaws accepted them and received their medals and red knives; but the other half refused them, saying they did not have or want to have any other fathers than the Spaniards, and that if the Americans did not retire immediately, they would kill them." Indeed, said the messenger, the Shawnees, Cherokees, Creeks, and their allies, as well as the rest of the Chickasaws, to whom he had already carried the wampum belt, were even now ready to descend on Chickasaw Bluffs and destroy the Americans' post, and with it their Chickasaw allies. The envoy contradicted himself so often in answering questions that Grand-Pré did not know what to make of it all and discounted the whole report.[118]

---

[114] Samuel Cole Williams, *History of the Lost State of Franklin* (New York: Press of the Pioneers, 1933), 142.

[115] Coker and Watson, *Indian Traders*, 78, citing Corbitt and Corbitt, eds., "Papers from the Spanish Archives," vol. 10: 335–7; Roper, "Revolutionary War on the Fourth Chickasaw Bluff," 8. Sevier was eager to persuade the Chickasaws "to rent some of your vacant land." *North Carolina State Records*, vol. 22: 704–8, 719–21.

[116] McGillivray to Miró, July 25, 1787, AGI, PC, leg. 200–9; O'Neill to His Excellency, Aug. 3, 1787, and Miró to O'Neill, Oct. 6, 1787, AGI, PC 37–30; Miró to O'Neill, Aug. 12, 1787, AGI, PC, leg. 4–4 (all in North Carolina State Archives, box 26).

[117] Caughey, *McGillivray of the Creeks*, 238–40, 245–9; Coker and Watson, *Indian Traders*, 177–8; Gibson, *Chickasaws*, 84.

[118] *Spain in the Mississippi Valley*, vol. 3, pt. 2: 210–12.

The Chickasaws were also at this time at odds with the Kickapoos, Piankeshaws, Miamis, Illinois, and Abenakis or other eastern Indians,[119] many of whom had relocated to the Arkansas country. Emissaries from the eastern tribes attempted to mediate a peace, "for they had enough to do with the whites without shedding blood among themselves," but the Chickasaws paid little attention.[120] Chickasaws had a long-standing practice of hunting on the west bank of the Mississippi and they encroached increasingly on the Ozark hunting territory of the Osages.[121]

William Panton met Piomingo during a trip through Choctaw and Chickasaw country in 1790 and reported that though the Mountain Leader had agreed to the American request to build a post at the fork of the Tennessee River, "he had not the voice of the Nation on his side." Piomingo impressed him as "a sensible talkative little Indian," but Panton felt his influence did not extend beyond Tchoukafala, which contained about 150 warriors. Taski Etoka and the rest of the nation were ready to accept Spanish protection and obtain their trade from Mobile.[122] Piomingo was absent when James Wilkinson passed through Tchoukafala about the same time; the chief apparently was away raising arms for use against the Creeks. "Cannot you acquaint McGillivray of the circumstance & have this troublesome fellow cut off?" Wilkinson asked Miró.[123]

The Chickasaw nation remained in considerable turmoil in the early 1790s.[124] Agents, spies, and messengers passed in and out of their towns. "As to the Chickasaws," sighed McGillivray, "I do not well know what to think of them."[125] Even though Governor Manuel Gayoso invited him to Natchez, provided hospitality in his own home, and talked persuasively of supplying the Chickasaws with trade goods,[126] Piomingo remained solidly pro-American and opposed the pan-Indian alliance envisaged by McGillivray and Spain. Ugulayacabe's spies kept McGillivray informed of Piomingo's actions, and McGillivray's agents worked to undermine Piomingo, but Creek harassment and Spanish pressure only pushed Piomingo closer to the United States. He and his warriors even served

---

[119] The "Abenakis" identified in this area may have been Delawares or some other eastern group. The term Waupunaukie, very close to Waubanaki, was used to refer to the Delawares; e.g.: *PCC*, reel 65, item 51: 41.

[120] *Spain in the Mississippi Valley*, vol. 3, pt. 2: xxx, 292–3, 314, 316, 332, 364–5, 384, 408.

[121] Willard H. Rollings, *The Osage: An Ethnohistorical Study of Hegemony on the Prairie-Plains* (Columbia: University of Missouri Press, 1992), 181, 187–9.

[122] D. C. Corbitt, ed., "Some Papers Relating to Bourbon County, Georgia," *Georgia Historical Quarterly* 19 (1935), 261.

[123] Corbitt and Corbitt, eds., "Papers from the Spanish Archives" *East Tennessee Historical Society Publications* 22 (1950), 137; see also Draper Mss. 15U26.

[124] Secretary of War Henry Knox estimated the population at thirteen hundred at this time. American commissioners reported eight hundred warriors; others said twelve hundred. Massachusetts Historical Society, Timothy Pickering Papers, reel 59: 7; *ASPIA*, vol. 1: 49.

[125] Caughey, *McGillivray of the Creeks*, 336, 338, 345, 351–2.

[126] Jack D. L. Holmes, *Gayoso: The Life of A Spanish Governor in the Mississippi Valley, 1789–1799* (Baton Rouge: Louisiana State University Press, 1965), 148.

with American troops in campaigns against the northwestern Indian confederacy, and the United States presented him with a silver peace medal in recognition of his services.[127] Piomingo built up a substantial arsenal at Tchoukafala which, according to McGillivray, allowed him "rule the roost" among all but three of the Chickasaw villages. He also had support in some of the Choctaw villages.[128] In 1792, Dragging Canoe persuaded Taski Etoka to join the Indian alliance against the United States, but the next year Piomingo convinced the Chickasaw national council to reject confederation and make war on the Creeks.[129]

Ugulayacabe was increasingly receptive to Spanish courting. In 1790, shortly after visiting the Spanish governor in New Orleans, he received an American invitation to visit Cumberland. By his own account, he replied "that the Spaniards were his Whites," and he wanted no others, but he finally agreed to go to see if it was true that Piomingo had ceded lands to the Americans. William Blount, governor of the territory south of the Ohio, and superintendent of Indian affairs for the region, "carressed [sic] him much" and told him not to accept goods from the Spaniards or consider taking any action against the United States. Ugulayacabe refused Blount's proposal to establish a trading post on Chickasaw land, saying Spain furnished all the goods they needed, at which Blount "looked at him with evil eyes." Ugulayacabe said that if there was war between Spain and the United States he would "stand back and let them fight one another," but he would never allow the Americans to advance further into Chickasaw territory. On his return, Ugulayacabe boasted that if his Spanish father wished, "I will Send him Piomingo, who has Never given his Hand to the Spaniards, that I have only to Open my Mouth, and he will Obey, because he Is one of my Warriors."[130] On the urging of Governor Gayoso, Baron de Carondelet provided Ugulayacabe with a pension of $500 in recognition of his services.[131] Taski Etoka rejected Piomingo's American alliance but did not embrace the Spanish connection with the enthusiasm of Ugulayacabe.

Carondelet regarded winning over both Piomingo and Ugulayacabe as a vital step to thwarting the American threat. In May 1792, with Gayoso presiding, he convened a conference of southern tribes at Nogales to build a four-tribe confederation under Spanish protection.[132] In August, Piomingo, Ugulayacabe,

[127] Gibson, *Chickasaws*, 84–7; Caughey, *McGillivray of the Creeks*, 344–6; Wiley Sword, *President Washington's Indian War: The Struggle for the Old Northwest, 1790–1795* (Norman: University of Oklahoma Press, 1985), 166, 168, 269, 271, 273; *ASPIA*, vol. 1: 247, 249. On the peace medal, dated 1793, and uncovered by road construction, presumably at the site of Tchoukafala, see Atkinson, "The Ackia and Ogoula Tchetoka Chickasaw Village Locations," 54.
[128] Caughey, *McGillivray of the Creeks*, 348–9.
[129] Champagne, *Social Order and Political Change*, 79.
[130] Corbitt and Corbitt, eds., "Papers from the Spanish Archives," *East Tennessee Historical Society Publications* 22 (1950): 146–7. Ugulayacabe's account of his visit to Cumberland is in *American State Papers, Foreign Relations*, 6 vols. (Washington, D.C.: Gales Seaton, 1832–59), vol. 1: 281.
[131] Holmes, "Anglo-Spanish Rivalry," 53.
[132] Serraño y Sanz, *España y los Indios Cherokis y Chactas*, 48–62, 90.

and others attended a conference called by William Blount at Nashville to discuss boundaries. Ever vigilant where Chickasaw lands were concerned, Piomingo reiterated the territorial boundaries and requested a new map of the country as made at the Treaty of Hopewell. "I am the man who laid of the boundary of that map," he said, "and to save my own land, I made it plain: I knew the fondness of the Cherokees to sell land." Ugulayacabe took a prominent role at the council, warning his people that the Americans "had hard shoes" and would tread on Chickasaw toes if they were ever allowed to establish a post in their country. Ugulayacabe again described Piomingo as "a great warrior under me," but also said "he is my father." At the end of the conference, as the Indians came forward to receive their presents, "the inhabitants of Long Town [Tchoukafala] first marched up, with Piomingo at their head"; the other towns and their chiefs followed "according to their order."[133] Meanwhile, Taski Etoka spent his summer arranging peace talks with the Creeks and set up a meeting between Piomingo and McGillivray. The meeting never happened, as McGillivray died in February 1793.[134] Tchoukafala in particular, and the Chickasaws in general, were in a precarious position. "The Chickasaws will never act against the Americans, and if they offer to join them They will be cut to pieces in one month," William Panton advised Carondelet in January 1793.[135] In June 1793, Choctaw intermediaries carried Creek peace belts to Tchoukafala. Piomingo accepted the peace talks but insisted that the Creeks were "thieves and Murderers." Sporadic hostilities continued for years.[136]

In October 1793, Ugulayacabe led a Chickasaw delegation to another conference with the Spaniards at Nogales. Piomingo was conspicuously absent.[137] McGillivray's death and the outbreak of war between Spain and France that same year did nothing to weaken Piomingo's position. Taski Etoka died in 1794. He was succeeded in traditional matrilineal fashion by his nephew Chinibee, who adhered to Ugulayacabe's Spanish alliance.[138] Chickasaw–Creek tension continued. In 1795 Tchoukafala, with its formidable supply of arms, repulsed a Creek war party that descended on Piomingo's headquarters.[139]

---

[133]  The proceedings of the Nashville conference, between William Blount, Andrew Pickens, and delegates from the Chickasaws and Choctaws, are in *ASPIA*, vol. 1: 284–8.

[134]  Coker and Watson, *Indian Traders*, 170–1; *Spain in the Mississippi Valley*, vol. 4, pt. 3: xxvii–xxviii, 76, 79–80, 82–3.

[135]  Corbitt, ed., "Papers Relating to the Georgia–Florida Frontier," *Georgia Historical Quarterly* 23 (1939), 201.

[136]  "Indian Speeches made at Long Town," *Spain in the Mississippi Valley*, vol. 4, pt. 3: 164–7.

[137]  *Spain in the Mississippi Valley*, vol. 4, pt. 3: 104; Coker and Watson, *Indian Traders*, 173, 180; Caughey, *McGillivray of the Creeks*, 343. The Treaty of Nogales, with the names of the chiefs who attended, is in *Spain in the Mississippi Valley*, vol. 4, pt. 3: 223–7. The Spanish text is in Serraño y Sanz, *España y los Indios Cherokis y Chactas*, 91–2.

[138]  Champagne, *Social Order and Political Change*, 79. At the Nashville conference in 1792, Chinabee was already described as "King of the Chickasaws." *ASPIA*, vol. 1: 284. According to Nutt, Chinibee was "an old weak well meaning man"; Jennings, ed., "Nutt's Trip," 47.

[139]  Gibson, *Chickasaws*, 89.

The intensified political conflict between 1777 and 1795 did not produce disintegration of the Chickasaw polity. The divisions the Revolution generated evidently were little more than continuations of the cleavages that had developed during an earlier period of Anglo-French rivalry, and that the traditional kinship–political structure was capable of accommodating.[140] Moreover, it seems likely that Piomingo and Ugulayacabe were closer in their objectives than their American and Spanish backers and suitors believed. As Ugulayacabe said at Nashville, "Piamingo and myself are one." Both sought to keep their people well supplied and independent. Ugulayacabe opposed American requests for land, "saying that if he gives them an inch they will take four."[141] But he reacted in surprise to Spanish requests that he send warriors to assist them against the Americans, asking why "I have Received two talks from you Where you Mention of Lifting the Sharp Wapons, Which Seems for me to propose as a Contradiction to our first Established Maxim of pease."[142] Piomingo sold the Americans land at Muscle Shoals,[143] but he wanted to keep "the white people . . . at some Distance from us facing of [f] Each other."[144]

The Chickasaw diplomatic landscape took another change, however, in 1795. At the Treaty of San Lorenzo – Pinckney's Treaty – Spain gave up the Yazoo strip, opened the Mississippi to free American navigation, and agreed to withdraw all garrisons from territory north of the thirty-first parallel. As Spain began to retreat from the Mississippi Valley, the Chickasaws were no longer caught in a tug-of-war. Nor were they able to operate the old system of playing rival powers against each other.[145] The influence of the American party rose considerably, and the Spanish party had to reconcile themselves to a future dominated by the Americans. Exasperated, Ugulayacabe demanded to know why the Spaniards intended to leave them at such a critical time and abandon them to the Americans "like the smaller animals to the jaws of the Tiger and the bear." He added, "We perceive in them the cunning of the Rattle snake who caresses the Squirrel he intends to devour."[146] His apprehensions were well founded.

For generations, the Chickasaws had survived in a world they shared with competing European powers that recognized their power and courted their allegiance. Tchoukafala stood at the diplomatic hub of this world. They had steered their course through turbulent waters, always managing to maintain

---

[140] Champagne, *Social Order and Political Change*, 50, 79.
[141] *ASPIA*, vol. 1: 287; Corbitt and Corbitt, eds., "Papers from the Spanish Archives," *East Tennessee Historical Society Publications* 22 (1950), 146.
[142] Corbitt and Corbitt, eds., "Papers from the Spanish Archives," *East Tennessee Historical Society Publications* 40 (1968), 101.
[143] Houck, ed., *Spanish Regime in Missouri*, vol. 2: 112.
[144] Corbitt and Corbitt, eds., "Papers from the Spanish Archives," *East Tennessee Historical Society Publications* 38 (1966), 81.
[145] Gibson, *Chickasaws*, 90–5.
[146] Talk of the Chickasaw Chiefs at Silver Bluffs, represented by Wolf's Friend . . . [1797], Clements Library, McHenry Papers.

their independence. They emerged from the Revolution with their independence intact, and survived a dozen years more by cultivating relations with both Americans and Spaniards. Now they confronted shrinking foreign-policy options as the United States emerged as their only "available" foreign power. Piomingo's opposition to the Spanish–Indian alliance promoted by McGillivray had helped to ensure American victory in the lower Mississippi Valley. The final triumph of the United States ushered in a new world.

Without international rivals in the area, the United States was free to replace gift giving – for generations the lubricant of Chickasaw diplomacy – with hard trade. The Chickasaws were encouraged to run up debts at government trading posts because "whenever in that situation," said Thomas Jefferson, "they will always cede lands to rid themselves of debts." The plan worked. In July 1805, the Chickasaws ceded all claim to lands north of the Tennessee River in exchange for $20,000 "for the use of the nation at large, and for the payment of the debts due to their merchants and traders." Without Britain or Spain as actual or potential allies, the Chickasaws also resorted to land cessions as a means of diverting American expansion and keeping American settlers temporarily at arm's length. The United States proceeded to strip the Chickasaws of their ancient domain. Many Chickasaws began to turn from the deerskin trade to participation in the expanding cotton economy.[147]

Moreover, Americans no longer saw a place for the Chickasaws as a people, let alone as a power in the Mississippi Valley. They proceeded to implement a social revolution that aimed to destroy Chickasaw cultural independence. As mixed-bloods exerted increasing influence in tribal affairs, Chickasaw people came under pressure to adopt new ways in the new American nation. Presbyterian missionary Rev. Joseph Bullen lived at Big Town at the turn of the century and found a society in crisis: "Deaths are frequent among children in this place, and the voice of mourning all around us," he wrote. Ugulayacabe, formerly anti-American in all things, now gave his two youngest sons to live with Bullen's family "and learn good things."[148] Dr. Rush Nutt, who visited Tchoukafala five years later, found the district situated in a prairie about fifteen miles long, with 166 men, 197 women, and 108 children. Government agents had urged them to move out of their towns and settle in different parts of the country, where they built cabins, ran fences around their fields, and turned their attention to farming, manufacturing, and stock raising. "The men have laid down their gun and tomahawk & taken up the implements of husbandry," Nutt wrote. "The women have exchanged their little hoes and skin aprons, for spining wheels, & home manufactured cloth."[149]

[147] Gibson, *Chickasaws*, 103–5; Daniel H. Usner, Jr., "American Indians on the Cotton Frontier: Changing Economic Relations with Citizens and Slaves in the Mississippi Territory," *Journal of American History* 72 (1985), 297–317, esp. 299–301.
[148] Phelps, "Excerpts from the Journal of the Reverend Joseph Bullen," 273, 276.
[149] Jennings, "Nutt's Trip," 42–3, 49.

However, after a century of war to preserve their identity and independence, the Chickasaws were not finished. They were, said Bullen, still very much "their own men," conscious of their reputation and the figure they cut:

> The Chickasaw men are very effeminate and dressy – the head is, in a hot summer day, bound with a handkerchief, over it a thick binding of fulled cloth, covered with broaches; to the nose hang six bobs, one in each ear, the outer curl of which is slit, and enraped [sic] in silver. One bunch of hair is tied on top of the head, to which is fastened, in seven locks, enclosed in silver and beads, the hair of a deer's tail coloured red: this hangs over the face and eyes: the face is painted with streaks and spots of red and black; the beard is pulled out; the neck adorned with a dozen strings of beads of different sorts, besides a silk handkerchief, the arms and wrists adorned with silver bands; the body and arms covered with a calico shirt: the dress of the lower limbs is various. The women have no covering or ornament on the head but that of nature, unless a little paint, and the hair clubbed behind with binding. The men have a bunch of white feathers fastened to the back part of the neck, and if a person of note, a black feather; and lest the dress or colouring should be discomposed, carries his glass in his pocket, or hanging to his side.[150]

Fortescue Cuming noted similar traits among the Chickasaw warriors he saw several years later, "drest each according to his notion of finery, and most of them painted in a grotesque but not a terrifick manner. Many of them had long feathers in the back part of their hair, and several wore breast plates formed of tin in the shape of a crescent, and had large tin rings in their ears."[151] Missionaries and government agents were at work, mixed-bloods influenced the direction Chickasaw society would go in the new nation, and their world was changing before their eyes. But, among the people who had held off the French, British, Spanish, and American empires, there were some who remained defiant. They remained "a people to our Selves."

[150] Phelps, ed., "Journal of the Reverend Joseph Bullen," 273–4.
[151] Fortescue Cuming, "Sketches of a Tour to the Western Country (1807–1809)," in Reuben G. Thwaites, ed., *Early Western Travels, 1784–1846* (Cleveland: Clark, 1904), vol. 4: 294.

# 9

## *Cuscowilla: Seminole loyalism and Seminole genesis*

By the end of the American Revolution many Indian villages – in Iroquoia, the Ohio Valley, the Smoky Mountains, and elsewhere – lay in ruins. Their inhabitants were dead, huddled in refugee camps, or had fled to new homes beyond the reach of American expeditions. Survivors faced a harrowing future in the new nation. The winning of American independence meant destruction and dependence for many Indian people. But the revolutionary era witnessed community creation as well as community destruction. Refugees rebuilt war-torn lives and constructed new towns, often amalgamating in one community the dispersed survivors of several villages. Warriors from different tribes joined forces in towns that the Americans described as "renegade strongholds." And some Native American communities were developing their own independence and asserting a separate identity.

The Seminole Indians did not figure prominently in the Revolutionary War; indeed the standard book on southern Indians in the Revolution barely mentions them.[1] Nevertheless, Seminoles did play a role in the war, and the Revolution did have an impact in Seminole country. Florida was one of the British provinces that did not seek independence from George III during the Revolution.[2] Its fate at the war's end was not independence but continuing colonial status with a return to Spanish dominion. However, the changing colors on the political map of East Florida as one European monarch handed the province to another did not reflect the continuing loyalism to Britain of many of the Seminole Indian inhabitants. Moreover, it obscured political changes at the tribal level, as the people who actually controlled most of Florida took

---

[1] James H. O'Donnell, III, *The Southern Indians in the American Revolution* (Knoxville: University of Tennessee Press, 1973). See also idem, "The Florida Revolutionary Indian Frontier: Abode of the Blessed or Field of Battle?" in Samuel Proctor, ed., *Eighteenth Century Florida: Life on the Frontier* (Gainesville: University Presses of Florida, 1976), 60–74.

[2] J. Leitch Wright Jr., "British East Florida: Loyalist Bastion," in Samuel Proctor, ed., *Eighteenth-Century Florida: The Impact of the American Revolution* (Gainesville: University Presses of Florida, 1978), 1–13, considers the reasons for East Florida's loyalty. See also idem, *Florida in the American Revolution* (Gainesville: University Presses of Florida, 1975).

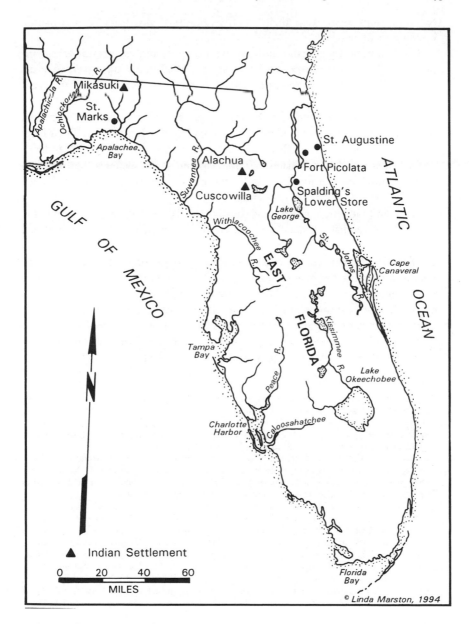

Map 11. Cuscowilla and Seminole Florida.

tentative steps away from their "mother country" and toward some nation building of their own.[3]

The Seminole Indians did not exist before 1700, and the groups that composed the Seminoles did not coalesce into a unified polity until well after the American Revolution.[4] In the early sixteenth century several hundred thousand Indians lived in Florida. Timucua, Apalachee, Tocobago, Tequesta, Calusa, and other tribes constituted a rich array of Indian civilizations before Spanish invaders and catastrophic epidemics sent populations plummeting. Then English slave traders from South Carolina, often accompanied by Creek Indians, virtually destroyed the Apalachee, Timucua, and other societies that had survived in northern Florida. Florida by the early eighteenth century had been virtually emptied of Indian population.[5]

Creek individuals, families, and bands, themselves seeking to escape the pressures of English traders, began to cross the international border between British and Spanish possessions and moved into the emptied regions of northern Florida. Perhaps at first making temporary trips for winter hunting, they later formed more permanent settlements. These migrations went on for more than a century as southward-moving newcomers settled on the abandoned lands of people who were now nearly extinct. Most of the migrants came from the area of the lower Chattahoochee River and the Oconee and Ocmulgee rivers in central Georgia. In some cases, they absorbed the scattered remnants of northern Florida's native population.[6] The Alachua Seminoles said they evacuated Oconee

---

[3] For an excellent study of ethnogenesis on the Great Plains, together with good comments on the nature and evolution of tribes, nations, and tribal nations, see John H. Moore, *The Cheyenne Nation: A Social and Demographic History* (Lincoln: University of Nebraska Press, 1987). Moore views citizenship, territory, political unity (which does not exclude disagreements), and language as the major determinants of both tribal nations and nation-states.

[4] Richard A. Sattler, "*Siminoli Italwa*: Socio-Political Change among the Oklahoma Seminoles between Removal and Allotment, 1836–1905," Ph.D. dissertation: University of Oklahoma, 1987, 17 et passim. Technically, the Seminoles in the Revolutionary era should better be described as "proto-Seminoles," but for style and convenience I have used "Seminoles."

[5] Jerald T. Milanich and Charles H. Fairbanks, *Florida Archaeology* (New York: Academic, 1980) 213, and ch. 9. Henry F. Dobyns, *Their Number Become Thinned: Native American Population Dynamics in Eastern North America* (Knoxville: University of Tennessee Press, 1983) gives a controversial study of native population collapse in Florida; Peter H. Wood provides a convenient overview in "The Changing Population of the Colonial South: An Overview by Race and Region, 1685–1790," in Peter Wood, Gregory A. Waselkov, and M. Thomas Hatley, eds., *Powhatan's Mantle: Indians in the Colonial Southeast* (Lincoln: University of Nebraska Press, 1989), 51–5. On the destruction and dispersal of the Apalachee after 1704, see John H. Hann, *Apalachee: The Land Between the Rivers* (Gainesville: University Presses of Florida, 1988), 264–317, and Mark F. Boyd, Hale G. Smith, and John W. Griffen, *Here They Once Stood: The Tragic End of the Apalachee Missions* (Gainesville: University Presses of Florida, 1951).

[6] Charles H. Fairbanks, "The Ethno-Archaeology of the Florida Seminole," in Jerald Milanich and Samuel Proctor, eds., *Tacachale: Essays on the Indians of Florida and Southeastern Georgia during the Historic Period* (Gainesville: University Presses of Florida, 1978), 166; Milanich and Fairbanks,

about 1714 because of the encroachments of white people, and drifted southeast toward the coast until they came to the fertile hills and plains of Alachua. The territory was then claimed by the Yamassees and other remnants of ancient Floridian tribes, but in the 1730s and 1740s Oconee and other Creek bands raided into northern and central Florida, striking the Spanish and their Yamassee and other Indian allies. Reinforced by other emigrants from the Creeks, the Oconees eventually established a line of settlements stretching from the Alatamaha to Apalachee Bay.[7]

The "colonization" of northern Florida by people who became known as Seminoles was well under way by the middle of the eighteenth century, but the transformation of Creek into Seminole was not sudden, nor was it complete by the time of the Revolution. In some ways it represented a natural outgrowth of the loose and flexible political arrangements that constituted the Creek confederacy. The Creek confederacy was a voluntary association of towns or, in Muskogee, *italwa*, bound together by custom and mutual interest and not by centralized coercion. Rather than a physical group of residences in the European sense of the term "town," the *italwa* represented a group of people associated with a particular political and ceremonial center or square ground, a concept closer to the European notion of a "tribe." These semiautonomous towns or tribes comprised one or more settlements (*talofa*) that could establish their own square ground and sacred fire. Each *italwa* received its sacred fire from one of the "mother towns," but in time it could establish its independence from the parent community. This built-in "process of band fission" gave the Creek confederacy a supple strength; it also meant that towns could gradually "secede" from the loose configuration without ever formally declaring their secession.[8] The Seminole Indians living in northern Florida at the time of the Revolution were part of a tradition of movement and fission within the Creek confederacy; they were also part of an ongoing southward colonization movement and incipient separation from the confederacy.

Our historical view of the Seminoles tends to be dominated by images from a later period: portraits of Osceola and Billy Bowlegs, and the jungle warfare of

*Florida Archaeology*, 253; Sattler, "*Siminoli Italwa*," 18–20; J. Leitch Wright Jr., *Creeks and Seminoles: Destruction and Regeneration of the Muscogulge People* (Lincoln: University of Nebraska Press, 1986), 5–6. William C. Sturtevant, "Creek into Seminole," in Eleanor Burke Leacock and Nancy Oestrich Lurie, eds., *North American Indians in Historical Perspective* (New York: Random House, 1971), 92–128; James W. Covington, "Migration of the Seminoles into Florida," *Florida Historical Quarterly* 46 (1968), 340–57; idem, *The Seminoles of Florida* (Gainesville: University Presses of Florida, 1993), ch. 1.

[7] William Bartram, *Travels through North and South Carolina, Georgia, East and West Florida* (Charlottesville: University Press of Virginia, 1980; facsimile of London 1792 ed.), 378–9.

[8] Sturtevant, "Creek into Seminole," 93, 103; Michael D. Green, *The Politics of Indian Removal: Creek Government and Society in Crisis* (Lincoln: University of Nebraska Press, 1982), 4; Sattler, "*Siminoli Italwa*," 34, 44.

the Second Seminole War.[9] But, at the time of the Revolution, the Cuscowilla Seminoles lived on the Alachua plains of northern Florida, rode horses, and herded cattle. Life in a new country demanded some change in traditional patterns, but such adjustments were nothing new for the newcomers, who traced their roots back to precontact Mississippian culture and were heirs to historical processes that preserved and transformed that culture pattern through time.[10] Agriculture remained the mainstay of Seminole communities, supplemented by hunting, fishing, and gathering, but by the second half of the century Seminoles were also herding the feral cattle that ranged the Alachua region after the collapse of the Spanish ranches, adding cowhides to their deerskin trade.[11] Whether the crucial determinant of emerging Seminole ethnicity is regarded as cultural,[12] environmental,[13] or political,[14] the new Seminole communities in northern Florida preserved important ties with their Creek relatives and heritage. A separate Seminole ethnic and political identity was still a long way off in 1775.[15] As Richard Sattler explains, Seminole sociopolitical organization at this time was more a process than a state.[16]

After the transfer of the Floridas to Britain in 1763, almost the entire Spanish population of about thirty-seven hundred people moved, along with the surviving Yamassee Indians, who "left Florida at their own request." Most of these remnant Indian groups in southern Florida went with the Spanish to Cuba. The Indian population of Florida now comprised primarily the migrant Creeks in the northern settlements around Apalachee and Alachua.[17]

The British takeover and Indian policy contributed to the creation of a separate Seminole identity, at least in European eyes, as the British began to make use of the name "Seminole" to distinguish the Indians of northern Florida from those in Georgia, Alabama, and elsewhere. Seminole appears to be a

---

[9] George Catlin's portraits of Osceola are reproduced in Brian W. Dippie, *Catlin and His Contemporaries: The Politics of Patronage* (Lincoln: University of Nebraska Press, 1990), 89, 116; Carl Wimar's picture "Chief Billy Bowlegs (Holatamico)" is in Rick Stewart, Joseph D. Ketner II, and Angela L. Miller, *Carl Wimar, Chronicler of the Missouri River Frontier* (New York: Abrams, 1991), plate 19.

[10] Brent Richards Weisman, *Like Beads on a String: A Culture History of the Seminole Indians in Northern Peninsular Florida* (Tuscaloosa: University of Alabama Press, 1989), xi, 14–36, 163.

[11] Milanich and Fairbanks, *Florida Archaeology*, 254; Fairbanks, "Ethno-Archaeology of the Florida Seminole," 168–9; Sattler, "*Siminoli Italwa*," 23–7; Sturtevant, "Creek into Seminole," 94–5; Alan K. Craig and Christopher S. Peebles, "Ethnoecologic Change Among the Seminoles, 1740–1840," *Geoscience and Man* 5 (1974), 87; Wright, *Creeks and Seminoles*, 67.

[12] Sturtevant, "Creek into Seminole."

[13] Craig and Peebles, "Ethnoecologic Change Among the Seminoles."

[14] Charles H. Fairbanks, *Ethnohistorical Report on the Florida Indians* (New York: Garland, 1974).

[15] Weisman, *Like Beads on a String*, 13.

[16] Sattler, "*Siminoli Italwa*," 17.

[17] Robert L. Gold, "The Settlement of the Pensacola Indians in New Spain, 1763–1770," *Hispanic American Historical Review* 45 (1965), 567–76; Fairbanks, *Ethnohistorical Report on the Florida Indians*, 139–40.

corruption of *cimarron*, the Spanish word for "wild" or "runaway," although "pioneer" may be a better designation. Since there is no "r" in Hitchiti or any of the Muskhogean languages, the term became *cimallon*, and eventually "Seminole." In time, whites applied the term "Seminole" to almost any Indian in northern Florida, not just to the Oconee Creeks who spearheaded the migration, but as J. Leitch Wright pointed out, when the Hitchiti-speaking Oconees called themselves Seminoles, they were telling the British that they were Hitchitis, not Muskogee-speaking Creeks from Coweta and its vicinity.[18] In the 1760s and well into the Revolution, the British still recognized their basic relationship to the Lower Creeks. Indian Superintendent John Stuart referred to them as Seminole Creeks and "the Seminolies or East Florida Creeks." The emergence of the Seminoles as a distinct ethnic group had more to do with developments in Indian country than with the attempted interference and apparent confusion of outsiders, but the application of a new name recognized an existing and growing geographic separation.[19] In time, geographic separation translated into political and cultural distinction, but during the Revolution some outsiders still regarded the Seminoles as renegades, outlaws, "the scum of several tribes."[20]

Moreover, although the western Seminoles at Tallahassee and Mikasuki tended to be pro-Spanish and traded toward Saint Marks, the eastern groups in the Alachua region were steadfastly pro-English and gravitated toward Saint Augustine and British trading posts stretching to Apalachee. John Stuart dealt with the eastern Seminoles around Alachua and Saint Augustine as separate from the western groups.[21]

A key individual in maintaining the British loyalism of the Alachua Seminoles in the revolutionary era, and a dominant character in the early development of a separate Seminole identity, was Ahaya of Cuscowilla, known to the British as Cowkeeper.[22] When Oglethorpe besieged Saint Augustine in 1740, Cowkeeper led a group of his Creek allies from Oconee. By midcentury, Cowkeeper and his Oconees had created a permanent settlement, the largest of a number of migrant

[18] Wright, *Creeks and Seminoles*, 4.
[19] John Stuart to Gage, Dec. 14, 1771, Clements Library, Gage Papers, vol. 108; Clements Library, Clinton Mss., vol. 31: 4; Fairbanks, *Ethnohistorical Report*, 137–8, 145, 149; idem, "Ethno-Archaeology of the Florida Seminole," 170–1.
[20] *PCC*, reel 87, item 73: 8; C.O. 5/560: 455.
[21] Howard F. Cline, *Provisional Historical Gazetteer with Locational Notes on Florida Colonial Communities (Florida Indians II)* [hereafter *Notes on Colonial Indians*] (New York: Garland, 1974), 75, 102, 212; Sturtevant, "Creek into Seminole," 102.
[22] See Kenneth W. Porter, "The Founder of the 'Seminole Nation:' Secoffee or Cowkeeper,"*Florida Historical Quarterly* 27 (1949) 362–84, and idem, "The Cowkeeper Dynasty of the Seminole Nation," *Florida Historical Quarterly* 30 (1952), 341–9. Stuart to Gage, July 19, 1764, plus enclosure: "An Account of Presents delivered to the Latchewie Indians, June 22, 1764," Gage Papers, vol. 21.

Creek communities around the Alachua prairies.[23] In September 1757, Cowkeeper arrived from the south at the head of fifty warriors for a special meeting with the governor of Georgia in the council chamber at Savannah. Cowkeeper said he had not been in the Creek nation for four years, but he was described as a Creek chief, and it was evident that he felt uncomfortable engaging in a "talk" without authorization from the confederacy. He added that "he was a Stranger to the State of Affairs in the Indian Nation having been so long absent," but assured the governor that he would always be ready to join with the Creek nation in the service of the English.[24]

In June 1764, John Stuart held a conference at Saint Augustine with Seminole headmen. Writing to General Gage, Stuart reported both Seminole separateness and Cowkeeper's support. The Lower Creek towns were about 370 miles from Saint Augustine, but about 130 "Creek Families" had "Detached themselves from their Nation" and were settled at "Latchewie" (Alachua) about seventy miles away. Stuart noted that the inhabitants had always been warm allies of Britain and "irreconcilable Enemies to the Spaniards." He handed out gifts and after six days the Indians left well satisfied. Cowkeeper and Long Warrior [Weoffkee] expressed strong attachment to the British "and declared that they would always hold the white people fast, even if their Nation should behave otherwise." "They know but little of what passes in their nation not having heard from them for several months," Stuart wrote. Cowkeeper alerted his British friends to possible hostilities by the Choctaws and Upper Creeks. Gage confessed that he had never heard of the Alachua Indians before Stuart's report, but urged prudent measures to "fix them in our Interest."[25]

In the fall of 1765, Governor Grant and Stuart met with chiefs of the Upper and Lower Creeks at Picolata. The Indians at first seemed uncooperative and "were very tenacious of their lands," but finally ceded "a very handsome and extensive territory" to Georgia and East Florida. Cowkeeper declined to attend because of the ostensible sickness of his family. Grant bestowed a small medal on Long Warrior and told him "that a great Medal was reserved for the Cowkeeper the Headman of his Town." Cowkeeper's "diplomatic illness" had cleared up in December and he traveled to Saint Augustine with an entourage of sixty

[23] Fairbanks, "Ethno-Archaeology of the Florida Seminole," 167; Cline, *Notes on Colonial Indians*, 30, 69; Sturtevant, "Creek into Seminole," 102–3. Sattler, "*Siminoli Italwa*," 19–20, lists at least four villages in the Alachua region by the 1760s, with five more in the Apalachee area.

[24] Porter, "Founder of the 'Seminole Nation,'" 382; Allen D. Candler, ed., *Colonial Records of Georgia*, 26 vols. (Atlanta, 1904–16), vol. 7: 626–30.

[25] Stuart to Gage, July 19, 1764, plus enclosures, Gage Papers, vol. 21; Major Francis Ogilvie to Gage, July 28, 1764, Gage Papers, vol. 22; Gage to Stuart, Aug. 8, 1764, Gage Papers, vol. 23; C.O. 5/66: 5; C.O. 323/18: 44; John Alden, *John Stuart and the Southern Colonial Frontier* (Ann Arbor: University of Michigan Press, 1944, reprited New York, 1966), 190, n. 42, 198; Fairbanks, "Ethno-Archaeology of the Florida Seminole," 170; Louis De Vorsey, Jr., *The Indian Boundary in the Southern Colonies, 1763–1755* (Chapel Hill: University of North Carolina Press, 1961), 187.

people. Grant made him a Great Medal Chief and presented him with many gifts and provisions.[26] Such diplomatic gifts and the funneling of British trade goods into the region encouraged continued Creek expansion into Florida.[27]

Relations with the British were not always harmonious, however. In 1767, Alachua Seminoles killed nine colonists after a settler whipped two Indians who had tried to steal his horses. Stuart reported that the Alachua Seminoles were "Notorious Horse thieves" who had tried to steal British officers' mounts around Saint Augustine. He also said the Seminoles were considered "Out laws" by the Creeks, and that Creek chiefs at Augusta had requested him to deprive "the detached Villages" of trade, "which would force them to rejoin their Nation for in their present situation they cannot be answerable for their Conduct."[28]

Cowkeeper's headquarters at "Allatchoway" or Cuscowilla was the principal town of the Seminoles and closest to Saint Augustine, some seventy miles to the west of the city.[29] It is also the Seminole town about which we know most in this period, thanks to the pen of William Bartram, who accompanied a trading expedition to Cuscowilla in 1774. The inhabitants had moved to Cuscowilla, near present-day Micanopy, from "the ancient Alachua town on the borders of the savanna" a few miles father north, where alligators, mosquitoes, and the stench of reptiles and fish had made life intolerable in the summer months. Now they enjoyed a beautiful situation on "a high swelling ridge of sand hills," overlooking a lake in the fertile Alachua savanna, which provided pasture for their herds of cattle and horses, as well as for deer. Fields of corn, beans, potatoes, pumpkins, and melons surrounded the village. "Waving forests" of magnolias, palms, poplars, oaks, and "fragrant Orange groves" bordered the savanna, and the lake was rich in fish and fowl.[30] At the time of Bartram's visit, Cuscowilla contained about thirty habitations, "each of which consists of two houses nearly the same size, about thirty feet in length, twelve feet wide, and about the same in height."[31]

Cowkeeper welcomed Bartram's party on their arrival and passed around the pipe. He made a striking impression:

[26] Stuart to Gage, Jan. 11, 1766; Grant to Gage, Jan. 13, 1766; and Proceedings of Congress at Picolata in Stuart to Grant, Jan. 21, 1766, Gage Papers, vol. 47; Porter, "Founder of the 'Seminole Nation,'" 376; Robert L. Gould, *Borderland Empires in Transition: The Triple Nation Transfer of Florida* (Carbondale: Southern Illinois University Press, 1969), 180; Fairbanks, *Ethnohistorical Report* 154.

[27] Sturtevant, "Creek into Seminole," 103–4.

[28] C.O. 323/24, pt. 2: 23, 25, and 37–8.

[29] "Table of Distances of Indian Towns from St. Augustine and Pensacola [1777]," LC, C.O. 5/78: 315.

[30] Bartram, *Travels through North and South Carolina, Georgia, East and West Florida*, 185–6, 188, 190–1. See also Charlotte M. Porter, "William Bartram's Travel in the Indian Nations," *Florida Historical Quarterly* 70 (1992), 434–50.

[31] Bartram, *Travels*, 189–90.

The chief is a tall well made man, very affable and cheerful, about sixty years of age, his eyes lively and full of fire, his countenance manly and placid, yet ferocious, or what we call savage, his nose aquiline, his dress extremely simple, but his head trimmed and ornamented in the true Creek mode. He has been a great warrior, having then attending him as slaves, many Yamassee captives, taken by himself when young. They were dressed better than he, and served and waited upon him with signs of the most abject fear.

Slaves were allowed to intermarry with the Seminoles. Though they remained slaves for life, their children were free "and considered in every respect equal to [the Seminoles]."[32]

Bartram's party met with the assembled chiefs in the public square or council house, the existence of which suggests that the town was at least quasi-independent by this time. They partook of a banquet that included wild oranges sweetened with honey. Bartram's trading companions left him to renew their acquaintance with "some female friends," something Bartram acknowledged to be important "in matters of trade and commerce."[33]

The Seminoles were not yet independent of the Creeks, but distance was permitting them increased autonomy. Bartram said their towns were small and self-governing, but he believed they were influenced by the Creek nation in matters of consequence. He hit upon the ambiguous and flexible nature of the relationship when he called the Seminoles "a treacherous people, lying so far from the eye and controul of the nation with whom they are confederate." Governor Patrick Tonyn remarked on the same phenomenon at about the same time. Writing to the earl of Dartmouth in September 1774, he said, "The Indians settled in this province my Lord, are separated from the Creek Nation, and are not considered by them to be of it: although we cannot entirely hold them, as a free People, independent of that Nation."[34] A British map prepared a few years later still referred to towns of "the Seminolies or Wild People" as "Collonies from the Muscogees Alias Creek Nation."[35]

Individual independence may also have been on the rise. According to Brent Weisman, young warriors, freed from the restraints of a clan moiety system that was in the process of disintegrating, were flexing their muscles in the new world of opportunities provided by the colonial frontier. The sketch Bartram made of Long Warrior [Fig. 9] and the graphic descriptions he provided of Seminole

---

[32] Ibid., 183–4.
[33] Ibid., 189, 192–3; Fairbanks, *Ethnohistorical Report*, 170.
[34] William Bartram, "Answers to Queries about Indians, 1789," Bartram Papers, Historical Society of Pennsylvania, Philadelphia, cited in Porter, "William Bartram's Travels in the Indian Nations," 445; Fairbanks, *Ethnohistorical Report*, 172–3; Bartram, *Travels*, 436; LC, C.O. 5/555: 178.
[35] Mark F. Boyd, "A Map of the Road from Pensacola to St. Augustine, 1778," *Florida Historical Quarterly* 17 (1938), 22–3.

Figure 9. According to William Bartram, Long Warrior was chief of "a predatory band of Seminoles." He was reputed "to have communion with powerful invisible beings or spirits," and on one occasion threatened to summon up thunder when a trader refused him credit. From William Bartram, *Travels Through North and South Carolina, East and West Florida* (London, 1792).

costume illustrate the social changes the Seminole were experiencing. "In an atmosphere of wildly fluctuating partisanship, on a frontier increasingly peopled with half breeds and cunning entrepreneurs, the grand and gaudy Seminole costume (plumes, silver gorgets, and the like) immediately announced ethnic affiliation and marks of individual personality and achievement."[36]

The Seminoles, however, were keeping themselves independent of both the

[36] Weisman, *Like Beads on a String*, 40–1.

British and the Spanish. Archaeological finds of iron tools, guns, and glass (rum) bottles indicate the extent to which Seminoles relied on trade, and the British had trading posts on the Saint Marys and Saint Johns rivers, as well as one in the immediate vicinity of Cuscowilla.[37] Despite Cowkeeper's early allegiance to Britain and his people's avowed hostility to Spain, however, the Cuscowilla community showed plenty of evidence of Spanish influence a full ten years after the Spanish withdrawal. Bartram said their manners and customs were "tinctured with Spanish civilization." Most of the people spoke Spanish, and many of them wore silver crucifixes, "affixed to a wampum collar round their necks, or suspended by a small chain upon their breast." Such things may have been surviving evidence of the Spanish missions in Florida, but the Seminoles also continued to trade with the Spanish on the eve of the Revolution. Cuban fishing boats plied the Florida coast and Seminoles paddled large seagoing canoes made of cypress trunks to Cuba, the Florida Keys, and the Bahamas, trading deerskins, honey, and dried fish for coffee, rum, tobacco, and sugar.[38] Creeks and Seminoles helped to preserve Spanish culture traits and diffuse them into the developing Anglo-American culture of the Southeast.[39]

Moreover, all was not harmony between Seminoles and British traders: the party Bartram accompanied to Cuscowilla was a delegation sent to reestablish trade relations, which the firm of Spalding and Kelsall had suspended after young Seminoles had plundered their post on the Saint Johns River, in apparent retaliation for mistreatment at the hands of the traders there. With trade restored, Long Warrior and a party of Seminoles appeared at James Spalding's post on the Saint Johns that autumn: they were off to fight the Choctaws and requested blankets, shirts, and other supplies. The post agent, Charles McLatchie, agreed to let them have what they needed on half payment.[40] In such situations, the American Revolution opened up new opportunities for Seminoles: the

[37] Fairbanks, "Ethno-Archaeology of the Florida Seminole," 172–3.
[38] Bartram, *Travels*, 184; Helen Hornbeck Tanner, "Pipesmokes and Muskets: Florida Indian Intrigues of the Revolutionary Era," in Samuel Proctor, ed., *Eighteenth-Century Florida and Its Borderlands* (Gainesville: University Presses of Florida, 1975), 17–18; Sattler, "*Siminoli Italwa*," 31–2; Stuart to Gage, Dec. 14, 1771, Gage Papers, vol. 108; Stuart to Gage, May 26, 1775, Gage Papers, vol. 129; Clarence Edwin Carter, ed., *The Correspondence of General Thomas Gage*, 2 vols. (New Haven, Conn.: Yale University Press, 1931–3), vol. 1: 320; James W. Covington, "Trade Relations between Southwestern Florida and Cuba, 1660–1840," *Florida Historical Quarterly* 38 (1959), 114–28; idem, "The Cuban Fishing Ranchos: A Spanish Enclave within British Florida," in William S. Coker and Robert R. Rea, eds., *Anglo-Spanish Confrontation on the Gulf Coast During the American Revolution* (Pensacola: Gulf Coast Humanities Conference, 1982), 17–24. Mark F. Boyd and Jose Navarro Latorre, trans. and eds., "A Spanish Interest in British Florida and the Progress of the American Revolution. I: Relations with the Spanish Faction of the Creek Indians," *Florida Historical Quarterly* 32 (1953), 121–2, 128–9, speculate that a Captain Wacapuchase who visited Havana in 1778 may have been Cowkeeper.
[39] Terry G. Jordan, "The Creole Coast: A Multi-Ethnic View of the American South," paper presented at the thirty-second annual meeting of the Western History Association, New Haven, Conn., 1992.
[40] Wilbur Henry Siebert, *Loyalists in East Florida, 1774 to 1785*, 2 vols. (Deland: Florida State Historical Society, 1929), vol. 1: 9–12.

British encirclement they had dealt with for a dozen years was now replaced by Anglo/Spanish/American competition.[41]

According to Bartram, there were nine towns of Lower Creeks or Seminoles in East Florida by the beginning of the Revolution, plus some smaller villages. Assimilating survivors of local groups and adding runaway slaves to their number, the Seminoles may have numbered about fifteen hundred by 1775.[42] Bartram said they were "but a weak people with respect to numbers," with a total population no bigger than that of a single Creek town, yet they possessed a vast territory and enjoyed "a superabundance of the necessaries and conveniences of life." The deerskin trade furnished them with additional material comforts and they lived undisturbed in the midst of plenty, with "no cruel enemy to dread."[43] The Revolution did little directly to disturb this way of life, since Seminoles fought away from home and their trade was not seriously disrupted. Forty years later, however, Cuscowilla lay in ruins.

In March 1774, Governor Tonyn had a friendly meeting with Cowkeeper, Long Warrior, and other headmen "of the Creek Nation."[44] Nevertheless, he recognized a distinction between these people and the Creeks. In September, Tonyn reported to the earl of Dartmouth that the Indians in his province were anxious to be friends with the British and had offered to carry talks to the Creek nation. "They are settled," said Tonyn, "amongst our Plantations, they have daily intercourse with them, and are as it were a People interwoven with us." He thought that "they actually depend on us, for food and support," but warned, "with these Indians, my Lord, the string may be stretched too tight. If they be drove to despair, they may commit a violence? One hostile act, or a scalp taken, wou'd throw a confusion, into this Province, little short of destruction." Tonyn felt it was necessary "to draw a line of difference, between this People, and the Creek Nation." He endeavored to do so by giving each a different reception, "one meeting with no favours, the other having them from a sparing retentive hand, and are made to comprehend the distinction."[45]

Tonyn's concerns about potential upheaval in the province were not without foundation. The Indians in northern Florida were not immune to the pressures of land speculators and settlement that sparked violence elsewhere, and Seminoles and Creeks were not the only people looking to northern Florida as an area of opportunity.

In October 1774, Jonathan Bryan of Georgia obtained from the Creeks a lease to several million acres in northwest Florida known as the Apalachee Old

[41] Wright, *Creeks and Seminoles*, 113.
[42] Wood, "Changing Population of the Colonial South," 55–6. A British map of 1778 gives the population of several Seminole towns by families and gunmen; Boyd, "Map of the Road from Pensacola to St. Augustine," 15–24.
[43] Bartram, *Travels*, 209–10.
[44] *DAR*, vol. 7: 72; C.O. 5/554: 18–29.
[45] LC, C.O. 5/555: 178–9.

Fields. Governor of Georgia Sir James Wright later persuaded the Indians that they had been deceived, and they tore their marks and seals from the document; but Bryan subsequently got a second lease, granting him the lands for ninety-nine years. Hostile British sources accused Bryan of plying the signers with alcohol, Stuart said the lease was "a mere Forgery," and most historians have regarded it as a fraud; but as Alan Gallay has argued, the Creeks may well have seen in Bryan's schemes an opportunity to escape the British trade monopoly. Bryan then turned to winning the support of the Seminoles; he traveled to Cuscowilla in November 1774 only to find the men away at war. He left a message for Cowkeeper and promised to return in two months with boats full of presents. The Creeks apparently asked Governor Wright to warn Cowkeeper of Bryan's schemes "and prevent his being imposed on by Mr. Bryan." As the political storm burst over Bryan's lease, implicating Chief Justice William Drayton and Dr. Andrew Turnbull of the Council of East Florida, Bryan fled the province and never made it back to Cuscowilla. In September 1775, he sent mixed-blood Thomas Grey to try and secure the Seminoles' approval, but Tonyn got word of it and warned the Seminoles against dealing with Grey. The Seminoles turned Grey over to Tonyn for questioning, but as Grey was related to many of the Creek and Seminole headmen, they and Tonyn both knew there was nothing the governor dared do against him. Grey reported that Cowkeeper was angry that Bryan "had thrown Talks at a Distance to him," and that the Seminoles were adamant they did not intend to grant the lands to Bryan. Grey may well have been telling Tonyn what he wanted to hear, and he willingly furnished the governor with ammunition for his political assault on Drayton, but Cowkeeper's Seminoles were certainly less receptive than their northern relatives to Bryan's arguments.[46]

The crisis passed when Bryan retreated, claiming that he had leased only a small area, and the outbreak of the Revolution overshadowed his schemes. But Bryan never took his eyes off northern Florida, and the disputed lease seems to have added another increment to the growing political division of Creek and Seminole.[47] Meanwhile, Stuart advised Governor Tonyn that, rather than call

[46] The best discussion of Bryan's schemes is in Alan Gallay, *The Formation of A Planter Elite: Jonathan Bryan and the Southern Colonial Frontier* (Athens: University of Georgia Press, 1989), ch. 6, with a map of Bryan's lease on 140. See also: Charles Loch Mowat, *East Florida as a British Province, 1763–1784* (Gainesville: University Presses of Florida, 1964), 88–9, 94; Siebert, *Loyalists of East Florida*, vol. 1: 14–5; Martha Condray Searcy, *The Georgia–Florida Contest in the American Revolution, 1776–1778* (University: University of Alabama Press, 1985), 20–1. Pertinent documents are contained in C.O. 5/76, C.O. 5/555–6, and Gage Papers, vol. 125. See especially LC, C.O. 5/76: 274–84; C.O. 5/546: 25–39; C.O. 5/555: 7–37, 225–7, 273–5; C.O. 5/556: 337; *DAR*, vol. 9: 23–4, vol. 10: 159, 236; *PCC*, reel 65, item 51, vol. 6: 83–5; and Stuart to Gage, Jan. 18, 1775 plus enclosures, Gage Papers, vol. 125. Copies of Bryan's lease are in LC, C.O. 5/555: 19–23, 35. Thomas Grey's depositions are in LC, C.O. 5/555: 277–9, 281–6; C.O. 5/556: 137–9, 329–36.

[47] Wright, *Creeks and Seminoles*, 109–10; Gallay, *Formation of a Planter Elite*, 141, 145.

the Creeks down for general congresses and seek more land cessions from them, "his Indian Fund will be better Employed in Cultivating a good understanding with the Seminollies & detached Tribes in his own neighborhood."[48]

The outbreak of the Revolution in the colonies to the north sent Loyalist refugees scurrying to East Florida for safety, and Saint Augustine quickly became a center of counterrevolutionary sentiment and activity. Among the refugees were Indian superintendent John Stuart, as well as subordinates Yorkshireman Thomas Brown and backcountry Loyalist (and former South Carolina regulator) Moses Kirkland.[49]

In December, Governor Tonyn met visiting Creek and Seminole chiefs and explained the causes of the war, attributing it to American villainy and assuring them that the king's troops would deal with the rebels in short order. He told the Indians that the English would hold on to them like a mother nursing her child and would never forsake them, any more than "the Head can forsake the Body and both live." He then took Long Warrior and Usitchie Mico, the Pumpkin King, on board one of the king's schooners for private talks about Bryan and possible land cessions to the crown, and formally presented them with commissions "as Captains of their Towns, and of east Florida."[50]

Stuart wanted to keep the Indians neutral in the early months of the war, but Tonyn advocated employing Indians from the first, and their disagreement over the role of Indian allies grew into personal animosity. Tonyn, and then Brown and Kirkland, argued that all Indians in East Florida were Seminoles and thus under their jurisdiction and not that of the Creek agents, and Tonyn felt no need to consult Stuart in his dealings with the Seminoles. British Indian administration thus added another perceived distinction between Creek and Seminole.[51] Tonyn made Alexander Skinner his principal agent and gave him the title of commissary of Indian affairs. After Stuart moved to Pensacola in the summer of 1776, the center of British Indian trade and diplomacy shifted west, but Cowkeeper's Alachua Seminoles continued to deal with Tonyn at Saint Augustine.[52]

East Florida never really became a theater of war, but it was often on the verge, as Georgia and South Carolina, enthusiastically supported by Jonathan Bryan and his associates, threatened invasion, and Britain called on Cowkeeper and the eastern Seminoles for assistance. In October 1778 Moses Kirkland proposed a scheme to liberate Georgia and the Carolinas by marching north

[48] Stuart to Gage, Jan. 18, 1775, Gage Papers, vol. 125.

[49] Siebert, *Loyalists of East Florida*, vol. 1: 23–5.

[50] LC, C.O. 5/556: 97–103, 111, or C.O. 5/556: 141, 154, 161–3; also Raleigh, North Carolina, Department of Cultural Resources, Division of Archives and Records, Secretary of State General Records, box 306.

[51] Clements Library, Clinton Mss., vol. 16: 35; LC, C.O. 5/556: 456; H.M.C., *Report on American Mss.*, vol. 1: 39; Mowat, *British East Florida*, 113; Wright, *Creeks and Seminoles*, 113.

[52] Mowat, *British East Florida*, 113; C.O. 5/559: 140–1; Searcy, 30.

with a force of regulars, rangers, and Indians, and linking up with Scottish Loyalists from North Carolina. Before the British recaptured Georgia in 1778, the East Florida–Georgia frontier experienced some bitter partisan warfare, with warriors from Cuscowilla playing a prominent role.[53]

In February 1776, Tonyn (who hoped the Seminoles and other East Florida Indians could furnish two hundred warriors for the king's service[54]) asked the Seminoles to station their warriors between Saint Augustine and the Saint Johns and Saint. Marys rivers; but Cowkeeper hesitated to commit his people to armed assistance until he knew the sentiments of the Creek nation. While Bryan worked to win Creek allegiance to the rebels and sent presents for the Seminoles, Cowkeeper and his people waited in Saint Augustine, assuring the British of their support but refusing to stir until they heard from the Creeks. Determined that "the Seminoly Indians must join with us and keep all Rebels out of the Province," Governor Tonyn sent urgent messages to David Taitt, the British agent among the Creeks, pressing him to get the Creeks to send a talk to Cowkeeper and the Seminoles, expressing their loyalty to the king. The Seminoles, said Tonyn, were "very much afraid and stand in great awe of the Creek Nation," and wanted to know how they should act "so as to regulate their actions on those of the Nation."[55]

In April, Thomas Brown reported that the major Seminole groups – Oconee King and King of Mikasuki, as well as Cowkeeper's Alachuas – were firmly attached to Britain, but that the Lower Creeks were not likely to give any military assistance. Assembling the Lower Creek chiefs and headmen at Chiaha in May, Taitt secured a promise from all except the Cowetas, Hitchitis, and Cussitas that they wold not listen to rebel talks. The headmen also nominated Oconee King – a renowned warrior with "great Influence among the wild People" – to lead a large group of Seminoles to Saint Augustine.[56]

In July, when a rebel raiding party crossed the Saint Marys River, Tonyn sent a courier asking Cowkeeper to cut them off, but the rebels escaped.[57] In

[53] Wright, *Creeks and Seminoles*, 113–14, 129; Robert Stansbury Lambert, *South Carolina Loyalists in the American Revolution* (Columbia: University of South Carolina Press, 1987), 80–1. Kirkland's proposals are in Clinton Papers, vol. 43: 24, 28, reprinted in Randall L. Miller, ed., "A Backcountry Loyalist Plan to Retake Georgia and the Carolinas," *South Carolina Historical Magazine* 75 (1974), 207–14. Searcy, *Georgia–Florida Contest*, 28, 108, 177.

[54] Clinton Mss., vol. 13: 46.

[55] *DAR*, vol. 10: 315, vol. 12: 109; LC, C.O. 5/556: 411–15; Clinton Mss., vol. 16: 38 39; Searcy, *Georgia–Florida Contest*, 26–8.

[56] Searcy, *Georgia–Florida Contest*, 28–9; LC, C.O. 5/556: 419, 429; Clinton Mss., vol. 16: 36, 37, 40, 41.

[57] Edgar Legare Pennington, "East Florida in the American Revolution," *Florida Historical Quarterly* 9 (1930), 25; C.O. 5/557: 161–72; Searcy, *Georgia–Florida Contest*, 43. The Americans despatched militia to the area on reports that five or six hundred soldiers and Indians came to the Saint Marys River to invade Georgia; Lilla M. Hawes, ed., "The Papers of Lachlan McIntosh, 1774–1779," *Collections of the Georgia Historical Society* 12 (1957), 51.

August, Tonyn turned to the Seminoles to help repel another anticipated raid from Georgia. He assembled a large force of Seminoles on the west bank of the Saint Johns River, but a group of Mikasukis arrived saying that the Creek national council did not sanction the action, as they intended to let the whites fight their own quarrels. Again, Tonyn had to write urgently to Taitt:

> Pray use every means to bring the Creeks down here & that they will lay strong Injunctions on all the Symmonolies & these people of the lower Towns, to Cooperate with me for his Majesty's service, I always knew the Symmonolies would regulate their Conduct by that of the Nation & the Meccasukies pretend they know the Sentiments of the Nation & have given it out as described already.[58]

Once again, the widening division between Creeks and Seminoles was apparent. Bryan was able to exert his influence to keep the Lower Creeks neutral, but the Seminoles, more dependent for trade upon British East Florida, had more reason to support the crown. Unlike their Creek relatives, they could send warriors to participate in the border fighting, knowing that their villages in Florida were relatively safe.[59]

As vicious raids and counterraids continued between Georgia and East Florida, Thomas Brown's East Florida rangers and Seminole warriors fought in a common cause, albeit for somewhat different reasons.[60] In February 1777, Brown's rangers and Seminole warriors, led by Cowkeeper and Perryman, joined Lieutenant Colonel Lewis Fuser and seventy-three regulars in a raid across the Georgia border. The raiders captured and burned the American stockade at Fort McIntosh, but Fuser's contemptuous attitude toward the rangers and Indians so affronted the Seminoles that Brown was obliged to "mollify" them on their return.[61]

In July, Stuart, who two years earlier had believed the garrison at Saint Augustine strong enough that the Indians were not needed there, declared that "the Seminollie Creeks," who could raise eight hundred gunmen, were Saint Augustine's only reliable source of assistance in the event of a sudden attack, since the Upper and Lower Creeks were too far away.[62] In August, Cowkeeper

---

[58] Searcy, 57; LC, C.O. 5/78: 63–4.
[59] Gallay, *Formation of a Planter Elite*, 151–2.
[60] LC, C.O. 5/557: 247. On Brown see Gary D. Olson, "Thomas Brown, Loyalist Partisan, and the Revolutionary War in Georgia, 1778–1782," *Georgia Historical Quarterly* 54 (1970), 1–19, 183–208; idem, "Thomas Brown, the East Florida Rangers, and the Defense of East Florida," in Samuel Proctor, ed., *Eighteenth Century Florida and the Revolutionary South* (Gainesville: University Presses of Florida, 1978), 15–28; and Edward J. Cashin, *The King's Ranger: Thomas Brown and the American Revolution on the Southern Frontier* (Athens: University of Georgia Press, 1989).
[61] Siebert, *Loyalists of East Florida*, vol. 1: 44–5; C.O. 5/557: 257–8; LC, C.O. 5/557: 253; Cashin, *King's Ranger*, 61–2.
[62] Clinton Mss., vol. 16: 32; *DAR*, vol. 14: 148–9; C.O. 5/78: 208.

and a large Seminole war party raided beyond Fort Barrington and killed eighteen men; "he bid the Interpreter assure me," Tonyn told Stuart, "that his people had done strictly as I had desired, and had attacked only Rebels, that were out in Arms," and had harmed no women and children.[63] But not all Seminoles were as ready or able as Cowkeeper's band to defend Saint Augustine. In September, Seminoles from the Flint River responded to Stuart's call for warriors but pointed out that "Our Path to Saint Augustin is far out of our way and a great Distance to go," whereas Cowkeeper and his men were "always about St. Augustin." Stuart could depend on them "defending our Land & keeping it safe," but they made it clear they expected to keep any horses, slaves, or cattle they captured.[64]

While Tonyn worked to keep the Seminoles loyal and immune to the rebels' "infectious impressions," his political enemy William Drayton maintained that the Indians' visits to Saint Augustine were a source of only nuisance and expense. Courted with "a Degree of Servility, loaded with Presents, and fatigued with long, unintelligible Talks," he said, the Indians had come to despise the governor and constituted a "domestic enemy," camping near the town, where they plundered the inhabitants and stole slaves.[65]

Although Stuart complained that the Creeks were "a mercenary People," governed by their own self-interest, the Seminoles continued to impress the British with their loyalty early in 1778. The British now estimated Seminole warrior strength at about a thousand.[66] John Stuart had appointed Moses Kirkland his deputy among "the Seminollie Creeks," and in February Kirkland set off on a tour through Seminole country. He was to take a few headmen with him to Saint Augustine and keep the Seminoles primed for any campaign General Augustine Prevost might mount.[67] By April, Cowkeeper was on his way to Saint Augustine with many warriors, accompanied by their women and children. "The Old Fellow has behaved well and deserves to be taken notice of," said Alexander Skinner. Meanwhile, young Perryman and some fifteen hundred men, women, and children from Flint River were en route to assist the British at the Saint Marys, and expected that British provisions would be waiting for them.[68] Such influxes would have placed a great drain on British resources, and Stuart let the Indians know that their services would not be needed.[69]

[63] LC, C.O. 5/558: 474, or C.O. 5/558: 706.
[64] DAR, vol. 13: 185; LC, C.O. 5/79: 48, 59.
[65] Cited in Mowat, British East Florida, 114. On Drayton, see J. Russell Snapp, "William Henry Drayton: The Making of a Conservative Revolutionary," Journal of Southern History 57 (1991) 637–58; and William Dabney and Marion Dargon, William Henry Drayton and the American Revolution (Albuquerque: University of New Mexico Press, 1962).
[66] Report on American Mss., vol. 1: 190, 199, 225; DAR, vol. 15: 34.
[67] Clinton Mss., vol. 31: 4; Report on American Mss., vol. 1: 190.
[68] LC, C.O. 5/79: 247.
[69] Report on American Mss., vol. 1: 251–2.

No sooner had Stuart's agents spread the word than news came of Robert Howe's expedition against Florida. The British scrambled to rally Indian support and the Seminoles were quick to respond. "The Seminoly Indians have ever shown their attachment to his Majesty," Tonyn reported as the Americans retreated.[70] "Sixty Seminolies have joined our Rangers," he wrote in July, "more Gangs are marching west of St. John's river for the same purpose and I have despatched messengers to Cowkeeper and Oconey King to rouse all their People which I hope will have effect."[71]

The British experienced more difficulty in enlisting Creek and Seminole support for David Holmes's expedition against the rebels that summer. The campaign had to wait until after the Busk or Green Corn ceremony, "no Indian being allowed to go out on any expedition until that feast was over." Holmes drank the black drink in the square at Mikasuki and waited.[72] Cowkeeper and Oconee King did not take part in the expedition. Tonyn advised Holmes not to disturb them, as they had recently returned from campaign. Holmes, with 213 warriors in his command, deemed it no great loss, dismissing Cuscowilla as "composed Chiefly of a parcel of renegadoes, who, for their misbehaviour were obliged to leave their respective Towns and go down there, for the purpose of being out of the way of Justice, which people from the best Accounts I can learn, do not exceed forty Gunmen."[73] Later that year, Tonyn sent Skinner to collect the Alachua Seminole warriors and take them to Fort Barrington, where they were to rendezvous with a force of Loyalists. Finding no Loyalists there, the Seminoles returned home in disappointment, while Skinner was killed by a party of Creeks who mistook him for a rebel.[74] Jonathan Bryan also was removed from the scene that year. Captured at the fall of Savannah in December, Bryan spent twenty months, in old age and ill health, aboard a British prison ship.[75]

Indians who had been called away on campaign during the 1778 spring planting season, turned up in great numbers at Saint Augustine the following winter "upon a pretext of not having raised any corn." The next winter, 1778–9, was one of near famine among the Lower Creeks, and they joined the

---

[70] DAR, vol. 15: 122, 168; Siebert, Loyalists of East Florida, vol. 1: 57–9; Report on American Mss., vol. 1: 275–6

[71] LC, C.O. 5/558: 216–17.

[72] DAR, vol. 15: 180; Holmes's journal of his expedition is in LC, C.O. 5/80: 51–80; see esp. 53, 64. For twentieth-century descriptions of the ceremony, see Louis Capron, "The Medicine Bundles of the Florida Seminoles and the Green Corn Dance," Bureau of American Ethnology Bulletin 151 (1953), 155–210; William Sturtevant, "The Medicine Bundles and Busks of the Florida Seminole," Florida Anthropologist 7 (1954), 31–70; and Charles Hudson, The Southeastern Indians (Knoxville: University of Tennessee Press, 1976), 365–75.

[73] LC, C.O. 5/80: 73–4, 80–1.

[74] Searcy, Georgia–Florida Contest, 165; DAR, 16: 63–5; C.O. 5/559: 173; William Moultrie, Memoirs of the American Revolution, 2 vols. (New York, 1802), vol. 1: 334.

[75] Gallay, Formation of a Planter Elite, 156–9. Bryan was released late in 1780 and died in 1788.

large numbers of Seminoles dependent on Saint Augustine. While the British struggled to feed the Indians, Spanish emissaries became increasingly active among the tribes. However, they failed in their effort to introduce an agent into the Seminole towns near Saint Marks: "The Indians, rather too politic for the Spaniards, permitted their agent to land, received his presents, and put him to death," reported Thomas Brown with considerable satisfaction.[76] At the end of 1779, the British prepared to rally the Seminoles ("wild Indians") to repel a rumored Spanish attack on Saint Marks.[77]

Tonyn's authority over East Florida Indian affairs increased in July 1780: "The Simonolies being so entirely dependent on Saint Augustine," Lord Germain placed their management in the hands of the governor.[78] With a weak garrison, Tonyn continued to need the Seminoles to help defend his city. The Seminoles nearest Saint Augustine remained loyal but, with their economy disrupted by the war, they needed supplies that Tonyn did not have. Spanish emissaries continued their work. "In the military and Indian departments," lamented Tonyn in December 1781, "I find myself invested with the mere shadow of authority without power."[79]

The problems increased with the British evacuation of Savannah and Charleston in 1782. Steady numbers of refugees from the neighboring rebel colonies had fled to Florida throughout the war years, altering the composition of its population with a marked increase in the number of blacks. Minorcan immigrants, brought to the east coast of Florida in 1768 to help populate the settlement of New Smyrna, suffered terrible hardships there, and the survivors fled to Saint Augustine in 1777.[80] Now the trickle of new peoples became a flood. Charleston itself had been a refugee center for backcountry Loyalists and their families. More than two hundred of these people, almost half of them children, had died in the crude shelters and steaming summers around the city. Now they fled again. By Christmas 1782, more than 6,000 refugees had arrived in East Florida from Georgia and South Carolina; the final total reached as high as 13,375, including more than 8,000 black slaves. The white and black population of East Florida, which had formerly approximated 1,000 and 3,000 respectively, exceeded 17,000 by the end of the war.[81] The refugees to Saint Augustine also included 2,000 Choctaws, who had been with the garrison at Savannah for

[76] *Report on American Mss.*, vol. 1: 403, 414, 424, 427, 455; vol. 2: 39, 130, 152, 359; *DAR*, vol. 17: 184–5; vol. 18: 57–8.

[77] C.O. 5/81: 152.

[78] *Report on American Mss.*, vol. 2: 152.

[79] *DAR*, vol. 19: 57; C.O. 5/560: 188–9, 288.

[80] Patricia C. Griffin, *The Mullet on the Beach: The Minorcans of Florida, 1768–1788* (Jacksonville: University of North Florida Press, 1991).

[81] Lambert, *South Carolina Loyalists in the American Revolution*, 259–62; Mowat, *British East Florida* 125–6, 137; Siebert, *Loyalists of East Florida*, vol. 1: 101, 130–2; *DAR*, vol. 21: 145; Sylvia Frey, *Water From the Rock: Black Resistance in a Revolutionary Age* (Princeton, N.J.: Princeton University Press, 1991), 179–81.

six months, and 150 Creeks who had fought in the city's defense.[82] The massive rise in population generated Florida's first land boom, but it also put tremendous strain on institutions and resources. With the white population badly outnumbered, the General Assembly enacted a slave code, which applied to both black and Indian slaves. Free Indians, free blacks, mestizos, and mulattoes were to be distinguished by wearing a silver badge with the word "free" on the left arm.[83]

The war in the southern colonies also created a surge in the number of African people living among the Seminoles. Slaves from the British colonies had fled to Spanish Florida in the past, and, though Creek Indians often cooperated with the British in returning runaway slaves, southern Indian communities had developed a tradition of taking in escapees. Now the British campaigns in the South offered the chance of freedom to many more slaves who fled to the British lines, and also introduced Creeks and Seminoles to slavery as practiced on large and prosperous plantations on the Atlantic coast. Some Creeks took slaves as spoils of war, and by the end of the Revolution, Creeks appear to have absorbed some of their white neighbors' concepts of slavery. More black people sought refuge in Creek and Seminole country after Yorktown, and those who joined Seminole communities appear to have experienced a relatively mild form of servitude. Others formed their own communities of free blacks or "maroons," and lived in separate villages close to Seminole towns. One such community allied itself to the Alachua Seminoles. African influence in Seminole communities became considerable. Africans dressed like Seminoles, and in later wars they fought together against American invaders. Whereas white colonists elsewhere in the Southeast deliberately tried to foment fear and hostility between Indians and blacks as a way of keeping them divided, in Florida both Britain and Spain encouraged Seminole–black solidarity as a buffer against American expansion after the Revolution.[84]

---

[82] Siebert, *Loyalists of East Florida*, vol. 1: 107.
[83] Mowat, *British East Florida*, 132–3; Wilbut H. Siebert, "Slavery in East Florida, 1776–1785," *Florida Historical Quarterly* 10 (1931), 139–61.
[84] Wright, *Creeks and Seminoles*, 6, 20, 84–90; idem, "British East Florida," 12; Lambert, *South Carolina Loyalists in the American Revolution*, 240–4. Kenneth Porter, "Negroes and the East Florida Annexation Plot, 1811–1813," *Journal of Negro History* 30 (1945), 9–29, discusses runaway slaves among the Seminoles, pp. 12–15, and suggests that they enjoyed a very mild form of servitude, paying only a portion of their annual crop to the Seminoles. For Seminole–black alliance, see Kenneth W. Porter, "Florida Slaves and Free Negroes in the Seminole War," *Journal of Negro History* 28 (1943), 390–421, and idem, "Negroes and the Seminole War," *Journal of Negro History* 36 (1836), 249–80. For contrasting policies toward Indians and blacks, see William S. Willis, "Divide and Rule: Red, White and Black in the Southeast," *Journal of Negro History* 48 (1963), 157–76; cf. William G. McLoughlin, "Red Indians, Black Slavery and White Racism: America's Slaveholding Indians," *American Quarterly* 26 (1974), 370. See also: Lawrence Foster, *Negro–Indian Relationships In the Southeast* (Philadelphia: 1935, New York: AMS Press reprint 1978); Martha Condray Searcy, "The Introduction of African Slavery into the Creek Nation," *Georgia Historical Quarterly* 64 (1982), 21–32; Kathryn E. Holland Braund, "The Creek Indians, Blacks, and Slavery," *Journal of Southern History* 57 (1991), 601–36; Daniel F. Littlefield, Jr., *Africans and Seminoles: From Removal to Emancipation* (Westport, Conn.: Greenwood, 1977), 4–6, 8–9. American agent Benjamin Hawkins said that British agents also

Saint Augustine was accustomed to ethnic diversity and the comings and goings of different population groups long before the Revolution. The Indian population around the city had increased significantly during the last decades of the seventeenth century, when Christian Guales sought refuge from nonmission Indians; moreover, Europeans, Africans, and American Indians had mingled and mixed in its streets for generations. The city had an "Indian Church."[85] Now, however, Saint Augustine became choked with refugees. Old residents and new arrivals, soldiers and sailors, African slaves, resident Indians, and visiting delegations from allied tribes added immeasurably to the bustle and confusion in the town.[86] There were serious food shortages in East Florida in the winter of 1782–3, and, when a delegation of twelve hundred Cherokees, together with representatives of the Mohawks, Senecas, Delawares, Shawnees, Mingoes, Tuscaroras, Creeks, and Choctaws, came to Saint Augustine to learn the state of affairs, promote an intertribal confederation, and confirm their allegiance to King George, the British were in considerable consternation, as they had little in the way of presents or supplies. Fortunately, the delegation stayed for only ten days.[87]

East Florida's sudden emergence as a Loyalist population center led many people to hope or assume that its place in the empire was secure, but the view from London was different. At the Paris peace talks, the earl of Shelburne suggested that Britain keep Gibraltar and offer Spain East Florida and Minorca in compensation. West Florida had already fallen, and the eastern province seemed of little value without it. Spain agreed, and by the fifth article of the treaty, East Florida was ceded to Spain; British subjects were allowed eighteen months to settle their affairs and leave. In reality, the evacuation dragged on for two and a half years.[88]

The use of East Florida as a diplomatic counter brought the second change of sovereignty in twenty years and disrupted the lives of thousands of its inhabitants, white, Indian, and African. Governor Tonyn issued a proclamation announcing the cession of the province on April 21, 1783; eight days later he

gave Indians black slaves in payment for their services during the Revolution; Hawkins, "A Sketch of the Creek Country, in the Year 1798 and 1799," *Collections of the Georgia Historical Society* 3 (1848), 66. For detailed examination of relations between black runaways and the British army, see Frey, *Water From the Rock*.

[85] John R. Dunkle, "Population Change as an Element in the Historical Geography of St. Augustine," *Florida Historical Quarterly* 37 (1958), 3–32; Charles H. Fairbanks, "From Missionary to Mestizo. Changing Culture of Eighteenth-Century St. Augustine," in Samuel Proctor, ed., *Eighteenth-Century Florida and the Caribbean* (Gainesville: University Presses of Florida, 1976), 88–99; Kathleen Deagan, "Mestizaje in Colonial St. Augustine," *Ethnohistory* 20 (1973), 55–65; Kathleen Deagan, ed., *Spanish St. Augustine: The Archaeology of a Colonial Creole Community* (New York: Academic, 1983); and esp. J. Donald Merritt, "Beyond the Town Walls: The Indian Element in Colonial St. Augustine," 125–47; *Report on American Mss.*, vol. 3: 395.

[86] Mowat, *British East Florida*, 138.

[87] *Report on American Mss.*, vol. 3: 277, 322, 325–7; Carleton Papers, PRO 30/55/60: nos. 6728, 6742, 6953.

[88] *DAR*, vol. 21: 166–9; Mowat, *British East Florida*, 140–1.

announced shipping would be available to take the inhabitants to England and the West Indies. Saint Augustine in 1783 began to resemble Saigon in 1973. The brief land boom created by the influx of refugees collapsed, the "utmost confusion" reigned, and people thronged into the city in anger, fear, disbelief, and resentment. Some people turned to plundering; a group of soldiers plotted to arm the slaves, seize the fort and hold on to the country; and groups of "banditti" from the American states began to raid the northern plantations. Tonyn feared disaster if the troops were removed before the final evacuation took place. The evacuation of Florida produced a Loyalist and African American diaspora that cast "throngs of homeless people" into the Bahamas, the southern states, and the lower Mississippi Valley, as well as to Britain, Nova Scotia, Jamaica, Dominica, and "other Foreign Parts."[89]

In this confused and charged atmosphere, the response of the Indians assumed enormous importance. British traders were ordered out of Indian country and to repair to Saint Augustine, lest they fall victim to Indians who were rumored to be contemplating vengeance.[90] Retaining Seminole allegiance, and providing them with presents so as not to offend them, became more important than ever.[91] Indian delegations arrived in Saint Augustine throughout the spring of 1783. Cowkeeper and others were said to have sworn vengeance against the king for giving away their land, and vowed that when the English departed they would kill every Spaniard who ventured out of Saint Augustine.[92] But Cowkeeper and other chiefs also declared their determination to evacuate Florida along with the British rather than stay and live with the Spaniards.[93] General Guy Carleton, stung by accusations of betrayal from Indians and officers, declared

---

[89] Joseph Byrne Lockey, comp. and trans., *East Florida 1783–1785: A File of Documents* (Berkeley and Los Angeles: University of California Press, 1949), 156–7, 173, 214–17; Mowat, *British East Florida*, 138–43, 147; Joseph B. Lockey, "The East Florida Banditti, 1783," *Florida Historical Quarterly* 24 (1945), 87–107; Siebert, *Loyalists of East Florida*, vol. 1: 101, 152; Alfred J. Morrison, trans. and ed., *Travels in the Confederation* by Johann David Schoepf, 2 vols. (New York: Bergman, 1968), vol. 2: 240–1. Not all Britons evacuated Saint Augustine; see Joseph B. Lockey, trans. and ed., "The St. Augustine Census of 1778," *Florida Historical Quarterly* 18 (1939), 11–31; Frey, *Water From the Rock*, ch. 6. The most prominent bandit leader was Daniel McGirt, or McGirth, a former Loyalist who led an interracial band; Frey, *Water From the Rock*, 99, 102–3; Robert Scott Davis, Jr., "Daniel McGirth," in Richard L. Blanco, ed., *The American Revolution, 1775–1783: An Encyclopedia*, 2 vols. (New York: Garland, 1993), vol. 2: 997–8.

[90] *Report on American Mss.*, vol. 3: 358; vol. 4: 58–9, 350–1; C.O. 5/82: 367–70, 392–3; C.O. 5/111: 51–2; Carleton Papers, PRO 30/55/81, nos. 9094, 9098; Lockey, *East Florida*, 111, 138, 154–7.

[91] Siebert, *Loyalists of East Florida*, vol. 1: 136; C.O. 5/547: 135; 560: 288; *DAR*, vol. 19: 391, vol. 21: 168.

[92] Siebert, *East Florida Loyalists*, vol. 1: 144; *Report on American Mss.*, vol. 4: 75, 83; Lockey, *East Florida*, 173.

[93] Siebert, *Loyalists of East Florida*, vol. 1: 139; *Report on American Mss.*, vol. 4: 119, 351; C.O. 5/82: 369, 372–3, 397, 432; Carleton Papers, 7688: 6, 7717; Morrison, trans. and ed., *Travels in the Confederation*, by J. Schoepf, vol. 2: 240. See also Peter Marshall, "First Americans and Last Loyalists: an Indian Dilemma in War and Peace," in Esmund Wright, ed., *Red, White and True Blue: The Loyalists in the Revolution* (New York: AMS, 1976), 33–53.

that Britain had had no choice but to cede the province and denied any breach
of faith toward "those deceived Indians as you are all so fond to stile them."
Indians who insisted on going to the Bahamas should be furnished with the
means to do so, but Carleton ordered his officers to use every argument to
"dissuade them from a measure destructive of their happiness."[94] As late as
February 1784, Indians around Saint Augustine still could not believe the
British intended to leave them.[95]

Unlike the Chickasaws and others who responded to the British defeat by
seeking to come to terms with Spain or the United States, Cowkeeper and the
Alachua Seminoles remained steadfastly pro-British at the end of the war,
asserting their independence against Spaniards and Americans alike. Patrick
Tonyn said they possessed an "unextinguishable spark of ardent Love and
faithful attachment, to the British name; which may rise into a Flame, and be
improved upon to advantage, on some future occasion," and he took pains to
cultivate the various Seminole bands who visited Saint Augustine prior to the
Spanish takeover.[96] Cowkeeper, who must have been in his seventies, died early
in 1784. Even though his dying words ostensibly urged his people to continue
fighting the Spaniards, his death eased to some degree the transition from the
British to the Spanish regime.[97]

The new governor, Vicente Manuel de Zéspedes, arrived in August, and the
fort at Saint Augustine was transferred the next month. Despite acrimonious
relations with his replacement, Tonyn followed orders and tried to cultivate a
good disposition among the Indians toward the Spaniards, a policy exactly the
opposite of that he had pursued for the past several years and one he found to
be "a very unpleasant task." Zéspedes quickly appreciated that his best policy
was to continue the procedures established by his British predecessors, holding
Indian congresses and distributing presents as required. He met with the
Seminoles in September, and held a larger congress at Saint Augustine in
December. Zéspedes recognized the necessity of following established protocol
if the path between Spain and the Seminoles was to be kept "bright and clear,"
and he endeavored to resolve subsequent interruptions in generally peaceful
relations by working with and through headmen from Cuscowilla.[98]

[94] C.O. 5/111: 39–40; *Report on American Mss.*, vol. 4: 165; Carleton Papers, 8084: 7.
[95] C.O. 5/82: 430–3.
[96] Lockey, *East Florida*, 325; C.O. 5/561: 37.
[97] Porter, "Founder of the Seminole Nation," 383–4; Cline, *Notes on Colonial Indians*, 86–7;
Tanner, "Pipesmokes and Muskets," 29; idem, *Zéspedes in East Florida, 1784–1790* (Jacksonville:
University of North Florida Press, 1989 reprint), 83; LC, East Florida Papers, bundle 116L9,
doc. 1784–5.
[98] Mowat, *British East Florida*, 144–6; Siebert, *Loyalists of East Florida*, vol. 1: 178; Lockey, *East
Florida*, 324; C.O. 5/561: 35–6, 359–61; Tanner, *Zéspedes in East Florida*, 83–5. Zéspedes's
conferences with the Seminoles (A los tetes y guerreros de los Indios Seminolies, Sept. 30, 1784,
and A los tetes y guerreros de los Crikes interior y Seminolies, Dec. 8, 1784) are in LC, East
Florida Papers, reel 43, bundle 114J9, translated and reprinted in Lockey, *East Florida*, 280–3,

Zéspedes's deference to British procedures and his efforts to maintain good relations with the Indian inhabitants of his new province illustrates a broader pattern of continuity in the midst of apparent change. Despite political revolution to the north and transfers of sovereignty in Saint Augustine, in Seminole country during and after the Revolution, there was plenty of "business as usual." Beyond Saint Augustine and San Marcos de Apalachee, Spanish East Florida after the Revolution really consisted of no more than a strip of land stretching about ninety miles below the Saint Marys River along the Atlantic coast. The rest of Florida remained Seminole country.[99]

The American Revolution generated changes in the Creek and Seminole deerskin trade, but they were changes of direction rather than of content or ultimate market, and seem to have affected the Seminoles less than the Creeks. Many of the traders operating in Indian country at the beginning of the Revolution were loyal subjects of George III. Some abandoned their businesses and lost their property during the war. Others, wealthy merchants in the coastal cities of Georgia and South Carolina, fled south, bringing their connections and expertise with them. Scots like William Panton, Thomas Forbes, John Leslie, and James Spalding took refuge in East Florida, and British dominance of the southern Indian trade continued. The Seminoles followed traditional patterns of hunting and trading, and dealt with the same factors in their villages. Their pelts went to Pensacola and to posts on the Saint Marys and Saint Johns rivers, not to Charleston, Savannah, or Silver Bluff; but as before, they ended up in London. As J. Leitch Wright said, "Winning the Revolution had cost Americans much of the southeastern Indian trade," and essentially the same people did business with the Seminoles after the Revolution as before it.[100] The influence of Scottish merchants on Creek and Seminole trade and culture continued.[101]

European trade had become a fundamental factor in Seminole life by the time of the Revolution. Lists of goods traded to southern Indians indicated the extent to which the Seminoles were becoming tied into a wider Atlantic economy that produced goods specifically for the Indian trade and simultaneously

---

428–9. On subsequent relations see, for example, Governor of St. Augustine to Headmen and Warriors, Oct. 13, 1789, and "A Talk from the Oconee King and Warriors of the Seminolie Indians of the Tribe of Latchaway and Villages Adjacent to the Governor of St. Augustine" (Oct. 19, 1789), Library of Congress, East Florida Papers, reel 43, bundle 114J9.

[99] David J. Weber, *The Spanish Frontier in North America* (New Haven, Conn.: Yale University Press, 1993), 278.

[100] Wright, *Creeks and Seminoles*, 43–5, 49–53, 115; William S. Coker and Thomas D. Watson, *Indian Traders of the Southeastern Spanish Borderlands: Panton, Leslie and Company and John Forbes and Company, 1783–1847* (Pensacola: University of West Florida Press, 1986), ix–xi (fwd. by J. Leitch Wright). Cf. Kathryn Holland Braund, *Deerskins and Duffels: Creek Indian Trade with Anglo-America, 1685–1815* (Lincoln: University of Nebraska Press, 1993), 169–70, sees rather more disruption in the deerskin trade.

[101] Wright, *Creeks and Seminoles* 36, 42; Dorothy Downs, "British Influence on Creek and Seminole Men's Clothing, 1733–1858," *Florida Anthropologist* 33 (1980), 46–65.

introduced into Indian country elements of an increasingly uniform Western consumer culture. In 1783, Thomas Forbes compiled a list of "articles of British Manufacture absolutely necessary for the Indians inhabiting the Western frontier of East and West Florida" which included blue and red stroud; Welsh plain cloth; Yorkshire broadcloth; Irish linen and coarse white linen; checked and striped linen and cotton; printed, checked, and silk handkerchiefs; Scotch osnaburgs; saddles; shoes; smooth-bore muskets; gunpowder; lead bars; flints; iron pots; kettles; pans; axes; carpenters and coopers' tools; locks; hinges; nails; needles; scissors; knives; razors; ribbons; silver trinkets; vermilion and lamp black; hand mirrors; tobacco and pipes; hats; cheap rum and brandy; and salt.[102] During the Revolution, Alachua Seminoles went on campaign "dressed in scarlet coats, armed with steel knives and hatchets, wearing silver armbands and gorgets, and equipped with new muskets and rifles, all recently made in England."[103]

Maintaining access to sources of such things was vital to Seminole survival. The Seminole chiefs who met Zéspedes in Saint Augustine in December 1784 accepted his offers of peace and said they were not opposed to the transfer of power, but made clear that they wanted "to have the same goods come to them over the salt water as in the time of the English."[104] Obtaining some kind of hold on the Indian trade was vital to Spanish hopes of transferring paper sovereignty into any kind of meaningful presence in Seminole country. Barely had Zéspedes arrived in Saint Augustine than the resident Scottish firm, Panton, Leslie and Company, submitted a memorial, pointing out that only they had the capital and the credit, the knowledge and the experience, the personnel and the connections necessary to carry on the Indian trade. Zéspedes agreed. Two weeks later he wrote to Bernardo de Galvez regarding the remarkable influence of Panton and Leslie among the Creeks and Seminoles: "If it is desired to win the friendship of these Indians efficaciously, it would be risky to expel this company suddenly or until several years have passed so as to give time to introduce among the Indian tribes Spaniards experienced in the trade with them and knowing something of the language." To attain this end, Zéspedes recommended sending orphans and children of soldiers, between eight and ten years old, to live for a year or two among the Indians, "returning for two months each year to the city in order not to forget the Christian Doctrine." Such children might grow up to become "men of means and useful to the state."[105]

---

[102] Coker and Watson, *Indian Traders*, 34–5; cf. similar lists in Wright, *Creeks and Seminoles*, 54–5; Tanner, *Zéspedes*, 90; Lockey, *East Florida*, 162, and D. C. Corbitt, trans. and ed., "Papers Relating to the Georgia–Florida Frontier, 1784–1800," *Georgia Historical Quarterly* 21 (1937), 275–8. See Braund, *Deerskins and Duffels*, for a broader view of the impact of the trade on Creeks and Seminoles.

[103] Wright, "British East Florida," 7.

[104] Lockey, *East Florida*, 429–30.

[105] Ibid., 161–3, 254–60; *Spain in the Mississippi Valley*, vol. 3, pt. 2: 108–12, 114–16.

Spain did not grant the Panton firm a formal monopoly of the Indian trade, but it had little choice but to allow them an effective one. Britain had lost much of its political control over the southeastern Indians, but it still dominated their economy, and a Scottish firm became the "quasi-official agency of the Spanish government handling Indian relations."[106] In 1788, when Loyalist adventurer William Augustus Bowles attempted to turn the Indians against Panton, Leslie and Company, the Cuscowilla Seminoles not only refused to help but actively thwarted his plans.[107] As the Seminoles anchored themselves to newly established trade networks around Alachua and the Saint Johns River, they took another step away from the network of alliances that constituted the Creek confederacy.[108]

By the end of the Revolution, the British, Spanish, and Americans still regularly referred to the Seminole groups in Florida as part of the Creek confederacy, but they were unclear as to the exact relationship. In November 1788, American treaty commissioners Richard Winn, Andrew Pickens, and George Mathews wrote to Alexander McGillivray and the headmen of the Creek Nation, complaining that the Seminoles were doing a great deal of mischief: "We know not whether they belong to any part of the Creeks, but wish to be informed." A year later, American commissioners Benjamin Lincoln, Cyrus Griffin, and David Humphreys distinguished clearly between Upper Creeks, Lower Creeks, and Seminoles in their report to the secretary of war. Ten years after that, however, U.S. Indian agent Benjamin Hawkins listed seven Seminole towns and explained that "they are Creeks."[109]

Seminoles themselves continued to act and speak as though they were Creeks. With Alexander McGillivray rebuilding the unity of the Creek confederacy as an effective power in the complex international diplomacy of the Southeast, it seemed for a time as if Seminole ties to the confederacy would be strengthened. But, though McGillivray summoned the Seminoles to meet with the Creeks in assembly, he admitted to Governor Zéspedes, "As for the Semanolies I have but little Acquaintance with the present leaders, the former ones I knew are dead." The Creek chief deferred to British trader John Leslie, who knew the

---

[106] Coker and Watson, *Indian Traders*, ix–xi; Wright, *Creeks and Seminoles*, xii; Tanner, *Zéspedes*, 104. Josef de Espeleta to O'Neill, Aug. 18, 1784, Library of Congress, East Florida Papers, reel 41, bundle 114J9, doc. 1785–27; McGillivray to O'Neill, July 24, 1785, AGI, PC, leg. 198; O'Neill to Miro, Dec. 29, 1786, AGI, PC, leg. 37–13; Charles McLatchey to His Excellency, Dec. 15, 1783, AGI, PC, leg. 196; O'Neill to Galvez, Sept. 4, 1785, AGI, PC, leg. 37–36 (all in North Carolina State Archives, box 26).

[107] Siebert, *East Florida Loyalists*, vol. 1: 178–9; Sattler, *"Siminoli Italwa,"* 68; Corbitt, ed., "Papers Relating to the Georgia–Florida Frontier," *Georgia Historical Quarterly* 21 (1937), 280. On Bowles, see J. Leitch Wright, Jr., *William Augustus Bowles: Director General of the Creek Nation* (Athens: University of Georgia Press, 1967).

[108] Fairbanks, *Ethnohistorical Report*, 173; idem, "Ethno-Archaeology of the Florida Seminole," 171; Weisman, *Like Beads on a String*, 9–10.

[109] *The New American State Papers: Indian Affairs*, vol. 6 (Wilmington, Del.: Scholarly Resources, 1972), 36, 92; Sturtevant, "Creek into Seminole," 103.

Seminoles better than he.[110] Even before McGillivray's death in 1793, it was clear that the physical separation of the Seminoles was translating into something else. Spanish sovereignty did little to interfere with the increasing autonomy and independence of Seminole communities. Seminole sociopolitical organization at the band level remained unchanged, and there was not yet a unified Seminole "tribe"; nevertheless, unlike Cowkeeper at the beginning of the Revolution, Seminoles no longer seem to have felt bound by the decisions of the Creek national council.[111]

Separation brought separate developments in Seminole country. When Cowkeeper died in 1784, the leadership, following matrilineal succession, went to his sister's son, Payne.[112] As more migrants came from the north, Seminole towns proliferated. In 1774 Bartram had counted nine towns, of which Cuscowilla was the largest. By 1821, there were perhaps four times as many, and Mikasuki, under Chief Kinache or Tom Perryman, had surpassed Cuscowilla in size and importance.[113] According to Weisman, this proliferation of towns was itself a response to the increase in traders and trade opportunities in Seminole country, which encouraged individuals and families to depart from the traditional *talwa* pattern of settlement, establish their own towns, and strike deals of their own with outsiders.[114] Though the Creek migrants seem to have transplanted in full the traditional *talwa* plan in the settlements they created across Florida, by the late eighteenth century Seminoles adopted more diffuse settlement patterns instead of the cohesive village political organization of the ancestral Creek culture. Town squares and council houses began to disappear, ultimately producing concomitant changes in the political and religious practices of the Florida people.[115]

The prosperity that the Seminoles created through participation in the deerskin and cowhide trade and development of a mixed subsistence economy also brought about a deterioration in their situation. The deerskin trade went into sharp decline in the 1790s and came to a grinding halt when the Napoleonic Wars closed off European markets.[116] Moreover, the Seminoles' rich villages and crops became targets of American assault. Although the Alachua Seminoles seem to have avoided direct participation in the Creek War of 1813–14, they fell victim to an American assault in 1813. The Seminoles and their black allies

[110] John Walton Caughey, *McGillivray of the Creeks* (Norman: University of Oklahoma Press, 1938), 125, 147.

[111] Sturtevant, "Creek into Seminole," 104–5; Sattler, "*Siminoli Italwa*," 29, 64, 69, 71, 82; Cline, *Notes on Colonial Indians*, 230; Fairbanks, "Ethno-Archaeology," 172; idem, *Ethnohistorical Report*, 181, 187; Weisman, *Like Beads on a String*, 8–10; Searcy, *Georgia–Florida Contest*, 179.

[112] Sattler, "*Siminoli Italwa*," 83, 97–8; Cline, *Notes*, 93.

[113] Weisman, *Like Beads on a String*, 60; Wright, *Creeks and Seminoles*, 126.

[114] Weisman, *Like Beads on a String*, 58–9, 79–81.

[115] Ibid., 41; Fairbanks, "Ethno-Archaeology of the Florida Seminole," 174–5.

[116] Sattler, "*Siminoli Italwa*," 78–80, 94; see also documents in Lockey, *East Florida*.

helped the Spaniards defeat an American attempt to annex East Florida, but the octogenarian Chief Payne was killed in the fighting, and an American force destroyed the Alachua villages. The Seminoles subsequently abandoned the Alachua prairies and withdrew south toward Tampa Bay, or moved closer to the western Seminoles.[117] Wars with the United States continued, and a "harried guerilla existence" became an increasingly normal way of life for Seminole bands. Forced into a "gypsy life-style," Seminoles changed settlement patterns, house types, and, according to one interpretation, "progressively divested themselves of those customs unsuitable to their deteriorating situation."[118]

Cuscowilla survived the Revolution unscathed. It remained prosperous and prominent among a growing number of Seminole communities that exercised increasing independence during the revolutionary era but had not yet developed a unity of their own. Thirty years after the Revolution, it fell victim to the American aggression that ultimately pushed the separate Seminole bands into a unified Seminole "tribe."

---

[117] Porter, "Negroes and East Florida Annexation Plot," 22, 25–7; Fairbanks, "Ethno-Archaeology," 179–80; Cline, *Notes on Colonial Indians*, 113, 173, 230; Sattler, "*Siminoli Italwa*," 73, 83.
[118] Craig and Peebles, "Ethnoecologic Change Among the Seminoles," 88, 91–2.

# 10

## *The peace that brought no peace*

For all the devastation the American Revolution brought to Indian country, Indians remained a force to be reckoned with at the war's end. In reading the reports of American invasions of Indian country, it is easy to assume, as did some American commanders, that burning Indian villages and destroying crops constituted a knockout blow. But burning homes, razing fields, and killing noncombatants does not necessarily destroy people's will to fight or even their ability to win. Geoffrey Parker's observation about the resilience of peasant communities victimized by European wars – "as in Vietnam, what was easily burnt could also be easily rebuilt"[1] – sometimes held true for Indian communities during the Revolution. Many survived the destruction of their villages. George Rogers Clark recognized the limitations of the American search-and-destroy missions, and an officer on Sullivan's campaign agreed that burning crops and villages was not the same as killing Indians: "The nests are destroyed but the birds are still on the wing."[2] A British officer reviewing the American campaigns against the Iroquois and the Cherokees agreed that such a system of warfare was "shocking to humanity," and as sound military strategy was "at best but problematical."[3] The Indians in the West were holding their own in 1782. The real disaster of the American Revolution for Indian peoples lay in its outcome.

Speaking on a war belt in council with the British in Detroit in December 1781, the Delaware war chief Buckongahelas declared that his warriors had been making blood "fly" on the American frontier for five years.[4] The next year,

---

[1] Geoffrey Parker, *The Military Revolution: Military Innovation and the Rise of the West, 1500–1800* (Cambridge University Press, 1988).

[2] Draper Mss. 26J27–8; James Alton James, ed., *George Rogers Clark Papers 1771–1781* (Springfield: Illinois State Historical Society, 1912), 383; Frederick Cook, ed., *Journals of the Military Expedition of Major General John Sullivan against the Six Nations of Indians* (Auburn, N.Y.: Knapp, Peck and Thomson, 1887), 101.

[3] R. Lamb, *An Original and Authentic Journal of Occurrences During the Late American War* (Dublin, Ireland: Wilkinson & Courtney, 1809; reprint ed., New York: Arno and New York Times, 1968), 291–2.

[4] *MPHC*, vol. 10: 544.

1782 the last of the war, witnessed even bloodier conflict. Indians routed American forces at Blue Licks and Sandusky. Americans slaughtered Moravian Delawares at Gnadenhütten and burned Shawnee villages. Delawares ritually tortured Colonel William Crawford and, as atrocities mounted, they and the Shawnees pushed "their retaliation to great length by putting all their prisoners to death."[5]

Then the British and Americans made peace. The Peace of Paris recognized the independence of the thirteen colonies and transferred to the new United States all land east of the Mississippi, south of the Great Lakes, and north of the Floridas. Wyandot chiefs, who had heard rumors of peace, told Major De Peyster "we hope your children [i.e., the Indians] will be remembered in the Treaty,"[6] but the peace terms made no mention of the Indian people who had fought and died in the Revolution and who inhabited the territory to be transferred. The Peace of Paris brought a temporary lull in hostilities, but it brought no peace to Indian country. Rather, by ending open conflict between non-Indian powers, it deprived Indians of allies and diplomatic opportunities as they continued their struggle for independence against Americans who claimed their lands as the fruits of victory.

If a speech that John Heckewelder attributed to Captain Pipe is accurately dated and recorded, Indians were apprehensive of British betrayal even as they carried war to the Americans in 1781. "Think not that I lack *sufficient sense to convince me*," the Delaware chief told Major De Peyster at Detroit, "that altho' You *now* pretend to keep up a perpetual enmity to the Long Knives (American People), you may, e'er long, conclude a Peace with them!" The British, he said, had set him on their enemy like a hunter setting his dogs on his quarry, but he suspected that if he glanced back, "I shall probably see my Father shaking hands with the Long Knives."[7] Pipe's worst fears were now realized. As news of the peace terms filtered into Indian country, Indian speakers in council after council expressed their anger and disbelief that their British allies had betrayed them and handed their lands over to their American and Spanish enemies. The head warrior of the Eufalees refused to believe that the English would abandon the Indians; another Creek chief dismissed reports of the treaty as "a Virginia Lie." The Iroquois were "thunderstruck" when they heard that British diplomats had sold them out to the Americans without so much as a reference to the tribes. Little Turkey of the Overhill Cherokees concluded, "The peacemakers and our Enemies have talked away our Lands at a Rum Drinking." Okaegige of

---

[5] E.g.: Haldimand Papers, 21762: 13–14; 21775: 49. On the Kentuckian disaster at Blue Licks, see John Mack Faragher, *Daniel Boone: The Life and Legend of an American Pioneer* (New York: Holt, 1992), 215–24. Quote from J. Watts De Peyster, ed., *Miscellanies by an Officer. Arent Schuyler De Peyster* (Dumfries: Munro, 1813), XXXIV.

[6] *MPHC*, vol. 11: 355.

[7] James H. O'Donnell, III, ed., "Captain Pipe's Speech: A Commentary on the Delaware Experience, 1775–1781," *Northwest Ohio Quarterly* 64 (1992), 126–33.

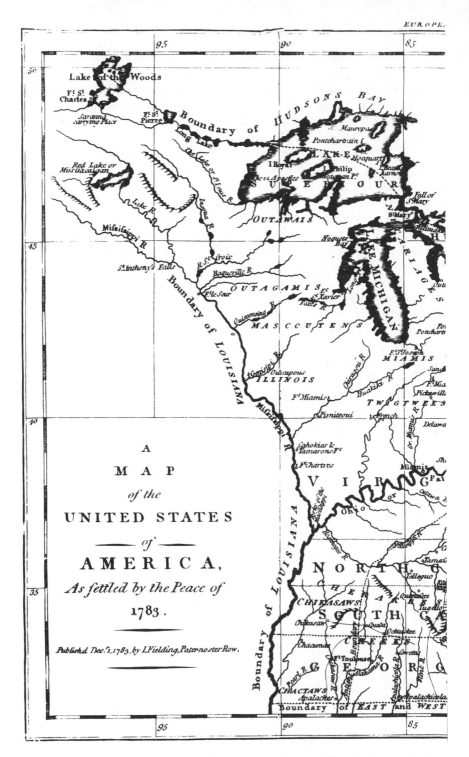

Map 12. Map of the United States's boundaries as determined by the Peace of Paris. Courtesy National Archives of Canada, NMC. 7456. The map shows the location of some of the Indian peoples who were affected by the peace settlement but not mentioned in it.

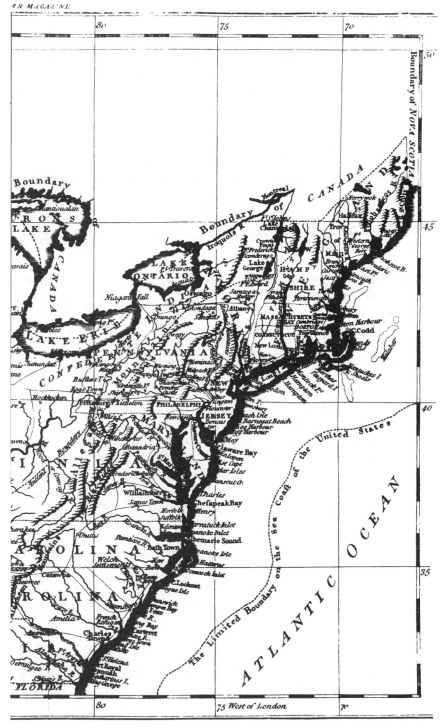

the Flint River Seminoles reminded the British that the Indians took up the hatchet for the king "at a time we could scarce distinguish our Friends from our Foes," and asked if the king now intended to sell them into slavery. Fine Bones, speaking for his Cowetas and other Upper Creeks, said they could not now turn around and take the Spaniards and Virginians by the hand; if the English intended to evacuate, the Indians would accompany them.[8]

Alexander McGillivray told the British he could no longer keep his people in the dark. After nine years of faithful service, "at the Close of it to find ourselves & Country betrayed to our Enemies & divided between the Spaniards & Americans is Cruel & Ungenerous." The Indians had done nothing to permit the king to give away their lands, "unless . . . Spilling our blood in the Service of his Nation can be deemed so." The Indians had been "most Shamefully deserted." Turning to the Spaniards, McGillivray reiterated that Britain had no right to give up what it did not own, and that the Creeks as a free nation had the right to choose what allies they thought most appropriate. "The protection of a great Monarch is to be preferred to that of a distracted Republic," he said, courting Governor Estevan Miró, but making it clear he would turn to the Americans for trade if necessary.[9] Spanish officials referred patronizingly to McGillivray as "nuestro mestizo," but McGillivray deftly pursued Creek, not Spanish, interests in the decade after the Revolution.[10]

Many southern Indians – "having made all the world their Enemies by their attachment to us" – expressed their determination to evacuate along with the British rather than stay and come to terms with the Americans and Spaniards, but the British discouraged them.[11] William Augustus Bowles, masquerading as a Creek chief in London eight years later, summed up the situation: "The British Soldier, when he left the shore of America, on the proclamation of peace, had peace indeed, and returned to a Country where Peace could be

[8] On Indian reactions to the peace terms, see: Colin G. Calloway, "Suspicion and Self-Interest: British–Indian Relations and the Peace of Paris," *Historian* 48 (Nov. 1985), 41–60; idem, *Crown and Calumet: British–Indian Relations, 1783–1815* (Norman: University of Oklahoma Press, 1987), 3–23; Carleton Papers, PRO 30/55/69: doc. 7564 (Eufalies); C.O. 5/82: 368, 448 (Virginia lie); Haldimand Papers 21717: 146–7, or *DAR*, vol. 21: 126 (Six Nations); C.O. 5/82: 446–7 (Little Turkey); C.O. 5/82: 372–3, LC, C.O. 5/560: 55–7, or Joseph Byrne Lockey, ed. *East Florida, 1783–1785: A File of Documents* (Berkeley and Los Angeles: University of California Press, 1949), 109–10 (Okaegige and Fine Bones). Additional Indian responses are in PRO, Foreign Office Records, F.O. 4/1: 143–6; 3: 83–5; C.O. 5/82, and Ernest Cruikshank, ed., "Records of Niagara, 1784–87," *Publications of the Niagara Historical Society* 39 (1928), 64.

[9] C.O. 5/82: 405; McGillivray to Miró, March 20, 1784, McGillivray to O'Neill, March 26, 1784, AGI, PC, leg. 197 (North Carolina State Archives box 26); John Walton Caughey, ed., *McGillivray of the Creeks* (Norman: University of Oklahoma Press, 1938), 73–4, 92.

[10] O'Neill to Zéspedes, Nov. 2, 1786, AGI, PC 40–3 (North Carolina State Archives, box 26).

[11] C.O. 5/82: 368, 373, 397, 432; Carleton Papers, PRO 30/55/69, docs, 7688, 7717, 8084: 7; PRO 30/55/92, doc. 10116; Peter Marshall, "First Americans and Last Loyalists: An Indian Dilemma in War and Peace," in Esmund Wright, ed., *Red, White and True Blue: The Loyalists in the Revolution* (New York: AMS, 1976), 37–8.

enjoyed; But to the Creek & Cherokee Indians was left, to drain to the dregs the remainder of the bitter cup of War, unassisted & alone." McGillivray asked the British army at least to leave the Creeks military stores so that they could defend themselves against the Americans.[12]

Indian people farther from the center of revolutionary conflict felt the betrayal equally hard. The Chippewa chief, Matchekwis, visited Michilimackinac in September 1784, and when Captain Daniel Robertson refused his requests for presents, the Indian

> abused me in a very particular manner, as all our great men below, saying we were all Lyers, Impostures &c. that had encouraged him and others to go to Canada &c. to fight and loose their Brothers and Children, now despise them, and let them starve, and that they, the Indians ought to chasse us and our connections out of the country.[13]

British officers and Indian agents scrambled to save face and reconcile the Indians to "this unfortunate event," fearing that their former allies might with good reason turn and vent their rage on the people who had betrayed them. British traders prepared to leave Indian villages even as British officers stressed the need to maintain the usual supplies to the Indians although the war was over.[14] Sir John Johnson's speech to the Iroquois, in which he naively or cynically reassured them that he could not believe the United States intended to deprive them of their land on pretext of having conquered it, was relayed to other tribes. The Indians were advised to bear their losses with fortitude, forget what was past, and look forward to the blessings of peace.[15] Not too sure themselves about the peaceful intentions of the new republic, and determined to protect their interests among the Indians, the British resolved to hold on to the frontier posts that were supposed to be handed over to the United States "with all convenient speed" under the peace terms. Retention of these posts, which stretched from Lake Champlain to Michilimackinac, conveyed the impression that the British were on hand to support the tribes in continuing resistance to the United States, even though Britain carefully avoided renewed war with the United States.[16] Spain operated a similar policy to check American expansion in the south: Spanish officials encouraged McGillivray "by word of mouth" and did their best to "help the Indians without the Americans being able to prove that we have done so."[17]

[12] PRO, Foreign Office Records, F.O. 4/9: 9; McGillivray to O'Neill, Feb. 8, 1784, AGI, PC, leg. 197 (North Carolina State Archives, box 26).

[13] MPHC, vol. 11: 453.

[14] C.O. 5/82: 367–70, 413, 444; Lockey, ed., East Florida, 154–5; Haldimand Papers, 21717: 168–9; MPHC, vol. 20: 124.

[15] Haldimand Papers, 21779: 123–9; MPHC, vol. 20: 177.

[16] Calloway, Crown and Calumet, 13.

[17] Miró to O'Neill, Apr. 20, 1786, AGI, PC, leg. 4–14 (North Carolina State Archives, box 26).

Meanwhile, Americans made the most of British perfidy. They told the Shawnees that Britain had cast them aside "like Bastards."[18] Virginian emissary John Dodge told the Chickasaws that the English had been forced to withdraw from the country and "their Poor foolish Indians which refused to make Peace with us, is miserable on the Earth, Crying & begging for mercy Every Day."[19] General Philip Schuyler told the Six Nations Indians that the British deceived them if they told them they were included in the peace; "the treaty does not contain a single stipulation for the Indians, they are not even so much as mentioned." At the beginning of the war, Schuyler said, he had asked the Six Nations to sit still and they had not listened. Now, like the Loyalists, they had forfeited their lands. "We are now Masters of this Island, and can dispose of the Lands as we think proper or most convenient to ourselves," the general declared.[20] Six Nations delegates listened in bewilderment. From what he heard from his messengers, Joseph Brant (Fig. 10) thought Schuyler "as Saucy as [the] very devil," and thought the Iroquois delegates behaved shamefully. "After our friends the English left us in the lurch, still our own chiefs should make the matter worse," he wrote to Major Robert Mathews. "I do assure you I begin to prepare my death song for vexation will lead one to rashness."[21]

The peace signed in Paris did little to change things in the backcountry world inhabited by Indians and American frontiersmen. Frontier vendettas continued and old scores remained unsettled. Some people on the eastern seaboard were appalled by the massacre of the Moravian Delawares in 1782, but William Irvine, commanding at Fort Pitt, knew that people who lived closer to the Indians and had lost relatives in the war felt very differently. He warned his wife to keep her opinions about the massacre to herself, as he would: "No man knows whether I approve or disapprove of killing the Moravians."[22] The Indianhating that produced and sanctioned the Moravian massacre paid no regard to words of peace exchanged in Paris and made real peace impossible in Indian country. Commander De Peyster at Detroit warned his superiors in the fall of 1782 that the backcountry settlers would continue to make war on the Delawares, Shawnees, and Wyandots even after Britain and her revolted colonists made peace. Allan MacLean at Niagara feared that while he was busy preventing the Indians from going to war in the spring of 1783, the rebels "were preparing to cut the throats of the Indians."[23]

[18] Haldimand Papers, 21779: 117.
[19] *Virginia State Papers*, vol. 3: 500.
[20] NYPL, Schuyler Papers, reel 7, box 14, items dated July 2, 1783 and Jan. 11, 1784.
[21] Haldimand Papers, 21772: 223–4.
[22] Consul W. Butterfield, ed., *The Washington–Irvine Correspondence* (Madison, Wis.: Atwood, 1882), 343–5.
[23] Alfred J. Morrison, trans. and ed., *Travels in the Confederation*, by Johann David Schoepf. 2 vols. (New York: Bergman, 1968) vol. 1: 277–81; Butterfield, ed., *Washington–Irvine Correspondence*, 149; De Peyster, ed., *Miscellanies by an Officer*, XI; Haldimand Papers, 21756: 91–2.

Figure 10. Joseph Brant in 1786, by Gilbert Stuart. Oil on canvas. Courtesy New York State Historical Association. By the time this portrait was painted, Brant and most of his people were living in exile in Ontario, where they built new homes and lives on the Grand River.

Nor were all Indian people eager to embrace the peace. Warriors with relatives to avenge paid little attention to formal peace terms worked out by men far from the bloodletting. A Potawatomi, singing the war song, told Major De Peyster he was eager for action in 1781 because "you see me here in mourning and I am ashamed to remain so." Another asked De Peyster "for means to enable him to revenge himself" for the loss of his kinsman.[24] John Montour, a mixed-blood Delaware who flits in and out of the records, "was one of Seven Brothers, all of them reckoned able good Warriors at the Commencement of the Rebellion, five of them have been Since killed in the service." While the war drew to a close and the British tried to keep their allies at peace, John and his surviving brother were out in Indian country, anxious for revenge. In November 1782, they came into Fort Niagara with four scalps and three young female prisoners, saying they knew nothing about the suspension of hostilities.[25]

The end of the Revolution produced a new phase of conflict between Indians and Americans in the Ohio country. Murders, horse thefts, raids, and counterraids continued with little abatement. "While empires and states went about making peace," explains Richard White, "the villages continued to act on their own." Like the British after 1763, American policymakers could no more control their citizens than Indian chiefs could control their young men. A flood of backcountry settlers invaded Indian country, broke down what remained of the "middle ground" arrangements of coexistence that had been built up over generations, and knocked the heart out of federal attempts to regulate the frontier. Many of these people, reported a congressional committee, had no more desire for peace with the Indians than the British had for peace between Indians and Americans.[26] As revolutionary violence gave way to postwar peace and a future of prosperity in some other areas of the country, vengeance and strife continued to be a way of life and of getting things done in Indian country, even in relations between whites. Tension between frontier settlers and eastern elites resulted in western demands for autonomy, separatist movements, violent confrontations, and the breakdown of normal means of redress.[27]

---

[24] NAC, C-1223, vol. 13: 18, 34.

[25] Haldimand Papers, 21762: 213. John Montour was described as "an Outcast" from the Delawares "on account of his foolish Conduct," who went to live with the Delawares at Detroit. His brother Che cheas was driven from Kuskuskias by Edward Hand's campaign – "He is a foolish Fellow & for revenge went & join'd the Wiandots." *Frontier Advance*, 343–4; Morgan Letterbook, vol. 3: 178–9; see also Butterfield, ed., *Washington–Irvine Correspondence*, 168–9. A certain John Montour also held a captain's commission in the United States Army and served with a contingent of Delaware soldiers in 1781: "Pay Roll of the Delaware Indians in service of the United States, June 15, 1780–Oct. 31, 1781," National Archives, Revolutionary War Rolls, 1775–83, Microfilm M246, reel 129. See also Draper Mss. 3H19–20, 76–7; 1AA201–2; and Neville B. Craig, ed., *The Olden Time*, 2 vols. (Cincinnati, Ohio: Clarke, 1876), vol. 2: 310, 378, 389. In December 1779, Guy Johnson opened a council at Niagara with a ceremony of condolence for the death of "two young warriors and a woman of the family of Montour." NAC, C-1223, vol. 12: 92.

[26] Richard White, *The Middle Ground: Indians, Empires, and Republics in the Great Lakes Region, 1650–1815* (Cambridge University Press, 1991), 410–11, 418–20, and chs. 9–11; Faragher, *Daniel Boone*, 249–55.

[27] Robert Gross, *The Minutemen and Their World* (New York: Hill & Wang, 1976), ch. 7; cf. Slaughter, *Whiskey Rebellion*, ch. 2, esp. 57; George E. Connor, "The Politics of Insurrection: A Comparative Analysis of the Shay's, Whiskey, and Fries' Rebellions," *Social Science Journal* 29 (1992), 259–81.

During the war, American soldiers had returned from expeditions into Indian country with stories of the rich lands awaiting them once independence was won. With the Peace of Paris under their belts, Americans now set about taking over Indian lands as the spoils of victory. Peace initiated a new era of land speculation and unleashed a new land rush into Indian country. Between 1783 and 1790, the white population of Pennsylvania's three western counties grew by 87 percent; by the end of the century, western Pennsylvania's population had jumped from around thirty-three thousand to ninety-five thousand.[28] Governor Benjamin Harrison of Virginia confessed to Governor Alexander Martin of North Carolina that he was "shocked when I reflect on the unbounded thirst of our people after Lands that they cannot cultivate, and the means they use to possess themselves of those that belong to others." Frenchman Francois Jean de Chastellux, traveling in North America as the war wound down, predicted that an inevitable consequence of the peace for the Indians "must be their total destruction, or their exclusion at least from all the country within the lakes."[29] A delegation of 260 Iroquois, Shawnee, Cherokee, Chickasaw, Choctaw, and "Loup" Indians visiting the Spanish governor of Saint Louis in the summer of 1784 already felt the effects of the American victory:

> The Americans, a great deal more ambitious and numerous than the English, put us out of our lands, forming therein great settlements, extending themselves like a plague of locusts in the territories of the Ohio River which we inhabit. They treat us as their cruelest enemies are treated, so that today hunger and the impetuous torrent of war which they impose upon us with other terrible calamities, have brought our villages to a struggle with death.[30]

Faced with an empty treasury and no means of replenishing it except by selling off Indian lands, the United States government focused its attention on the Old Northwest, where individual states relinquished their claims to western lands to the national government.[31] A congressional committee, reporting in October 1783, noted that the Indian tribes of the northwest and the Ohio Valley seriously desired peace, but cautioned that "they are not in a temper to relinquish their territorial claims, without further struggles." Nevertheless, the report continued, the Indians were the aggressors in the recent war. They had ignored American warnings to remain neutral and "had wantonly desolated our villages and destroyed our citizens." The United States had been obliged, at

---

[28] Slaughter, *Whiskey Rebellion*, 65.
[29] *North Carolina State Records*, vol. 16: 442; Francois Jean de Chastellux, *Travels in North America, in the Years 1780, 1781, and 1782*, 2 vols. (London: G. G. J. and J. Robinson, 1787), vol. 1: 404.
[30] *Spain in the Mississippi Valley*, vol. 3, pt. 2: 117.
[31] Reginald Horsman, *Expansion and American Indian Policy, 1783–1815* (East Lansing: Michigan State University Press, 1967), chs. 1–2, provides a concise analysis of American Indian policy in the postwar years.

great expense, to carry the war into Indian country "to stop the progress of their outrages." The Indians should make atonement and pay compensation, "and they possess no other means to do this act of justice than by compliance with the proposed boundaries." Rather than continue a costly war, the report recommended that the United States make peace with the tribes and negotiate boundaries that could then be renegotiated as Indians retired west before the inevitable press of settlement.[32]

Acting on the assumption of Indian war guilt and eager for the spoils of victory, American commissioners demanded lands from the Iroquois at Fort Stanwix in 1784; from the Delawares, Wyandots, and their neighbors at Fort McIntosh in 1785; and from the Shawnees at Fort Finney in 1786. They brushed aside Indian objections in arrogant confidence that Indian lands were theirs for the taking by right of conquest. In 1775, Congress had instructed its treaty commissioners to "speak and act in such a manner as they shall think most likely to obtain the friendship or at least the neutrality of the Indians."[33] Times had changed. James Duane, chairman of the Committee on Indian Affairs in the Continental Congress and mayor of New York City from 1784 to 1789, urged the United States not to continue the British practice of cultivating relations with the Indians as if they were nations of equal standing. The Six Nations should be treated as dependents of the State of New York. They should adopt American diplomatic protocol, not vice versa. Unless the United States seized the opportunity to implement this new hard-line approach, said Duane, "this Revolution in my Eyes will have lost more than half its' [sic] Value."[34] American treaty commissioners followed Duane's advice and dispensed with wampum belts and elaborate speeches. "In their place," writes James Merrell, they "substituted blunt talk and a habit of driving each article home by pointing a finger at the assembled natives."[35] Moreover, the federal government was just one player in the competition, as individual states, land companies, and speculators scrambled for Indian lands.

Iroquois delegates at Fort Stanwix tried to argue for the Ohio River as the boundary to Indian lands, but the American commissioners would have none of it. "You are a subdued people," they lectured the delegates. "We are at peace with all but *you*; *you* now stand out *alone* against our *whole* force." Lest the

---

[32] Washington C. Ford and Gaillard Hunt, eds., *Journals of the Continental Congress*, 34 vols. (Washington: Government Printing Office, 1904–37), vol. 25: 681–3; *Revolution and Confederation*, 290–4.

[33] Ford and Hunt, eds., *Journals of the Continental Congress*, vol. 10: 110–11.

[34] Hugh Hastings, ed., *Public Papers of Governor George Clinton* 10 vols. (Albany N.Y.: State Printers, 1899–1914), vol. 8: 328–32, quote at 329; *Revolution and Confederation*, 299–301.

[35] James H. Merrell, "Declarations of Independence: Indian–White Relations in the New Nation," in Jack P. Greene, ed., *The American Revolution: Its Character and Limits* (New York University Press, 1987), 201. References to the kind of arrogant attitude Merrell describes are also in Consul Willshire Butterfield, ed., *Journal of Captain Jonathan Heart . . . to Which is Added the Dickinson–Harmar Correspondence of 1784–5* (Albany: Munsell, 1885), 53, and in Clements Library, Harmar Papers, Letterbook A: 33.

Indians miss the point, American troops backed up the commissioners.[36] At Fort McIntosh, when chiefs of the Wyandots, Chippewas, Delawares, and Ottawas said they regarded the lands transferred by Britain to the United States as still rightfully belonging to them, the American commissioners answered them "in a high tone," and reminded them they were a defeated people.[37] At Fort Finney, when Shawnees balked at the American terms and refused to provide hostages, one of the American commissioners picked up the wampum belt they gave him, "dashed it on the table," and told them to accept the terms or face the consequences.[38]

Indian representation at these treaties was partial at best, and the Americans exploited and aggravated intratribal divisions. Six Nations delegates who returned home from Fort Stanwix were denounced by their own people, and the Six Nations in council at Buffalo Creek refused to ratify a treaty made under such duress. Western Indians were furious at the Six Nations for making a treaty without consulting them. In 1785, the Seneca chief Cornplanter delivered up his copy of the articles of peace concluded at Fort Stanwix, saying they had become "burdensome."[39] Chiefs who made cessions lost face with their people. Captain Pipe, who lost his place to other Delaware war captains in 1782, tried to regain standing by acting as a mediating chief rather than a warrior, and signed the Treaty of Fort McIntosh, which only cost him more support.[40] Nevertheless, chiefs had little choice but to make land cessions. Their ability to act as chiefs by backing up their words with the distribution of gifts to their followers had long made them dependent on outsiders. The British had provided them with gifts as allies seeking their support, but the Americans demanded land in return for the few gifts they offered. Some chiefs signed treaties knowing that others would do so if they refused.[41]

"If ever a peace failed to pacify, it was the peace of 1783," observed historian Arthur Whitaker in reference to the South. The end of the Revolution marked the beginning of years of turmoil as the region became an arena of competing national, state, and tribal interests, international intrigues, land speculation, and personal ambitions.[42] The principal result of the war in the southern backcountry

---

[36] Craig, ed., *Olden Time*, vol. 2: 424; *Revolution and Confederation*, 305–27.

[37] *Penn. Archives*, 1st series, vol. 10: 395. The treaty is in *Revolution and Confederation*, 329–31.

[38] Craig, ed., *Olden Time*, vol. 2: 524; *Revolution and Confederation*, 340–8, esp. 347; treaty at 349–51.

[39] Butterfield, ed., *Journal of Captain Jonathan Heart*, 51, 78, 89–90; Clements Library, Harmar Papers, Letter Book A: 81.

[40] White, *Middle Ground*, 436–7, 439; Graig, ed., *Olden Time*, vol. 2: 515–16, 518.

[41] White, *Middle Ground*, 496.

[42] Arthur P. Whitaker, *The Spanish–American Frontier, 1783–1795*, reprint ed. (Lincoln: University of Nebraska Press, 1970), 1; Lawrence Kinnaird, "International Rivalry in the Creek Country," *Florida Historical Quarterly* 10 (1931), 57–79; J. Leitch Wright, Jr., *Creeks and Seminoles: The Destruction and Regeneration of the Muscogulge People* (Lincoln: University of Nebraska Press, 1986), ch. 4; *Revolution and Confederation*, chs. 5–6. See also Alexander McGillivray's review of treaties, *ASPIA*, vol. 1: 19–20.

was to transfer control of a vast frontier from the Indians and their British allies and associates to the Whigs and the new men who emerged to lead them in the course of the Revolution.[43] Until the southern states yielded their claims to western lands, the federal government had no lands to sell in the South and simply hoped to prevent full-scale Indian war. North Carolina did not cede its western land claims to Congress until 1789; Georgia not until 1802. These states, plus the "state" of Franklin, made their own treaties with the Indians, generally refused to cooperate with the federal government in its attempts to implement a coherent Indian policy in the region, and sometimes tried to sabotage federal treaty-making efforts. Meanwhile, the aggressions of Carolinian and Georgian backcountry settlers threatened to embroil the whole frontier in conflict.[44] The United States negotiated the Treaties of Hopewell, with the Cherokees in late 1785 and with the Choctaws and Chickasaws in January 1786. The treaties confirmed tribal boundaries but did little to preserve them.[45] Cherokee leaders appealed for assistance to Patrick Henry of Virginia in 1789: "We are so Distrest by the No. Carolina People that it seems Like we sho'ld soon become no People. They have got all our Land from us. We have hardly as much as we can stand on, and they seem to want that little worse than the Rest."[46]

The Creeks emerged from the Revolution with their lands relatively intact, but Georgia demanded all the lands between the Oconee and Ocmulgee rivers as war damages. At the Treaty of Augusta in November 1783, a handful of compliant Creek chiefs, primarily from the neutral and pro-American groups in the nation, led by Hopoithle Mico (the Tame King) of Tallassee and Cussita Mico (the Fat King) of Cussita ceded roughly eight hundred square miles to Georgia. McGillivray and the rest of the Creeks condemned the treaty, and in June 1784 signed the Treaty of Pensacola, placing themselves under Spanish protection. The Creeks entered the postrevolutionary era further divided into bitter factions. Factionalism had helped them avoid exclusive dependence on one ally throughout much of the eighteenth century and had secured them multiple outlets for trade. But as European allies began to fall away after the Revolution, McGillivray recognized that without Spanish support, "we may be forced to purchase a Shameful peace & barter our Country for a precarious Security." Now factionalism became dangerously dysfunctional, and the

---

[43] Edward J. Cashin, "'But Brothers, It Is Our Land We Are Talking About': Winners and Losers in the Georgia Backcountry," in Ronald Hoffman, Thad W. Tate, and Peter J. Albert, eds., *An Uncivil War: The Southern Backcountry during the American Revolution* (Charlottesville: University Press of Virginia, 1985), 240–75.

[44] *Revolution and Confederation*, ch. 5.

[45] For the texts of the treaties and related documents see *ASPIA*, vol. 1, and *Revolution and Confederation*, 393–410, 412–16, 418–26. Papers relating to the Hopewell conferences are also in Draper Mss. 14U

[46] *Virginia State Papers*, vol. 4: 620.

conflict between McGillivray and Hopoithle Mico augured the civil strife of 1813.[47]

Treaties made over the opposition of the majority of the tribes left boundaries in dispute. Indians punished intruders whom the United States government failed to keep off their lands, and settlers retaliated. Even where there was no conflict, the fiction that all Indians had fought for the British in the Revolution justified massive dispossession of Native Americans in the early republic, whatever their role in the war. Catawbas derived maximum mileage from their revolutionary services, and by wrapping themselves in the flag used their record of service in the patriot cause "to carve a niche for themselves in the social landscape of the Carolina piedmont."[48] However, they were an exception. Whereas other revolutionary veterans were granted land bounties, Indian veterans lost land. The Mashantucket Pequots served and suffered in the patriot cause, but in 1785 they were complaining to the government of Connecticut that "our Tribe find ourselves Interrupted in the Possession of our Lands by your People round about Cutting & Destroying our Timber & Crowding their Improvements in upon our Lands."[49] Neighboring Mohegans found that both "white strangers & foreign Indians" encroached on their land and sold their timber from under them in defiance of state laws.[50] In Massachusetts, Indians had fought and bled alongside the colonists in their struggle for liberty, but in 1788 the state reinstituted its guardian system for Indians, and deprived Mashpee of its right of self-government by establishing an all-white board of overseers.[51] The Penobscots and Passamaquoddies found their Maine hunting territories invaded by their former allies. Passamaquoddies appealed for justice to Congress, "that we may Enjoy our Privileges which we have been fighting for as other Americans," but Congress dismissed John Allan from his role as superintendent of eastern Indians, and Massachusetts resumed its pursuit of Indian lands in Maine. The state stripped the Penobscots and Passamaquoddies of most of their land in a series of post-Revolution treaties.[52] New England Indians

[47] Randolph C. Downes, "Creek–American Relations, 1782–1790," *Georgia Historical Quarterly* 29 (1937), 142–81; David H. Corkran, *The Creek Frontier, 1540–1783* (Norman: University of Oklahoma Press, 1967), 322–5; the Treaty of Augusta is in *Revolution and Confederation*, 372–3; Caughey, *McGillivray of the Creeks*, 75–6; McGillivray to Zéspedes, Apr. 15, 1787, Library of Congress, East Florida Papers, reel 43, bundle 114J9; Joel Martin, *Sacred Revolt: The Muskogees' Struggle for a New World* (Boston: Beacon, 1991), 81–3.

[48] James H. Merrell, *The Indians' New World: Catawbas and Their Neighbors from European Contact through the Era of Removal* (Chapel Hill: University of North Carolina Press, 1989), 215–22.

[49] Connecticut State Archives, Hartford, Connecticut Archives, Indian Series I, vol. 2: 248.

[50] Ibid., 329.

[51] Barry O'Connell, ed., *On Our Own Ground: The Complete Writings of William Apess, A Pequot* (Amherst: University of Massachusetts Press, 1992), 239; Jack Campisi, *The Mashpee Indians: Tribe on Trial* (Syracuse, N.Y.: Syracuse University Press, 1991), 88–91.

[52] *PCC*, reel 71, item 58: 59–63, 67–8, 75–9; reel 163, vol. 149, part 2: 561–2; James S. Leamon, *Revolution Downeast: The American War for Independence in Maine* (Amherst: University of Massachusetts Press, 1993), 218–20; Colin G. Calloway, ed., *Dawnland Encounters: Indians and*

who had moved to Oneida country only to be driven back by the war, and "who for their Fidelity and Attachment to the American Cause, have suffered the Loss of all things," petitioned the Connecticut Assembly for relief at the war's end.[53]

The Oneidas had suffered mightily in the American cause during the war. General Philip Schuyler had assured them during the Revolution that "sooner should a fond mother forget her only son than we shall forget you." Once they had helped the Americans win independence, the Oneidas would "then partake of every Blessing we enjoy and united with a free people your Liberty and prosperity will be safe." But the Oneidas fared little better than their New England friends or their Cayuga and Seneca relatives in the postrevolutionary land grabbing conducted by the federal government, New York State, and individual land companies. Schuyler interceded on their behalf, and Congress guaranteed the territorial integrity of their Oneida and Tuscarora allies at the Treaty of Fort Stanwix, a guarantee the United States confirmed at Fort Harmar in 1789, and at Canandaigua and Oneida in 1794. But paper commitments gave little protection. In 1794, the government absolved its obligations to the Oneidas with an award of $5,000, an annuity of $4,500, and promises to build a sawmill, a gristmill, and a church. The State of New York meanwhile negotiated a string of treaties, illegal under the Indian Trade and Non-Intercourse Act of 1790, that by 1838 had robbed the Oneidas of their entire homeland.[54] The bitter divisions the Revolution produced within the Oneidas were "not yet forgotten" by 1796.[55]

As many Revolutionary War veterans, often illiterate, signed away their land grants for a pittance to more powerful and prosperous citizens of the new nation, so too Indian veterans, who had fought to win the United States's independence, often found themselves reduced to selling off land simply to survive. Simon Joy Jay, or Choychoy, a Mohegan who was wounded in the Revolution, "fighting for the Country," had to sell his land to support himself in old age and infirmity. The widow of Indian Daniel Cyrus, a white woman named Sarah, who lost two sons in the war, likewise had to sell her land to

*Europeans in Northern New England* (Hanover, N.H.: University Press of New England, 1991), 128–31; Paul Brodeur, *Restitution: The Land Claims of the Mashpee, Penobscot and Passamaquoddy Indians in New England* (Boston: Northeastern University Press, 1985).

[53] Connecticut Archives, Indian Series I, vol. 2: 227a.

[54] *Revolution and Confederation*, 69–70; *PCC*, reel 173: 551–5; Ford and Hunt, eds., *Journals of the Continental Congress*, vol. 29: 806; Maryly B. Penrose, comp., *Indian Affairs Papers: American Revolution* (Franklin Park, N.J.: Liberty Bell, 1981), 135–7, 265–6, 269; Franklin B. Hough, ed., *Proceedings of the Commissioners of Indian Affairs . . . for the Extinguishment of Indian Titles in the State of New York* (Albany, N.Y.: Munsell, 1861), 39–44, 84–108; Jack Campisi, "Ethnic Identity and Boundary Maintenance in Three Oneida Communities," Ph.D. diss., SUNY Albany, 1974, 88–94; J. David Lehman, "The End of the Iroquois Mystique: The Oneida Land Cession Treaties of the 1780s," *William and Mary Quarterly*, 3d series, 48 (1990), 524–47.

[55] *Collections of the Massachusetts Historical Society*, 1st series, 5 (1798), 16.

support herself in old age.[56] Abenaki Indian patriots in Vermont fell on equally hard times.[57]

The widows of men from Mashpee who had given their lives in the struggle for independence were forced to look outside their communities for husbands. By 1793, Indian towns like Mashpee included not only Africans and Anglo-Americans, but also Germans who had served in the war as mercenaries and had since married into the community and were raising families.[58]

Many Indian peoples clung to their ancestral lands, even where those lands had been in the middle of war zones. Some Mohawk families returned and remained in their Fort Hunter and Canajoharie homes until the 1790s.[59] But most Mohawks found new homes at Grand River or the Bay of Quinté. The peace that ended the Revolution did not end the vast movement of people that scattered Loyalists and African Americans across the globe and displaced Indian populations throughout North America.[60] The war's end found Indian refugees at Niagara, Schenectady, Detroit, Saint Louis, Saint Augustine, and Pensacola, and the peace continued to dislocate thousands of Indians. Indian peoples pressured by Anglo-American expansion continued, as they had in the past and would in the future, to seek refuge in Canada. The Moravians established a new Delaware mission village at Moraviantown on the Thames River. Indian Loyalists moved to new homes at Grand River and the Bay of Quinté in Ontario rather than return to homelands engulfed by the Americans.[61] By the end of the Revolution, Shawnees who remained in Ohio were crowded into the northwestern reaches of their territory. In time they joined other Indians in

[56] Connecticut Archives, Indian Series II, vol. 1: 70; vol. 2: 150.

[57] Colin G. Calloway, *The Western Abenakis of Vermont, 1600–1800: War, Migration, and the Survival of an Indian People* (Norman: University of Oklahoma Press, 1990), 231–3.

[58] O'Connell, ed., *On Our Own Ground*, 240; Gideon Hawley, "An account of the number of Indian houses in Mashpee, July 1, 1793," Harvard University, Houghton Library Ms., autograph file.

[59] David K. Faux, "Iroquoian Occupation of the Mohawk Valley During and After the Revolution," *Man in the Northeast* 34 (Fall 1987), 27–39.

[60] Sylvia R. Frey, *Water from the Rock: Black Resistance in a Revolutionary Age* (Princeton, N.J.: Princeton University Press, 1991), ch. 6; John N. Grant, "Black Immigrants into Nova Scotia, 1776–1815," *Journal of Negro History* 58 (1973), 253–61; Mary Beth Norton, *The British-Americans: The Loyalist Exiles in England, 1774–1789* (Boston: Little, Brown, 1972). Some former slaves who migrated to Nova Scotia later moved to Freetown in Sierra Leone, where they were known as the Nova Scotians. Gary B. Nash, *Race, Class, and Politics: Essays on American Colonial and Revolutionary Society* (Urbana: University of Illinois Press, 1986), 274–80; James W. St. G. Walker, *The Black Loyalists: The Search for a Promised Land in Nova Scotia and Sierra Leone, 1783–1870* (New York, 1976). Highland Scots who had migrated to John Johnson's estate in New York and taken his side in the Revolution now moved to Glengarry, Ontario. Marianne McLean, *The People of Glengarry: Highlanders in Transition, 1745–1820* (Montreal: McGill-Queen's University Press, 1991); ch. 6; *NYCD*, vol. 8: 682–3.

[61] Robert S. Allen, *His Majesty's Indian Allies: British Policy in the Defence of Canada, 1774–1815* (Toronto: Dundurn, 1992), 196–98; Carleton Papers, reel 17, No. 6742: 18, 23; No. 6476: 3; Charles M. Johnston, ed., *Valley of the Six Nations: A Collection of Documents on the Indian Lands of the Grand River* (Toronto: Champlain Society, 1964).

creating a multitribal, multivillage world centered on the Glaize. There some two thousand people lived around three Shawnee towns, two Delaware towns, a Miami town, and British–French trading communities, along with some Nanticokes, Mingoes, and Chickamauga Cherokees.[62] Stockbridge Indians, unable to secure relief from their former allies after the Revolution, joined other Christian Indians from New England in moving to lands set aside for them by the Oneidas in New York, joining "People of many Nations" at New Stockbridge.[63] Hundreds of refugee Indians drifted west of the Mississippi and requested permission to settle in Spanish territory. Abenaki Indians, dispersed by previous wars from northern New England into the Ohio Valley, turned up in Arkansas and Missouri in the decade after the Revolution, testimony to the continuing dislocation of Indian communities that the conflict occasioned in eastern North America.[64] The migrations of Indian peoples across the Mississippi generated repercussions on the plains and threatened to disturb "the tranquility of the Interior Provinces of New Spain."[65]

For American Indians, the new republic was still very much a revolutionary world in which their struggles continued with little abatement. For many Indian peoples, the Revolution was one phase of a "Twenty Years' War" that continued at least until the Treaty of Greenville in 1795. Before it was over, a whole generation had grown up knowing little but war.[66] The Indians' war of independence went on until 1795, 1815, and beyond, and it took many forms, as Indians mounted "spirited resistance" and "sacred revolts."[67] Confronted with renewed pressures and aggressions, spurred on by the murder of mediation chiefs like Moluntha and Old Tassel, and encouraged by the presence of Britons and Spaniards waiting in the wings for the experiment in republicanism to fail, many of the tribes renewed their confederacies. Shawnees, Chickamaugas, and Creeks carried war belts throughout the eastern woodlands; Indian ambassadors traveled from Detroit to Saint Augustine and back, urging united resistance. Warriors from a host of tribes continued a war of independence that was multitribal in character.[68] In council held at the mouth of the Detroit River

[62] Colin G. Calloway, "'We Have Always Been the Frontier': The American Revolution in Shawnee Country," *American Indian Quarterly* 16 (1992), 44–5; Helen Hornbeck Tanner, "The Glaize in 1792: A Composite Indian Community," *Ethnohistory* 25 (1978) 15–39.

[63] Harold Blodgett, *Samson Occum* (Hanover, N.H.: Dartmouth College Publications, 1935), 195.

[64] *WHC*, 18: 434–5; *Spain in the Mississippi Valley*, xxix–xxx, 186, 203–8, 255, 269, 280, 292; Louis Houck, ed., *The Spanish Regime in Missouri*, 2 vols. (Chicago: Donnelley, 1909), vol. 2: 70–1; Dubreuil to Miró, Dec. 14, 1785, AGI, PC, leg. 107.

[65] Elizabeth A. H. John, ed. *Views from the Apache Frontier: Report on the Northern Provinces of New Spain, By José Cortés, Lieutenant in the Royal Corps of Engineers, 1799* (Norman: University of Oklahoma Press, 1989), 42–6.

[66] Craig, ed., *Olden Time*, vol. 2: 515.

[67] Gregory Evans, Dowd, *A Spirited Resistance: The North American Indian Struggle for Unity, 1745–1815* (Baltimore: Johns Hopkins University Press, 1992); Martin, *Sacred Revolt*.

[68] Dowd, *Spirited Resistance*, ch. 5; Draper Mss. 13S6–7; James Alton James, ed., *George Rogers Clark Papers, 1781–84* (Springfield: Illinois State Historical Society, 1926), 189–90; *North Carolina State Records*, vol. 16: 924–5; vol. 17: 83–4, 92, 159–60; *Virginia State Papers*, vol. 4: 118.

in November and December 1786, delegates from the Five Nations, as well as Hurons, Delawares, Shawnees, Ottawas, Chippewas, Potawatomis, Miamis, Cherokees, and Wabash allies, sent a speech to the United States from the "United Indian Nations," declaring invalid all treaties made without the unanimous consent of the tribes.[69] Led by capable chiefs who had risen to prominence during the Revolution – Joseph Brant, Little Turtle, Buckongahelas, Blue Jacket, Dragging Canoe, and McGillivray – revived Indian confederacies continued the wars for their lands and cultures into the 1790s and exposed the American theory of conquest for the fiction it was.

Americans in the new republic, like their British and Spanish rivals, were often hard-pressed to keep up with the political changes the Revolution generated in Indian country, as new communities emerged, new power blocs developed, and new players called different tunes. "Tribes" ceased to be the functioning unit of Indian politics and diplomacy, if they ever had been. Young warriors continued the war from multitribal communities. "Banditti of several tribes find asylum in the Lower Towns of the Cherokees," Arthur Campbell reported to George Washington; Cherokees removed to new homes with the Creeks, a nation that "seems always to have been the receptacle for all distressed Tribes," said the Cherokee Turtle at Home, who had joined the Chickamauga resistance and had spent so much time in Shawnee country that he spoke Shawnee fluently.[70]

Not until the mid-1790s did the Indian war for independence as waged by these warriors come to an end. General Josiah Harmar and General Arthur St. Clair met with defeat and disaster in their campaigns against the northwestern confederacy. Only in 1794 did the Americans inflict a telling victory on the tribes at Fallen Timbers and get at the extensive cornfields on the Auglaize and Maumee rivers, which had sustained the Indian war effort for years. Anthony Wayne described this as "the grand emporium of the hostile Indians of the West," and claimed he had never seen "such immense fields of corn, in any part of America, from Canada to Florida."[71] Defeated in battle and abandoned by the British, the Indians could only watch as Wayne's troops put the area to the torch. A dozen years after the end of the Revolution, the American strategy of burning Indian food supplies finally ended the Indians' war for independence. Before the war, said Little Turtle to the French scientist Constantin-Francois de Volney several years later, "We raised corn like the whites. But now we are poor hunted deer."[72] Cherokees had voiced similar sentiments after the Revolution

[69] *ASPIA*, vol. 4: 8–9; *MPHC*, vol. 11: 467–70; *Revolution and Confederation*, 356–8.
[70] Draper Mss. 13S6–7; Carl F. Klinck and James J. Talman, eds., *The Journal of John Norton, 1816* (Toronto: Champlain Society, 1970), 33, 47.
[71] *ASPIA*, vol. 1: 490.
[72] C. B. Brown, ed., *A View of the Soil and Climate of the United States by C. F. Volney* (1804; reprint, New York, 1968), 382, quoted in Leroy V. Eid, "'The Slaughter was Reciprocal': Josiah Harmar's Two Defeats, 1790," *Northwest Ohio Quarterly* 65 (1993), 63.

and the devastation of their crops: "We are now like wolves, ranging about the woods to get something to eat."[73]

By 1795 the war for Ohio was lost. Little Turtle and others who had been on the forefront of resistance joined the old chiefs in making peace at the Treaty of Greenville, and ceded most of Ohio to the United States. That same year, the Treaty of San Lorenzo effectively deprived southern Indians of Spanish support in their resistance to American expansion.

In the Northwest Ordinance of 1787, the United States had committed itself to expansion while simultaneously treating Indian people with "the utmost good faith." Men like Henry Knox and Thomas Jefferson wrestled with the dilemma of how to take Indian lands and still act with "justice and humanity." With their victory finally secured and Indians no longer a major military threat, Americans finally resolved the dilemma inherent in their belief that United States Indian policy could combine "expansion with honor." Since too much land encouraged idleness and presented an obstacle to "civilization," and Indian people could survive in the new nation only by becoming "civilized," the United States would deprive them of their lands for their own good. Not surprisingly, the good intentions of a few men became lost amid the pressure to rid the Indians of their lands.[74]

Burned villages and crops, murdered chiefs, divided councils and civil wars, migrations, towns and forts choked with refugees, economic disruption, breaking of ancient traditions, losses in battle and to disease and hunger, betrayal to their enemies, all made the American Revolution one of the darkest periods in American Indian history. The emergence of the independent United States as the ultimate victor from a long contest of imperial powers reduced Indians to further dependence and pushed them into further dark ages. Two Mohegans, Henry Quaduaquid and Robert Ashpo, petitioning the Connecticut Assembly for relief in 1789, expressed the sentiments and experiences of many Native Americans as the new nation came into being: "The Times are Exceedingly Altr'd, Yea the Times have turn'd everything Upside down."[75] Seneca communities, in Anthony Wallace's words, became "slums in the wilderness," characterized by poverty, loss of confidence in traditional certainties, social pathology, violence, alcoholism, witch fear, and disunity. Cherokees, reeling from the shock of defeat and dispossession, seemed to have lost their place in the world, and the very fabric of their society seemed to be crumbling around them.[76]

---

[73] *ASPIA*, vol. 1: 48; *Revolution and Confederation*, 475.
[74] Francis Paul Prucha, ed., *Documents of United States Indian Policy* (Lincoln: University of Nebraska Press, 1975), 10; Horsman, *Expansion and American Indian Policy, 1783–1815*; idem, "The Indian Policy of an 'Empire for Liberty,'" paper presented at the United States Capitol Historical Society Symposium, 1992.
[75] Connecticut Archives, Indian Series I, vol. 2: 330.
[76] Anthony F. C. Wallace, *The Death and Rebirth of the Seneca* (New York: Knopf, 1969), ch. 7; William G. McLoughlin, *Cherokee Renascence in the New Republic* (Princeton N.J.: Princeton University Press, 1986), 3–4.

And yet, in the kaleidoscopic, "all-change" world of the revolutionary era, there were exceptions and variations. Despite new colors on the map of Florida, political change in Seminole country reflected not new dependence on a foreign power so much as increasing independence from the parent Creek confederacy. While Alexander McGillivray continued traditional Creek policies of playing off competing nations with considerable skill, the Seminoles emerged by the new century as a new player and an unknown quantity in the Indian and international diplomacy of the southeast. Many Indian communities succumbed and some disappeared in the new world produced during the Revolution, but others were in process of formation and asserting their separate identity.

Like the Shawnees who built and rebuilt Chillicothe, Indians adjusted and endured. Contrary to predictions of extinction and assumptions of stasis, Indian communities survived, changed, and were reborn. The Revolutionary War destroyed many Indian communities, but new, increasingly multiethnic, communities – at Niagara, Grand River, Chickamauga, and the Glaize – grew out of the turmoil and played a leading role in the Indian history of the new republic. The black years following the Revolution saw powerful forces of social and religious rejuvenation in Handsome Lake's Longhouse religion among the Iroquois, far-reaching stirrings of cultural assertiveness, political movements like the northwestern Indian confederacy of the 1780s and 1790s, a renascence in Cherokee country, and pan-Indian unity under the leadership of Tecumseh and the Shawnee Prophet in the early years of the new century.[77]

The American Revolution was a disaster for most American Indians, and the turmoil it generated in Indian country continued long after 1783. But by the end of the eighteenth century, Indian peoples had had plenty of experience suffering and surviving disasters. They responded to this one as they had to others and set about rebuilding what they could of their world. But now they were building on quicksand, for the new America had no room for Indians and their world.

---

[77] Wallace, *Death and Rebirth of the Seneca;* Dowd, *Spirited Resistance*; McLoughlin, *Cherokee Renascence in the New Republic*; R. David Edmunds, *The Shawnee Prophet* (Lincoln: University of Nebraska Press, 1983).

# Epilogue

## *A world without Indians?*

Indian peoples experienced, interpreted, and defined the American Revolution in a variety of ways. Freedom, in Indian country, often meant siding with the British against revolutionaries whose independence was sure to imperil Indian lands and cultures. Many Mohawks, tied to the Johnson dynasty by marriage and to the crown by perceived common interest, joined other Loyalists in moving to Canada rather than return to life as dependents in the new republic. Chickamauga, Mingo, and many Shawnee warriors tried in the Revolution to regain some of the independence they had lost, by turning back the tide of settlement. On the other hand, Stockbridge and many other New England Indians spoke as if the cause of American liberty was their own and sacrificed as much as any of their patriot neighbors in the struggle. White Eyes of the Delawares saw in the Revolution and an American alliance the opportunity to assert his people's independence from Iroquois claims of hegemony. Dragging Canoe and younger Cherokees saw it as a chance to declare their independence from the policies and authority of an older generation of chiefs. Chickasaws pursued a variety of diplomatic options in an effort to prevent their independence slipping away in a world of shifting geopolitical power. Seminoles increased their independence from the parent Creek confederacy. The Iroquois, past masters at surviving by diplomacy, saw their confederacy torn apart in the Revolution. Abenakis, formerly the "shock troops" of New France, developed effective tactics to keep this conflict at arm's length. Some communities were destroyed in the Revolution; others grew out of it.

With the Revolution won, however, Americans reduced the diverse experiences of Indian peoples to a single role. In a sense, the Revolution became the United States' creation story. The myths spun around that story proved lethal for the peoples whose creation stories in America reached back thousands of years. As Kenneth Morrison has pointed out, "For many Americans, the story of who they are winds back to the Revolution."[1] It is equally true that for many Americans

---

[1] Kenneth M. Morrison, "Native Americans and the American Revolution: Historic Stories and Shifting Frontier Conflict," in Frederick E. Hoxie, ed., *Indians in American History* (Arlington Heights, Illinois: Davidson, 1988), 95.

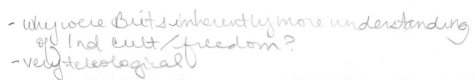

the story of who Indians are winds back to that time. While embattled patriots fought for freedom against a tyrannical monarch in the East, "merciless savages" ravaged American settlements in the West. The agony of the American Revolution for American Indians was lost as the winners constructed a national mythology that simplified what had been a complex contest in Indian country, blamed Indians for the bloodletting, and justified subsequent assaults on Indian lands and cultures. In the aftermath of the Revolution, new social orders were created and new ideologies developed to explain which groups of people were included and excluded, and why. In the long run, the legacy the war produced in the minds of non-Indians proved almost as devastating to Indian peoples as the burned towns, fractured communities, and shattered lives of the war itself.

Americans at different times invented versions of Indian people to suit their particular policies and purposes,[2] but the Revolution had particularly enduring influence and fueled ambivalence about the future place of Native Americans in the new republic that was being created. After all, the Declaration of Independence depicted Indians as savage allies of a tyrannical monarch, who "endeavored to bring on the inhabitants of our frontiers, the merciless Indian savages, whose known rule of warfare is an undistinguished destruction of all ages, sexes, and conditions." The congressional committee whose report influenced the shape of United States Indian policy throughout the confederation era echoed Jefferson's sentiments: The Indians were "aggressors in the war, without even a pretence of provocation," and "determined" to join forces with the British.[3] Embodied in the document that marked the nation's birth, the image of Indians as vicious enemies of liberty became entrenched in the minds of generations of white Americans. Siding with the redcoats meant opposing the very principles on which the new nation was founded: having fought to prevent American Independence, Indians could not expect to share in the society that independence created.

The vicious border warfare of the Revolution produced atrocities and lasting impressions on both sides. Benjamin Franklin admitted in 1787 that "almost every War between the Indians and Whites has been occasion'd by some Injustice of the latter towards the former."[4] The Shawnee warriors Richard Butler encountered at Fort Finney in 1786 had grown to manhood knowing nothing but war, and they would live through another decade of conflict before their Twenty Years' War was over. When United States Indian agent Benjamin

---

[2] Roy Harvey Pearce, *Savagism and Civilization: A Study of the Indian and the American Mind* (Baltimore: Johns Hopkins University Press, 1965); Robert F. Berkhofer, *The White Man's Indian: Images of the American Indian from Columbus to the Present* (New York: Vintage, 1979).

[3] Washington C. Ford and Gaillard Hunt, eds., *Journals of the Continental Congress.* 34 vols. (Washington: Government Printing Office, 1904–37), vol. 25: 683.

[4] Albert Henry Smyth, ed., *The Writings of Benjamin Franklin*, 10 vols. (New York: Macmillan, 1907), vol. 9: 625.

Hawkins visited a group of Cherokees in 1796, he found the women fearful of him and "the children exceedingly alarmed at the sight of white men." In one cabin, a little boy of eight years old "was especially alarmed and could not be kept from screaming out until I got out of the door, and then he run and hid himself." Asking the child's mother the reason for his fright, Hawkins learned that these Cherokees were refugees from Keowee and Tugelo, towns that "had been much harrassed by the whites" in the Revolution. The old people frequently spoke of their sufferings and "those tales were listened to by the children, and made an impression which showed itself in the manner I had observed." As Tom Hatley points out, Cherokees and Americans alike resorted to caricatures of the other.[5]

*nat'l memory*

However, in the emerging national memory of the Revolution, responsibility for the brutality and destruction of the Revolutionary War on the frontier lay squarely on the shoulders of the Indians and their British backers. In American eyes, the Gnadenhütten massacre and rumors of American atrocities at Onondaga and Piqua paled in comparison with descriptions of white "Women and Children strip'd, scalped, and suffered to welter in their gore"; whole families "destroyed, without regard to Age or Sex – Infants are torn from their mothers Arms & their Brains dashed out against Trees."[6] The well-worn story of William Crawford's capture and torture by Delaware warriors in 1782 featured prominently in narratives of border warfare;[7] the frantic and often more typical peace-keeping efforts and shuttle diplomacy of Cornstalk, White Eyes, and Kayashuta tended to be forgotten. After the war, lurid accounts tended to increase rather than diminish, and the growing popularity of narratives of Indian captivity fueled stereotypes. Stories of Indian atrocities became implanted in the minds of an entire generation so that by the time James Seaver published his *Narrative of the Life of Mary Jemison* in 1824, there were few Americans of middle age who could not "distinctly recollect of sitting in the chimney corner when children, all contracted with fear, and there listening to their parents or visitors, while they related stories of Indian conquests, and murders, that would make their flaxen hair nearly stand erect, and almost destroy the power of motion."[8]

Bernard Sheehan, who sees the Indians' role in the Revolution as minor,

[5] "Letters of Benjamin Hawkins, 1796–1806," *Collections of the Georgia Historical Society* 9 (1916), 23; Tom Hatley, *The Dividing Paths: Cherokees and South Carolinians through the Era of the Revolution* (New York: Oxford University Press, 1993), 235–9.

[6] *Virginia Magazine of History and Biography* 27 (1919), 316; *Calendar of Virginia State Papers* 2 (1881), 48.

[7] Archibald Loudon, ed., *A Selection of Some of the Most Interesting Narratives, of Outrages Committed by the Indians, in Their Wars with the White People.* (Carlisle, Pa., 1808; reprinted New York Times and Arno, 1971).

[8] June Namias, ed., *Narrative of the Life of Mary Jemison. By James E. Seaver* (Norman: University of Oklahoma Press, 1992), 53. For example: Josiah Priest, *Stories of the Revolution, with an Account of the Lost Child of the Delaware; Wheaton and the Panther, &c* (Albany: Hoffman & White, 1838) contains anecdotes of Indian savagery and a frontispiece depicting an Indian massacre of fourteen prisoners.

emphasizes the importance for propaganda purposes of the image of the Indian as a savage, which their participation in that conflict created, or at least perpetuated. The story of the murder of Jane McCrea by Indians accompanying Burgoyne's army around Saratoga rallied American militia at the time and justified American policies in later years. "Jane McCrea became one of those important images used by white men to explain the meaning of the Indian in relation to the Americans' struggle to preserve their liberty," writes Sheehan. John Vanderlyn's painting (1804, Fig. 11) of the event "impressed it on the American imagination and made it legendary." A young white female, her breasts partially exposed, kneels beneath dark, muscular, half-naked Indians who grab her long hair and wield tomahawks with murderous intent. One of the first major artworks of the new nation, the painting fueled sexual and racial anxieties and vividly reminded Americans that Indians during the Revolution were "merciless savages." Few Americans remembered, if they ever knew, that if McCrea did die at Indian hands – and even that is debatable – the killers were probably Christian Indians, recruited from French mission villages on the Saint Lawrence.[9] Looking back from nineteenth- and twentieth-century vantage points, their view obscured by chronicles of border warfare, racist writings of Francis Parkman and Theodore Roosevelt, and romanticized depictions of conflict in paintings like Vanderlyn's *Death of Jane McCrea*, or the many versions of Indians abducting Daniel Boone's daughter, Americans telescoped the Revolution and the colonial wars into one long chronicle of bloody frontier conflict. Periods of peace, patterns of interdependency, and Indian efforts to remain neutral were ignored as racial war took a dominant place in the national mythology.

Such stories and images provided a rationale for dispossession of surviving Indians. Foreign visitors to the new nation regularly commented on the Americans' desire for Indian lands and their genocidal tendencies toward Indian people. "Certainly no effort is made to hide plans to strip the Indians of everything," observed Louis Philippe, future king of France, during a visit to the southern states in 1797, "and their eagerness to get on with it leads the whites often to paint the Indians in false colors."[10] When Andrew Jackson, arch exponent

[9] Bernard W. Sheehan, "The Problem of the Indian in the American Revolution," in Philip Weeks, ed., *The American Indian Experience* (Arlington Heights, Ill.: Forum, 1988), 68–80, quote at 71; Brian Burns, "Massacre or Muster?: Burgoyne's Indians and the Militia at Bennington," *Vermont History* 45 (1977), 133–44. June Namias discusses "Jane McCrea and the American Revolution" in her *White Captives: Gender and Ethnicity on the American Frontier* (Chapel Hill: University of North Carolina Press, 1993), ch. 4. Robert W. Venables, "The Iconography of Empire: Images of the American Indian in the Early Republic, 1783–1835," U.S. Capitol Historical Society Symposium, 1992, shows how images of Indian atrocity like the murder of Jane McCrea served the purposes of empire building.

[10] Louis Philippe, *Diary of My Travels in America*, Stephen Becker, trans, (New York: Delacorte, 1977), 97; William Strickland, "Journal of a Tour in the United States of America 1794–1795," *Collections of the New York Historical Society* 83 (1950), 167–8; Isaac Weld, *Travels Through the States of North America and the Provinces of Upper and Lower Canada, During the Years 1795, 1796, and 1797* (London: Stockdale, 1799), 370–1; Jack D. L. Holmes, ed., *Journal of a Tour in*

Figure 11. *The Death of Jane McCrea*, by John Vanderlyn. Courtesy The Wadsworth Atheneum, Hartford, Conn. Vanderlyn's painting graphically imprinted on the minds of generations of Americans the notion that Indians in the Revolution were, in the words of the Declaration of Independence, "merciless Indian savages, whose known rule of warfare is an undistinguished destruction of all ages, sexes, and conditions."

of Indian removal, looked back to the Revolution, he recalled "the scalping knife and Tomhawk [raised] against our defenceless women and children."[11] Powerful images and long memories of Indian violence primed subsequent generations for trouble with new Indian groups encountered farther west.[12] The psychology of conflict and dispossession became fixed.

As Indian peoples confronted the new American nation, outright resistance often gave way to more subtle forms of cultural resistance in Indian communities and Indian souls. But Indian cultural resistance only reinforced the inherited view that Indians fought against civilized people and civilized ways, and it was just as damning as bloody warfare in the minds of many Americans. "Civilization or death to all American savages!" had been the Fourth of July toast of Sullivan's officers as they prepared to invade Iroquoia in 1779.[13] "Civilized and uncivilized people cannot live in the same territory, or even in the same neighborhood," Benjamin Lincoln told historian Jeremy Belknap in 1792, voicing much the same sentiments, albeit in less strident tones, and ignoring the interconnectedness of Indian and white lives that had characterized large areas of colonial America.[14] Indian resistance to the expansion of American "civilization," whether it manifested itself as frontier warfare or adherence to traditional ways, only furthered the conviction that Indians must be "savages." Having fought against freedom at the republic's birth, Indians continued to fight against the very civilization on which the republic prided itself. Refusing civilization, as Sullivan's officers made clear, left only one alternative. As Bernard Sheehan has pointed out, frontiersmen murdered Indians; so-called humanitarians demanded

---

*Unsettled Parts of North America in 1796 and 1797. By Francis Bailey* (Edwardsville: Southern Illinois University Press, 1969), 106; Durand Echevirria, trans. and ed., *New Travels in the United States of America 1788. By J. P. Brissot De Warville* (Cambridge, Mass.: Harvard University Press, 1964), 418, 420; Antonio Pace, ed., *Luigi Castiglioni's Viaggio: Travels in the United States of North America, 1785–87* (Syracuse, N.Y.: Syracuse University Press, 1983), 232. Though his own travels in America had been on the eve of the Revolution, John D. F. Smith wrote after the war that "white Americans have the most rancorous antipathy to the whole race of Indians; nothing is more common than to hear them talk of extirpating them totally from the face of the earth, men, women, and children." John Dalziel Ferdinand Smith, *A Tour of the United States of America*, 2 vols. (London, 1784), vol. 1: 345–6.

[11] John S. Bassett, ed., *Correspondence of Andrew Jackson*, 6 vols. (Washington, D.C.: Carnegie Institution, 1926–35), vol. 1: 500.

[12] Cf. Peter Mancall, *Valley of Opportunity: Economic Culture along the Upper Susquehanna, 1700–1800* (Ithaca, N.Y.: Cornell University Press, 1991), 158–9. Russell Bourne, *The Red King's Rebellion: Racial Politics in New England, 1675–1678* (New York: Oxford University Press, 1990), sees a similar phenomenon in New England after King Philip's War. John D. Unruh, Jr., *The Plains Across: The Overland Emigrants and the Trans-Mississippi West, 1840–1860* (Urbana: University of Illinois Press, 1979), ch. 5, esp. 120–1, 136.

[13] Frederick Cook, ed., *Journals of the Military Expedition of Major General John Sullivan* (Auburn, N.Y.: Knapp, Peck, & Thomson, 1887), 225–6.

[14] *Collections of the Massachusetts Historical Society*, 6th series, vol. 4: 514; cf. Richard White, *The Middle Ground: Indians, Empires, and Republics in the Great Lakes Region, 1650–1815* (Cambridge University Press, 1991); Colin G. Calloway, ed., *Dawnland Encounters: Indians and Europeans in Northern New England* (Hanover: University Press of New England, 1991).

that they commit cultural suicide. "Ultimately, the white man's sympathy was more deadly than his animosity. Philanthropy had in mind the disappearance of an entire race."[15] In the new society, American frontiersmen, soldiers, agents, and missionaries continued to deal out heavy doses of both civilization and death to Indians.[16] In American eyes, Indian resistance, military or cultural, was a war Native Americans had no chance of winning after 1783, and the American future was something they had no chance of surviving. In a society and an age with a vision of "progress," Indians belonged to the past, and it was a violent past.[17] A future of peace and prosperity held no place for them.

In the propaganda of the Revolution, Indian figures and accoutrements frequently symbolized the American cause. One school of thought even maintains that Indian influence was so pervasive among the founding fathers' generation that the League of the Iroquois provided a model for the framing of the United States constitution.[18] Confronting the question of where Indian people fit in the new republic, however, Americans found their answer to be explicitly negative. Indian influences endured in the new republic, but the United States had no place for Indian people.

Of course, Native Americans were not the only people to find that the new world created by the Revolution was a world of closed opportunities and exclusion. Other groups – women, backcountry farmers, and ordinary laborers, as well as African slaves – found that the Revolution and the republic to which it gave birth did not free them from restraints of gender, region, class, and race. For many, the victory in the war for independence meant continued, if not increased, dependence.

While ordinary working people struggled to keep themselves employed, and their families clothed and fed, in an economy that was sliding into postwar depression, the rich and the wellborn reaffirmed their domination of social, political, and economic life. "In less than a generation," writes Ronald Schultz, "Revolutionary hopes for a republic of small producers had been defeated by merchants and speculators in land, currency, and human needs." In Philadelphia, laborers began to organize to bring about the kind of society the Revolution had promised, but that their revolutionary leaders withheld.[19]

[15] Bernard W. Sheehan, *Seeds of Extinction: Jeffersonian Philanthropy and the American Indian* (New York: Norton, 1974), 277–8.

[16] James H. Merrell, "Declarations of Independence," in Jack P. Greene, ed., *The American Revolution: Its Character and Limits* (New York University Press, 1987), 217.

[17] Pearce, *Savagism and Civilization*, 154, 160.

[18] E.g.: Donald A. Grinde and Bruce E. Johansen, *Exemplar of Liberty: Native America and the Evolution of Democracy* (Los Angeles: UCLA American Indian Studies Center, 1991); Bruce E. Johansen and Elisabeth Tooker, "Commentary on the Iroquois and the U.S. Constitution," *Ethnohistory* 37 (1990), 279–97.

[19] Ronald Schultz, *The Republic of Labor: Philadelphia Artisans and the Politics of Class, 1720–1830* (New York: Oxford University Press, 1993), chs. 3–4, quote at 90.

In western Massachusetts in 1786, small farmers whose debts brought them to the verge of ruin appealed for relief to a state government controlled by commercial and creditor interests. When their appeals fell on deaf ears, Massachusetts farmers did as they had done eleven years earlier and took matters into *farmers* their own hands. They mobbed county courthouses to prevent creditors from foreclosing on their farms and marched on the federal arsenal in Springfield before the state militia restored order.[20] Almost twenty years after Americans had rebelled to secure self-determination, protection from unjust taxes, and more representation in government, settlers in western Pennsylvania did much the same thing. Disenchanted with the fruits of the Revolution, they invoked much of the same rhetoric in an effort to secure similar goals from a distant and seemingly unresponsive government. The "heroes of the Revolution" were now defenders of order, and the new federal government dispatched troops to suppress the revolt.[21] In Maine, postwar hard times and continuing contests for land between men of wealth and influence and desperate farmers produced violence and radicalism. Impoverished backcountry squatters organized secret groups to defend their property and liberty against powerful proprietors. In the eyes of these 'white Indians," a new breed of Tories was denying the people the rights they had fought for in the Revolution.[22]

The Revolution broke down many barriers to women's participation in public *women* and political life, but, as the citizens of the republic redefined roles in the new society, they determined that a woman's role should lie in domestic responsibilities and raising republican sons rather than in political participation. Restricting women's politicization, in Linda Kerber's words, was "one of a series of conservative choices that Americans made in the postwar years as they avoided the full implications of their own revolutionary radicalism." For American women, the legacy of the American Revolution was ambiguous at best.[23]

Limiting the Revolution's revolutionary implications was especially important

---

[20] David Szatmary, *Shay's Rebellion: The Making of an Agrarian Insurrection* (Amherst: University of Massachusetts Press, 1980).

[21] Thomas P. Slaughter, *The Whiskey Rebellion: Frontier Epilogue to the American Revolution* (New York: Oxford University Press, 1986).

[22] James S. Leamon, *Revolution Downeast: The War for American Independence in Maine* (Amherst: University of Massachusetts Press, 1993), ch. 7; Alan Taylor, *Liberty Men and Great Proprietors: The Revolutionary Settlement on the Maine Frontier* (Chapel Hill: University of North Carolina Press, 1990).

[23] Elaine F. Crane, "Dependence in the Era of Independence: The Role of Women in a Republican Society," in Greene, ed. *American Revolution*, 253–75; Mary Beth Norton, *Liberty's Daughters: The Revolutionary Experience of American Women, 1750–1800* (Boston: Little, Brown, 1980); Linda K. Kerber, *Women of the Republic: Intellect and Ideology in Revolutionary America* (Chapel Hill: University of North Carolina Press, 1980), 287; Joan Hoff-Wilson, "The Illusion of Change: Women and the American Revolution," in Alfred F. Young, ed., *The American Revolution: Explorations in the History of American Radicalism* (De Kalb: Northern Illinois University Press, 1976; Ronald Hoffman and Peter J. Albert, eds., *Women in the Age of the American Revolution* (Charlottesville: University Press of Virginia, 1989).

*- slaves*

in race relations. As Gary Nash has pointed out, most Americans were no more willing to extend the Revolution's principles to Indian people than they were to fulfill the revolutionary ideal of abolishing slavery. Indeed, the Revolution gave slave owners new mechanisms to protect their human property, and the post-revolutionary era witnessed a dramatic expansion of slavery across the Georgia and Carolina low country and into lands acquired from Indians in Kentucky, Alabama, and Mississippi. Freed blacks in the North took new names, rebuilt their families, and created new communities and institutions, but even in states that abolished slavery, emancipation did not free black people from constricted

*- free blks*

opportunities, nor did it deprive white society of their labor. African labor, like Indian land, was a vital resource for the new republic, and Americans would not and could not forego its exploitation.[24] In the wake of a revolution that left social and racial arrangements in disarray, southern whites moved quickly to redefine the status of African Americans, and made clear that the promise of the Revolution did not apply equally to all men.[25]

Pequot William Apess bitterly understood that "the Revolution which en-shrined republican principles in the American commonwealth, also excluded African Americans and Native Americans from their reach." Referring to the guardian system reinstituted by Massachusetts, placing Indian settlements under the authority of state-appointed overseers, he wrote, "The whites were no sooner free themselves, than they enslaved the poor Indians."[26] The new republic needed African labor, and it excluded African Americans from its definition of "free and equal" on the basis of supposed racial inferiority. The new republic needed Indian land and excluded Native Americans on the basis of supposed savagery.

American Indians could not expect to be accepted in a nation that denied the fruits of an egalitarian revolution to so many of its citizens and that lived with the contradiction of slavery in a society built on principles of freedom. Native

---

[24] Gary B. Nash, "The Forgotten Experience: Indians, Blacks, and the American Revolution," reprinted in Richard D. Brown, ed., *Major Problems in the Era of the American Revolution* (Lexington, Mass: Heath, 1992), 277–83; Ira Berlin and Ronald Hoffman, eds., *Slavery and Freedom in the Age of the American Revolution* (Charlottesville: University Press of Virginia, 1983). Even in Pennsylvania, where slavery declined in the revolutionary era, tensions continued between the rhetoric of natural rights and the power of economic interests. Emancipation there was a gradual and complicated business that had less to do with the application of republican principles than with demographic and economic developments; see Gary B. Nash and Jean Soderland, *Freedom by Degrees: Emancipation in Pennsylvania and Its Aftermath* (New York: Oxford University Press, 1991). On the revolutionary aspirations of black people in Philadelphia and their struggle to translate emancipation into independence, see Gary B. Nash, *Forging Freedom: The Formation of Philadelphia's Black Community, 1720–1840* (Cambridge, Mass.: Harvard University Press, 1988), esp. chs. 2–3.

[25] Jeffrey J. Crow, *The Black Experience in Revolutionary North Carolina* (Raleigh: North Carolina Historical Commission, 1977), 82–95.

[26] Barry O'Connell, ed., *On Our Own Ground: The Complete Writings of William Apess, a Pequot* (Amherst: University of Massachusetts Press, 1992), lxix, lxxiii, 239–40.

Americans had been heavily dependent on, and interdependent with, colonial society and economy before the Revolution. But as Indian land became the key to national, state, and individual wealth, the new republic was less interested in their dependence than in their absence. Indian country, and the intermingling of cultures it involved, did not cease to exist. Indeed, as the new nation became increasingly biracial rather than triracial in character, consigning most nonwhites to the status of blacks, many Indian communities became increasingly multiethnic in nature.[27] But by the nineteenth century, Indian country was envisioned as a place beyond the Mississippi.

Indian people had been virtually everywhere in colonial America, building new worlds on the ruins of old worlds. Despite recurrent conflicts, many British officials had envisaged Indians as part of their North American empire. Southern Indian superintendent John Stuart had recommended to the lords of trade in 1764 that the government continue French policies of gift-giving and evenhanded dealings as the means of "fixing the British Empire in the Hearts of the Indians."[28] Stuart's vision was never realized, of course, but British officials did appreciate the imperial importance of Indian trade and presence, and that meant extending a measure of protection to Indian hunting grounds. The United States looked to build an empire on Indian land, not on Indian trade, and that required the Indians' removal.[29]

The United States looked forward to a future without Indians. The Indians' participation in the Revolution guaranteed their exclusion from the new world born out of the Revolution; their determination to survive as Indians guaranteed their ultimate extinction. Artistic depictions of Indian people showed them retreating westward, suffused in the heavy imagery of setting suns, as they faded from history.[30]

Fortunately for us all, Indian people had other ideas.

[27] Hatley, *Dividing Paths*, 225, 240.
[28] C.O. 323/17: 264–70, quote on 270.
[29] Cf. Edward J. Cashin, ed., *Colonial Augusta: "Key of the Indian Country"* (Macon, Ga.: Mercer University Press, 1986), 123: "Whatever else the American Revolution meant for Americans, for those in the Georgia backcountry it meant the end of a British policy that favored Indians' [*sic*] retaining their hunting grounds and the beginning of the American policy of Indian removal."
[30] E.g.: Rick Stewart, Joseph D. Ketner II, and Angela L. Miller, *Carl Wimar: Chronicler of the Missouri River Frontier* (Fort Worth, Tex.: Amon Carter Museum / Abrams, 1991), plates 1–2, 4–15; Brian W. Dippie, *Catlin and His Contemporaries: The Politics of Patronage* (Lincoln: University of Nebraska Press, 1990), plate 12.

# Index

on whites as Indians, 18
visits Shawnees, 163
McCrea, Jane, murder of as policy
  justification, 295
McDonald, John
  living on Chickamauga Creek, 200
  views war as generational, 196
McDowell's attack on towns, 206
McGary, Col. Hugh
  attacks Maquachakes, 177
  court martialed, 177
  kills Moluntha, 177
McGillivray, Alexander
  as Creek leader, 60
  asks British to leave supplies for
    Creeks, 277
  contest with Piomingo, 236–40
  denounces Augusta treaty, 284
  on Seminoles, 269
  plays off nations, 291
  tells British of Indian service, 276
  views of Spaniards, 276
McIntosh, Gen. Lachlan, warnings by,
  38
McLoughlin, William, on Cherokee
  disorder, 212
medals
  as sign of authority, 60
  Stuart gives to Choctaws, 7–8
medical supplies, 140
mercenaries, Hessian, 55
Merrell, James
  on diplomacy, 282
  on "new world," 3
Meslamonehonqua, on women's views of
  food shortages, 57
Miami Indians, attempts to unite against
  U.S., 40
Michilimackinac
  DePeyster report from outpost at, 25
  Matchekwis visits, 277
  Sioux visit, 42
Micmac
  service with U.S., 36
  take allegiance to King George, 36
migrations, 8–9
  during American Revolution, 61,
    287–8
  effect on Western tribes, 61
  Shawnees, 169–70

militants, increasing role of, 59
military service
  at Fort Niagara, 133
  Indian enlistment in, 28
  Indians in, 4
  Maine tribes in, 36
Mingo
  American Revolution for, 292
  at Pluggy's Town, 32–3
  killed, 24
  Shawnee groups favor joining, 169
Mingo Houma, 220, 225, 231, 233–4
  death of, 235
Minorcan, immigrants, 262
Minutemen, Stockbridge Indians
  volunteer as, 92
Miró, Gov. Estevan
  McGillivray courts, 276
  views on Chickasaws, 229–30
missionaries
  conversion of to Indian ways, 16
  among Indians, 14, 15
  to Mahicans, 86
  at Oquaga, 112, 113–21
  work disrupted by war, 62–3
Missisquoi, as true Abenaki center, 68
Missisquoi Abenakis, 79–80
mixed bloods, Chickasaw, 221
Mobile congress, 11
moccasins, continued use of, 14
Mohawks
  bring news to Chota of events in
    north, 194
  concern for American encroachments,
    122
  found new homes, 287
  Loyalists move to new homes, 287
  migration to Oquago by, 122
  move to Canada, 292
  prayer books destroyed, 63
  quality of life of Fort Hunter, 12
  remained in homes after war, 287
  rum sales to, 13
  sharing villages and valley, 3
  urge united resistence, 195
  warfare with Mahicans, 86
Mohegans
  American Revolution casualties
    among, 34
  land losses by, 285